The Cultural Legacy of María Zambrano

LEGENDA

LEGENDA is the Modern Humanities Research Association's book imprint for new research in the Humanities. Founded in 1995 by Malcolm Bowie and others within the University of Oxford, Legenda has always been a collaborative publishing enterprise, directly governed by scholars. The Modern Humanities Research Association (MHRA) joined this collaboration in 1998, became half-owner in 2004, in partnership with Maney Publishing and then Routledge, and has since 2016 been sole owner. Titles range from medieval texts to contemporary cinema and form a widely comparative view of the modern humanities, including works on Arabic, Catalan, English, French, German, Greek, Italian, Portuguese, Russian, Spanish, and Yiddish literature. Editorial boards and committees of more than 60 leading academic specialists work in collaboration with bodies such as the Society for French Studies, the British Comparative Literature Association and the Association of Hispanists of Great Britain & Ireland.

The MHRA encourages and promotes advanced study and research in the field of the modern humanities, especially modern European languages and literature, including English, and also cinema. It aims to break down the barriers between scholars working in different disciplines and to maintain the unity of humanistic scholarship. The Association fulfils this purpose through the publication of journals, bibliographies, monographs, critical editions, and the MHRA Style Guide, and by making grants in support of research. Membership is open to all who work in the Humanities, whether independent or in a University post, and the participation of younger colleagues entering the field is especially welcomed.

ALSO PUBLISHED BY THE ASSOCIATION

Critical Texts
Tudor and Stuart Translations • *New Translations* • *European Translations*
MHRA Library of Medieval Welsh Literature

MHRA Bibliographies
Publications of the Modern Humanities Research Association

The Annual Bibliography of English Language & Literature
Austrian Studies
Modern Language Review
Portuguese Studies
The Slavonic and East European Review
Working Papers in the Humanities
The Yearbook of English Studies

www.mhra.org.uk
www.legendabooks.com

STUDIES IN HISPANIC AND LUSOPHONE CULTURES

Studies in Hispanic and Lusophone Cultures are selected and edited by the Association of Hispanists of Great Britain & Ireland. The series seeks to publish the best new research in all areas of the literature, thought, history, culture, film, and languages of Spain, Spanish America, and the Portuguese-speaking world.

The Association of Hispanists of Great Britain & Ireland is a professional association which represents a very diverse discipline, in terms of both geographical coverage and objects of study. Its website showcases new work by members, and publicises jobs, conferences and grants in the field.

Editorial Committee
Chair: Professor Trevor Dadson (Queen Mary, University of London)
Professor Catherine Davies (University of Nottingham)
Professor Andrew Ginger (University of Bristol)
Professor Hilary Owen (University of Manchester)
Professor Christopher Perriam (University of Manchester)
Professor Alison Sinclair (Clare College, Cambridge)
Professor Philip Swanson (University of Sheffield)

Managing Editor
Dr Graham Nelson
41 Wellington Square, Oxford OX1 2JF, UK

www.legendabooks.com/series/shlc

STUDIES IN HISPANIC AND LUSOPHONE CULTURES

1. *Unamuno's Theory of the Novel*, by C. A. Longhurst
2. *Pessoa's Geometry of the Abyss: Modernity and the* Book of Disquiet, by Paulo de Medeiros
3. *Artifice and Invention in the Spanish Golden Age*, edited by Stephen Boyd and Terence O'Reilly
4. *The Latin American Short Story at its Limits: Fragmentation, Hybridity and Intermediality*, by Lucy Bell
5. *Spanish New York Narratives 1898–1936: Modernisation, Otherness and Nation*, by David Miranda-Barreiro
6. *The Art of Ana Clavel: Ghosts, Urinals, Dolls, Shadows and Outlaw Desires*, by Jane Elizabeth Lavery
7. *Alejo Carpentier and the Musical Text*, by Katia Chornik
8. *Britain, Spain and the Treaty of Utrecht 1713-2013*, edited by Trevor J. Dadson and J. H. Elliott
9. *Books and Periodicals in Brazil 1768-1930: A Transatlantic Perspective*, edited by Ana Cláudia Suriani da Silva and Sandra Guardini Vasconcelos
10. *Lisbon Revisited: Urban Masculinities in Twentieth-Century Portuguese Fiction*, by Rhian Atkin
11. *Urban Space, Identity and Postmodernity in 1980s Spain: Rethinking the Movida*, by Maite Usoz de la Fuente
12. *Santería, Vodou and Resistance in Caribbean Literature: Daughters of the Spirits*, by Paul Humphrey
13. *Reprojecting the City: Urban Space and Dissident Sexualities in Recent Latin American Cinema*, by Benedict Hoff
14. *Rethinking Juan Rulfo's Creative World: Prose, Photography, Film*, edited by Dylan Brennan and Nuala Finnegan
15. *The Last Days of Humanism: A Reappraisal of Quevedo's Thought*, by Alfonso Rey
16. *Catalan Narrative 1875-2015*, edited by Jordi Larios and Montserrat Lunati
17. *Islamic Culture in Spain to 1614: Essays and Studies*, by L. P. Harvey
18. *Film Festivals: Cinema and Cultural Exchange*, by Mar Diestro-Dópido
19. *St Teresa of Avila: Her Writings and Life*, edited by Terence O'Reilly, Colin Thompson and Lesley Twomey
20. *(Un)veiling Bodies: A Trajectory of Chilean Post-Dictatorship Documentary*, by Elizabeth Ramírez Soto

The Cultural Legacy of María Zambrano

EDITED BY
XON DE ROS AND DANIELA OMLOR

LEGENDA
Studies in Hispanic and Lusophone Cultures 24
Modern Humanities Research Association
2017

*Published by Legenda
an imprint of the Modern Humanities Research Association
Salisbury House, Station Road, Cambridge CB1 2LA*

*ISBN 978-1-910887-20-2 (HB)
ISBN 978-1-78188-360-0 (PB)*

First published 2017

All rights reserved. No part of this publication may be reproduced or disseminated or transmitted in any form or by any means, electronic, mechanical, photocopying, recording or otherwise, or stored in any retrieval system, or otherwise used in any manner whatsoever without written permission of the copyright owner, except in accordance with the provisions of the Copyright, Designs and Patents Act 1988, or under the terms of a licence permitting restricted copying issued in the UK by the Copyright Licensing Agency Ltd, Saffron House, 6–10 Kirby Street, London EC1N 8TS, England, or in the USA by the Copyright Clearance Center, 222 Rosewood Drive, Danvers MA 01923. Application for the written permission of the copyright owner to reproduce any part of this publication must be made by email to legenda@mhra.org.uk.

Disclaimer: Statements of fact and opinion contained in this book are those of the author and not of the editors or the Modern Humanities Research Association. The publisher makes no representation, express or implied, in respect of the accuracy of the material in this book and cannot accept any legal responsibility or liability for any errors or omissions that may be made.

Trademark notice: Product or corporate names may be trademarks or registered trademarks, and are used only for identification and explanation without intent to infringe.

© Modern Humanities Research Association 2017

Copy-Editor: Charlotte Brown

CONTENTS

❖

Acknowledgements ix
List of Contributors xi

Introduction 1

PART I: ENCOUNTERS AND EXCHANGES

1 María Zambrano and Rosa Chacel: The Paradigms and Paradoxes of Female Modernity
   SHIRLEY MANGINI 15

2 In the Dark Night of the Human: María Zambrano and the Avant-Garde
   INMACULADA MURCIA SERRANO 34

3 The Anti-Fascist Origins of Poetic Reason: Genealogy of a Reflection on Totalitarianism
   ANTOLÍN SÁNCHEZ CUERVO 51

4 Eros's Desire: Some Aspects of the Relationship Between José Ángel Valente and María Zambrano
   ANTONIO MOLINA FLORES 63

5 Hope beyond Hope: The Motif of Ruins in María Zambrano and Luis Cernuda
   FEDERICO BONADDIO 77

6 Poetry and Realization: Towards a Knowledge of the Poet's Place in María Zambrano
   ALBERTO SANTAMARÍA 89

PART II: IDENTITY AND REPRESENTATION

7 Melancholy and Loss in María Zambrano's Journals
   GORETTI RAMÍREZ 107

8 *La tumba de Antígona*: Psychoanalysis and Feminism
   XON DE ROS 122

9 Metaphor in María Zambrano: Theory and Practice
   ROBERTA JOHNSON 139

10 About Painting and Dialectical Images of María Zambrano
   ELIDE PITTARELLO 156

11 The Ethics of Exile and Memory in Zambrano
   DANIELA OMLOR 171

12 María Zambrano: Philosophy, Literature, and Democracy
   FRANCIS LOUGH 185

Bibliography 200
Index 215

ACKNOWLEDGEMENTS

The project was awarded a grant from the Hispanex Program (2016) by the Spanish Ministry of Education, Culture and Sport. The editors are also grateful to the Director of the Fundación María Zambrano, Luis Ortega Hurtado, for providing and granting permission to reproduce the portrait of Zambrano included here, also to Dr Pablo Aparicio Durán of the Universidad de Granada for his photograph of Málaga railway station featured on the cover. We would also like to acknowledge the support at different stages of the book of the following: Diane Garvey, Rhys Vaughan Williams, María José Giménez, Pablo Sauras, to Joanne Ferrari, of the Taylor Institution at Oxford, for her bibliographical assistance, and Dr Mari Paz Balibrea at Birkbeck College London for her encouragement in the first stages of the project, to Graham Nelson and the Editorial team at Legenda for their exacting professional standards, especially to Charlotte Brown for the acuity and thoroughness of her work as copy-editor. Last but not least to Chris Reid and Jamie McKendrick for their constant support and encouragement.

X.R. & D.O., Oxford, January 2017

LIST OF CONTRIBUTORS

Federico Bonaddio is Senior Lecturer in Modern Spanish Studies and Head of Department at King's College London. Amongst his recent publications are the monograph *Federico García Lorca: The Poetics of Self-Consciousness* (Tamesis, 2010) and the edited volume *A Companion to Federico García Lorca* (Tamesis, 2007).

Roberta Johnson is Professor Emerita at the University of Kansas, and Adjunct Professor in the Department of Spanish and Portuguese at UCLA. She is the translator and commentator of several works by Zambrano. Among her publications are *Crossfire: Philosophy and the Novel in Spain 1900–1934* (University of Kentucky Press, 1993) and *Gender and Nation in the Spanish Modernist Novel* (Vanderbilt University Press, 2003). She is the co-editor of *Antología del pensamiento feminista español 1726–2011* (Cátedra, 2013).

Frank Lough is Professor of Hispanic Studies at the University of Birmingham, and Director of the Centre for the Study of the Hispanic Exile. His research interests are the literature of the Spanish Civil War and the Republican diaspora. He is the co-editor of *Spanish Republican Exile Geographies / Geografías del exilio republicano español* (University of Birmingham, 2013).

Shirley Mangini is Professor Emerita at the California State University, Long Beach, and has published extensively on modern Spanish literature and politics with a focus on women and gender studies. Her books include: *Memories of Resistance: Women's Voices from the Spanish Civil War* (Yale University Press, 1995), *Las modernas de Madrid* (Península, 2001), and *Maruja Mallo and the Spanish Avant-Garde* (Ashgate, 2012).

Antonio Molina Flores is Associate Professor of Aesthetics at the Universidad de Sevilla and has published on contemporary Spanish culture. He is the author of *Doble teoría del genio: sujeto y creación de Kant y Schopenhauer* (Universidad de Sevilla, 2001) and he is the co-editor of *Tendencias estéticas y literarias en la cultura contemporánea* (Renacimiento, 2014).

Inmaculada Murcia Serrano is Associate Professor of Aesthetics and Theory of the Arts at the Universidad de Sevilla in Spain. She is the author of *La razón sumergida: el arte en el pensamiento de María Zambrano* (Luso-Española de Ediciones: 2009) and *Agua y destino: introducción a la estética de Ramón Gaya* (Peter Lang, 2010).

Daniela Omlor is Lecturer in Modern Spanish Literature at the University of Oxford and Tutorial Fellow at Lincoln College, and has published on exile and historical memory. She is the author of *Jorge Semprún: Memory's Long Voyage* (Peter Lang, 2014).

Elide Pittarello is Professor of Spanish Literature at the Universita Ca' Foscari, Venice. She has published widely on twentieth-century Spanish literature and the visual arts. She is the co-editor of *(En)claves de la transición: una visión de los Novísimos. Prosa, poesía, ensayo* (Iberoamericana, 2009).

Goretti Ramírez is Assistant Professor in Modern Spanish Literature and Culture at Concordia University, Montreal, Canada. Her research focuses on twentieth-century Spanish poetry and intellectual history, with particular emphasis on María Zambrano and the Republican exile under Franco's dictatorship. She is the author of *María Zambrano: crítica literaria* (Devenir, 2004) and co-editor of volume VI of María Zambrano's *Obras completas* (Galaxia Gutenberg, 2014).

Xon de Ros is Professor of Modern Spanish Studies at Oxford and Tutorial Fellow at Lady Margaret Hall. She has published on modernism, poetry, and women's studies. Recent publications include *The Poetry of Antonio Machado: Changing the Landscape* (Oxford University Press, 2015). She is the co-editor of *A Companion to Spanish Women's Studies* (Tamesis / Boydel & Brewer, 2011).

Alberto Santamaría is Associate Professor in the Facultad de Bellas Artes of the Universidad de Salamanca. He has published several books on the latest tendencies in Spanish poetry. He is the co-editor of *Malos tiempos para la épica: visiones y revisiones de la poesía española 2000–2012* (Visor, 2012).

Antolín Sánchez Cuervo is Tenured Researcher at the Institute of Philosophy of the Spanish National Research Council (CSIC). He is author and editor or co-editor of several books on Spanish and Latin-American cultural studies, especially on the Spanish Republican exile, and director of the following research projects: 'El pensamiento del exilio español de 1939 y la construcción de una racionalidad política' (MINECO, FFI2012–30822) and 'Exilio, ciudadanía y deber de memoria' (CSIC, i-link 09851). He is editor of *Las huellas del exilio: expresiones culturales de la España peregrina* (Tébar, 2008).

María Zambrano in Madrid circa 1930

INTRODUCTION

The Spanish philosopher María Zambrano (1904–1991) belongs to the group of twentieth-century women whose work has left an enduring mark on a culture defined as masculine, without compromising either their freedom or their individuality. The singularity of her contribution and her uniqueness in the arena of Spanish academia makes her achievement exceptional. Even more so when considering her forty-five years in exile, mostly spent without an institutional affiliation and writing free-lance. She devoted her philosophical career, with more than thirty books from the 1930 essay *Horizonte del liberalismo* to the final version of *Los sueños y el tiempo*, published posthumously in 1992, to thinking through the crisis of modernity and reflecting on its alternatives.[1] A heterodox philosopher who conceived her role as that of an agent for ethical change, she sought to reconcile philosophy and poetry, and wrote not only essays on philosophy, but also plays, poetry, literary criticism, art reviews, and a memoir. Her influence on her contemporaries and on subsequent generations of Spanish poets was seminal. Her biography could easily join the ranks of the female case-studies on which Julia Kristeva postulates the idea of a feminine genius: Hannah Arendt, Melanie Klein, and Colette (2004).[2] Like Zambrano, none of them openly espoused the feminist cause but their legacy has turned them into icons for feminism. It was through their alignment with a male-normative perspective that they achieved an equitable subjectivity which enabled them to question and challenge the socio-historical conditions of their identity as women. Their work is seen as 'rooted in the biography of their experience' (Kristeva 2001: x), and Zambrano's life and writing are tightly interconnected with her experience of exile, both as a philosopher in the context of male hegemony, and from 1939 to 1984 as a Republican exiled from Spain. Zambrano's case is closer to that of Arendt (1906–1977) who was also a philosopher and, after having fled Nazi Germany in 1933, spent most of her adult life in exile. Both were witness to the devastation of Europe in the aftermath of the Second World War and to the effects of totalitarian rule, and their work addresses in different ways the contemporary crisis of values; both started their careers under the aegis of charismatic and prominent mentors — Ortega and Heidegger, respectively — who exerted a strong influence on their philosophical trajectories and to whom they professed a life-long loyalty despite their ideological differences. From an engagement in political activism in their youth, their interest moved on to metaphysical reflection without abandoning ethical concerns. Neither of them produced a systematic philosophy which may explain the fact noted by Kristeva in all her examples that even though professionally these women 'were not truly excluded or marginalized, they nevertheless lay outside the norm' (2001:

xix). Philosophy, in any case, seems to be a particularly fraught field for women, whose relative absence, or what has been described as 'ambiguous presence' in the discipline has been the object of on-going debate (see Lloyd 2002: 21; Le Doeuff 2007; Hutchinson and Jenkins 2013; see also Maillard 1998). One of the obstacles highlighted by feminist critics is that 'women are correlated with the very elements against which philosophy defines itself' (Grosz 1989: 208). Philosophical theory helped to articulate and naturalize gender dichotomies asserting the supremacy of reason associated with masculinity, while the feminine was relegated to the inferior spheres of imagination and emotion. It is precisely Zambrano's questioning of the primacy of rationality for a proper understanding of human reality and her championing of a phenomenology based on empathy and open to the irrational that sets her work outside the parameters that have defined the disciplinary boundaries of philosophy from the Enlightenment onwards.

The model presented by Kristeva may provide further insight into the set of practices that separate the female genius from the masculine paradigm.[3] In contrast to the solipsist isolation traditionally associated with the latter, the feminine genius according to Kristeva is realized through the attachment to others, and in Zambrano we find a compelling illustration of the acting and speaking with others that also characterized Arendt's attitude (Kristeva 2001: 173). From the strong bond with her sister, in whose company she spent most of her life and to whom she refers repeatedly in her writings, often through the figure of Antigone, her biography is constituted within a 'web of human relations', to use Kristeva's phrase, where she found intellectual sustenance, as well as material support when confronting the hardships of exile.

Through her father, the socialist educator Blas Zambrano, she was introduced early in her life to the older generation of writers and intellectuals such as Antonio Machado, Unamuno, and Azorín, whose work she surveyed in *Pensamiento y poesía en la vida española* (1939) and invoked elsewhere in her writing. The long list of her own acquaintances from her time as a university student in Madrid in the late 1920s and 1930s attests to her intellectual curiosity and sociability. Apart from frequenting the many *cafés tertulias* which were centres of social and literary life conducted by prominent cultural figures, from the modernist Valle-Inclán in *Granja del Henar* to the avant-gardist Ramón Gómez de la Serna in *Café Pombo*, she was also invited to the more select circles generated around publications such as *Cruz y Raya* and *Revista de Occidente*. From 1926 she opened her own *salón tertulia* in her family home in Madrid where figures of the intelligentsia mixed with the younger generation of writers. The flurry of activities that marked the years before the Civil War saw Zambrano attending to and participating in events at the Atheneum, the Lyceum Club Femenino, the Residencia de Señoritas, and other cultural institutions. She was an active member of the students' union and contributed with public lectures, seminars, and articles to current debates. Her increasingly public standing when she became a university lecturer in 1931 under the auspices of Zubiri and Ortega, is reflected in a number of manifestos and public declarations where her name figures among the signatories, as in the *Alianza de Intelectuales para la Defensa de la Cultura*

(AIDC), but also ill-advisedly in *Manifiesto del Frente Español,* whose statutes were later absorbed by the Falange.

Zambrano's support for the Republic escalated from her engagement in the Pedagogical Missions project of spreading culture to rural areas, to her work on the editorial board of the journal *Hora de España* (1937–38), a fulcrum of literary and artistic Republican resistance. Her political activism crystallized in her appointment as a delegate in the Ministry of Propaganda. During the war, her circle extended to international figures such as Simone Weil, Octavio Paz, and Nicolás Guillén who came to Spain in solidarity with the Republican cause. After leaving Spain in 1939 and during her exile she would re-encounter many of these acquaintances among the Republican diaspora and with some of them she would form a deep attachment, based on common recollections and shared ideas. This is the case of the Eugenicist Gustavo Pittaluga, the painter Ramón Gaya, and the writer Rosa Chacel, as well as the poets Luis Cernuda, José Bergamín, Jorge Guillén, Miguel Altolaguirre, and Rafael Alberti among other members and epigones of the 1927 group of writers. To this constellation of exiles there would be other additions from her time in Mexico, Puerto Rico and Cuba in the 1940s; in the latter, a particular bond of friendship was established with the writer José Lezama Lima and the group of poets linked to his magazine *Orígenes* (1944–1956). Her early experience of a vibrant intellectual community in Spain may have contributed to her discomfort in the relative tranquillity of her first academic destination abroad in 1939, the University of Morelia in Michoacan, missing the buzz of intellectual activity of the *Casa de España* in Mexico City, with its traffic of visiting lecturers and seminars, and also of the more cosmopolitan Havana, where the first meeting of exiled Spanish academics was held in 1943 which resulted in the *Declaración de La Havana* condemning the Franco regime. The sense of belonging to a large community of equals, united in a common intellectual endeavour, is expressed by Zambrano in her article 'Persona y democracia' where she links friendship with philosophy through their etymological root in the Latin *filia*, described as 'una dedicación constante, continua que proviene, aunque nazca de la misteriosa simpatía, de la comunidad de pertenecer a un mismo reino del espíritu; es una especie de confraternidad que nace de ir en busca de las mismas cosas' [a constant and continuous dedication, which may have its origins in a mysterious fellow-feeling, but comes from the feeling of belonging to the same spiritual realm; it is a kind of confraternity born out of seeking after the same goals] (2011d: 374).[4]

From the early 1950s in the course of her peripatetic existence in Europe, with long stays in Rome, Paris, the French Jura, and Geneva, she would befriend among others Albert Camus, Elena Croce, and Emil Cioran. Later on, among her visitors there would be a number of young Spanish poets from the 1960s such as Jaime Gil de Biedma and José Ángel Valente on whom she would leave a lasting impression, and through them on subsequent poetic generations. Her prolific correspondence shows an on-going dialogue with three generations. The self-realization through companionship is reflected most eloquently in the process of cross-fertilization effected in those relationships. Zambrano's essays on several of the poets of 1927, and her reviews of work written by contemporaries are only the most superficial part of this exchange.[5] Some of her interlocutors, as in the case of Cioran, Paz, or Valente openly acknowledged her influence. This dialogue is an important part of Zambrano's legacy that is explored in some of the contributions to this volume.

For Zambrano exile was also associated with the idea of rebirth which is a recurrent theme in her writing: 'El exiliado está ahí como si naciera [...] sí como si naciera [...] qué remedio tiene sino nacer?' [the exile is there as if she was being born [...] yes, as if she was born [...] what could she do but be born?] (in Moreno Sanz 2003: 383).[6] In fact this is an experience that preceded her exile and is described in her autobiography *Delirio y destino*, written in 1952 and published in 1989, where references to her early years' precarious health led to the conception of self-begetting through creation and writing.[7] The notion of a constant process of re-birth of the self and of society is at the centre of some of her meditations, particularly prominent in *Persona y democracia* (1958). This emphasis on the temporality of birth is another aspect which Kristeva identifies with the feminine genius, expressing 'the rhythm of renewal, as against the linear time of the realisation of destiny' (2004: 502). But above all, a commitment to the life of the mind, the identification of thought with life, is manifest in Zambrano's writing, where the process of thinking is often ostensibly conveyed. While the density of metaphor at times makes reading her work a challenging task, her style is part of a poetics intended to elicit in the reader an affective recognition which does not exclude perplexity and bewilderment, a response associated in her work with the motif of ruins.

The confluence of life and thought is encapsulated in her vindication of a sentient thought conveyed in the concept of 'razón poética', first formulated in 1937 and developed in *Claros del bosque* (1977).[8] It has been described as a 'creative reason able to endow the reasoning of human life with feeling, a reasoning that takes account of feeling' (Illán 2002: 242). This notion of 'razón poética' also informs her approach to literature and art, as demonstrated in her reflections on painting collected in *Algunos lugares de la pintura* (1989), and in her essays on Spanish literature.

In 1984 Zambrano returned to Spain. Three years earlier she had been awarded the first Príncipe de Asturias Prize for Communications and Humanities, and in 1988 she became the first woman and the first philosopher to be presented with the prestigious Miguel de Cervantes Prize. Until her death in Madrid in 1991 she carried on with her work in dialogue with those around her. After the relative obscurity of her life in exile, Zambrano's genius began to be recognized in the final decade before her death, and since then, both in Spain and Latin-America, her reputation as a major thinker has been steadily consolidated.

The Fundación María Zambrano was created in 1987 in her birthplace, Vélez-Málaga, to preserve and disseminate her work, and among the activities under its aegis is the edition of the complete works in eight volumes, of which three have already been published.[9] In 2004 on the centenary of her birth a number of major studies were published, and a biographical film was released, *María querida*, by José Luis García Sánchez, based on the later years of her life.[10] While the early reception of her work in Spain was primarily aimed at offering a survey of her philosophical texts, exploring the philosophical ideas in her writings, critical attention in Anglo-American academia has taken a more interdisciplinary approach, from the pioneering translation of Zambrano's autobiographical work by Carol Maier to the more recent *Two Confessions* translated by Noël Valis and Carol Maier which gathers together the essays on the genre by Zambrano and Chacel. Other landmarks have been the two bi-lingual monographs co-edited by Madeline Cámara Betancourt (2011) and Luis Pablo Ortega Hurtado (2015), as well as *María Zambrano in Dialogue*, a special issue in 2015 of the *Journal of Spanish Cultural Studies*, edited by Lena Burgos-Lafuente and Tatjana Gajic.[11]

Following this lead, the present volume, without excluding her contribution to philosophy, focuses on Zambrano's role as a cultural agent, considering her relevance in relation to the avant-garde, feminism, psychoanalysis, literary comparativism, art criticism and semiotics, autobiographical writing, political theory, historical memory, and exile.[12]

Kristeva celebrates the legacy of the female geniuses in her biographical studies, for their exceptionality as well as for their ability to transform the lives of those who encounter it, and her words can be easily applied to Zambrano's legacy:

> At the heart of the precarious solitude of their pioneering work, which was the price they paid for their unique creativity, [they] managed to create the conditions that give rise to a necessary public opinion and, why not, a school and, at best, create an effect of seduction that solicits a communion of readings and a communion of readers. (Kristeva 2004: 503)

Following this cue, the present volume seeks to extend the readership for Zambrano's work beyond national and disciplinary boundaries through a communion of readers whose contributions are gathered here. While the general focus of this collection gravitates toward Spanish and European contexts, Zambrano's legacy can equally be considered from the perspective of its projection in Latin America, where many of her works were first published, and where many important friendships were forged. This is an area that deserves a full-length volume of its own.

The book is structured in two sections. The first — Encounters and Exchanges — explores the dialogue Zambrano establishes through her work both with her contemporaries and with subsequent generations. In these essays her figure functions as a point of intersection or crucible for cultural currents in the twentieth century and beyond.

The second section — Identity and Representation — focuses on different aspects of Zambrano's writing with a comparative and intertextual approach that investigates the interconnection between subjectivity, poetics, politics, and ethics. In particular, contributors show how by problematizing traditional ways of conceiving the relationship between the self and culture the figure of Zambrano becomes a space for the articulation of a paradigm.

In the first essay, writing within the area of Women's Studies, **Shirley Mangini** argues that Zambrano became not only a role model for the young female students who had begun their education in the twenties and thirties, but also a strong reference for the cohort of women associated with the *Residencia de Señoritas* (1915–1936) [Young Ladies' Residence] and the Lyceum Club Femenino (1926–1939) [Lyceum Women's Club]. These writers and artists were the first generation of Spanish women who entered the cultural scene and became active agents in the process of modernization, paving the way for social and political reform. Their experience in a male-dominated environment fostered an *esprit de corps* among them — a communality truncated by Franco's victory and put under strain with the dislocations of exile. Drawing from her previous work on these Madrid-based artistic and intellectual women's circles identified with modernity, Mangini discusses Zambrano's position within this community and her relation with some of the leading figures: the avant-garde artist Maruja Mallo, the poet Concha Méndez, the educator Concha Albornoz, and especially the writer Rosa Chacel, whose rapport was first established within the orbit of Ortega y Gasset and the *Revista de Occidente*. Both Chacel and Zambrano taught at the liberal educational establishment *Instituto-Escuela* and at the *Residencia de Señoritas*, and published in the Republican magazine *Hora de España*. Whereas their friendship floundered in exile despite their sporadic correspondence (Zambrano 1992c), their writing shows what has been described elsewhere as an ongoing 'secret, subterranean dialogue passing between the two' (Valis 2015: 2) conducted through a network of interconnections, which, as Mangini demonstrates in her essay, are informed by their respective intellectual trajectories.[13]

Among the interests shared by both Chacel and Zambrano was the avant-garde that had emerged in the 1920s in Spain and would become a determining factor in the definition of their own generation. In Madrid, Zambrano met with a number of young artists and writers, some of whom became friends, in some cases well into her years of exile. She was not, however, a champion of the phenomenon that would so influence European culture in the twentieth century, yet she reflected on its significance and throughout her life she made several forays into the subject in essays and in reviewing the work of some of its leading figures. **Inmaculada Murcia Serrano** surveys Zambrano's views on the avant-garde, offering an insight into this complex transformation in the cultural history of the West, while also shedding new light on some fundamental aspects of Zambrano's ideology, starting with one of her earliest pieces on the artistic avant-garde, 'Nostalgia de la tierra', of 1933. Seven years before, the philosopher José Ortega y Gasset (1883–1955), had published in the *Revista de Occidente* his famous essay on *La deshumanización del arte*, to which María Zambrano refers indirectly in hers. More than a decade later, she published another essay, with her attention still fixed on Ortega — though not only on him — entitled 'La destrucción de las formas', which closes, so to speak, the intellectual cycle dedicated to the avant-garde by the author. In these texts Zambrano explores the aesthetics of primitivism and the continuity of tradition with reference to several Spanish artists of the twentieth century, and in particular to Surrealism, one of the avant-garde movements which was closer to her own poetics. Murcia Serrano's perceptive discussion of Zambrano's critique is organized around these thematic axes.

The critique of Idealism articulated in the texts on the avant-garde is shifted by **Antolín García Cuervo** to the terrain of political philosophy with a discussion of Zambrano's notion of 'poetic reason', which was first formulated as a response to a supra-national experience of war and developed later on in relation to exile and the recovery of suppressed traditions of Spanish thought. Challenging the spiritualist interpretations prevalent among Zambrano's critics, García Cuervo vindicates the unequivocal political dimension of 'poetic reason'. He argues that for Zambrano, the Spanish Civil War was not so much the consequence of archaic violence or fratricidal instincts supposedly rooted in the psyche of a nation which had not experienced the Enlightenment, but rather the outcome of a totalitarian logic incubated for a long time at the heart of modern reason, and whose most brutal contemporary expression was fascism. Zambrano's interpretation of fascism, first introduced in her work in the 1930s and further developed, albeit implicitly, in the late 1950s in relation to the category of the sacred, exceeds therefore the conventional hermeneutic framework of her formative years in Spain. In her analysis, fascism is not simply an accidental, incidental, or random phenomenon within the civilizing ways supposedly paved by modern rationality, but a catastrophic experience rooted in logical reason itself. In line with thinkers like Rosenzweig and at a remove from Ortega, Zambrano proposes a critique of fascism that connects directly with a critique of Idealism and, in particular, of modern reason, which, as García Cuervo demonstrates, is implied in her notion of 'poetic reason'.

Federico Bonaddio brings into the discussion the figure of Luis Cernuda, indisputably the most important poet of the Republican diaspora, and very much admired by Zambrano. They frequented the same literary circles in Madrid and had many friends in common, such as Rosa Chacel and Concha de Albornoz, but their relationship crystallized when they met again in Cuba in the early 1950s. Despite the differences in temperament, their mutual support and reciprocal references in their work, and the fellow-feeling evinced in their correspondence, suggest a deep affinity kindled by their status of exiles. Bonaddio's analysis focuses on the treatment of the ruin motif in their work of this period, highlighting the significance it acquires in each case.[14] While their reflections on ruins can be seen as a displaced working-through of their experience in the wake of the Spanish Civil War and the Second World War, they also articulate a concern with historical consciousness. An image of the triumph either of time, or over time, the ruin represents, in Bonaddio's argument, a marker for an understanding of their respective poetics. While for Cernuda, the vision of impermanence is counteracted by existential affirmation, Zambrano's sentiment of ruins becomes a referent for the conceptual and perceptual creativity implied in her philosophy of 'poetic reason'.

Among the many encounters during her long exile, her friendship with the Cuban writer and poet José Lezama Lima was the most enduring and intellectually fruitful. The strong bond between them, forged during the fourteen years of her American exile spent mostly in Cuba, continued from a distance through letters and publications once she settled in Europe and up to 1959 at the victory of the Cuban Revolution. After an eight-year hiatus their correspondence resumed in 1967 with a letter in which Zambrano introduced Lezama to the Spanish poet José Ángel Valente, whom she had met and befriended in 1964 after moving to La Pièce, on the French-Swiss border. Valente was at the time living in Geneva, and on this occasion had been invited to visit Havana.[15] Zambrano's gesture initiated a dialogue within and among the three writers which lasted till Lezama's death in 1976. **Antonio Molina Flores** explores the relationship between the younger poet and Zambrano, tracing the impact of their collaboration in their respective work. His analysis highlights ideological convergences in their shared interest in mysticism and in particular in the quietist philosophy of Miguel de Molinos, as well as divergences in their respective approaches to the articulation between transcendence and desire. Despite the breakdown of their friendship in 1983, the confluence of Zambrano's philosophy and Valente's poetics would become a strong reference for younger generations of Spanish poets.

The prevailing tendency in Zambrano criticism celebrates the inspirational and transformative potential of her doctrine, but she has also been criticized for the reactionary implications of privileging a poetic form of cognition divorced from the realities of contemporary politics (Mayhew 2012). This critique assimilates Zambrano's thought to the cultural essentialism of the previous generation of Spanish intellectuals represented by Unamuno. Circumventing the charges of exceptionalism, **Alberto Santamaría** realigns Zambrano's perspective with Ortega's universalism, through the concept of realization, which had its origins in Ortega and which she reconstructs and reconfigures to make it her own. Santamaría's essay places her position within the debate around the moot question of the poet's relation to society in the context of the rise of fascism in Europe, which engaged thinkers such as Heidegger, Gombrowicz, and Adorno, as well as poets such as T. S. Eliot and Wallace Stevens. Zambrano's intervention is postulated on a new historical sensibility that challenges entrenched ideologies. From this vantage point, even though the connection is not made explicit, Zambrano's advocacy of a new sensibility comes closer to the nomadic subjectivity theorized by Rosi Braidotti as one which subverts 'the settled and conventional nature of theoretical and especially philosophical thinking' (Braidotti 2011: 14).

In the first essay of the second section, **Goretti Ramírez** takes the cultural legacy of melancholia and introspection as her starting point for the reading of Zambrano's diaries, which have hitherto been understudied. She proposes to locate Zambrano's melancholy within a modern (psychological) understanding of this notion, which establishes an intimate connection between melancholia and loss. In Zambrano's diaries, references to loss are recurrent, not least because she lived through the death of her father, mother, sister, and many different friends and companions in exile, heightening her sense of survival. Rather than turning inward and withdrawing from the world in mourning, however, Zambrano's melancholy is a constant reminder of the absence left behind by loss but also of the bond that continues to exist with those who are no longer. Melancholy then acts as a trigger for renewed creativity and can initiate the recovery of the link with the divine. In addition to these personal losses, Zambrano's writing also comments on the experience of collective loss brought about by the loss of meaning in the modern world. Melancholy emerges thus as a key component of Zambrano's thought, representing another form of criticism directed at all-encompassing rationalism and continuing to advocate a more significant role for emotions in our understanding of human life. Melancholy is drawn on as a means of expressing a renewed interest in the world for Zambrano and as a tool for exploring the relationship between self and other.

The interaction between self and other is also fundamental for **Xon de Ros**'s exploration of the gender politics in Zambrano's work. Although the philosopher never defined herself as a feminist, her concern with women's consciousness is manifest in her treatment of literary and mythological female characters, particularly insistent in her reflections around the figure of Antigone, most extensively in her play *La tumba de Antígona*, which is the subject of this essay. De Ros suggests that the association between delirium and Antígona's discourse can be interpreted in the context of the engagement with hysteria across feminist theory and criticism of the 1970s and 1980s. Just as hysteria articulates both the malady and the cure in the foundational texts of the major French feminist theorists, Irigaray, Cixous and Kristeva, Antígona's delirium is both a symptom of the dis-ease of patriarchy and a discourse of subversion and resistance. From these premises, de Ros offers a psychoanalytical interpretation of Zambrano's play underscoring the similarities with Julia Kristeva's approach to subject-formation, which vindicates the semiotic maternal bond. While both philosophers relate the feminine to the position of exile, and, as in Zambrano's exploration and practice of melancholia, her engagement with Antigone is another opportunity to think through the implications of being, in Kristeva's phrase, 'strangers to ourselves'. For Zambrano, however, women's position is determined by cultural and historical circumstances rather than psycho-somatic, and the open-ended conclusion of her play casts doubts on the efficacy of psychoanalysis in challenging the patriarchal structures of the polis.

A 'female aesthetic predicated on metaphorical thinking and poetic writing' (de Ros), as posited by Cixous finds an echo in **Roberta Johnson**'s contribution, which situates Zambrano's thought at the crossroads of that of Ortega y Gasset and the poststructuralist thinkers, particularly Merleau-Ponty. With this objective she explores the interplay between world, consciousness, and language. Johnson underlines that Zambrano differs significantly from Ortega in her consideration of the metaphor of the heart as embodied, thereby criticizing the primacy given to consciousness and establishing a direct association with the notion of 'poetic reason'. The heart as a space of recesses and depth, which can open and close like a door and yet is not independent of other organs, comes to symbolize dawning consciousness. Metaphors as a philosophical way of thinking, which find their culmination in *Claros del bosque*, have a direct impact on Zambrano's thought processes and also her style. In the end, form and content are inseparably intertwined. In order to demonstrate this Johnson focuses on *La tumba de Antígona* and the extensive use of metaphors that Zambrano makes within this play. On the one hand, Antigone's liminal position in her entombment is linked to the role of the heart with its implication of depth and openness. Antigone's 'vital state' becomes a metaphor for Zambrano's notion of the way in which consciousness functions both in its pre-conscious and fully conscious state. On the other hand, the sustained employment of light and fire metaphors develops the problematic of the 'representation of auroral consciousness'.

Continuing on from this idea that images might be a 'main device for thinking' **Elide Pittarello** stresses the importance of metaphors and the gaze as speech acts in the Ricoeurian sense within Zambrano's *oeuvre*. Her art criticism and her interpretation of paintings as visions of visions constitute an application of her philosophy to the visual arts. Uniquely, Zambrano opposes mimetics to revelation and does away with the traditional division between subject and object, creating a personal hermeneutics of painting influenced by the overarching concept of 'poetic reason'. Zambrano's comments forego logical, linguistic exegesis in order to open up the chasm between the visible and the invisible for the viewer, foreshadowing in some sense an understanding of art laid out in the iconic turn. Through Ramón Gaya's paintings, hybrid creations which reject temporality and strive to reveal the 'sacred nature of reality', Zambrano becomes aware of the emotional movement that passes between the painter and the beholder. This revelation was perhaps influenced by direct contact with Gaya, once the latter had also moved to Rome in the 1950s. Zambrano's approach to art then culminates in an essay on Giorgione's *The Tempest* in whose unfathomability she inscribes features of her own, prolonged exile. Finally, Pittarello argues that *Algunos lugares de la pintura*, which spans Zambrano's art criticism from as early as 1933 up until 1989, should be subjected to a renewed reading to come closer to the itinerancy during which these essays were produced.

Zambrano did indeed spend more than forty years in exile and its importance for the development of her thought is not to be underestimated. **Daniela Omlor** traces the evolving understanding of exile in a range of Zambrano's works. In these writings the focus is not on the exile's spatial and temporal dislocation or even linguistic alienation in a new land, instead the exile's liminal position is accorded an ethical dimension by likening her casting out to a sacrifice. Her complete dispossession is akin to a sacrifice as the exile loses herself and forcibly becomes other. In order to forge herself a new identity the exile has to negotiate with her own history. Yet, exile as the story of survival also appears as profoundly traumatic. Thus, as a survivor, the exile's suffering turns her into a living dead, which she must accept in order to live exile as a revelation which can lead to complete transformation. Memory is necessary for this process, given that it constitutes a means of accessing alternative histories. As a tool for active contemplation memory represents a connection to lived experience that cannot be severed. In her discussion of exile, Zambrano draws comparisons with the expulsion from paradise and the trials of Job, linking individual experience to a more universal sense of loss. However, in the last instance, exile bears within it the possibility of complete freedom, once the exile has accepted her dispossession as a new state of being.

In exile, Zambrano's philosophy developed and changed, but, as **Frank Lough** argues the association she established between politics, literature, and philosophy remained valid throughout her life. Whereas previously her initial interests in liberalism and democracy were triggered by the crisis of rational thought, which influenced the relationship between individual and society, her later inquiry into the nature of democracy was 'more detached from the real world of politics' and more concerned with philosophical discussions on ethics and metaphysics. To an extent, this is mirrored by her employment of increasingly metaphorical language, fundamental to her key concept of 'poetic reason'. Nonetheless, the political ideas behind her philosophy should not be ignored. Lough re-evaluates Zambrano's political thought in the light of recent critical debates, namely the aesthetic turn and affect theory. On the one hand, the connection between poetry and love is located at the core of Zambrano's politics, because it culminates in 'a belief in co-existence' in the social realm. On the other hand, politics as a creative and bodily practice whose aim is change is identified as a fundamentally human activity. Underlying Zambrano's engagement with politics, literature, and philosophy is ultimately the hope for 'the possibility of a repeated encounter with alterity' (Attridge 2004: 28).

One of the challenges that the contributors to this volume confront is that of translating Zambrano's prose, which is characterized by an accumulation of abstractions and metaphors, a poetic style which does not always find an easy equivalent in English. The translators' skills are often tested in passages that brush against obscurity, drawing attention to absences and uncertainties, which require a steady hand that refrains from imposing a deceptive order on the original, or from filling in the gaps. The reader will also find that phrases, and even titles, are translated differently in different contexts offering alternative meanings which are not mutually exclusive — for instance 'tierra' in 'Nostalgia de la tierra' is translated as 'land' thus referring more specifically to the experience of exile, but elsewhere as 'earth' which gives the word a more cosmic and mythic significance. Likewise, inevitably, many of the contributions refer to 'poetic reason' and define it in different but complementary ways. These multiplicities attest to the fluid vision promoted by Zambrano's philosophy with its emphasis on affects, imagination, and creativity. Furthermore, even though the emphasis in this volume is on Zambrano's cultural legacy and her intervention in fields other than the discipline of philosophy, a critical approach based on rigid demarcations would stand against her own holistic philosophical practice which defies disciplinary boundaries, as the essays collected here demonstrate, and the breadth of reference brought to bear in these essays illustrates the range and variety of approaches elicited by her work.

As a fitting image to conclude this introduction to Zambrano's cultural legacy, we might choose one she cherished — that of ruins, which she described as metaphors of hope, in a manner not dissimilar to the old elm tree in Antonio Machado's poetry, the contemplation of which should fill the observer with both awe and renewed creative energy.

Notes to the Introduction

1. For a bibliography see: <http://cvc.cervantes.es/actcult/zambrano/bibliografia/> [accessed 15 December 2016].
2. In this article Kristeva refers to her trilogy of biographies published under the general title: *Le Génie féminin: la vie, la folie, les mots: Hannah Arendt, Melanie Klein, Colette*, 3 vols (Paris: Fayard, 1999–2002); on the subject of genius and gender, see also Battersby 1989.
3. Even though Kristeva makes a point in distancing her investigation from the presupposition of a binary sexual system, in her discussion on genius she uses the categories of female and feminine indistinctly, see a version of this essay published as 'Female Genius, Freedom and Culture', *Irish Pages*, 2/2, The Earth Issue (Autumn/Winter, 2004), 214–28.
4. In the same essay Zambrano refers to friendship as 'una relación que está más allá de los que así se relacionan; se trata de un frecuentar los mismos lugares del pensamiento, de ir por un mismo camino, aunque a veces sea con diferente paso' [a relationship which goes beyond those connected by it; it is about recurrence of the same places in their thinking, to walk the same path, although sometimes at a different pace] (2011d: 74).
5. Already in 1936 Zambrano published an anthology of García Lorca's poetry in Chile where she travelled with her husband, a Spanish diplomat, but they would return to Spain the following year. The marriage was short-lived.
6. This anthology of texts edited by Moreno Sanz includes a detailed biographical section, 'Cronología y genealogía filosófico-espiritual', which has been a useful tool for this introduction, pp. 673–730
7. The first English translation by Carol Maier was published in the US in 1999.
8. The phrase 'razón poética' first appeared in Zambrano's review of Antonio Machado's *La Guerra*, in *Hora de España* (Zambrano 1986a: 82).
9. <http://www.fundacionmariazambrano.org> [accessed 15 December 2016].
10. Salient contributions to the scholarship on Zambrano in Spain are those of Chantal Maillard (1992); Ana Bundgaard (2000), Carmen Revilla Guzmán (2005), and José Luis Abellán (2006).
11. Luis Ortega Hurtado is also the editor of the periodical *Antígona: Revista cultural de la Fundación María Zambrano* (2007-).
12. The increasing interest in Zambrano's work in British Hispanism is attested by the number of scholarly essays published in peer-reviewed journals, and more recently by the international symposium organized by M. Paz Balibrea at the University of London (Birkbeck College), 'María Zambrano Amongst the Philosophers' (21–22 May 2015).
13. After her return to Madrid in 1977, in an interview with José Miguel Ullán in *El País* (21 July 1979), Chacel referred to Zambrano as the only other Spanish woman of her generation whose writings were worth reading.
14. Bonaddio's essay takes issue with Bruce W. Wardropper's claim that 'The Spaniards [...] never really learned to like ruins. They remained for them a grim reminder of the fragility of man's life. The lessons which the poets of the Golden Age taught the Spanish people were never forgotten' (1969: 305); Wardropper also overlooks Bécquer's unfinished *Historia de los templos españoles* which is an earlier example of the same *sentiment des ruins*.
15. Zambrano's letter to Lezama Lima of 12 November 1967 states: 'Y como Ángel Valente, poeta, escritor, amigo, también recibo siempre algo bueno, me parece muy natural el que se conozcan, sean amigos para siempre. Y me alegra el que este encuentro se verifique teniéndome presente como si los presentara y no por azar' [Because Ángel Valente, poet, writer, and friend, always brings me something good, I find it natural that you two meet, that you become friends forever. And I'm glad that this meeting should take place through me as if I were introducing the two of you in person and not by chance] (in Fornieles Ten 2005: 137).

PART I

Encounters and Exchanges

CHAPTER 1

María Zambrano and Rosa Chacel: The Paradigms and Paradoxes of Female Modernity

Shirley Mangini, California State University, Long Beach

In 1921 the young María Zambrano lived in Segovia; she was seventeen. Fully supported by her parents, she had been commuting to Madrid for studies in philosophy at the Central University of Madrid. Her cousin and first love, the poet Miguel Pizarro, introduced her to his close friend, the poet Federico García Lorca, and spoke to her enthusiastically of attending a lecture at the Atheneum in Madrid, given by a brilliant young writer, Rosa Chacel. María describes Pizarro's admiration for Chacel:

> María, he conocido y oído en Madrid a una muchacha, tan joven como tú, hablar de Nietzsche en el Ateneo. Ya no eres única, ella se te ha adelantado. Tiene talento, belleza y el hado del genio en su frente. (Zambrano 1988d: 11–12)

> [María, I have met and heard a girl, as young as you are [Chacel was six years older than Zambrano] in Madrid speak of Nietzsche at the Atheneum. You are no longer the only one; she has surpassed you. She has talent, beauty and genius written on her forehead.][1]

Through her father's political and intellectual activities, María also met the poet Antonio Machado, and other well-known writers who passed through the ancient city of the great Roman aqueduct, such as Miguel de Unamuno and the endocrinologist and writer Gregorio Marañón (Zambrano 2004c: 674).[2] Her father had arranged for María to move to Madrid to live at the *Residencia de Señoritas* in order to complete her studies in philosophy at the Central University; but by September of that fateful year, Blas Zambrano wrote to the director, the well known pedagogist María de Maeztu, that his daughter would not be arriving for the autumn course because of the 'neuralgia and neck pain' that was afflicting her (Marset 2004: 270). Although some critics have attributed these health problems to the heartbreak over Pizarro, we now know that María had already found a new love, a young military man at the Academy of Artillery, Gregorio del Campo Mendoza, and that she had become pregnant with his child.[3]

It appears that the sad event was never discussed outside the Zambrano home, and we fast-forward to 1924. Although it is possible that María continued the relationship with Gregorio for several more years (Zambrano 2012c: 12), she and her family were now installed in Madrid, and she had begun her trajectory toward prominence, returning to her coursework at the Central University, which she completed in 1926. In the mid to late twenties, María met several other outstanding women in Madrid, such as swimming champion-cum-poet Concha Méndez and the literature professor Concha de Albornoz, as well as the writer María Teresa León.[4] These friends had begun to meet at the various *tertulias* and in the *Cacharrería* at the Atheneum over the years.[5] While Zambrano had misgivings about her career on some occasions because of the societal pressures that dissuaded female intellectuals from attempting to join the male enclave, she was saved by a somewhat unlikely ally: the 'liberal' but misogynistic José Ortega y Gasset. Zambrano — along with many young male intellectuals — was invited to form part of his *tertulia* around the journal *La Revista de Occidente* in 1924. There she would meet the brilliant Chacel, who in 1927 had just returned from a sojourn in Rome begun in 1922, as well as the entertaining and subversive avant-garde artist Maruja Mallo.[6] As discussed later, Ortega y Gasset was very interested in the 'difference between the sexes' at this time, and given that fact, these would be formative years for the development of Zambrano's and Chacel's philosophical ideas on gender and their resistance to patriarchal injunctions.[7]

The year 1927 would mark the zenith of avant-garde activity in Madrid, characterized by the flourishing artistic and literary movement of several groups, especially the 'The Generation of 1927', whose venue was primarily the all-male *Residencia de Estudiantes* where many of the fellows lived. The newly mechanized world prompted a zest for spontaneity and artistic freedom. The inventions of the communications and transportation industries, the introduction of the Parisian art movements into Spain, and the advanced techniques of the Seventh Muse became part of the avant-garde aesthetic of 'Roaring Twenties' Madrid.

In 1927–1928, Zambrano plunged into politics, well ahead of her female colleagues. She became a member of the Federación Universitaria Escolar (FUE) and then the Liga de Educación Social.[8] She also began teaching at the first co-educational high school in Spain, the Instituto Escuela. But she was again deterred from fully pursuing her careers — as a philosophy instructor and political activist — at the end of 1928, this time by tuberculosis. Yet she continued to collaborate with the FUE, and began writing a column on women in the Madrid daily *El Liberal* called 'Fresh Air', in which she not only demands equal rights for women, but also elucidates the direction her philosophy would take.[9] In 1929 she began her first book, *Horizonte del liberalismo*, where she prognosticates the inevitability of a republic and calls for political action. This book and her articles placed Zambrano at the forefront of the group of young intellectuals seeking the end of monarchy and dictatorship and a new socialist democracy. She describes the year 1929 in her 'novelized' autobiography, *Delirio y destino*:[10]

Era la historia de España que se despertaba en aquella hora precisa, que se ponía en movimiento, desde el corazón y el ánimo esperanzado y enigmático, se proyectaba sobre el cielo implacablemente azul de Madrid, 1929. Sí, toda la vida y también la historia parecía aguardarla. (Zambrano 1989b: 27)

[It was the history of Spain awakening at that very hour, set in motion from a heart and a hopeful enigmatic spirit, projecting itself on Madrid's implacably blue sky in 1929. Yes, all life and all history seemed to await her.] (Zambrano 1999: 14)[11]

In the meantime, the frivolous Roaring Twenties had turned the corner and Spain began to experience an era of deep political engagement, a search for a more humanistic approach to all things cultural, and an energy and commitment to a more democratic economic process for Spain. These, of course, were the main preoccupations of the Republican and leftist women and men in Madrid. Among those at the vanguard of this charge was María Zambrano, who as we have seen had already begun organizing and writing about women's equality and the class struggle in various venues, as well as moving toward her unique philosophical vision which would later be dubbed 'poetic reason', a revolutionary divergence from the maestro Ortega y Gasset's dominant rational historical philosophy.[12]

In 1930, with the collapse of the Primo de Rivera dictatorship, the pieces were falling into place. By 1931, Primo's replacement, Dámaso Berenguer, resigned, and King Alfonso fled Spain. Thus the democratically-elected Second Republic (1931–1939) was proclaimed, while its supporters listened in awe. Zambrano describes the ambience as she walked through the streets of the city centre and observed. Reminiscent of Walter Benjamin's *flâneur*, the philosopher depicts the restless crowds running to and from Madrid's hot spots, spilling out of bars, everyone shouting about the king's abdication.[13] She explains the joy and hopefulness of the crowds as they hear the proclamation of the Republic at the city centre, the Puerta del Sol:

Bajando por un costado de Gobernación llegó un grupo de obreros como danzando. Uno de los que formaban el grupo se destacó dirigiéndose a alguien que pasaba y gritó: '¡Viva la República!,' mientras los demás revolteaban en su danza improvisada, '¡Viva España!' (Zambrano 1989b: 233)

]A group of workers came prancing down the street toward the Puerta del Sol alongside the Ministry of Interior. One of them broke away from the group, addressed a passerby, and shouted 'Viva la República!' while the others whirled about in their improvised dance: 'Viva España!'] (Zambrano 1999: 165)

With the establishment of the Republic, many educated women saw themselves suddenly elevated to public positions. Most significantly, Victoria Kent, Margarita Nelken, and Clara Campoamor were the first females to be elected to parliament. Other women became more visible as journalists and writers of fiction, poetry, and non-fiction, such as Chacel, Zambrano, and poets Ernestina de Champourcín and Concha Méndez. Some gained visibility and prestige as teachers and school functionaries, such as the writer and teacher Carmen de Burgos and Professor Concha de Albornoz. Of utmost importance is that many of these prominent women were active in cultural institutions like the Lyceum Club,[14] the Residencia de Señoritas, the United States-sponsored Spanish Institute, and the Atheneum. They also commingled in political and intellectual *tertulias,* like the one at the café Granja del Henar, formerly frequented by men only. To the consternation of many of their male colleagues, including the so-called liberals, the Republic was a defining moment for women as they were forging intellectual and political bonds.[15]

María Zambrano's importance as a teacher and role model at the Residencia de Señoritas in 1935 was essential for the young female students of Madrid. For example, we have the testimony of one of her students, Conchita Zamacona (later a librarian at Madrid's Complutense University), who some six decades later describes the indelible impression the philosopher made on her:

> Las clases de María Zambrano en la Residencia eran muy diferentes de las clases de la facultad. [...] Maria [...] explicaba desde una nueva forma de entender la filosofía: como una necesidad de lo poético en toda búsqueda intelectual. [...] María Zambrano me enseñó a pensar, a captar el asombroso misterio de todo acto creativo. [...] Pero además de esta deslumbrante indagación filosófica, que dejó una profunda huella, María fue mi guía. Me contaba todo lo que estaba ocurriendo en Madrid: lo que tenía que ver, los conciertos a los que debía asistir, las exposiciones, los teatros, las películas... Era mi maestra. Mis diálogos con ella han permanecido siempre en el recuerdo. Se acabaron sus clases, pero nunca su inolvidable magisterio. No volví a verla nunca ¡Qué pena, qué inmensa pena! (Alcalá Cortijo 2009: 252)

> [María Zambrano's classes at the Residence were very different from those at the University. [...] María [...] explained a new way of understanding philosophy: like a need for the poetic in all intellectual enterprises. [...] María Zambrano taught me how to think, to capture the amazing mystery of all creative acts. [...] But besides this dazzling philosophical inquiry that left a profound mark on me, María was my guide. She told me about everything that was happening in Madrid: the shows to see, the concerts I should go to, exhibitions, theatre, movies... She was my teacher. My dialogues with her have forever remained in my memory. Her classes ended, but never her unforgettable teaching. I never saw her again. What a pity, what an immense pity!]

The female friendships and cultural liaisons formed in those years would last throughout the lives of Madrid's accomplished women in many cases, in spite of the exile of most of those mentioned here. For instance, the case of Concha de Albornoz and Rosa Chacel is notable. Concha was from an illustrious political family. Her father Alvaro de Albornoz was a powerful leftist lawyer who during the Republic became Minister of both Justice and Public Works. After obtaining her doctorate, Albornoz became a literature professor at a prestigious institute in Madrid, secretary of the Philosophy Section at the Madrid Atheneum, and, during the early part of the war, she held various political posts.[16] She became a close friend to Rosa Chacel both in Spain and in exile after the war; Concha was Rosa's bridesmaid in 1922 and godmother to Rosa's son. Chacel describes her friendship with Zambrano as 'intellectual', while she considered Albornoz a 'fraternal girlfriend'. Chacel, in fact, includes poet Luis Cernuda in this friendship: 'Con Cernuda me unió una gran amistad; desde muy jóvenes, él, Concha de Albornoz y yo formábamos un trío inseparable, y además siento gran admiración por su obra' [I had a great friendship with Cernuda; from when we were very young, he, Concha de Albornoz and I formed an inseparable trio, and besides, I feel great admiration for his work] (quoted in Mateo 1993: 73).[17] Chacel dedicated several poems to Albornoz, one of which was the first sonnet in her book *A la orilla de un pozo* (1936), another in her book *Versos prohibidos*, published some fifty years later. In the lengthy prologue to the latter book, Chacel speaks of 'secrets' and something 'prohibited'. Both Chacel and Albornoz married and the couples were neighbours and summered together. But it appears that even before Concha's divorce and Chacel's separation from her husband, they had begun a sexual relationship.[18]

Chacel describes the risqué and innovative ambience of Madrid upon her return in 1927, above all the excitement of the new literature, the surrealist movement, the many pop-up journals, the groups that had formed, and especially the eschewing of social mores which she sums up with the statement: 'Sería absolutamente falso sostener que *en aquel entonces* nos detenían escrúpulos morales cuando, en realidad, éramos la avanzada de todas las subversiones' [It would be absolutely false to maintain that *in those days* we were deterred by moral scruples when, in reality, we were at the vanguard of all [types of] subversion] (Chacel 1980: 36). While it is true that Concha Méndez, Rosa Chacel, and Maruja Mallo were very transgressive in their behaviour in those years, refusing to conform to patriarchy's rules for women, María Zambrano did not strive to be 'scandalous'.[19] As we have observed, she had several male love interests in her years in Segovia and also in Madrid, but did not personally flaunt her resistance to patriarchal mores. In fact, in 1984 she spoke of how she had felt about such matters in her youth, stating that she had not wished to be 'a free woman', because it would have been her 'most destructive error' (Cruz 1984). Her public 'deviance' from norms was only to be found in her journalistic writing and in her philosophy, when she broke away from Ortega's dominance and began creating her unique 'poetic reason'.

Perhaps Zambrano's remarks about being a free woman as a destructive endeavour were influenced by Maruja Mallo's lifestyle. They had become good friends and María respected Maruja as an artist, but obviously did not approve of Mallo's promiscuity, which was highly criticized by her peers. They had some intellectual pursuits in common, such as their mutual interest in esoterica, especially theosophy.[20] Zambrano was also an admirer of Pythagorean theorem and as María Escribano notes, her friendship with Mallo had a great deal to do with that common interest.[21] Escribano writes that in her many years of conversations with Mallo, the artist often spoke of the Sunday *tertulias* that Zambrano held in her Madrid home in 1935 and said of the philosopher: 'Era gran amiga mía y muy helénica' [She was a great friend of mine and very Hellenic] (Escribano 2009: 26). Yet, Escribano cautions that their ideology was not similar because Zambrano was interested in 'suprarational knowledge', while Mallo was a 'racionalista, pese a que su creencia en el orden interno del universo la fuera llevando [...] a una especie de panteísmo materialista' [rationalist, in spite of the fact that her belief in the internal order of the universe led her toward [...] a sort of materialistic pantheism] (Escribano 2009: 26).

There is a telling anecdote that perhaps best illustrates the socio-intellectual bond between Mallo and Zambrano. On May Day in 1936 the two women attended the parade celebrating International Workers' Day. At the Colón Plaza, a woman from the countryside appeared among the marching proletariat who was holding up an enormous loaf of bread. Mallo asked for an explanation, and the farm woman told her that it meant that 'they needed bread' (Vidal 1999: 59). This vision motivated Maruja to paint 'Surprise of the Wheat', an immense canvas that elucidates the new humanism that had taken hold among Spanish Republicans — visible in Zambrano's developing 'poetic reason'. Monolithic in size, a theosophically-inspired female figure holds up her right hand, out of which three spikes of wheat appear to be sprouting from three fingers, while in her left hand she holds three grains of wheat. This wheat goddess mythologizes 'the ubiquitous grain of Castile that for centuries was the main sustenance of the masses' (Mangini 2010: 135) and immortalizes that moment on May Day, 1936, when the artist and the philosopher witnessed the last peaceful democratic convergence held in Spain until after the death of Franco.

When the war broke out in July, Zambrano began to write her war essays, a series of intermittently hopeful and desperate diatribes on the working-class soldiers and the liberal Spanish intellectuals who she felt could save Spain from fascism.[22] Mallo, who had fled Spain at the end of 1936, would continue — in exile in Buenos Aires — the paintings that began with 'Surprise of the Wheat', canvasses that glorified farm workers and those who toiled in the fishing industry. Known as 'The Religion of Work' series, she explains its origins (in her typically elliptical prose):

> *Sorpresa del trigo* (mayo 1936) que anuncio como prólogo de mi labor sobre los trabajadores de mar y tierra, compenetración de elementos materiales. El trigo, vegetal universal, símbolo de la lucha, mito terrenal. Manifestación de creencia que surge de la severidad y la gracia de las dos Castillas, de mi fe materialista en el triunfo de los peces, en el reinado de la espiga. (Mallo 1939: 40)

> ['Surprise of the Wheat' (May 1936) that I announce as a prologue to my work on the labourers of the sea and the land, a natural interpenetration of material elements. Wheat, a universal grain, a symbol of the struggle, an earthly myth. A manifestation of the faith that arises from the severity and grace of the two Castiles, of my materialistic faith in the triumph of the fish, in the reign of the wheat spike.]

Both Mallo and Zambrano spent more time with men than with women. This was logical, given that both the fields of philosophy and art were largely populated by men. But in Mallo's case, it was also because she preferred male company to female. They both appeared to be attracted to poets — Rafael Alberti (Mallo's great love interest in the late twenties), Miguel Hernández, Luis Cernuda, Chilean Pablo Neruda, Galician Rafael Dieste, among them — more than any other intellectuals; and these relationships in some cases inspired collaborations and/or inter-influences. Mallo had a surrealist period when she painted her 'Cesspools and Belfries', after which she was introduced into Andre Breton's surrealist circle in Paris in 1931 and 1932. Zambrano, although not a Surrealist, was attracted to some of the elements of Spanish surrealism, especially the idea of 'impurity', as Moreno Sanz notes:

Desde 1929 a 1934, Zambrano tematizará filosóficamente este nietzscheano tema de la 'impureza' de la tierra, al compás de muchos de sus coetáneos como R. Dieste o Rosa Chacel, y en la pintura toda de la llamada Escuela de Vallecas, y especialmente su amiga Maruja Mallo.[23] (Zambrano 2004c: 65)

[From 1929 to 1934 Zambrano philosophically makes this Nietzschean concept of the 'impurity' of the land a main subject, in step with many of her contemporaries like R. Dieste or Rosa Chacel, and in the paintings of the so-called School of Vallecas, and especially her friend Maruja Mallo.]

We observe Zambrano's admiration of the 'impure' poetry of her friend Neruda in an article first published in 1938 entitled 'Pablo Neruda o el amor a la materia' [Pablo Neruda or the Love of Matter]. In the essay, she speaks of his materialism as a 'realidad hirviente [...] de seres que aún no son; [...] de muertas y quietas cosas que nos muestran en su abandono y desgaste el vacío de la existencia' [boiling reality [...] of beings that do not yet exist; [...] of dead and quiet things that show us the vacuity of existence through their abandon and erosion] (Zambrano 1977: 157–58). She emphasizes that Neruda's poetry (in the book *Residencia en la tierra*) is 'rebellious', not 'platonic, contemplative, idealistic, idealizing' (158), that it brings with it an 'immense avalanche' (160) of matter, matter that is associated with death. Zambrano explains that Neruda transformed Spanish poetry, and associates that transformation with Spain's imminent tragedy: the defeat of the Republic and the imposition of fascism, one of Zambrano's greatest fears. His poetry is akin to Mallo's nightmarish series, 'Cesspools and Belfries', or to the stark, osseous paintings of the artist Benjamín Palencia. Zambrano, as critic and astute observer of the connection between art and politics, has been recognized in recent years as not only one of the great modern Spanish philosophers, but also as one of Spain's outstanding modern literary critics, a fact not lost on the many poets who admired her in Spain and those she befriended throughout her odyssey in exile and after her return to Spain in 1984.[24]

Zambrano and Mallo's mutual friend Concha Méndez became a poet, a dramatist, a filmmaker, and was an active member of the Lyceum Club; she was also one of the first female editors in Spain. Concha also became an informal ambassador for other Spanish female writers during her trip to London in 1929 and then her long sojourn in Buenos Aires from December 1929 to June 1931 (Valender 2001: 156–57).[25] She became close friends with both Mallo and Zambrano in the late twenties and in the thirties, when Zambrano occasionally joined them in their *flâneuserie* around Madrid.[26] Zambrano and Méndez corresponded during the many years of exile (they coincided in Havana in the early 1940s and later in Mexico, where María taught briefly and where Méndez lived out her life in exile). And it would be Zambrano who would preface Méndez's autobiography in 1990, where she affectionately evokes her memories of Concha's wedding to poet Manuel Altolaguirre in Madrid in 1932 and the publishing house the couple founded while they lived in Havana from 1939 to 1943 (Ulacia Altolaguirre 1990: 9–12).

Yet of all the cultural exchanges among the friends mentioned here, perhaps the most illuminating were those of Chacel and Zambrano which, as mentioned, partially originated in the discussions on gender at the *Revista de Occidente* salon, where Ortega held court. Not only did they both write about female-male relationships, but they both also theorized about confessional writing, literature, and art.[27] In addition, Chacel, although not considered a philosopher in her own right, was truly a philosophical writer, as attested to by many critics.[28] She also wrote several autobiographical novels about the lives of young females in Madrid in the 1920s and 1930s in her later years. Both Chacel and Zambrano, while in exile, were able to capture what that world of Madrid was like for the intellectual and artistic women who showered their riches on that vibrant Madrid of the avant-garde era and the short-lived Republic. In addition, they were the two most provocative female thinkers shaped by the liberating, yet limiting, avant-garde period in the 1920s and 1930s. While they had a close relationship, it was an intellectual one and not always civil. In various encounters and even in their subsequent letters when they went into exile, they had serious disagreements about life, philosophy, and politics, especially on issues pertaining to the Civil War.[29]

The limitations I mention were based on the patriarchal attitudes that persisted into the 1920s. World War I, in which Spain did not participate, had ended, but it had left painful residuals in most of Europe. As Gilbert and Gubar describe in their three volumes, *No Man's Land*, men returned broken and shell-shocked, while women had gained agency because they had gone out into the public sector during the war as breadwinners, and they learned skills that had previously been the domain of men. While feminism had begun in the mid-1900s in the United States and England above all, it was a disquieting phenomenon even in places where the movement had made very little impact, such as Spain. The Weimar period in Germany had illustrated the fluctuating gender roles that modernity brought with it and the 'modern woman' became an object of temerity for patriarchy all over Europe. The so-called Roaring Twenties introduced a stereotype: the flapper, that young, slim, short haired, and dance-crazed female who grew from the collective imagination of those who experienced the upheaval of those years. The flapper was athletic; she wore skimpy dresses and even trousers, deemphasizing the curves that defined a 'real' woman. This new look responded to the perceived or existing female liberation that came with the radical social transformations after World War I.

The male thinkers picked up their pens as warriors do their swords. Georg Simmel led the way in Spain. His essay on sexual difference, 'The Masculine and the Feminine', was translated and published in the *Revista de Occidente* in 1923. As Françoise Collin writes:

> Simmel no duda en absoluto la capacidad de las mujeres para participar en el mundo existente y desempeñar en él un papel. [...] Pero niega la posibilidad de una cultura específicamente femenina que viene a duplicar la cultura masculina o substituirla. [...] Hay dos sexos, sí; pero solo hay una cultura, que es la cultura de uno de ellos, en la cual el otro participa. (Collin 2000: 322)

> [Simmel in no way doubts the capacity of women to participate in the existent world and to play a role in it. [...] But he doubts the possibility of a specifically feminine culture that could duplicate or substitute male culture. [...] There are two sexes, yes; but there is only one culture, which is the culture of one of them, in which the other participates.]

Collin's assessment of Ortega y Gasset's interpretation and embracement of Scheler and Simmel is that Ortega's ideas are retrograde in comparison: 'la lectura de Ortega y Gasset parece simplificar y reducir las iluminadoras tensiones que pueblan las reflexiones de Simmel' [Ortega y Gasset's reading appears to simplify and reduce the illuminating tensions that populate Simmel's reflexions] (2000: 323). In fact Collin demonstrates how Ortega has taken 'a step backwards': 'La posición de Ortega y Gasset (que sin embargo hizo en la práctica mucho en favor de la promoción de las mujeres, entre otras cosas en su revista) es una mezcla de denigración y celebración' [Ortega y Gasset's position (that nevertheless in practice did much in favour of the promotion of women, among other things, in his journal) is a mixture of denigration and celebration of women] (324).

The deep contradictions in Ortega's ideas on gender were especially conflictive for the women who had a close intellectual relationship with him and listened to his and other male colleagues' opinions on the inferiority of females.[30] They were fuel for Zambrano and Chacel, but they also deprived them of some of their oxygen, as Laurenzi explains. While under the influence of Ortega and collaborating in his journal, they did not feel they could contradict him. And given that men — according to Scheler — possessed 'spirit' and were 'the maker[s] of culture' and women were pure 'soul', 'emotion', and 'nature' and, therefore, the makers of nothing (Laurenzi 2012: 19), Laurenzi observes that both Zambrano and Chacel had to separate their femininity from their professional and cultural lives, while eschewing any notions of feminism (21).[31]

Both women had confrontations with Ortega — as we have noted with Zambrano. Chacel describes hers vividly in a 1983 essay on Ortega, where she admits that she was 'hard to deal with', which was true of many of Chacel's relationships, as I observed personally in her final years. As mentioned, she had returned to Madrid in 1927 after a long stay in Rome, with her first novel, *Estación. Ida y vuelta*. Since she felt that it was a novelized version of Ortega's philosophy, she was very excited to show it to him, hoping he would publish it. Ortega praised the short novel, but said that it was clearly influenced by the French dramatist Jean Giraudoux. Chacel insisted that she had not read Giraudoux, and described her reaction: 'Mi indignación fue casi colérica' [My indignation was almost wrathful] (Chacel 1993a: 421). She explained that the encounter marked her friendship with Ortega, who never mentioned it again, but who Chacel felt was always thinking: 'Usted es una persona intratable. Sufra las consecuencias...' [You are an intractable person. Suffer the consequences...] (424). While Zambrano had intellectual, as well as — it would appear — emotional ties to Ortega, Chacel's relationship with the philosopher seemed to be purely intellectual and almost competitive in its contentiousness.

There is an interesting anecdote about how Chacel and Zambrano were perceived by their colleagues in the early days. Chacel comments on an article by the philosopher José Luis Aranguren and her resentment when he associated her and Zambrano (whom he hints are 'too intellectual') with the superficial high-society women who, according to Aranguren, frequented Ortega's lectures because they found them to be sexually provocative. Chacel writes ironically in her essay

'Volviendo al punto de partida':

> En cuanto a la pareja que formamos mi queridísima María Zambrano y yo, ¿por qué resulta que somos *muy* intelectuales? [...] Lo cierto es que, tanto María Zambrano como yo, siempre fuimos intelectuales, lo bastante para satisfacer nuestra vocación, y no creo que ello llegase a tanto como para dar motivo a ese adverbio de cantidad. Pero resulta que ahora nos enteramos de que era 'el solo hecho de hablar de *esas cosas*' lo que nos daba acceso a la alta sociedad. (Chacel 1993a: 279)

> [As far as the couple that my darling María Zambrano and I form, why is it that we are *very* intellectual? [...] The truth is that, both María Zambrano and I always were intellectuals, enough to satisfy our vocation, and I do not think that it was so exaggerated that there is a motive for that adverb of quantity. But now it seems that we find out that it was 'the very fact that speaking of *those things*' [sexual themes] that gave us access to high society.]

Both began writing philosophical/literary works while in Spain, but actually developed their unique theories once they were in exile, no doubt because of the pressure they felt from their male contemporaries, especially Ortega.

As mentioned, Zambrano had already begun to write about women in her 1928 articles in *El Liberal*. Two in particular stand out because of her modern stance on the plight of women. In 'Gender Violence', she discusses how modern women were rebelling and acquiring their own personality. She claims that because of this new phenomenon, men were jealous of women, and that there was only one 'remedy' for the situation: 'the spiritual integration of their lives' (Zambrano 2007b: 103). In the next article, 'Conjugal Fidelity', Zambrano talks about the fact that the Penal Code of 1928 had removed the section of the law that permitted a man to murder his wife if she committed adultery, but then discusses the fact that nothing else had really changed for women (105–06). Zambrano would often speak of this subject, the need for marital harmony through mutual understanding, addressing precisely the causes — according to male thinkers — of Europe's dysfunction after World War I. As Laurenzi comments:

> En la percepción de los más destacados intelectuales de la época, la decadencia y la crisis de la identidad que Europa sufría se reflejaba en la confusión de los roles y papeles de género, en la crisis del matrimonio burgués y en la pérdida de la armonía en las parejas: en fin, en el desorden de las casas y de las camas. (Laurenzi 2012: 19)

> [From the perception of the most salient intellectuals of the era, the decadence and crisis of identity that Europe suffered was reflected in the confusion of gender roles, in the crisis of the bourgeois marriage and in the loss of harmony among couples: in summary, in the disorder of homes and beds.]

Laurenzi goes on to describe the real reasons for this post-war dysphoria: the discomfort men felt about the new reality, that is to say, the introduction of women into public life, which they decided was harmful to females, because they could lose their feminine identity and become more masculine (2012: 19).

Both Chacel and Zambrano later became conscious of the ways in which men were responsible for this malaise, and both, to differing degrees, elucidate the phenomenon in their writing as chroniclers of the female intellectual's condition in pre-Civil War Spain.[32] Zambrano, in *Delirio y destino* reveals the mobility that she and other women had in those years; she speaks of many of the intellectual forums that she frequented: the Atheneum, the Student Residence, the Central University, the Prado Museum among them. Yet in *Delirio y destino* she also speaks ironically of the difficulties of being a woman within the intellectual world, and reveals her struggle as a female who aspired to become a philosopher:

> Si no fuera por la Filosofía, por aquella tonta ambición, ella — pensaban algunos que la querían — hubiera sido o hecho esto, aquello, lo otro, estaría casada por lo menos y en eso, podía ser verdad . . . Sí, esto que no había dependido enteramente de ella, como el hacer o el ser. Pero . . . estaba bien, todo había pasado y ahora solo le quedaba este ánsia de verdad y de justicia, de vivir adecuadamente a su pobreza íntima, de no sobrepasarse. (Zambrano 1989b: 23–24)[33]

> [If it weren't for philosophy, for that foolish ambition — thought some of the people who loved her — she would have been or done this, that, or the other thing, she would at least be married, and that might have been true . . . Yes, that had not depended entirely on her, like doing or being. But . . . it was all right, everything had passed, and now the only thing left was this longing for truth and justice, for a way of life suitable to her inner poverty, for a way to keep from going too far.] (Zambrano 1999: 11)

When warned by a male colleague that as a woman, she should avoid the dangers of being a leftist activist, Zambrano reveals in the book that gender should not be a consideration when it comes to political commitment. She responds to the man: 'No, no valdría ser mujer en este caso; el destino es para todos nosotros y yo lo siento asi' (1989b: 106–07) [No, being a woman won't save anyone in this instance; our destiny is for all of us, and that's how I feel it] (1999: 72). She also describes university life as a gender-neutral, utopian place. The ethics of her friends included 'horror y repugnancia de la coquetería, de la conquista' (1989b: 47) [a horror of and an aversion to both coquetry and conquest] (1999: 28). Zambrano explains that the students wanted radical change from the double standards of nineteenth-century Spain: 'Huían del delirio y de la consiguiente asfixia; querían encontrar la medida justa, la proporción según la cual la convivencia fuese efectiva, viviente, según la cual España fuese un país habitable para todos los españoles' (1989b: 48) [They were escaping from delirium and the resultant suffocation; they wanted to find the happy medium, the ratio that would make it possible to live with others effectively and vitally, that would permit Spain to become a habitable country for all Spaniards] (1999: 28).

Rosa Chacel's rendering of women's intellectual life within the stifling patriarchal climate is visible in a number of her essays and novels, and is perhaps best reflected in the novels, *Barrio de maravillas* (1976), which deals with the early teen years of her protagonists, Isabel and Elena, and *Acrópolis* (1984), which largely depicts their lives between the end of World War I and the establishment of the Spanish Republic. The novels are 'ontologically autobiographical' and a-chronological, as is

Zambrano's *Delirio y destino* (Mangini 2009: 171). They also, in great part, employ Madrid as a main character in the texts, with an emphasis on its socio-political reality. But Chacel's viewpoint, as an autodidact, is startlingly divergent from that of the university-schooled Zambrano. *Acrópolis* is the novel that best describes Chacel's artistically and erotically formative years through Elena and Isabel, when Chacel's 'university' consisted of the School of Fine Arts of San Fernando, Madrid's museums, the Atheneum activities, the Residencia de Estudiantes (the 'acropolis' where the avant-garde males were *creating* modern art), and the streets of both modern and old Madrid.[34] At the same time, it contrasts this typically female intellectual education — on the periphery of academic institutions — with the university and social milieu that enriched and legitimized the intellectual lives of her male contemporaries, specifically the Generation of 27.

In the text there is a fusion of female and male voices and a kaleidoscopic view of their lives, which often results in an 'androgynous' voice. As outsiders who longed to be insiders, the girls are *flâneuses*, as well as apprentices in their urban environment. They were teased and denigrated by the young men who felt superior to them because, although the girls had access to art, they had little access to 'masculine' fields of study or male-only venues in general. Elena and Isabel also express their longing to create their own 'theories', which as mentioned, was the domain of men in 1920s and 1930s Madrid.[35] While neither Zambrano nor Chacel considered themselves feminists, and while their later theories on women and gender were resolved in very different ways, in their 'ontologically autobiographical' prose they both reflect the dilemmas and concerns that young intellectual women like them faced as they worked to insert themselves into the cultural spheres that were the domain of men in interwar Madrid.[36] In Chacel's case, she reflects the more typical 'outsider' upbringing of the aspiring female artist in those years, while Zambrano describes an intellectual woman's elite education that afforded the unusual advantage of studying side by side with her male contemporaries.

Given her ideas on eroticism and its ties to the intellectual life, Chacel resolved her concerns in her writing and in her life in what might be considered a somewhat androgynous fashion by creating protagonists who are veiled versions of Chacel herself.[37] Perhaps the best example of this is represented in the unsavoury love triangle she portrays in the novel *Memorias de Leticia Valle*. The precocious and wilful child protagonist, Leticia (portrayed through Chacel's typically inscrutable and cryptic voice), narrates a life-changing incident she has recently experienced. Raised by an aunt and an alcoholic father, the child is taken under the 'wings' of an educated, but bored married couple, Luisa and Daniel, who are living in a remote and intellectually unchallenging village in Spain (in Chacel's home province of Valladolid). Luisa becomes Leticia's music teacher and friend, as well as a role model in domestic affairs. The stern 'Don' Daniel, an archivist, insinuates himself into the role of history instructor. As the novel progresses, there are constant signs of the strict divisions between male and female roles in the household, and the growing possessiveness of Luisa and Daniel as regards their 'student'. Daniel suggests that Leticia has masculine qualities (because of her attentions to Luisa). He stares at her with penetrating looks, while he lectures her in a condescending manner. Leticia also fixates on his physical attributes. It is suggested that they are mutually attracted in an obsessive, diabolical way. While Daniel keeps the child locked in his study during lessons, his wife plays the piano, seemingly attempting to attract Leticia to the music room and out of the clutches of Daniel.

An air of eroticism pervades the home where this triangular situation occurs, creating a crescendo effect.[38] Luisa, after a bad fall (or had she been pushed by Daniel?), recovers in her room, and Leticia begins to study music more frequently, nearly abandoning her history lessons, at which time Daniel furiously accuses her of being 'an artist' and threatens to kill her. Then there is a confrontation between Daniel and Leticia's father, a shot is heard (presumably Daniel's suicide), and Leticia is whisked off to live with relatives in Switzerland. The denouement is as ambiguous as the plot itself. Did Daniel seduce Leticia or was it the other way around? Maier acknowledges the autobiographical aspect of the novel: Chacel's confrontations with Ortega y Gasset and the admiration she felt for the philosopher (in Chacel 1994: 169–70).[39] What is of utmost interest here is the profound impact that Ortega had on Chacel, prompting her to write a novel that insists on the domestic domain of the female, and the worldly, yet bookish sphere of the male. The author clearly describes, as she does in other works, how conflicted she felt about her legitimate place in the intellectual world and the domestic life to which Spanish patriarchy had attempted to relegate women — even accomplished women — in the 1920s and 1930s.

In spite of their vast differences, María Zambrano and Rosa Chacel had a life-long intellectual friendship; it was not constant, nor was it always convivial, but it was always crucial to both of them. The proof of their mutual admiration can be found in two articles written in the 1980s. Chacel published an open letter to Zambrano in 1984 — the year Zambrano returned from exile — entitled 'Rosa mística'. In the letter/essay Chacel excuses herself for her silence of some thirty years. She also notes that they had chosen different paths for their intellectual pursuits, suggesting (through allusions to poets Antonio Machado and Ruben Darío) that María had chosen the poetic life — as Chacel labels it, a 'magic cauldron' — and that it was far from the 'tactile geometry of my prose' (Chacel 1993a: 526). The novelist discloses that these diverging paths were the reason for 'la falla de nuestro epistolario y el coloquio de nuestros vivires' [the failure of our collected letters and the colloquium of our lives] (526).[40] Chacel then confesses that she had always seen Zambrano as more advanced; she demonstrates that she felt that things came to the philosopher more easily, and that Zambrano was more admired and accepted than she was. She also points to María's political commitment in 1935 and 1936 (which she did not agree with), while Rosa wrote sonnets. Chacel explains the sonnet she dedicated to Zambrano at that time, which she published in her book of poetry *A la orilla de un pozo*. Referring to Zambrano as 'the ivory rose', it is a classical ode to beauty, desire, and ecstasy; but she cautions that the rose also has a thorn, and that thorn was Zambrano's militancy, 'tu canto a la belleza ante la muerte' [your song to beauty in the face of death] (530).[41] Chacel softens her reproach at the end of the article, by noting their mutual search for the ineffable and for freedom, and reminds her friend that her sonnet was a true interpretation of Zambrano's purity and constancy (531).

Four years later Zambrano published a response to Chacel's 'Rosa mística', a short article entitled 'Rosa' in the journal *Un Ángel Más*.[42] Always more diplomatic than Chacel, she brushes aside the years that had passed, and addresses her by stating: 'para mí, tú estabas siempre presente, desde antes de conocerte en persona' [for me, you were always present, even before knowing you in person] (Zambrano 1988d: 11). Zambrano then goes on to describe the timidity she felt when she met Chacel in 1927 and explains: 'Siempre tu viste sobre mí un cierto poder' [You always held a certain power over me] (12). Referring to Chacel's sonnet, Zambrano describes why she could not believe that she was the 'ivory rose', since she felt that Rosa was 'la única Rosa, la rosa de Alejandría [...] Como una reina de esas que rara vez se han dado en la historia' [the only Rose, the Rose of Alexandria [...] Like one of those queens who have rarely appeared in history] (12). Zambrano does not refer to the Civil War, but demonstrates the inscrutability, the uniqueness, the sheer mental power of her old friend, with whom she would be reunited in Madrid some sixty years after their first encounter.

Zambrano and Chacel were connected by exile and by their exceptionalism. After so many decades of being forgotten in their own country and after so many odysseys, agonizing losses, and the existential suffering of displacement, they returned triumphant. Unlike many other female intellectuals of their generation, some of whom never returned, others who returned in failing mental health, these groundbreaking women of the avant-garde reappeared with their full mental powers. They thus became the living representations of what their female friends and colleagues had accomplished in that turbulent pre-war era in Spain, as well as what they endured as women who sought to be accepted and appreciated as equals among their peers.

Notes to Chapter 1

1. All translations are my own unless otherwise stated.
2. Blas Zambrano was both a Republican and a Mason, and a well-known educator who was involved in numerous cultural and pedagogical entities throughout his career.
3. Zambrano's unedited and infrequently dated letters to the young man were acquired and published by María Fernanda Santiago Bolaños, a member of the María Zambrano Foundation. The young philosopher carried the birth to term, but the boy died shortly afterwards; her letter to del Campo on the tragedy is heart-rending (Zambrano 2012c: 104).
4. Méndez had known Concha de Albornoz (who also studied at the Central University, like Zambrano) since grade school days at the *Institución Libre de Enseñanza*. While León had cultural connections to the group of women discussed here, after she met the poet Rafael Alberti in 1930, she appeared to distance herself. This is in great part because one of Zambrano's friends, the painter Maruja Mallo, had had a long, culturally productive, but tormented relationship with Alberti between 1925 and 1929. León was irrationally jealous of the painter, and took extreme measures to avoid coinciding with Mallo in Madrid; this persisted when all three were in exile in Buenos Aires after the war. See Mangini 2010: 100–01.
5. The *Cacharrería* or 'Crockery Shop' was thus named because the room held a collection of Greek vases, which were negatively referred to as 'cacharros', or cheap pottery.

6. Maruja and Concha Méndez were already accomplished *flâneuses* in the late twenties, when they would subversively parade around Madrid — without the required hats or chaperones. Méndez explains in her memoirs how they would traipse around town, going to highbrow places like the Prado Museum and to lectures; but their actions also included peeking into bars and frequenting street fairs in the working-class *barrios* of Madrid. While none of these activities was permissible for 'proper' young ladies without an escort, Mallo and Méndez purposely devised strategies in order to scandalize everyone they could (Ulacia Altolaguirre 1990: 51).
7. Zambrano had clear thoughts about the double standard from an early age. Although we do not have del Campo's responses to Zambrano's letter in which she explains that she is with child, her angry reactions to his apparently accusatory letters make apparent that he blamed her for her 'sexual promiscuity' and the pregnancy. She expresses her furious reaction to his letter for placing the 'blame' on her: '¡Que te he ensuciado yo! yo que en esos momentos he albergado en mi alma sentimientos tan puros e inegoístas como tú 'el limpio' jamás podrías ni soñar. Y si ha habido disparidad en estos actos, es a mi favor, puesto que tú, según se deduce, los hacías empujado por la vil necesidad material y por debilidad de oponerte, y yo, yo la 'sucia' ni sacaba nada materialmente' [I have besmirched you! In those moments I harboured such pure and unselfish sentiments in my soul that you 'the clean one' could never dream of. And if there has been disparity in those acts, it is in my favour because you, according to what can be deduced, you acted driven by the vile material necessity and by the weakness to resist and, I, I 'the dirty one', got nothing material out of it' (Zambrano 2012c: 79–80).
8. The Federación was created in 1926 in resistance to the dictatorship of Primo de Rivera. The Liga was a reform movement by liberal intellectuals whose aim was to modernize the austere attitudes towards sexuality in Spain. Zambrano was one of the two female founders of the Liga.
9. On Zambrano's writing on women, see, for example, Revilla Guzman 2001.
10. Zambrano wrote her novelized autobiography *Delirio y destino* in Havana in 1952, but it was not published until 1989, after the philosopher had returned to Spain. It describes her life — without chronological order — from the prologue to the Second Republic, 1929–1930, to 1931, the year of its proclamation. The final section describes the trauma of exile. The translations of *Delirio y destino* employed here are by Maier. For an analysis of the text, see Caballero Rodríguez 2014 and Johnson 1996.
11. Interestingly, her friend Mallo would also describe those years, which she portrayed in her series of paintings, 'Cesspools and Belfries', from a surrealistic perspective, emphasizing the decay of the Monarchy-Military-Church alliance: 'Éstos eran los panoramas necrológicos que encontraba en el centro y en los vertederos de los alrededores de la capital, 1929–1931. Las edificaciones de los templos derrocados, la destrucción de las cloacas establecidas. La realidad más frecuente y tangible con que tropezaba, la agonía de la superstición, la hecatombe de las basuras que ruedan hacia las alcantarillas buscando el subsuelo, al mismo tiempo que en los fúnebres campanarios reina el estertor de las representaciones rituales' [These were the mortiferous panoramas that I found in the centre of town and in the dumps on the outskirts of the capital, 1929–1931. The church buildings torn down, the destruction of the sewers completed. The most frequent and tangible reality I ran into, the agony of superstition, the great slaughter of the garbage that rolls toward the sewers in search of the subsoil, at the same time that the death rattle of ritual representation reigns in the funereal bells] (Mallo 1939: 26).
12. It was in 1934 that Zambrano clearly began to deviate from Ortega's 'historical reason'. In 1986, she described the encounter. She had asked the maestro to read her then unpublished essay entitled 'Hacia un sabre del alma'. When Ortega met with her after reading the manuscript, he exclaimed: 'Estamos todavía aquí y usted ha querida dar el salto al más allá' [We are still here and you have attempted to leap into the beyond] (Colinas 1986: 6). Zambrano then explains that she cried when she left Ortega, and that 'de ahí parten algunos de los malentendidos con Ortega' [henceforth there were misunderstandings with Ortega] (Colinas 1986: 6), because she had begun her trajectory toward her theory of 'poetic reason'. 'Poetic reason' can be defined as a phenomenological process that includes intuition, faith, poetry, and dreams as part of philosophical contemplation.

13. Mercedes Gómez Blesa describes the author's intentions in the book: 'La autora establece [...] un paralelismo entre el despertar de ella misma a su ser verdadero y el despertar de la nación; establece una simultaneidad de procesos: el renacer de España coincide con su propio renacer' [The author establishes [...] a parallel between the very awakening of her true self and the awakening of the nation; she establishes a simultaneity of processes: the rebirth of Spain coincides with her own rebirth] (2007: 136).
14. Several Zambrano scholars have alluded to her participation in the Lyceum in the late twenties and thirties, but we have no evidence that she was a member of the club, although we can assume Zambrano must have attended an event occasionally. She was invited to speak at the Havana Lyceum Club while in exile there.
15. All of this would be destroyed because of the Civil War; Franco's misogynistic enterprise saw to it that progressive women's visibility and prestige were eliminated by, at best, relieving them of their positions and sending them home, and at worst, by incarcerating them or forcing them into exile. See Mangini 1995.
16. After 1944, Albornoz left her exile in Mexico and moved to the United States, where she taught Spanish at Mount Holyoke College for many years. Her friend, the poet Juan Gil-Albert, wrote several novels in which Albornoz is a main character. See López García 2013.
17. It is noteworthy that a few of the friendships between the men and women of this era, like those of Albornoz, Chacel, and Cernuda, produced profoundly important personal, intellectual, and artistic collaborations and/or influences. In fact, the bond between Cernuda and Albornoz appears to have been so strong that during the war Concha proposed marriage to Cernuda, given that they were both gay and she thought their union would be a convenient and productive one. Although it never came to pass, they spent years in exile together in Mexico, and Albornoz invited Cernuda to teach at Mount Holyoke, which he did for a number of years. In fact, Albornoz was the glue that bound many of the intellectuals of the Generation of 27 in Spain in the early years, and then in exile until her death in 1972. See López García 2013. Cernuda actually appeared to be a sort of male 'muse' for not only Concha and Rosa, but also for Zambrano, who wrote in *La Caña Gris* that his poetry represented 'something essential for my ideas and feelings about poetry' (Zambrano 1962: 15). It should in addition be noted that Chacel also wrote an article on Cernuda's poetry for the same issue of *La Caña Gris*, as well as another published in her book of essays, *Los títulos*.
18. Luis Antonio de Villena makes reference to their liaison during the 1930s (Villena 2002: 32). Chacel often referred to her relationship with Concha de Albornoz in her diary *Alcancía. Ida*, when they were both in New York in the early sixties; among the references, there are veiled allusions to jealous intrigues. Rosa's bisexuality is a well-known fact; she has inserted the subject more overtly — although never explicitly, true to Chacel's style — into several of her essays and novels, as will be discussed. After Albornoz went into exile, she became a more openly gay person, and dressed in a masculine fashion (López García 2013: 494).
19. Mallo's erratic behavior and her many affairs are well documented. See Mangini 2010.
20. Theosophy — a word derived from the Greek *theos* (god) and *sophia* (wisdom) — which is not a religion, but rather a synthesis of religion, philosophy, science, and psychology largely appropriated from Eastern ideas, is a contemporary version of Gnosticism, grounded in a form of Hellenistic Christian thought (whose magic number is three). As Mejía Burgos remarks: 'En realidad, toda la estructura de su filosofía, a excepción de la que aportan los connotados autores occidentales [...] es semejante a la teosofía' [In reality, the entire structure of her [Zambrano's] philosophy, with the exception of what noted Western authors [...] contributed, is similar to theosophy] (2014: 182). See also Jesus Moreno Sanz in his book *El logos oscuro* on this subject. The Theosophical Society was founded in 1875 in New York by Helena Petrovna Blavatsky. It took hold in Spain at the turn of the twentieth century and there was a resurgence in Madrid during the Republic (a Theosophic Atheneum was established there between 1930 and 1937), when a number of statesmen and intellectuals took an interest in its teachings, including — it has been mentioned — María Zambrano. Her colleagues Arturo Serrano Plaja and Antonio Sánchez Barbudo, who would later work with her on the wartime journal *Hora de España*, actively participated in the Theosophic Atheneum's activities (Penalva Mora 2013: 217–18). Mallo had dabbled in esoterica since her sojourn in Paris in 1931–1932. Most of her life was spent seeking

alternatives to Catholicism, especially after she went into exile in Argentina, when she began studying various cults and astrology. See Mangini 2010.
21. Chacel was also interested in Pythagoras. See Pardo 2001.
22. Zambrano was one of the editors of *Hora de España*, in which she published many of her war essays, later collected in the book *Los intelectuales en el drama de España*.
23. The School of Vallecas was a group of rambling sculptors, painters, and writers headed by Benjamín Palencia and Alberto (Sánchez) who roamed the Madrid countryside in search of found objects and detritus to inspire their work. Mallo was the only woman who consistently accompanied them. See Mangini 2010: 102–04.
24. See Ramírez 2004 on Zambrano as literary critic. Of particular importance to María Zambrano were her friendships with the Cuban poet José Lezama Lima and Spanish poet José Angel Valente. As Roberta Johnson also points out, Zambrano discovered that immersing herself in the study of Spanish novelistic characters provided her with a vehicle for her philosophical analyses. See Johnson 1996.
25. It should be noted that there was another Spanish female 'modern' in Buenos Aires, the teacher, journalist, and translator Consuelo Berges, who accompanied Méndez in her intellectual endeavours there, and who would return to Spain when the Republic was established. Berges was an adventuresome young woman who travelled around Latin America and was unofficially involved in Spanish politics during the Republic. Her staunchly liberal journalistic writing made her well known among the *Revista de Occidente* salon members, including María Zambrano and Rosa Chacel. See Mangini 2001.
26. A number of critics affirm that Zambrano also accompanied the artists from the 'School of Vallecas' group on their jaunts in the countryside, but I have found no evidence to that effect.
27. Chacel had studied classical sculpture at the Royal Academy of Fine Arts of San Fernando in her youth and shared Zambrano's interest in Hellenistic themes. Her book of poetry, *A la orilla de un pozo*, is clearly influenced by ancient Greek culture.
28. See, for example, Pardo in Chacel, *Obras completas*.
29. In fact, according to Clara Janés, after Zambrano returned to Spain — Chacel had returned permanently in 1977 — she asked Janés to arrange a meeting with Chacel. It appears that the conversation with very 'spirited' and 'somewhat theatrical', with the usual reactions of the indomitable spitfire, Rosa Chacel (Janés 2002–2003).
30. It is a well known fact that Ortega y Gasset was a ladies' man. As Luis Carandell remarks: 'If he went to a restaurant or a public place and there were no beautiful women, he usually said: "I am a miserable man"' (1983: 4).
31. It should be mentioned that one of the women who most vigorously refuted these ideas about the inferiority of women in the twenties and thirties was the congresswoman and feminist writer Margarita Nelken. See Mangini 2009. It should be mentioned that while Chacel only indirectly contradicted Ortega y Gasset in her essay 'Esquema' (published in *La Revista de Occidente* in 1931), she clearly debunks his ideas in a later book based on the ideas in 'Esquema', *Saturnal* (1960). On this subject, see Mangini 1998.
32. Nevertheless, Chacel also faults females for their 'weakness' in some of her writings, which has caused her work to be perceived as highly misogynistic by several critics. See, for example, Freixas 2004. Yet Chacel clearly points out the misogyny prevalent in Spain in her era, especially in her novels written in exile.
33. Zambrano's reference to marriage perhaps alludes to the fact that when she became pregnant, there was talk of a possible marriage to the father, Gregorio del Campo, and based on her letters to him, it appears that she would have been amenable to that solution (Zambrano 2012c: 13).
34. Carretón Cano suggests that the protagonists are based on Chacel's friends, Margarita Villegas and Victorina Durán (one of the few openly lesbian women of the twenties and thirties), who studied together at the School of Fine Arts (2000: 15).
35. At the end of *Barrio de maravillas*, we find the girls — the younger version of the protagonists of *Acrópolis* — questioning how the fellows see them and how they envision themselves. One responds: 'Lo que me parece es que vamos a tener que ponernos a pensar en la teoría' [What I think is that we are going to have to begin thinking about theory] (Chacel 1985: 280).
36. See Laurenzi 2012 and Johnson 2012 on this subject. Only a few months before her death, Chacel

repeated her ideas to me about her theory that women must learn to join the world of men. She explained that she conceived of herself as an 'exceptional woman [who] gives sermons *to* women and never speaks *about* women, but rather *to* them' (conversation with Chacel, 6 December 1993).

37. Gómez Pérez discusses what she considers Chacel's novel of sexual guilt *par excellence*, *La Sinrazón*, which is based on a love triangle (written in the fifties and first published in 1960 in Buenos Aires). In the novel, as Rodríguez Fischer notes, 'hay una serie de sorprendentes coincidencias entre el diario ficticio que escribe Santiago y los cuadernos reales de la autora' [there are a series of surprising coincidences between the fictitious diary that Santiago writes and the real diaries of the author] (Chacel 1989: 39). More than simply ontological memory, Chacel is writing her own confessional story through the voice of a man because, as Gómez-Pérez sees it, Chacel considers confessional writing to be the business of men, not women (2001: 353). The critic adds: 'La complejidad sexual de esta situación [...] deja transparentar la subversión inconsciente de una escritora que aceptó [...] la necesidad de masculinizarse para pertenecer al orbe de cultura por derecho' [The sexual complexity of this situation [...] makes the unconscious subversion transparent of a writer who accepted [...] the necessity of masculinizing herself in order to belong to the cultural sphere in her own right] (2001: 354). It is possible that the *ménage à trois* she speaks of in *La Sinrazón* is inspired by a personal relationship that is obliquely suggested in Chacel's diary entries in *Alcancía. Ida* between 1959 and 1961, that she may have participated in with Concha Albornoz and Albornoz's ex-student and travelling companion in the 1950s, Clara James. Perhaps because of this, the Chacel-Albornoz friendship had ended by 1962. In November 1963, Albornoz wrote to Zambrano to lament Cernuda's death. At the end of the letter, she remarks: 'Rosa [Chacel] was here about a year or more ago. Since she returned to Brazil from the United States [...] I haven't heard anything from her and I hope not to hear from her again (quoted in López García 2013: 511).

38. The silence between the adults grows and a turning-point takes place during a homage to a teacher that Luisa and Leticia are planning. In a meta-literary subplot, the child decides to read a long poem on the legend of the thirteenth-century King of Granada, *Al-Hamar el Nazarita* (written by the famous nineteenth-century poet, José Zorrilla, who was Chacel's great uncle). The event, which deeply affects Daniel, causes him to leave in the middle of the recitation. Leticia had noted early on that Daniel resembled a 'Moorish king' (Chacel 1994: 31) and her reading perhaps was Chacel's (Leticia's) vehicle for denouncing Daniel's illicit seduction of the child or, conversely, Leticia's confession of seduction. Carol Maier, in her 'Afterword' to her translation of the book, reveals that Chacel was inspired by two stories of seduction, and that, as Chacel explains, she conceived a novel in which 'a thirteen-year old girl would seduce an older man and he would be the one who had to commit suicide' (Quoted in Chacel 1994: 168–69).

39. Maier remarks: 'I would also mention Daniel's arrogance and the humiliation Leticia suffers as his pupil, noting a resemblance between some of their interchanges and Chacel's descriptions of her meetings with Ortega' (in Chacel 1994: 169–70).

40. See Revilla Guzmán (2001: 102–07) on their epistolary relationship.

41. María was infinitely more political than Rosa, although they both were active in the Alliance of Anti-Fascist Intellectuals when the war broke out. Zambrano, though, would continue her militancy throughout the war, and moved from Madrid to Valencia to Barcelona as the Nationalist forces marched into the first two cities and the Republican government was finally relocated to Barcelona in late 1937. Only at the end of the war did she flee Barcelona across the French border. Zambrano had labelled her generation of writers who had opposed and suffered through the war and who had ended up in prison or in exile as the 'Generation of the Bull'. María, in fact, in June 1938 — when the Republic had suffered so many losses that most people were feeling hopeless — responded to a letter she received from Rosa, who had gone into exile in early 1937 with her young son. In her missive, Zambrano demonstrates her complete disagreement with Chacel on the war, as well as with Ortega y Gasset and a number of others for having fled Spain or for having become 'traitors' to their country. (On the subject of traitors, see in particular her 'Carta al Doctor Marañón' in *Los intelectuales en el drama de España*.) In a letter to Chacel from Barcelona on 26 June 1938, the philosopher vehemently describes how, in spite

of risking her life, she would remain in Spain until the end. She explains, expressing her hope against all odds, that she is: 'Ligada a la lucha por la *independencia* de España, por la existencia misma de España contra Italia [...] contra los bastardos del Norte [...] contra la degeneración y perversion + [más] grande de lo español que han conocido los siglos [...] *y con*, con mi pueblo en el que creo al par que en Dios' [Tied to the battle for Spain's *independence*, for the very existence of Spain against Italy [...] against the bastards of the North [...] against the greatest degeneration and perversion that has been seen in Spain in centuries [...] *and with*, with my people in whom I believe the same as [I believe] in God] (quoted in Fisher: 38).

42. In the article, Zambrano begins by describing the moment that her friend Pizarro spoke of Chacel's presentation at the Madrid Atheneum in 1921; it is startling that the anecdote from over sixty years before would be ever present in the mind of the philosopher.

CHAPTER 2

In the Dark Night of the Human: María Zambrano and the Avant-Garde

Inmaculada Murcia Serrano, Universidad de Sevilla

An analysis of the two main essays Zambrano devoted to the avant-garde, 'Nostalgia de la tierra' (1933) [Nostalgia for the Earth] and 'La destrucción de las formas' (1944) [The Destruction of Forms], suggests that one of her objectives was to criticize Ortega y Gasset's views on modern art expressed in *La deshumanización del arte* (1925) [The Dehumanization of Art].[1] After all, Zambrano had been his disciple and, although her intellectual trajectory following his tutelage, and especially once she had gone into exile, gradually departed from the philosophy of *raciovitalismo* [vital reason], Ortega's essay was too important to be ignored. Thus, in her initial approach to the avant-garde, 'dehumanized art' was to be equated to what she called 'arte desterrado' [unearthly art]. Before she progressively moved away to other more *pneumatic*, Gnostic, or spiritual modes of thought, Zambrano started from the initial premise that 'man' always refers to the 'earthly' (Zambrano 1989a: 20), a view which is essentially still rooted in materialism and Nietzschean thought.

Firstly, when comparing the stances of Ortega and Zambrano it is important to note that their attitudes towards the new art were generally opposed. Although, not always, Ortega generally showed a greater interest in aesthetic issues, while Zambrano sought in those artistic forms which interested her, answers to problems of a philosophical, existential, political, or historical nature. Whereas in 'Nostalgia de la tierra' Zambrano acknowledges the fact that the new art claimed for itself the tenets of rationalist intellectualism — an approach which, for Ortega, is capable of purifying the very essence of art — she objects to the latter's defence of aesthetic purity and artistic anti-realism, arguing that the results have been devastating.

The excess of consciousness, according to Zambrano, had resulted in an impoverished and weakened apprehension of reality. At no time does she refer to the dehumanizing techniques discussed by Ortega; nor is she concerned whether this rationalization of art caused a popularization or an elitist distancing in the aesthetic sensibility of the common beholder. What really interested her in Ortega's essay was the confirmation that the new artists captured the *idea* of reality rather than reality itself, that they were faithful, as Ortega had noted, to the *fictitious* nature of art. In her writing, this idea would take the form of a description of avant-garde art objects as 'pure content of consciousness'. That artistic and rational purity, which, according to Ortega, had turned the new art into 'artistic art' was not interpreted by Zambrano as a way of bringing art closer to its true condition. Instead, the intervention of intelligence in the interest of this purification represented a way of perpetuating the 'petrifying' and 'disintegrating' power of consciousness, which acted by dissolving the very same reality. Zambrano believed that the overall consequence was a limitation in the representation of the world of the senses.

This is why she changed the term 'dehumanized art' into 'arte desterrado'. On the one hand, in this essay Impressionism was seen as a movement that had transformed the surrounding world into something ghostly and unstable; on the other hand, Cubism was described as a movement in which the physical world had disappeared for the sake of pure reason. Impressionism and Cubism constituted, therefore, authentic 'desterradas' arts, because they transformed the earth, that is matter and reality, into pure sense impression, either frail and evanescent, or disembodied and coldly abstract.[2]

In 'Nostalgia for the Earth' the longed-for *humanization* of art consisted therefore, not in regaining popular appeal or emotional reactions in aesthetic reception, but in pure and simple reality, identified here with the term 'earth'. The 'dehumanized art' is, for Zambrano as it was for Ortega, 'escape' from this world, and 'dehumanized', precisely because 'human', in her essay refers to the 'earthly'. It could be said that Zambrano shares with Ortega the idea that the painter, rather than moving towards reality, is seemingly going against it. However, if Ortega thought that this made the new art a truer one, Zambrano believed that it had only led to a reductionist view of reality itself.

Zambrano concluded her essay by stating that it was not necessary for artists to promote the desirable return to the earthly, as the 'artes desterradas' carried within themselves their own destruction: Impressionism, firstly, would disappear, dazzled by its own light, its spectrality, and its phantasmagoria; and then Cubism in turn was doomed to disappear because of its 'abusive formulism' and absolute 'depersonalization'. Adding a third movement to those already mentioned, Zambrano then referred to how Expressionism, which was also guilty of externalizing an excessive subjectivism, had escaped, in a way, from that 'deterritorialization' because by showing objects in process, *in fieri*, it prevented their full absorption into consciousness. That was, however, also its undoing: in their desire not to destroy reality, the Expressionist artists had merely been able to show disjointed relationships or inarticulate screams.

The criticism of modern consciousness and the disappearance of the world of the senses which Zambrano elaborated in this first essay with a clearly nostalgic tone, shows some correspondence with the argument advanced by Friedrich Nietzsche (1844–1900) regarding the loss of the earthly brought about by a particular way of understanding Western culture, and expressed in books such as *Also sprach Zarathustra* (1886).[3] Nonetheless, while the objective is the same for both philosophers, in the case of Zambrano the redemption of the earth should not be considered a dream only realizable after the death of God. On the contrary, Zambrano's God is precisely a Spinozan God, residing in physical and material things; therefore, the nostalgia for the earth which Zambrano expresses here will be finally redeemed, not by an *Übermensch* who dwells in the cold age of nihilism, but by the *warm* recovery of reality carried out by committed artists, this time, taking into account the sensuality of the world surrounding us.[4] These artists from their vantage point of modernity would remain faithful to the Spanish tradition — an issue we will return to later.

A general assessment of 'Nostalgia for the Earth' makes it clear from the very beginning that the initial attitude of Zambrano towards the avant-garde displays a degree of conservatism (although modern Spanish art itself was, to a large extent, also traditionalist). We must bear in mind that, in this particular essay, the new art is interpreted from extra-artistic coordinates because it is used as an instrument to relaunch a critique against modern rationalism which Zambrano was elaborating at the time. That means that she was not interested so much in criticizing the artistic achievements of Impressionism or Cubism, as in denouncing the theory behind them. The same approach would be taken repeatedly by Zambrano when it came to offering an assessment of specific art works.

What Zambrano was seeking in this first engagement with the avant-garde was an artistic confirmation of her philosophical diagnosis: that the supremacy that European modernity had accorded subjectivity and reason had caused the disappearance of the world of the senses, whose qualities, abandoned by contemporary art, were symptomatically described as gravity, colour, corporeality, or mass.

These same qualities, namely body, substantiality, or weight, were those which Zambrano saw perfectly reflected in the works of some contemporary Spanish artists, who, despite being as avant-garde as the Cubists and Impressionists described in 'Nostalgia for the Earth', appeared, nevertheless, to be detached from that denaturalized and unearthly modernity.

From the Vanguard to the Rearguard: Modernity Viewed from the Past

It may seem surprising but the poets of 1927, and many artists who in Spain advocated and practised avant-gardist art, whatever the criteria applied, showed a marked interest in the Spanish artistic tradition. In the case of the poetry of the Generation of 1927, the tri-centenary of Luis de Góngora, to whom issues 5–7 of the magazine *Litoral* were dedicated, marked the beginning of a new style that saw Góngora's poetry as a symbol of an irreversible break with the poets of the previous generation, who were associated with academic tradition and thereby with an aesthetics which was seen as anchored in nineteenth-century historicism and *modernismo*. In addition to Góngora, the poets of 1927 mined other sources from the literary past, such as Lope de Vega, the *Romanceros* [collections of ballads], the *Cancioneros* [anthologies of lyrical poetry], folk verse, or Baroque literature in general. Against the historical backdrop of the Counter-Reformation, Baroque literature promoted a conspicuous pursuit of imaginative freedom, together with an unprecedented appreciation of wit, metaphor, and literary self-sufficiency. These features seemed more than suitable for a new poetry which, jaded by the sentimental pathos of the nineteenth century, intended to renew Spanish letters (Rozas and Torres Nebrera 1989).

In this respect, María Zambrano was also a faithful representative of the paradoxical rear-guard spirit characteristic of the Spanish avant-garde and of the Generation of 1927 in particular. Her approach to many Spanish artists of the twentieth century consisted precisely in placing them in a genuinely Spanish tradition which was being revalorized, although updated both in form and content to suit the new times. The writings dedicated to these artists therefore cannot be separated from her interest in searching, within that tradition, not only for that which could be salvaged from the proposals for a formal renewal aspiring to 'purity', but more pointedly for that which held a capacity to reveal the secret at the heart of Spanish culture, its *intrahistoria*, to use Unamuno's coinage. It was this secret that Zambrano was determined to unveil from the moment she embarked on her intellectual endeavour, and which became more urgent when she was forced to leave the country for political reasons.

Zambrano had contemplated writing a book about Spanish painting whose title was going to be *España, lugar sagrado de la pintura* [Spain, Sacred Space of Painting], in the same vein as her work on Spanish poetry and literature, *Pensamiento y poesía en la vida española* (1939) [Thought and Poetry in Spanish Life], and in *España sueño y verdad* (1965) [Spain Dream and Reality]. The project was never completed, but a number of texts dedicated to Spanish artists and an essay entitled 'España y su pintura' [Spanish Painting], which constitutes, together with 'Sueño y destino de la pintura' [The Dream and Destiny of Painting], the germ of the ideas Zambrano had planned to develop in her book, hail from it.[5] The book covers painters such as Pablo Picasso, Luis Fernández, Ramón Gaya, and Ángel Alonso whose attitude of looking back at the past is representative of the ideology of the national avant-garde.

In the essay 'España y su pintura' the section probing the 'place of painting in Spanish culture' reveals that, among Zambrano's many concerns about Spanish art, tracing the imprint that painting had left on Spain throughout its history up to modernity was particularly important to her. Spanish painting, she claims, 'has been present in all our historical moments, even the low points', from Zurbarán and Velázquez to Goya; during the Restoration, with Fortuny and Rosales; then with Solana and Picasso etc. This continuity uncovered qualities which made each painter unique, but which together produced a genuinely Spanish school of painting which transcended the artistic movements or fashions of each era: Zurbarán, for example, was the 'pintor español por antonomasia' [the Spanish painter par excellence], the foremost representative of the Spanish pictorial 'canon'. Goya became the painter of 'esplendor y del delirio' [of splendour and delirium]; Velázquez, the artist of 'el esplendor, el ensimismamiento y la objetividad' [splendour, self-absorption, and objectivity]; and El Greco, to cite another example, as the painter most given to 'extremismos estetizantes' [aestheticizing extremes] and 'delirios de espíritu' [deliriums of the mind] of the first half of the twentieth century.

In general, the main figures of Spain's pictorial tradition belonged primarily to the Spanish Baroque, and among them Zurbarán occupied a privileged place.

Zambrano therefore employed metonymy in her search for the specific traits of Spanish character in modern painting through her study of Baroque painting. With these assumptions she approached the works of many artists, both contemporary and associated with the avant-garde, but this essay will focus on only two: Juan Gris (1887–1927) and the aforementioned Luis Fernández.

The brief comments which Zambrano wrote on the paintings of Gris, of no more than one page, are contained in her autobiographical novel, *Delirio y destino: los veinte años de una española* [Delirium and Destiny: A Spaniard in Her Twenties], and deserve to be mentioned because therein a symptomatic analogy between this painter and Zurbarán is established. In the cases of both Gris and Luis Fernández, Zurbarán is used as a 'measure' for the evaluation and judgment of their aesthetic achievements.

Like many specialists (Calvo Serraller 1988: 54; Sérullaz 1963; Sureda and Guasch 1987: 37), Zambrano, who seems to recant what she formerly stated in 'Nostalgia de la tierra', now thinks that Cubism has a special connection not only with Spain, but particularly with Spanish painting of the seventeenth century, an art informed by realism and a devotion to the object. Nevertheless, the author is not oblivious to obvious differences between the paintings of Zurbarán and Juan Gris. The reasons for this discrepancy are explained in these terms:

> Porque Zurbarán creía en las cosas, en su sustancia, no en su apariencia, no había tenido que desnudarlas en formas matemáticas, mientras que Juan Gris pintaba la matemática de las cosas descarnadas. [...] En Zurbarán la materia es sagrada, porque Dios existe, y está cerca. En Juan Gris el espacio está vacío y las cosas son trasuntos matemáticos, ecuaciones; pero la precisión era la misma en los dos, lo único es que ahora Dios está lejos. (Zambrano 1989a: 154)
>
> [As Zurbarán believed in things, in their substance, and not in their appearance, he did not have to strip them down to mathematical forms, while Juan Gris painted the mathematics of disembodied things. [...] In Zurbarán the material is sacred, because God exists, and is near. For Juan Gris space is empty and things are mathematical transcripts, equations; but the precision was the same in both, the only thing is that, now, God is far away.]

The Cubist painter, Zambrano argues, still projecting much of his interest in seeking rigour, just like the realists of the seventeenth century, rids himself of everything revealing only the pure forms of things. That is why his painting is 'disembodied' and makes no concessions to the material (Zambrano 1989a: 228). This way, the idea never comes into being. Therefore, the 'realism' of Juan Gris, despite being comparable with the painting of Zurbarán himself, is not in fact an example of Spanish realism, of the national school, because it lacks the sensuality and metaphysical intensity which are qualities found in the objects of, for example, Zurbarán's work.

For Zambrano, the difference between Zurbarán and Gris proceeds, therefore, from a difference in world view which affects the technical and formal qualities and hinders the legitimate insertion of Gris in the Spanish tradition: the work of Zurbarán shows, according to Zambrano, an enormous sensuality because beneath it there is a religious world view engaged in showing the plenitude and dignity of all 'creatures' of God, however insignificant. By contrast, Juan Gris's Cubist painting, which also represents, in general, domestic and trivial utensils, and which strives for the same rigour as Baroque realism, takes place within a secularized context and vision of the world that leads to a loss of this warmly sensuous character. As a result, Gris comes to represent, for Zambrano, a kind of Spanish dissident.

Something quite different can be found in the work of another member of the Spanish avant-garde, Luis Fernández, about whom Zambrano wrote 'El misterio de la pintura española en Luis Fernández' (1951) and 'La escondida senda de Luis Fernández' (1973).[6] In these essays, Zambrano presents this painter as a representative of the Spanish school of painting and a 'true' follower of Francisco de Zurbarán.

Despite working mostly in Paris, and being influenced by some avant-garde tendencies, most of his critics, such as Valeriano Bozal (1995), agree in emphasizing that Luis Fernández always remained relatively faithful to the pictorial tradition of the Baroque. One of the most striking features of his painting is, for example, the solidity with which objects are represented, something reinforced by the use of an internal light that springs from within the object, and gives a subsidiary role to the use of external lighting. It is possible, even, to compare this use of light with that used by Zurbarán in his paintings, which was the primary source of their religious connotations for Zambrano. Effectively, one of the ideas that she highlights is that Luis Fernández had remained faithful to that 'mysterious' and incendiary light,[7] characteristic of Spanish painting, that rendered the work of this painter, in contrast to that of Gris, arcane, secret, and religious (Zambrano 1989a: 182).[8]

Zambrano also refers to a kind of artistic evolution in his works. The first paintings of Fernández, she affirms, represent the dark world of entrails, blood, nightmares, or dreams. During this period, the use of black as a background colour would play a major role. These first paintings expressed a sacred and hermetic world, closely related to Surrealism. But from the darkness of the inner world of dreams, the later works of Fernández would move on to show the 'space of the soul', populated no longer by objects but by their symbols and 'correspondences' which have nothing in common with the abstract space of the mind (Zambrano 1989a: 184). Later, Fernández painted objects losing their shape, or returning to the material from which they emanated, which, according to Zambrano, is also characteristic of traditional Spanish painting (186–87). Finally, Fernández painted the white paintings at the peak of his career. These are characterized by stillness and whiteness, and everything in them is in a state of 'perfect communion' (187).

Zambrano was especially interested by the canvasses included in the second stage of this itinerary, those which had some connection with the 'space of the soul', as she described them, a place beyond the darkness of the entrails, but also beyond any abstraction of the mind; an intermediate and Gnostic space where things appear in the 'integrity' of their being, like the 'beings' painted by Zurbarán. The 'space of the soul' would thus represent the natural place of things, where they are 'crystallized in their being', immersed in their truth, without violence and conceptualizations.

Zambrano found this space in the secret history of Spanish painting and it also informed her entire philosophical thought. This is also the point of departure for a better understanding of her approach to another important avant-garde trend: Surrealism.

From Cubism to Surrealism: Getting Deeper into the Interior Space

Of all the twentieth-century avant-garde movements, Zambrano was most interested in Surrealism both aesthetically and philosophically, as evidenced by the number of times it is mentioned in her works. It has also been said that of all the avant-garde movements, Surrealism appealed most strongly to women (Ballesteros García 2004: 9). In the case of Zambrano this preference can be understood simply by the fact that the aesthetic foundations of this movement were closely related to the poetic universe with which the thinker agreed philosophically — for instance, the prominent role accorded to the world of dreams, to which Zambrano devoted some works and a multitude of essays. As suggested by Albert Béguin, the Surrealists were indebted to the Romantic poets and writers, who also sought to give free rein to the spontaneous and uncontrolled use of words, because these alone revealed the rich 'treasure' of the soul.[9]

Despite this intellectual proximity, the attitude of Zambrano to Surrealism was ambivalent. She often alluded to and made use of some of the tenets of the movement, while at the same time she criticized others which, in her view, reduced and diminished the richness of the soul. Otherwise, with a few exceptions, such as the paintings of Wifredo Lam (1902–1982) or the painting *La Masía* by Joan Miró (1893–1983), Zambrano, just like Ortega y Gasset, was not enthused by Surrealist artworks (Zambrano 1949: 5–6).[10]

Her first explicit reference to Surrealism can be found in the book *Los intelectuales en el drama de España* (1937) [The Intellectuals in Spanish Drama]. This is mainly a text of a philosophical and political nature in which Zambrano examines the cultural and ideological reasons that favoured the spread of fascism, which also serves to make sense of some of the trends in modern European art.

Like Béguin, Zambrano was convinced that Surrealism shared the world view of the novelists and poets of Romanticism, who had wielded idealism as ideological and cultural sustenance, as never before in history. She took the opportunity to criticize the Surrealists for their excessive retreat into the idealism of an innocent, infantile, more benign past, and for their limited sensitivity towards immediate experience, which was diametrically opposed to a realistic or tragic sense of life, central to Zambrano's thought at the time.

In his *Manifeste du surréalisme*, André Breton (1896–1966) suggested, for example, that the majority of the images that we hold in our mind have their origin in a re-learning process or a memory of that which happened in a previous state, closely related to one's own childhood and youth, an idea that has been interpreted as an indirect allusion to the Platonic theory of reminiscence, albeit mediated by the Freudian theory of the unconscious (Rubio 1994: 106). The images that we 're-learn', as much for Freud as for Surrealism, constitute an encounter with ourselves, with the lost world of our childhood, our longings, desires, frustrations, and so on, with that world which Zambrano considered infantile for its excessive distance from real and immediate experience.

However, it should be noted that, by relating Surrealism to idealism, Zambrano intended to address issues of a cultural rather than theoretical nature. She was trying to explore the cultural reasons that had led European subjective and individual life to stagnate in such a childish and irresponsible way. For her, the real mistake of Surrealism was to respond to its particular circumstances of having been engendered within the European cultural horizon that had itself emerged out of idealism.

Zambrano began her critique by examining first the existential consequences brought about by an idealism that had become the dogma of Western culture. Idealism had cast a shadow over our knowledge of life, replacing direct experience with the distancing contemplation of ideas which ultimately ended up concealing reality.[11] As evidenced by the number of authors and characters stuck in adolescence who populated European Romantic and post-Romantic literature — Zambrano's examples include Werther, Rousseau, Byron, Joyce's artist as a young man, and Surrealism — the obfuscation of an otherwise rich and contradictory existence had caused European man to forge for himself a 'bad conscience' or 'the conscience of an adolescent' which foolishly eradicated its own possibilities of realization and experience.[12] To make matters worse, psychoanalysis, which shaped the tenets of the movement, had ended up defacing the soul itself.[13] The conflict between the European obstinate adherence to idealism and its fatal outcome was reflected in the creative sterility which afflicted contemporary art, particularly Surrealism (Zambrano 1998: 91).

Thus, for Zambrano, Surrealism had thrived on the conflict between the ideology of idealism and its failure and was bound to suffer the same outcome as a result. The Surrealists also ended up clashing with reality, as would become visible or had already become visible in the form of strict rejection of bourgeois lifestyles and morality.

Some years later, Zambrano substantially modified her opinion, if not exactly favourably, granting Surrealism a privileged place in her work *La confesión, género literario* (1943) [The Confession: A Literary Genre].[14] Here, Surrealism is seen as a movement that hinders the human possibilities of transcendence by circumscribing its influence to one part of the soul, the psyche, reduced to instinctual impulses. What in her earlier work is presented as a consequence of Western culture is here analyzed from a less cultural and more philosophical perspective.

Claros del bosque (1977) [Clearings] offers a definition of the psyche that may shed more light on this idea: this part of the soul is described here as always ready to respond when stimulated. It moves, but seems to be always in the same place and, ultimately, gives no impression of having the momentum to extend beyond itself (Zambrano 1986a: 31). By contrast, the soul is, for Zambrano, the true metaphysical organ that constitutes man and, conversely, manifests an unswerving tendency to always go further, precisely because man is defined by his own thinking as the 'ser que padece su propia trascendencia' [being who endures his own transcendence] (1992: 9).

Before examining this second proposal, we need to consider two questions: the first concerns the surprise of finding a chapter on Surrealism in a book about confession, a genre usually associated with personal and even religious introspection, which Surrealism went to great lengths to reject. Despite their ideological divergences, Zambrano was able to find one thing they had in common that did away with this problem, claiming that the same longing to illuminate the inner self can be perceived in both Surrealist practice and the confession (Zambrano 1989a: 202). For Zambrano, Surrealism was valuable above all as a true reflection of life as flow and germination. Surrealism was the 'arte de entrañas adentro' [the art of the inner depths] (202). However, this statement, so attuned to her own intimate thought, was, once more, not sufficient reason to generate a positive attitude towards the movement.

The second point has to do with how, by directing her thoughts to the way in which both activities could facilitate the revelation of the interior, Zambrano was again distancing herself from Ortega y Gasset's perspective on the nature of the aesthetic developed in *La deshumanización del arte*, in which the philosopher had referred specifically to the *confessional* and, in short, sentimental character of the artistic works of Romanticism, which the aesthetic purity favoured by the ideology of the new art opposed. Zambrano linked both activities, confession and Surrealism, precisely in view of the *confessional* and *romantic* component they shared, and in view of their capacity to provide revelatory or expressive possibilities of interiority. The only difference regarding Ortega and Romanticism is that, for Zambrano, the ability of both Surrealism and the confession to *express* does not have so much to do with the sentimental outpouring of the artist, as it does with the coming-into-being, testifying to his existential project. This is precisely the central argument in Zambrano's second critique of surrealism.

One of the issues explored in *La confesión* are the differences and similarities between the confessional genre and the novel. Although both give expression to an individual's (his-)story, Zambrano believes that the novel is conceived on a temporal plane closely related to myth and which could be qualified as virtual. By contrast, confession reflects intimate existential temporality, that is, the real time of life.[15] This turns confession into a privileged genre for relating the 'attempts of being/projections of Dasein'. Confessions attest to the 'coming into being' of a self because in them narrative time and the author's lived time are mapped onto one another.[16]

But what kind of creative subject or subjective unit is better equipped to give expression to this existential project, while avoiding the dangers of aesthetic narcissism and respecting the existential possibilities and needs of self-realization? Is the Surrealist artist one of them?

Zambrano believes that the 'I' which the confession takes both as its point of departure and return is, in effect, endowed with certain traits which are diametrically opposed to the Cartesian 'I', which as a mere thinking thing, a *res cogitans*, reduces the vastness of the soul and displaces the seat in which intimacy is located. According to Zambrano, confessions are constructed from a *poietic* subjectivity able to challenge the rationalist restrictions which only concede a narrow margin to the activity of the soul (Zambrano 2004a: 93). Any confession must let speak that authentic and integral voice of the soul, which constitutes a creative subjective and metaphysical unit, transcendent and broader than Cartesian consciousness.

In *La confesión*, Zambrano argues that Surrealism, much like confession, also arises from a subjectivity, a unit or a 'centre', clearly different from the Cartesian subject. She employs words drawn from the *Second manifeste du surréalisme* of André Breton:

> Todo lleva a creer que existe un cierto punto donde la vida y la muerte, lo real y lo imaginario, lo comunicable y lo incomunicable, lo alto y lo bajo cesan de ser percibidos contradictoriamente. Y es en vano que se busque a la actividad surrealista otro móvil que la esperanza de encontrar ese punto. (Zambrano 2004a: 91)

> [Everything points towards the existence of some point where life and death, the real and the imaginary, the communicable and the incommunicable, the high and the low cease to be perceived as opposites. And it is in vain that one looks for another motive in Surrealist activity than the hope of finding that point.]

Following this line of thinking, Zambrano argues that Surrealism was established with the purpose of finding a creative 'point' capable of uniting dispersity, that is: a creative subjectivity that also eludes the narrow metaphysics and cognition of the *res cogitans*. However, this creative point could not approach the rich entity which Zambrano called the 'soul'. Illustrative, in this respect, is the following definition of the artist extracted from the book on the confession:

> Artista es aquel que puede descender hasta tal profundidad de sí mismo donde encuentra unas visiones que al par son acciones; el arte verdadero disipa la contradicción entre acción y contemplación, pues es una contemplación activa o una actividad contemplativa, una contemplación que engendra una obra, de la que se desprende un producto. Por eso anula a la par la diferencia entre lo real y lo imaginario, entre lo natural y lo fingido. (Zambrano 2004a: 97)

> [The artist is he who can descend to such a depth within that he finds visions that are, at the same time, actions; true art dispels the contradiction between action and contemplation, it is an active contemplation or a contemplative activity, a contemplation which engenders a work, which produces something. Thus, the difference between the real and the imaginary, between the natural and the false, is also annulled.]

In that visionary 'depth' of the artistic interiority, Zambrano saw reflected a specific philosophical subjectivity, which had been postulated by an author who was, for her, essential: St Augustine (354–430). The Augustine creative impulse possessed, despite its immanent character, a clear direction towards the transcendental, allowing it to oppose the Cartesian 'I', and equally, for the purposes of our argument, the creative subject of Surrealism.[17] This centre or 'point' to which Breton referred, was able, like the Augustinian 'I', to dissolve binaries and oppose cold rationality, but it was not enough to be assimilated to the centre proposed as a model by Zambrano.

The strong influence of the 'modern religion' of Freudianism had led Surrealism to turn towards a subjective instance of less prodigality: the psyche.

Therefore, in this second approach to Surrealism, Zambrano again saw fit to criticize it for endorsing Freudian assumptions about human nature which, contrary to the Augustinian ones, defended the idea that the psyche was the only essential human reality, one in which transcendence, broadly defined, played no relevant role.[18] In her philosophy which defends the divine nature of man and his agonic striving for transcendence, the immanence of the Surrealist movement and its attachment to the creative subject detracted, inevitably, from the artistic, but also existential and philosophical, richness that could be attributed to this avant-garde movement.

The Loss of Form as a Symbol of the Artistic, Cultural, and Existential Decline of the West

Zambrano paid close attention to other aspects of the historical avant-gardes in her essay 'La destrucción de las formas', first published in 1944. Although the observations contained in 'Nostalgia de la tierra' received little attention thereafter, the view of contemporary art as destructive was upheld in 1944 and in subsequent writings in which Zambrano returned to the subject of twentieth-century painting.[19] Therefore one could say that 'La destrucción de las formas' expresses with greater resonance than 'Nostalgia de la tierra' the general opinion that Zambrano had of the avant-garde.

In this instance, as is the case with her earlier essay and the other writings discussed here, the most striking observations concern not so much the technical or artistic explanation of what led to the destruction of artistic forms, 'figurative art', as the philosophical implications that they entailed, and that on this occasion would go hand in hand with Zambrano's other interests during the forties and fifties, and also with the political and historical context in which they were made.

This context was marked by a political and social upheaval unprecedented in history, the Second World War. It is worth considering that, although 'La destrucción de las formas' was published in 1944 as an independent article for the Mexican magazine *El Hijo Pródigo*, only a year later Zambrano decided to include it in her book *La agonía de Europa* [The Agony of Europe], a collection of essays written during the summer of 1940, which originally were lectures she gave that year at the Instituto de Investigaciones Científicas y Altos Estudios [School of Advanced Studies and Scientific Research] of the University of Havana.[20] In those texts, the author tried to shed light on the causes of the crisis that afflicted the old continent as a result of its major modern crisis.[21]

In its attempt to explain what was happening, the work offers a critique of the cultural modernity of the West. Here Zambrano insists once again that the reason that led Europe to catastrophe, among other less important ones, was none other than the stagnation produced by rationalism and idealism. According to her, Europe had been built on violence and on the ambition, characteristic of Western man, to create history, science, knowledge, and creations in his own image, the greatest act of pride ever conceived:

> Hacerse un mundo es el anhelo más íntimo y ferviente del europeo, un mundo desde su nada. Bajo el afán de justicia y aun de felicidad se ha llamado revolución. Se ha llamado, a veces, nostalgia del Paraíso. Y no es sino afirmación del momento, del eterno momento: 'Seréis como dioses'. (Zambrano 2000a: 59)

> [Creating a world is the most intimate and fervent desire of the European, a world from nothing. Blinded by the desire for justice and happiness this has even been called revolution. It has been called, sometimes, nostalgia for Paradise. And it is nothing but affirmation of the moment, the eternal moment: 'Ye shall be as gods'.]

The inclusion of an essay on the avant-garde in that collection served to give it a specific, pertinent, and explanatory historical and hermeneutic context. In fact, the first essay included in the collection, already announces the main thesis Zambrano would defend four years later in 'La destrucción de las formas':

> Las últimas creaciones europeas se caracterizaban todas ellas por ser obras en que se ejecutaba una destrucción, en que se verificaba un perdimiento. La última pintura era la destrucción implacable de la pintura; la literatura se negaba a sí misma, y hasta la filosofía naufragaba en un vitalismo y existencialismo desesperados. Nada íntegro, nada entero. (Zambrano 2000a: 25)

> [The latest European creations were characterized as works in which destruction was carried out, in which a loss was verified. The latest and last painting was the relentless destruction of painting; literature denying itself, and even philosophy was drowning in a desperate vitalism and existentialism. Nothing integral, nothing whole.]

For Zambrano, an avant-garde art in which any trace of figurative representation had disappeared, reflected the inexorable dismemberment of a continent that had been built on pride and violence. The arts of the avant-garde constituted memories of our time, and the means by which it was possible to access the European inner soul coming into being, albeit on the way to its own destruction.

As in 'Nostalgia de la tierra', in 'La destrucción de las formas' Zambrano's allusions and even explicit references to *La deshumanización del arte* are very much in evidence, even including direct quotations from the text.[22] On this occasion, the author reinterpreted and corrected her mentor's position regarding the 'feigned' attraction that the new art seemingly felt for primitive and naive art, wherein artists sought, according to Ortega y Gasset, something extremely attractive from an ideological point of view: the lack of tradition. Even though *a priori,* the phenomenon which both philosophers appeared to acknowledge was the same and although the two of them succeeded in using it to describe one of the most widespread trends in contemporary art, the observations, assessments, and interpretations which they extracted were markedly different. Unlike the mostly aesthetic perspective adopted by Ortega, Zambrano wanted to make clear that such primitivism 'was neither refinement, nor stylization' (Zambrano 2000a: 90). Rather than constituting an aesthetic mode, she saw it as a phenomenon which, having spread equally to all contemporary arts, visual, literary, or musical, had to have reasons to go beyond the strictly formalist.[23] This artistic return to the origins represented a profound event beyond the elimination of artistic tradition itself, calling into question the fundamental basis on which Western history was built.

From an overall perspective, and taking into account these insights, it can be said that, for Zambrano, the destruction which the new art had imposed on forms embodied the return to an earlier stage of Western history itself, when it was possible to be in contact with the sacred. The sacred is a key concept in her thinking, defined especially in her work *El hombre y lo divino* (1955) [Man and the Divine], where the term is associated with the original *physis*, prior to all history, all thought, even all poetry. It represents a pre-humanistic state, standing as a kind of initial topos, uncorrupted, pure, and only recoverable through a non-violent exercise of philosophy, i.e. neither rationalist nor idealist. Furthermore, she interpreted the sympathy shown by the new artists towards primitive art as a symbolic regression precisely to that primordial hermeticism of the sacred, which would explain the annihilation of every kind of figurative representation.

Although this may be a general description of what the 'destruction of forms' meant for Zambrano, she also specifies some of its most revealing manifestations which are worthy of comment. According to her, the avant-gardes first destroyed *objectivity*, a prominent feature of Western culture, embraced by philosophy since Thales, deliberating on the nature of things, and divided them into subject and object (Zambrano 2000a: 98). The loss of representation, on the contrary, would allow for the recovery of the original (con-)fusion between subject and object, the return to a sort of Dionysian spirit which had been eradicated in the course of the development of artistic forms.

Another aspect that the avant-garde had destroyed was the *idealized vision of the world*, replaced, artistically, by uninhabited landscapes, deserts, or the 'residuos de lo humano' [residues of the human] (Zambrano 2000a: 99). The destruction of the idealized — and *humanized* — vision of the world, in contrast, made the constituent elements of the primitive and sacred matter appear, that which in her essay she calls 'the mineral', 'gravity without life space', 'rhythm', the 'babble' prior to the word, the ineffable, etc.

Last, but not least, avant-garde art had proceeded to eliminate the humanized representation of man. Faced with the revelatory artistic tradition of the human, *humanistic*, rationalist, and idealistic, in the new art, now more than ever a *dehumanized art*, deserts, hostile landscapes, and, above all, masks had become the shaping elements of a new representation from which man, consequently, was also bound to disappear. Thus emerged 'la noche oscura de lo humano', the dark night of the human.

This further feature of the 'destruction of forms', which is central to the essay in question, was evaluated by Zambrano on the basis of a symptomatic dichotomy, and one not devoid of ambiguity: that which exists between the *face*, symbol of man and of humanization, that is, the cultural history of the West, and the *mask*. For her, the practice of portraiture, common among artists prior to the 'destruction of forms', was the symbol of an era of enlightenment, the realm and culmination of humanism.[24] Portraiture was born in Greece with the intention of revealing man himself, though Zambrano felt that harnessing the form for that purpose was actually an act of masking. This aesthetic concealment which prioritized beauty in the face of reality, and of which the work of Phidias was the most outstanding representative, in fact achieved nothing other than covering up human being, falsifying and disfiguring it. In clear opposition to this fraudulent practice, faces, in avant-garde painting, have been replaced by masks. If the former had proved to be another way of masking, masks, paradoxically, came to reestablish direct contact with reality.

In her essay the mask represents one of the privileged ways of approaching and getting in touch with the sacred. Specifically, it facilitates contact through participation or mystical con-fusion, which, compared to the humanist division of subject and object, which inaugurates Greek rationalism and idealism, represents a loss of limits, depriving man of his face, transfiguring him or breaking the Apollonian principle of individuation.[25] In confronting the sacred, Zambrano claims, the mask is necessary because it does not present any resistance to enlightenment or knowledge, as it is not part of the original *physis* nor of its definition, and has not been subsumed by the principle of identity, nor has it been reduced to the concept of 'nature' or the idea of 'being'. (Zambrano 1989a). Only modern art, disregarding tradition and emulating the magical origins of art, has been able to redeem it.[26] The appearance of the mask in contemporary art thus recalled the primeval treatment of reality, a purer treatment, and one less tainted by history; renewed with a reality that must be understood as *physis* and not as *nature*, which allows the recovery, in our contemporary experience, of the ambiguous, the restless, the animate, and the Dionysian.

Considering the above, we may return to the idea that the 'destruction of forms' refers not only to the disappearance of the boundaries used to identify objects or people; 'form' is here equivalent to the thing itself, to its being. The 'destruction of forms' suggests, by contrast, uncertainty, deformity, non-being (Gilson 1972). Zambrano does not allude with this expression only to abstract art but also to contemporary figurative art — Surrealism itself, the metaphysical painting of Giorgio de Chirico, and even Expressionism, as stated in the text — where, although 'forms' are still discernible, there is also a type of representation at play whose effects are equally distorting. Therefore, the term 'form' must also be understood in a much broader sense as the symbol of a theoretical and a humanist imposition, belonging to the *humanist* history of the West, expressed in an abstract or figurative way, which man creates on the primordial chaotic background to control its movement; it constitutes, therefore, much more than a stylistic device (Zambrano 2000a: 97). Form is here synonymous with humanism and, through it, with a violent and deified cultural history. It is synonymous, in short, with the history of the West. Its literal destruction in the field of contemporary art, beyond denoting the formal loss of form, symbolically signals the demise of the historical dominance of the human. This destruction equally represents at the symbolic level the wearing-away of an epistemological and artistic power dominated by the subject, by extension, of the decline of the West.

Notes to Chapter 2

1. References to Zambrano's essay are to the edition published in the anthology *Algunos lugares de la pintura* (1989: 15–22), although it was first published in *Los Cuatro Vientos*, 2 (April 1933) 108–13; also in *Documents of Spanish Vanguard* (ed. by Paul Ilie, University of North Carolina, 1969); in *Anthropos* (Antologías Temáticas, 2 (Madrid, 1987), pp. 52–54); and in *Condados de niebla*, edited by César Antonio Molina as a supplement to the pre-Civil War articles of María Zambrano (6 (Huelva, 1988), pp. 89–101).
2. The word 'desterrado', as used by Zambrano, means at once 'removed from the earth' and 'exiled', a double meaning which it is difficult to convey through direct translation into English. Zambrano further differentiated, in her native tongue, between 'desterrado' and 'exilado'.
3. In the opinion of Nietzsche, as long as the death of God, which would provoke the recuperation of the earth and of the material world, is not known, Man's drive to become *Übermensch* would continue to be directed to the beyond, and continue to constitute 'infidelities' to the earth, coarse asceticism, and the unnatural disdain for the body. See 'Zarathustras Vorrede' (Nietzsche 1980).
4. It is highly likely that the years Zambrano dedicated to the study of Spinoza, on whom she planned to write her doctoral thesis, may have left their mark on this divine vision of reality in which the most petty and insignificant things appear surrounded by a halo of sanctity. Ana Bundgaard seemingly notes the same when she states that 'God is for Zambrano a radical, deeply felt reality which manifests itself in man as a feeling of absence, rather than presence. God is a mysterious resistance which appears with a deeply felt certainty in the context of man's being in the world' (Bundgaard 2000: 129).
5. 'España y su pintura' is a fragmentary text dated around 1960, yet unpublished until the publication of *Algunos lugares de la pintura* (1989a: 69–90); 'Sueño y destino de la pintura' was also written around that date, and unpublished until its inclusion in the same book (91–98). It was also published the same year in *Diario 16. Culturas*, June 1989.
6. Both are included in *Algunos lugares de la pintura* (1989a: 177–87 & 189–94), with the title 'A Luis Fernández en su muerte'; the former also appeared in *Índice*, 1 (August 1969). Fernández and Zambrano met in París during the 1940s. Their friendship was the first in a series of friendships which were crucial for the development of Fernández's art and, indeed, life. Through Zambrano, he came into contact with other Spanish artists living in the French capital, such as Javier Valls, Jaime del Valle-Inclán, and Rafael Lasso de la Vega, who, incidentally, was one of the first to write an article about him, entitled 'La peinture abstraite de Louis Fernández' (1949), published in the prestigious review *Cahiers d'Art*.
7. 'No era hija de la luz esta pintura, sino del fuego' [This painting was not born from light, but rather from fire] (Zambrano 1989a: 192).
8. Critics have tended to see other characteristics as points of comparison between Fernández's work, the Baroque, and Zurbarán, for example the plastic isolation of the objects (skulls, ox heads, etc.) whose obstinate presence is brought out by the vivacious and energetic use of colours in contrast to the dark and neutral backgrounds. The iconography of Fernández with a focus on temporality and the vacuity of life, in addition to the number of canvasses dedicated to still lives, in whose treatment the influence of contemporary artists like Picasso can be appreciated, refers equally to the Spanish Baroque. The absence of additional iconographic motifs, the tendency to animate the inert and objectify the living, and the reduced size of the works reveal a style of painting that has a definite connection with the dramatism of the Golden Age.
9. 'Le mouvement de l'esprit est à peu près le même: on proclame la valeur de connaissance inhérente aux groupements spontanés des mots et des images qui surgissent de l'ombre intérieure. El l'on tente d'amener à la conscience tout le trésor inconscient' [The spiritual movement is similar: one proclaims the value of knowledge inherent in spontaneous groupings of words and images

which emerge from the darkness within. And one tries to bring to the fore of consciousness the entire subconscious treasure] (Béguin 1939: 391).
10. See María Zambrano: 'El inacabable pintar de Joan Miró' (1989a: 171–76). In this article, Zambrano relates the first time she viewed the painting *La Masía*, which she came across at the estate of Ernest Hemingway in Santa María del Rosario, near Havana.
11. 'El idealismo: la altísima idea del hombre que el europeo se formó a través del cristianismo y del renacimiento, no le ha permitido contemplar la imagen clara del funcionar real de su vida; una repugnancia infinita le defendía de esta realidad. El hombre se evitaba a sí mismo y eludía su propia imagen' [Idealism: the highest idea of man, that the European formed through Christianity and the Renaissance, has not permitted him to contemplate the clear image of the real function of his life; an infinite repugnance protected him from this reality. Man avoided himself, and eluded his own image] (Zambrano 1998: 90–91).
12. 'Recuérdese que los héroes literarios de Europa, sus modelos y al par expresión de aquello de donde se querría escapar, si hubiese fuerzas para tal deseo, son siempre adolescentes. Werther abre camino, y Rousseau con sus pecaminosas confesiones, que se leen con avidez, que toda Europa devora. La poesía de Byron y Shelley, luego nuestro adorado Dostoievski hasta Joyce y Cocteau; el surrealismo [...] adolescencia al principio, fragancia todavía, luego cada vez más revuelta en sí misma, más descompuesta en atrayente perfume' [We must remember that the literary heroes of Europe are always adolescents. They were the models and equally express that from which one wanted to escape, if one were to have enough strength to accomplish said desire. Werther leads the way, and Rousseau, with his sinful confessions, avidly read, and devoured by all of Europe. The poetry of Byron and Shelley, then our adored Dostoyevsky, up to Joyce and Cocteau; Surrealism [...] adolescence in the beginning, still fragrant, then ever more muddled in itself, more decomposed by its seductive perfume] (Zambrano 1998: 92).
13. 'Han tenido que venir los médicos del alma, el psicoanálisis, para impedir que no nos ahogue ese mundo submarino' [It has taken the arrival of the doctors of the soul, psychoanalysis, to impede our drowning in this submarine world] (Zambrano 1998: 92).
14. The book was published for the first time in 1943 with the title *Confesión: Género literario y método*, but was corrected in 1965, acquiring its definitive form, and that of later editions. Reference is made to the 2004 edition.
15. 'El que hace la confesión no busca el tiempo del arte, sino algún otro tiempo real como el suyo' [He who confesses is not in search of the time of art, but another real time, like his own] (Zambrano 2004a: 27).
16. 'La confesión, más que ningún otro género literario, muestra lo que la vida tiene de camino, de tránsito entre aquel que nos encontramos siendo y el otro hacia el que vamos' [Confession, more than any other literary genre, displays what lies along the way of life, in transit between that which we find ourselves being, and that towards which we travel] (Zambrano 2000a: 73).
17. St Augustine is widely recognized as one of the first thinkers interested in the inner world of human beings. As a close follower of Platonism and neo-Platonism, his epistemology rejects empirical data/sensatory information, on account of the supposition that truth resides in oneself. In his opinion, thoughts are driven powerfully towards this truth which dominates them from within, getting around the doubtful knowledge which the external organs offer, and negotiating the contingency and mutability to which one's own subjectivity is subjected. For him, in man there is something transcendent, as this interior truth is a Truth in itself transcendent, intelligible, necessary, immutable, and eternal. This Truth is none other than God.
18. In fact, Zambrano would accuse Freud of precisely this in the text she dedicated to him one year before publishing her book on confession, *El freudismo, testimonio del hombre actual*. 'Hasta ahora, hemos caminado juntos sin tener nada que reprocharle. [...] Pero... no se detuvo aquí, sino que se lanza a definir esa subconsciencia dogmáticamente, y en seguida, va a definir al hombre por ella. [...] Y así, Freud desemboca en una clase típica de teoría, las teorías de la "superestructura", según las cuales, lo claro, lo aparentemente victorioso no es sino algo aparencial y derivado que descansa sobre la profunda y única realidad de una substancia o fuerza única desconocida, o de inferior rango, hasta el momento. Todas estas teorías deshacen la trascendencia, dejan la vida humana reducida a la pura inmanencia' [Until now, we have come to this point without

any necessity for reproach. [...] However... he did not stop there, but instead threw himself into defining this subconscious dogmatically, and then went on to define man by it. [...] Thus, Freud leads to a typical kind of theory, the theories of 'superstructure', according to which the clear, the apparently victorious is nothing but something apparent and derivative which rests on the profound and unique reality of a substance or force, either unknown or lesser, up until that moment. All of these theories dissolve transcendence, leaving human life reduced to pure immanence] (Zambrano 2004a: 134).

19. See 'Wifredo Lam' (1954), 'La aurora de la pintura en Juan Soriano' (1954), and 'Verdad y ser en la pintura de Armando Barrios' (1960), all collected in *Algunos lugares de la pintura*.

20. The first edition dates from the year 1945 and was published by the Sudamericana publishing house in Buenos Aires. Here, reference is made to the edition of Trotta, edited by Jesús Moreno Sanz, because it includes subsequent corrections made by Zambrano to the first edition. All of the essays were published separately in the review Sur of Buenos Aires: 'La agonía de Europa', 72 (September 1940); 'La violencia europea', 78 (March 1941); and 'La esperanza europea', 90 (March 1942).

21. Ana Bundgaard has analyzed the points of contact between Zambrano's concept of the destruction of Europe and authors such as Miguel de Unamuno and José Ferrater Mora. For further details, see Bundgaard 2000. See also Ortega Muñoz 1994: 232–53.

22. 'De las miradas más lúcidas, quizá en una hora tardía (punto demasiado avanzado en el proceso), está la del admirable ensayo *La deshumanización del arte*, de Ortega y Gasset' [Among the most lucid views, perhaps all too late (at a point too advanced in the process), is that of the admirable essay *La deshumanización del arte*, by Ortega y Gasset] (Zambrano 2000a: 88).

23. Zambrano also made some incursions, although very brief, into the 'destruction of forms' in the area of contemporary music, based on the appearance of atonality and twelve-tone music. In *El hombre y lo divino*, for example, she approached this matter, seeing it as yet another manifestation of contemporary nihilism (Zambrano 1986a: 185–86).

24. 'Forjar un rostro en el arte es consecuencia de haberlo forjado ya en la mente; es el espejo y el resultado de haberse decidido a ser hombre, y de haber encontrado ya una noción, un saber previo acerca de la consistencia humana' [To give form to a face in art is to have already given it a form in the mind; it is the reflection and the result of having decided to be human, and of already having found a notion, a previous knowledge about the human makeup] (Zambrano 2000a: 87).

25. For precisely this reason, the mask is an outstanding Dionysian symbol. It is in itself a coming-together, symbol, and appearance of that which is absent, and union of immediate presence and absolute absence; see Otto 1960.

26. 'Se cerraba el largo espacio en que el rostro humano se había enseñoreado del mundo, el tiempo en que había gozado de la luz y se había permitido mostrarse en todos sus modos posibles. Era el eclipse de "lo natural"' [The large space in which the human face had dominated the world, the time in which it had enjoyed light, and had allowed itself to be seen in all possible ways, was closing. It was the eclipse of 'the natural'] (Zambrano 1989a: 89).

CHAPTER 3

The Anti-Fascist Origins of Poetic Reason: Genealogy of a Reflection on Totalitarianism[1]

Antolín Sánchez Cuervo, Consejo Superior de Investigaciones Científicas

The term 'poetic reason', which is widely used to describe Maria Zambrano's thought, appears to draw on a semantic network wholly unrelated to politics, or at least remote from many other ways of understanding reason in a conventionally political sense. The ideas Zambrano puts forward in her early writings — in books such as *Horizonte de liberalismo* (1930) [Horizon of Liberalism] and essays such as 'Hacia un saber sobre el alma' (1934) [Towards a Knowledge of the Soul], which were published several years before she first employed the term, are certainly far more radical than a 'reform of reason' — in keeping with the 'vital reason' proposed by her mentor Ortega y Gasset. 'Poetic reason' involves, indeed, a break with canonical ways of thinking or a seemingly paradoxical reconciliation, not with reason itself or with the logical, formal, or empirical dimensions of reality, but with some of its dark areas, or with vital experiences that have been overlooked despite their crucial role in defining the human condition; in other words, a reconciliation with the experience of finiteness and death, of love and hatred, of despair and hopelessness, of the tragic nature of existence, or simply with what Zambrano called 'las formas íntimas de la vida' [the intimate forms of life]. These are: time or the multidimensional expression of hope beyond the linear or chronological sense of history; love or the primary approach to reality; empathy or the ability to deal with the other; resentment or the discharge of everything subjugated by conscience; envy or the craving for what is different; nothingness or that which is unfathomable and doomed to non-being; death or the radical limit of life, which forces the subject to think with authenticity; the immediacy of the senses and the sensibility that enables a true relationship with life, betrayed by consciousness (Zambrano 2004c: 617–68).

In short, and to use Zambrano's image, 'poetic reason' seeks to grapple with all the heterodox knowledge that Western philosophy forgot in prematurely leaving the Platonic cave to establish itself under the blinding light of rationalism. It is therefore a reason divorced from politics in the 'practical', 'critical', or 'discursive' sense found in canonical thinkers such as Kant, Habermas, and Rawls. Zambrano did not propose a theory of sovereignty or of the social contract, or a reflection on equal opportunities.

This detachment from politics in the conventional sense became more apparent in her writings from the 1950s onwards, as Zambrano began to delve into the experience of dreams and her thought turned towards mysticism. Exile then took on an intimate character, as she gave up her commitment to the Spanish Republic which she had maintained throughout the 1930s and the Civil War (even though she never belonged to any political party), and came to terms with the collapse of the Republic as a civil and cultural project, and, to a certain extent, with her marginal condition as an exile, in keeping with the values of Seneca, which she espoused in her 1942 book *El pensamiento vivo de Séneca*. It has been pointed out many times that Zambrano's notion of exile took on strong allegorical connotations and that she thus left behind the Republican vocation of earlier years: exile became something of a dark night and a quest for an inner and transcendent fullness, detached from concrete history; a metaphor for an off-centre and shipwrecked thought that seeks salvation on the margins of the Western philosophical tradition, or a return to the bottom of the Platonic cave in order to recover what was left there (Bundgaard 2000: 137–77; Sánchez Cuervo 2010; Moreno Sanz 2010).

However, none of this means that poetic reason is entirely non-political or has no connection with political thought. Zambrano's exile certainly has an allegorical and 'spiritual' quality, but there are other dimensions to it. Exile as a way of living and thinking can lead us to the mysticism of many dark nights, but also to the shadows of the political. In the case of Zambrano, exile is also a political figuration and a material experience that radically challenges many of the spaces and temporalities constructed by modern rationality. In line with other figures of contemporary critical thought, ranging from Jewish precursors of critical theory such as Franz Rozensweig to Walter Benjamin, and Hannah Arendt, Giorgio Agamben or Jean Luc Nancy, exile is also, for Zambrano, a privileged place from which to uncover the exclusive dimensions of the state and its great ally, the narrative of the nation; a 'no man's land', rather, that reveals the importance of the nation-state in the origin of the totalitarian logic and the dark connection between this logic and the social contract liberal thought has amply drawn on.[2] A utopian place or a place without topos in which a new citizenship based on the semantics of otherness and the culture of diaspora can germinate. An experience, also, of memory that exposes the violence of oblivion inscribed in the logic of progress, on which the philosophies of history have so often relied, as well as the continuities drawn by historicism in an attempt to escape that logic. Furthermore, exile forces one to address the hermeneutics of the past, which go beyond the methods of the scientific or conventional historian, and recapture the critical and subversive, ethical and political, significance of memory (Sánchez Cuervo 2014).

These critical interpretations are often to be found in Zambrano's works. In *La tumba de Antígona* [Antigone's Tomb] exile is defined as a way of constructing and experiencing the civic space that is distinct from the customs established by modern reason. Other writings, however, hint at the notion of exile as diaspora and a call to a new cosmopolitanism that does not reproduce the exclusions of the modern universalism (Mate 2014; Zambrano 2014c: 743–45 & 777–79). Zambrano's republican memory is more explicit. It emerges in a number of her writings in terms that remind one of Benjamin's thesis on history, as can be seen in a passage of *El hombre y lo divino* (1955) [Man and the Divine] devoted to ruins (Zambrano 2011d: 254–61) and, in a more complex and elaborate way, in her autobiographical essay *Delirio y destino* (1953) [Delirium and Destiny], where memory, both individual and collective, appears as a lens capable of illuminating sociological areas, symbolic records, political traces, and hermeneutical keys to the past which the scientific historian cannot perceive (Beneyto 2004; Sánchez Cuervo 2011). A memory that is strongly ethical and charged with political critique also appears, of course, in 'Carta sobre el exilio' (1961) [Letter on Exile], which is addressed not so much to the old enemies as to the new ones — 'los inconformistas de hoy' [contemporary non-conformists], that is to say, the new generation of technocrats who had begun to shape politics and to consider setting up a democracy after Franco's death while casting aside exiles and their memories, for to them 'el exiliado ha dejado de existir ya, vuelva o no vuelva' [the exile has already ceased to exist whether or not he returns] (1961: 68).[3] That memory is also present in 'La experiencia de la historia (Después de entonces)' [The Experience of History (After then)], her preface to the second edition of *Los intelectuales en el drama de España* [The Intellectuals in the Drama of Spain], which was published in 1977, when Spain was transitioning to democracy, a process partly based on deliberately forgetting — or at best 'managing' the memory of — the victims of Franco's regime. Zambrano coined the expression 'sueño creador', which she had used as the title of her 1965 book, to designate the Republican project, whereas in other writings of the same period, later included in her posthumous book *Los bienaventurados* (1991), she refers to the figure of the exile as a figure of radical otherness, capable of disrupting the logic of oblivion typical of linear time.

In short, in Zambrano's reflection on exile it is necessary to consider certain political features that are usually overlooked or blurred by a 'spiritualist' interpretation. The political dimension of Zambrano's exile tends, by and large, to be ignored, rather like the political dimension of her 'poetic reason'. It is certainly true that the reference to its political origin, in the article '*La guerra* de Antonio Machado' [Antonio Machado's War], published in 1937 in the journal *Hora de España*, is a commonplace in studies of Zambrano's work, but as a chronological and bibliographical pointer rather than as a crucial hermeneutic key. 'Razón poética, de honda raíz de amor' [Poetic reason, deeply rooted in love] (2015: 193), she said in a phrase that is usually decontextualized; incidentally, it was not the first time she explicitly formulated the notion of 'poetic reason': she had already done so a few months before, in the afterword to the collection of essays *Madre España*, which she herself prepared during her stay in Chile in collaboration with a number of Chilean poets supportive of the Spanish Republic, including Vicente Huidobro and Pablo Neruda.[4] Towards the end of that text, Zambrano points out that 'dolor' [grief], 'pasividad' [passivity], and 'fiera lucha armada' [fierce armed fight] are not enough to grapple with the Spanish tragedy; and that it is therefore necessary to exercise 'la razón poética que encuentra en instantáneo descubrimiento lo que la inteligencia desgrana paso a paso en sus elementos' [poetic reason finds in instant discovery what intelligence gradually breaks down into its elements] (Zambrano 2015: 378).

Zambrano thus formulates poetic reason for the first time in a radically political and belligerent way that is not merely incidental, but determines her vocation itself from within. This vocation is none other than a response to the war, to fascism, and the destruction of Europe, itself the result of reducing reason to analytical and instrumental intelligence. Like many other fellow exiles, Zambrano understood very soon that the tragedy of Spain arose from a conflict not only national, but of a European scope, the result of a violence that had been breeding in Western modernity and which found its most brutal expression in fascism. Poetic reason thus conveyed the civil and political commitment Zambrano had been developing since her first book, *Horizonte de liberalismo*, in keeping with her support for the Republican project and in opposition to the academic and patriarchal knowledge epitomized by her mentor Ortega y Gasset.[5] It further expressed a radically original philosophical approach, connected with the deep insights she was to develop over the next fifty years. At any rate, we are dealing with a reason shaped by a strong anti-fascism, where fascism is understood not only as a mass movement, but also — and mainly — as the collapse of modern rationality and of European bourgeois culture. Zambrano will stress this point in her writings on the Spanish Civil War, and subsequently in her study of absolutism, *Persona y democracia* (1958) [Self and Democracy] and in *El hombre y lo divino*, about the return of the sacred.

In the interpretation of fascism lies precisely one of the most famous differences between Zambrano and her mentor Ortega, who disagreed just as strongly over liberalism, or rather the 'new liberalism', an expression they both used to designate radically different ideas. Zambrano chose to end her essay *Horizonte de liberalism* with that term, which involved a conception of liberalism as novel as it was naive, and which pointed to a democratic socialism compatible with the recognition and exercise of moral and political, aesthetic and religious individual freedoms (Zambrano 2014c: 100–04). It was also the expression Ortega, a mature thinker though also ingenuous in his own way, employed in 1938, when the Civil War had clearly tilted in favour of the rebels, to refer to a liberalism that was soon to emerge as a result of the purifying or cleansing action of the totalitarianism of the time. 'Totalitarianism,' he stated in 'Concerning Pacifism', published in July 1938 in *The Nineteenth Century*, later included in *The Revolt of the Masses*, 'will save liberalism giving it some of its colours, cleansing it, and thanks to this process, we shall also see a new Liberalism temper the authoritarian regimes' (Ortega y Gasset 1938: 34).

Ortega addressed the problem of fascism early on, though not explicitly or profoundly. In his brief essay 'Sobre el fascismo' [On Fascism], published in 1925 (Ortega y Gasset 2004–2010: II, 497–505), he ascribed four features to fascism: its contradictory nature (in that it advocates authoritarianism and revolt at the same time, the State and its dissolution); its negative nature, since its strength derives from weakness, decline and ultimate fall of its enemy, namely liberalism; its revelation of a new process in the public life of contemporary Europe; and its replacement of law by force and, consequently, its open appeal to violence. Ortega would mention the latter feature again in an article entitled 'Instituciones', which was published in 1930 in the newspaper *La Nación* of Buenos Aires (Ortega y Gasset 2004–2010: IV, 654–59), and in which he linked the discrediting of liberal institutions to the 'insinceridad constitutiva' of that period, apparent in the new art and especially in politics and in parliamentary liberalism, whose increasingly hollow rhetoric had exacerbated public distrust for the culture of legality and led to its replacement by both fascist and communist appeals to resoluteness and direct action.

In any case, these reflections are not isolated. In *The Revolt of the Masses*, published a year before, in 1929, the references to fascism are few but significant. One may say that Ortega attributes fascism — and bolshevism too, in many respects — to the 'massification', and hence devaluation, of the enlightened subject, understood in a broad sense. Fascism is thus viewed mainly as a result of the emergence of the mass-man, a kind of irresponsible teenager, 'a type of man who does not want to give reasons to be right, but simply shows himself resolved to impose his opinions'; who feels entitled 'to rule the society without the capacity for doing so'; prefers submission to authority rather than reasoned discussion; 'lacks the faculty of ideation' (Ortega y Gasset 1957: 73) or to conceive his own ideas, and behaves like a 'spoiled child' (98) and a 'self-satisfied' person.[6] The mass-man is crude and uncivilized and mainly identifies with barbarism and the absence of moral rules, with a lapse into primitivism and lack of historical knowledge. He is thus inclined, however latently, to violence as *prima ratio* and to 'direct action' as a social and political strategy, as opposed to the 'indirect action' and 'civilizing force of liberalism' (75–76).

These features appear incongruous: the mass-man is self-satisfied and a conformist, and at the same time domineering, violent, and even subversive. He is contaminated to a certain extent by the contradictory nature of fascism, which Ortega pointed out in his 1925 article, as the prototype of the totalitarian movements of that time. The revolt of the masses spawned fascism as well as other social movements like trade unionism and bolshevism, whose origin, however, Ortega does not attempt to analyze: maybe he was aware of this shortcoming when he described these movements as 'strange things' or innovations wrapped in an 'extraordinary form' (73). His study of fascism is tangential to his discourse on the mass-man and certainly inadequate; it is based, to say the least, on crude sociological categories, vague historical digressions, and a simplistic political analysis that attributes the emergence of this new type of man comparable to a spoiled child primarily to the state, or rather to statism. Furthermore, the opposition he posits between culture and barbarism, and between liberalism and fascism, seems rather too sketchy: there certainly are grey zones or spaces where both coexist. Critical theory, from its Jewish precursors to its current epigones, radically challenges this clear-cut distinction: it is hardly surprising that Horkheimer emphasized the limitations of Ortega's analysis a few years later. As he pointed out in *Eclipse of Reason* (1947), Ortega, like Gabriel Tarde at the end of the nineteenth century, proposed a 'progressive' interpretation of collectivism, as opposed to the 'romanticist and anti-intellectualist' critique offered by the 'philosophy of French counter-revolution and that of German pre-fascism'; however its 'popular' and 'pedagogical' nature takes away its philosophical potential and contributes to the very historical process it critiques. His 'conservative' critique of culture may well become a 'repressive doctrine' if 'used for panaceas' (Horkheimer 1974: 164). In other words, Ortega's sketchy critique of the mass-man, which is quite apparent in those clear-cut distinctions that lack any dialectical tension, does not help us to penetrate into its interior and reveal its secret scheme. In the case of Frankfurtian analysis, the logic of domination and self-sustaining violence, following on from the evolution of modern capitalism and its current hegemony under the forms of the cultural industry, has deprived the subject of all autonomy.

Zambrano's analysis of fascism is quite different from that proposed by the Frankfurt School, though it is linked to the critique of idealism by the predecessors of critical theory like Franz Rosenzweig. In any case, it has great philosophical depth and is far more complex than that of Ortega. As we shall see, Zambrano also views the fascist as something of an adolescent, but her interpretation is more introspective, even psychoanalytical, than 'aristocratic' and 'neo-enlightened'. Admittedly, it was mainly her intellectual environment, historical perspective, and personal experience that allowed her to delve deeper into fascism. Unlike Ortega, who had written on this phenomenon very early, in the 1920s, Zambrano did not face the problems of urgency and novelty: by the time she devoted several sections in *Los intelectuales en el drama de España* to fascism, she already had a broad historical perspective, as well as a dramatic one, given the course of events in Spain and Europe in the 1930s. Her knowledge of fascism was not limited to books: she had personally encountered it in its most violent and revealing expression, namely war, a topic with which Ortega always avoided grappling. She never ceased to reflect on fascism while in exile, and she did so without the obvious restrictions and limitations Ortega faced in Franco's Spain. In any case, Zambrano did not regard fascism as a 'strange thing' or an unpredictable accident in the course of modernity, but as the outcome of a historical process connected with its very core, or that of the Western logos. Her philosophical starting point is idealism, understood as the falsifying and arrogant construction of an absolute knowledge aiming to explain and develop in a self-sufficient way, by means of speculative categories, the rational consistence of the world, of an unconditional intelligence which therefore excludes 'otras realidades no racionales [...] Y unas realidades, unas necesidades que el hombre tiene y que son las que en realidad mueven su instrumento racional, le dirigen y orientan hacia una finalidad a veces enmascarada' [non-rational realities [...] Certain realities, certain needs which every human being possesses and which drive his rational instrument towards an occasionally hidden goal] (Zambrano 2015: 143). Hence idealism, while presenting a rather elevated idea of the world that can be traced back to Christianity and the Renaissance, has kept man 'from clearly grasping the very reality of his life, since an infinite disgust protected him from this reality'. Man thus 'avoided himself and was his own image' (Zambrano 2014c: 143). For that, idealism, in spite of showing a very elevated idea of the world, inheritor of Christianity and the Renaissance, did not let man 'contemplar la imagen clara del funcionar real de su vida, pues una repugnancia infinita le defendía de esta realidad' [contemplate the clear image of the very working of his life, since an infinite repugnance was defending him from this reality] (2015: 143). In this way, 'se evitaba a sí mismo y eludía su propia imagen' [man avoided himself and was eluding his own image] (143).

According to Zambrano, idealism constructed a rationality that reduces the world to its measure and human beings to abstractions, thereby arousing a sense of guilt, a condition of permanent adolescence or a conflict between this ideal and 'la riqueza dispar de la realidad' [the multifarious richness of reality]. Idealism resulted in a withering of life, or a 'sedimentación de sueños, deseos oscuros, desilusiones no formuladas, requerimientos incumplidos, que van aumentando' [sedimentation of dreams, dark cravings, unexpressed disappointments, unfulfilled and ever stronger urges] (2015: 144). Hence the significance of psychoanalysis as an outlet for this suppressed secret world; of narratives like Dostoevsky's, which may be regarded as the expression of a hidden Christian resentment; and of Surrealism, which boldly forces bourgeois society to confront its miseries and its despair, as well as the solitude and the angst felt by human beings due to their being trapped in an idealist culture which has turned into dogma and 'por una parte, impide al hombre vivir una experiencia total de la vida, al no reconocer la realidad, y por otra, ofrece una máscara en la que esconderse, salvando las apariencias todavía con una cierta comodidad' [on the one hand, keeps human beings from fully experiencing life, as they fail to come to terms with reality, and, on the other, provides them with a mask behind which they can hide, thus keeping up appearances with a certain ease] (146). Hence its contradictory character, which results in an 'enemistad con la vida' [enmity to life]: the very feeling that erupted in the First World War without producing, however, a cathartic effect. For Zambrano, the violence of the Great War might have given vent to this pent-up animosity and thereby prevented the emergence of fascism, a post-war phenomenon that 'nace como ideología y actitud anímica de la profunda angustia de este mundo adolescente, de enemistad con la vida que destruye todo respeto y toda devoción hacia ella' [was born as an ideology and an expression of the deep anguish of this adolescent world, of a hostility to life that destroys all respect for it] (146).

Fascism thus reveals 'la desesperación impotente de hallar salida a una situación insostenible' [the impotent desperation of finding an exit from an untenable situation] (147), as a result of an increasing resentment, as well as the uncreativeness of the European bourgeoisie. Fascism violently persists in the idealistic concealment of reality, a mask which has cracked under the pressure and the resentment created by a stagnant vitality that strains to express itself. Fascists exploit and debase 'conceptos sin vida ya, de cosas que han sido y han dejado de servir' [concepts already drained of life and things that have ceased to be useful] (147); hence their bombastic and hollow rhetoric, their reduction of politics to aesthetics and spectacle, as critical theory points out. Fascists float among 'ideas de ideas, entre pálidas sombras de creencias, entre restos de grandezas' [ideas of ideas, shades of beliefs, remnants of grandeur] (147), and thereby disguise a spiteful vitality which twists and turns because it cannot express itself, and which they attempt to destroy. That is why fascists 'acaba[n] en matar, en querer matar lo que no se quiere reconocer' [ultimately kill or seek to kill that which they refuse to recognize] (157). Fascism has sprung 'de la impotencia del idealismo europeo para superarse, de la enemistad europea con la vida, de su adolescencia marchita y estancada. Es incompatible el fascismo con la confianza en la vida; por eso es profundamente ateo' [from the helplessness of European idealism, the European hostility to life, a withered and stagnant adolescence. It is incompatible with faith in life and hence strongly atheistic] (148). Why? Why does Zambrano equate hostility to life with atheism, or at least with a certain kind of atheism? How are we to interpret the strong atheism she ascribes to fascism?

If we link Zambrano's argument to the conceptual framework she draws in *El hombre y lo divino*, one of her crucial works, we may interpret Idealism, and its fascist outcome, as the last stage in the process that transformed the sacred into the divine — or the fear of the unknown into a religion of love — and which she identifies with the development of Western rationality from its inchoate origins in Greek mythology and tragic poetry. Hegelian philosophy is the final expression of idealism, of the gradual dissolution of the divine into an absolute knowledge, an intellectual god that absorbs and subdues life. As Zambrano points out in *Persona y democracia*, which covers much the same ground as *El hombre y lo divino*, there is the need for a 'sacrificial history', since that absolute knowledge must unfold in history. It is a knowledge — and appropriation — of the divine because it is realized historically. The philosophical or secularized Christianity which characterizes idealism shifts the divine to history, thus transforming history into a new deity, in which man participates actively and violently; an insatiable idol, insofar as it is never fully realized, for its inability to become a god is apparent all along. The divine thus appears 'hecho ídolo en suma, en la historia' [made idol, in short, in history], and its insatiability renders sacrifice necessary and finds its radical expression in absolutism, which Zambrano defines as the 'nudo trágico de la historia de Occidente' [tragic tangle of western history], and as:

> Una caída, un abismo que se abre en la historia, y que devora alucinatoriamente siglos enteros [...] sumiéndola en una situación pre-histórica, más bien infra-histórica, como ha sucedido en Europa en el periodo que acaba de transcurrir [...] Las ideologías totalitarias transcurrían este proceso de endiosamiento, de regreso a través de unos hombres y un pueblo a ese nivel en que el hombre devora al hombre literalmente. [...] Y como este endiosamiento no puede jamás cumplirse, necesita la renovación continuada de las víctimas; la víctima innumerable. Es el momento en que la historia es simplemente un crimen multiplicado alucinatoriamente. (Zambrano 2011d: 426)

> [A fall, an abyss that opens up in history, swallowing entire centuries in a hallucinatory fashion [...] plunging it into a prehistorical, or rather sub-historical situation, as we have seen in Europe in the period that has just ended. [...] The totalitarian ideologies have inspired this quest to become god and made a few men and a people return to a state in which man devours man. [...] Because that quest is never successful, it constantly needs new victims. History then becomes a multiplied hallucinatory crime.]

Zambrano thus posits an openly negative view of the logic of progress: the Enlightenment, which supposedly is its culmination, actually means a return to prehistoric barbarism or, as she points out in *El hombre y lo divino*, a return of the sacred, understood as the hermetic and opaque bedrock of reality, the illegible contact with a dark and impenetrable reality which overwhelms the conscience, leaving it in a state of radical strangeness. Or the deepest reality, not codified yet under the categories of the divine, which determined the evolution of Western thought until its unsuccessful conclusion under idealism. In Zambrano's view, the divine has been gradually constructed in terms of unity, identity, and rational clarity, thereby rejecting and suppressing 'la realidad oscura y múltiple' which conscience cannot grasp or define. The abandonment of 'lo otro de la vida lúcida de la conciencia' (2011d: 224) results in an incomplete and false construction of the divine, and one that is doomed to collapse; in a deicide whose immediate consequence will be the return of the sacred in the form of the distressing experience of nothingness. Contemporary nihilism, the absence of the gods, and the reduction of the human condition to a pale existentialism reflect this return:

> El fondo sagrado de donde el hombre se fuera despertando lentamente como el sueño inicial reaparece ahora en la nada [...] Es lo sagrado que reaparece en su máxima resistencia. Lo sagrado con todos sus caracteres: hermético, ambiguo, activo, incoercible [...] Lo sagrado puro, la absoluta mudez que corresponde a la ignorancia y al olvido de la condición humana: ser libre, activo, más padeciendo. (Zambrano 2011d: 218)
>
> [The sacred depths from which man woke slowly as the initial dream now reappears in nothingness [...] It is the sacred that reappears in his utmost resistance. The sacred with all its features: hermetic, ambiguous, active, impossible to suppress [...] The sacred in its purest form, the absolute silence that corresponds to the ignorance of the human condition: to be free, active, but suffering.]

Zambrano believes the opposition only between idealism and nihilism to be apparent, for they are both, in fact, expressions of the same phenomenon: the retreat of the divine and the impossibility of a human experience of life. Similarly, Nietzsche's *Übermensch* has much in common with that foreshadowed in Hegel. In this respect, the fascist mind trivializes evil and recoils from life, because it 'flota en el vacío' [floats in the emptiness] and reacts against 'la nihilidad que le rodea' [the surrounding nihilism] (Zambrano 2015: 157). Therefore, idealism, atheism, nihilism, and the return of the sacred make up a constellation of negations which emerges catastrophically in the form of fascism.

What was Zambrano's response to this infernal return?

According to *El hombre y lo divino*, empathy or 'piedad' is 'el saber tratar adecuadamente con lo otro' [to know how to interact correctly with the other] (Zambrano 2011d: 227), with the world of the different, which Western metaphysics, particularly idealism, has ended up reducing and destroying. In fact, 'poetic reason' is, among other things, an attempt to regain that ability, which logical reason has undermined in its systematic deployments. Considering the hermeneutical link between *Los intelectuales en el drama de España* and *El hombre y lo divino*, it is fair to say that, for

Zambrano, the Republican experience and the fight against fascism at the time of the war were historical expressions of empathy, or historical moments characterized by the emergence and prominence of otherness as opposed to identity. There was an empathic dimension to the Spanish Republic, in the sense of the appearance of diversity as opposed to uniformity, of hope as opposed to nihilism. It meant the liberating break from a dead pulse and the political-cultural vitality of a project that, despite its shortcomings, could be the beginning of something novel not just in Spain, but also in a Europe intimidated by fascism. Whether in an idealized way or not, Zambrano regarded the Republican experience as a new insight into the human condition and a new '*proyecto de hombría*' (Zambrano 2015: 149). It is described as such in the first part of her autobiographical essay *Delirio y destino*, mentioned before, in which she evokes Spain between 1928 and 1931, that is, the period leading up to (the founding of) the Republic. Those years laid the ground for the Republic in a political sense, but, more importantly, created the collective vitality that permeated it and made it possible. Zambrano remembers that period as an extraordinary landmark in Spanish history, in which the country acquired a remarkable self-awareness, and she does so not only because the dictatorship of Miguel Primo de Rivera was abolished and critical reason and modernization became possible, but also because of its intimate significance, namely the disappearance of the spell that until then had pervaded Spanish history, the disruption of the inertia and fatalism it had been subject to for centuries, and the expression of a collective hope that had always been dashed. The Republic wasn't just a political option or a system of government, but also the dawn of a new era in which 'a true history' (Zambrano 1999: 122) or 'a history with no serpent' (144) was lit up; an inspiring moment at which 'things condemned to the past' were carried 'into the light of the present' (112). The Republic was therefore like 'the presence of a much awaited guest who approaches our door' (117), a guest who is unknown but sensed beforehand, and thus welcome, someone who is summoned because he has something to reveal.

This revelation was a major one. The Republic was a figure of otherness and the symbolic expression of a long-suppressed cultural tradition: obviously not any tradition, and neither that of traditionalism nor the canonical one. Zambrano refers to a veiled and displaced tradition, a latent and forgotten one, reflected in forms of life rooted in popular culture, and, incidentally, always misunderstood by intellectuals.

In her defence of deep cultural tradition, Zambrano was subject to many influences: the 'intrahistoria' or 'real tradition' described by Unamuno; certain essentialist and late-Romantic elements inherited from the 1898 generation, along with historicist nuances linked to the 1914 generation; a certain nationalism that seeks to challenge the undue appropriation of the national culture by traditionalism and fascism; and also echoes of the interest in popular culture shown by the Institución Libre de Enseñanza, and shared by Zambrano. However, these influences fuse together and metabolize in an original interpretation. The tradition described by Zambrano cannot be reduced to the usual stereotypes of 'Hispanismo' and reveals a critical dimension that reminds one of the tradition of the 'nameless', to which

Walter Benjamin appealed at that time in the context of an heterodox and messianic interpretation of historical materialism (Mate 2006: 315); that is to say, the tradition of the oppressed, of those who, because of their marginal position in history, are able to provide a more critical and authentic knowledge of it.

The 'people', a vague and malleable concept, no doubt, but one which played a crucial role in Zambrano's thought during those years, was in her view the main repository of that tradition, of that which the rationalist reconstructions of history have always tended, if not to forget or despise in terms of the 'masses', according to the liberal intellectuals, at least to reduce and absorb, either in terms of 'spirit' or 'proletariat', in the former as Romantic nationalism of idealistic origin, whose remnants fascism sought to recycle, in the latter as the mechanized subject under the control of historical materialism. For Zambrano, the people are not confined to the 'demos' or to a general will liberated from traditional authoritarian yokes: they are, indeed, 'el máximo sujeto de la historia' [the ultimate subject of history] (Zambrano 2015: 203). 'Sujeto porque es a quien pasa todo lo profundo y esencial que pasa — aunque individuo genial lo preceda — y porque es quien realiza todo lo que pasa y nada puede pasar sin él' [the main subject of history, since everything deep and essential happens to them — whatever brilliant individual precedes it — and they realize everything that happens and nothing can happen without them] (203). That is why their enemies, as Zambrano points out in her 1937 essay 'El español y su tradición', 'no pasarán' (203).

Moreover, the people are the reliable repository of a tradition that cannot be reduced to the rational analysis of a conventional philosopher or historian, and demand to be grasped in literature. The novelist Benito Pérez Galdós had done precisely that: Zambrano rescued him from oblivion in her essay 'Misericordia' and devoted a good deal of attention to him in her later books, especially in *La España de Galdós*. Federico García Lorca's work also contributed greatly to that task: Zambrano dedicated the first selection of her poems to him (the book was published during her stay in Chile). Pérez Galdós and García Lorca — and Machado, obviously — extensively explored that deep tradition, and Zambrano was inspired by these writers to elaborate her own interpretation of Spanish culture, which began in the war years, developed at the outset of her exile, in essays such as *Pensamiento y poesía en la vida española* (1939), and matured along with her 'poetic reason'. To be more precise, her 'poetic reason' always drew on that deep tradition, which branched out in a complex way: Senecaism, mysticism, Cervantes's realism, Galdós's narrative, the cultural world of the Institución Libre de Enseñanza, Unamuno's tragic sense of life, Ortega's vital reason, Machado's Mairena, and García Lorca's romances are some of her references, which force us to reassess the relationship between philosophy and literature.

In conclusion, the analysis of the origins of fascism proposed by Zambrano coincides with her first explorations of Spanish thought, and this is no accident. That analysis linked Zambrano to critical contemporary thought and particularly to critical theory, as well as leading her to search in the deepest and most hidden Spanish cultural tradition for a response to totalitarian violence. Her tendency to cultural nationalism and to the idealization of the Republican project can be attributed to that quest, which she never gave up, at least definitely, and which yielded brilliant results we cannot presently dwell on.[7] If poetic reason was born during the Civil War as a response to the violence of modern reason, and completed in the interwar period, at the height of totalitarianism, the fact remains that the above-mentioned tradition was one of Zambrano's main sources of inspiration. In her view, thinking in Spanish was somehow tantamount to thinking against fascism.

Notes to Chapter 3

1. This chapter forms part of the research project *El pensamiento del exilio español de 1939 y la construcción de una racionalidad política* (FFI2012–30822), funded by the Spanish government.
2. Social contract here refers to a general concept beyond Rousseau or others.
3. All translations are my own unless otherwise stated.
4. On Zambrano's Chilean stage, see Sánchez Cuervo and Hernández Toledo 2014.
5. On the tensions, affinities, and breaks between teacher and disciple, see the edition of Zambrano's writings on Ortega, with an introduction by Ricardo Tejada (Zambrano 2011b).
6. See Chapter XI, 'The Self-Satisfied Age' (Ortega y Gasset 1957: 97–106).
7. See the excellent editions of *Pensamiento y poesía en la vida española* by Mercedes Gómez Blesa (Zambrano 2015: 517–656 & 913–68); of *España, sueño y verdad*, by Jesús Moreno Sanz (Zambrano 2011d: 613–828 & 1305–75); and of *España: pensamiento, poesía y una ciudad* by Francisco J. Martín (Zambrano 2008).

CHAPTER 4

Eros's Desire:
Some Aspects of the Relationship between José Ángel Valente and María Zambrano

Antonio Molina Flores, Universidad de Sevilla

María Zambrano's remains are buried in the cemetery of a small village in the Andalucian region of Axarquía, Vélez-Málaga, very close to the sea. Her life was marked by enforced exile following the 1936 Nationalist uprising, the Civil War, and the dreadful post-war period imposed by the military regime. José Ángel Valente, twenty-five years younger than the philosopher, became her friend, confidant, and collaborator, especially during the period in which their paths crossed when Valente lived in Geneva and Zambrano, with her sister Araceli, in the Canton of Jura.

Zambrano (who was born in Vélez-Málaga in 1904 and died in Madrid in 1991) is perhaps the most important Spanish philosopher of the twentieth century and an outstanding European intellectual, whose influence can be felt strongly in Latin America, particularly in Cuba, Chile, Puerto Rico, and Mexico, countries in which she lived. Referring to her ideology, Albert Camus wrote: 'I feel very close, although from a non-religious context, to your thought, which you express so beautifully [...] however, I don't have a sense of the sacred and do not believe in the afterlife' (letter of 12 August 1951, cited in Zambrano 2014c: 92). Zambrano's background was clearly academic, given that she had worked with Ortega y Gasset in her youth and always considered herself his disciple. In addition, she had been a student of Xavier Zubiri and García Morente, a translator of Kant. Her father, Blas Zambrano, was a close friend of Antonio Machado, whom Zambrano always treated as a family member. She also met García Lorca, Valle-Inclán and Unamuno. The breadth of her learning and reading ranged from Nietzsche to the mystics and the Greek classics and extended to Junichiro Tanizaki and Eastern thought, inspired by María's cousin, Miguel Pizarro, who travelled to Japan and studied and translated the classics of Eastern thought and whom Zambrano fell in love with at the age of twenty-six. A friend of Federico García Lorca, Pizarro wrote his doctoral thesis on Miguel de Unamuno and worked with Ortega on *El Sol*.

During the long exile from which she returned in 1984, Zambrano always remained faithful to the ideals of the Republic as well as to those of Catholicism. Although she was not a socialist, as she repeatedly maintained, she defended the cause of the legitimate government, defeated in the Civil War. She was also the last major Republican figure to return from exile. Prior to her return, she had been advised by her friend José Bergamín not to go back because it was still too early. Initially Zambrano had planned to return in 1983 to stay in the convent of the Madres Agustinas in Valdepeñas and there were talks to that effect with their prioress. This move would have been consistent with some facets of her life and work: her adherence to religious belief, though exerted with the utmost freedom, and her heterodox interpretation of tradition.

Zambrano's philosophy can be described as a poetic constellation connecting the mysteries of Gnosticism with mystical wisdom. Hers was not a philosophy of doubt or suspicion, nor one which purported to be a sociological description of what is perceived by the senses; instead, it established a deep connection with the truths revealed in dreams, in ecstasy, or in the workings of artistic creation in general and poetry in particular. Those thinkers from whom she drew inspiration had been forgotten for centuries, reduced to objects of study by a stale academic environment. She invigorated these sources through a life of the spirit which was at one with all creation, in an exaltation of the transcendental.

José Ángel Valente, who was born in Orense in 1929 and died in Geneva in 2000, was one of the most prominent Spanish poets and essayists of the second half of the twentieth century. Initially he had studied law and literature in Madrid, but he moved to Oxford in 1954 and stayed there for three crucial years, during which he met Alberto Jiménez Fraud. The latter had been the director of the Residencia de Estudiantes in Madrid, an educational establishment associated with the Institución Libre de Enseñanza, whose teachings, open to scientific enquiry and to the artistic avant-garde, were instrumental in the education of several generations of Spaniards in the early decades of the century. Valente decided not to return to Spain, and in 1958 he moved to Geneva in a sort of voluntary exile. Afterwards his relations with the regime soured as evidenced by a court-martial against him for the publication of the short story 'El uniforme del general' [The General's Uniform] in his collection *Número Trece* [Number Thirteen] in 1972. Valente eventually returned to Spain in 1985 and settled in Almería, far from the centres of literary and political power, of which he was always critical and from which he kept his distance.

Zambrano was a prolific writer but her work was not necessarily in all cases conceived with the objective of a book as the final product in mind, and therefore she often required the assistance of those intellectually attuned and closest to her to put in order the scattered material. This is what Juan Carlos Marset did with *Notas de un método* (1989) [Notes on a Method], and José Ángel Valente had done earlier with *Claros del bosque* (1977) [Clearings], one of Zambrano's most celebrated works, which is most representative of her thought.

No complete biography of María Zambrano exists. However, the first volume of her complete works, corresponding to her formative years, has already been published. In trying to understand the period in which her relationship with Valente unravelled, it is therefore essential to make use of the material available in the form of published letters and archives to glean insights into Zambrano's personal life.

In a letter dated 17 July 1959 to Juan Soriano, a painter Zambrano held in high esteem, she wrote:

> Pero soy María, si es que soy María como la azucena y la yerba ruda, el escarabajo o la lechuga, la piedra que rueda o la gota de agua [...] soy una criatura, espero que de Dios, que la echaron a nacer [...] y le dieron un cuerpo que ha de estar en algún lugar del espacio visible, donde se respira, se come aunque sea un poquito y también se viste [...] Y a veces pienso si lo honesto, lo justo no sería acabar de una vez, pero yo no puedo [...] porque estoy naciendo y amo, creo, espero, veo, siento, toco y adoro [...] La nada no me llama y, si me llama, es en amor y entonces se me vuelve ser. (Zambrano 2010: 114)

> [But I am María, if I am María as in the lily and the rue, the beetle or the lettuce, the rolling stone or the drop of water [...] I am a creature, I hope God's creature, that was given life [...] and to whom a body was given which has to be somewhere in the visible space, where one can breathe, eat, even if only a little, and also get dressed [...] And sometimes I wonder whether the honest thing, the fair thing would not be to get it over with once and for all, but I cannot [...] because I'm being born and I love, I believe, I hope, I see, I feel, I touch and I adore [...] nothingness does not call on me, and if it calls, it is in love and then returns me to being.]

The poet José-Miguel Ullán, towards the end of his foreword to the anthology of texts entitled *Esencia y hermosura* [Essence and Beauty], refers to Zambrano in these terms:

> Pero bien sé que ella, obediente al oído y al amor, fue enteramente libre en su singular decir, en el cual convivían, hermanados, la compasión, el humor y el enigma, entre otras muchas cosas todavía a la espera de algún nombre. Hablaba para ver por qué. Hasta reconocerse mediadora ('y no digo más') al sacar a la luz y entregarnos ese sonido que solo en sueños se deja oír. (Zambrano 2010: 104)

> [But I know only too well that, faithful to the sound and to love, she was entirely free in the singularity of her discourse where compassion, humour and mystery, among many other things still to be named, were gathered together. She spoke in order to find reasons. Until she realized she was a mediator (and I won't say anymore) to bring to light and give to us the sound that only in dreams makes itself heard.]

Compassion, humour, and mystery can be perceived and recognized, but there is something unfathomable which cannot be named. Like her mother, Zambrano is said to have possessed the power of divination, of anticipating events. Vision. But not only that, it is her tentative groping in the darkness, perhaps in hope of the light, that likens her to the mystic.

Independently of whether Valente had read the work of Zambrano before meeting her, the fact is that their personal, friendly, and conspiratorial relationship began in 1964 when the Zambrano sisters, Araceli and María, moved to La Pièce, in the Canton of Jura, after leaving Rome, the city where they had lived since the beginning of the 1950s. Zambrano had been visited in Rome by both Jaime Gil de Biedma, a poet also linked to Oxford, and the poet and publisher Carlos Barral, so it is likely that Valente knew the work of Zambrano through them. The first time her name appears in his *Diario anónimo* is in an entry from 23 December 1964, referring to an article she had published a year earlier, 'El Tiempo y la Verdad' [Time and Truth] in Puerto Rico. Valente frequented the house in La Pièce, initially with the poet and writer Aquilino Duque. The relationship intensified and became more intimate during the period in which Valente was helping Zambrano to sort through the notes which would constitute her central work in those years, *Claros del bosque*. The following letter, dated 26 August 1973, gives us an idea of the closeness and familiarity established between them, as Zambrano writes:

> Y las cuartillas todas se fueron a unir como levadura y parte al mismo tiempo del olvidado, relegado libro *Historia y revelación*, concebido un 2 de febrero, escrito esta fiesta de la Purificación de Nuestra Señora de la Virgen María, no sé si del 67 o del 68, al día siguiente de una grande, viva y fraterna discusión con José Ángel Valente. Discusión vivísima en la cual, creo llegué al delirio. (Zambrano 2014c: 516)

> [And all the pages came together like a yeasted dough to become part of the forgotten, abandoned book *History and Revelation*, conceived one 2nd of February, on the feast of the Purification of Our Lady the Blessed Virgin Mary. I do not recall whether it was 1967 or 1968, but it was a day after a long, lively, and fraternal discussion with José Ángel Valente. An extremely vivid discussion in which I think I became delirious.]

She considered Valente, whom she called just 'Ángel', her 'compañero en términos intelectuales y de pensamiento' [companion in terms of intellect and thought]. The relationship between Valente and Zambrano was not one of master-disciple, as that between Ortega y Gasset and Zambrano had been, as she always recognized. Though she introduced him to the work of Miguel de Molinos, which became extremely important for Valente later on, and in 1968 lent him books such as Herringer's *Zen in the Art of Archery* in its Italian edition, their relationship was one of equals. Valente settled in Geneva in 1958, having completed his previous education with his three years at Oxford, which would end up being decisive. He did not finish his doctoral thesis on the English lyric and this too they had in common: for neither did Zambrano complete her thesis on Spinoza. This was in fact the reason José Gaos was opposed to her application for the Chair of Metaphysics in Mexico, previously held by García Bacca. Despite the age difference of twenty-five years — the approximate span of a 'generation' according to Ortega — , the two decades from 1964, the year of La Pièce, to 1984 when Zambrano returned to Spain, were years of intense, parallel creativity, in full intellectual and personal camaraderie for Zambrano and Valente. However, a year before Zambrano's return to Madrid, in 1983, a final cataclysm in the relationship took place, which is worth examining.

The Fundación María Zambrano, based in Vélez-Málaga, holds the correspondence between Valente and Zambrano. From 1967 to 1979 there is a constant exchange of letters and postcards. Incidentally, in 1970 Valente would send Zambrano a postcard from Almería, of an aerial view of the city and the Alcazaba, the place where fifteen years later he would buy a house and settle in what was to become his last abode. Valente also sent her a letter (dated between 8 April and 28 August 1979) with the text 'El pasmo de Narciso' [Narcissus's Astonishment], which later was included in his book *La piedra y el centro* [The Stone and the Centre], and, most importantly, the full text of *Tres lecciones de tinieblas* [Three Lessons of Darkness], a fundamental work in Valente's poetic career, where his poetics are explicitly linked to musical forms, a connection also made by Zambrano.

This correspondence was abruptly interrupted in 1987, after a final, intense, and dramatic exchange in the summer of that year. On 30 June Zambrano wrote to Valente in Almería:

> Amigo José Ángel Valente: Me decido a escribirte, sabiendo que tú no lo haces, que pasas por aquí y no se te ha ocurrido, o has rechazado, el verme. Pero yo creo en tu lealtad y que aquella amistad que tuvimos te moverá a contestarme.
>
> [My friend José Ángel Valente: I have decided to write to you, as I'm well aware that you no longer write to me, that you come here and it doesn't occur to you, or you refuse, to visit me. But I believe in your loyalty, and hope that the friendship that we once had will move you to reply.]

And among other things she added: 'Me ha desolado vuestro apartamiento' [I am devastated by your withdrawal].

Zambrano asked her friend for the manuscript of *Claros del bosque*, most likely thinking of the newly established Foundation. She also asked for the letters they exchanged with Lezama Lima. Valente replied to her on 27 July from Geneva without the letter to hand but promising to look for the documents on his return to Almería — this was to be their last exchange. There is a heartfelt acknowledgement of the circumstances and death of Araceli, María's sister. Araceli was seven years younger than María, and had been admitted to a clinic. Although many years later the details are still not clear, neither for Zambrano nor Valente, judging by the hesitations and inconsistencies in their letters, the fact is that María Zambrano, after having been to the mortuary formally to identify her dead sister, had spent the night, according to Valente, at his home in Geneva. Zambrano stated specifically: 'in Antonio's bed' (Antonio was Valente's son). Araceli died on 20 February 1972. María Zambrano recalls that at the time she was writing 'El Delirio — El dios oscuro' [Delirium — The Dark God] section of the third chapter, 'Pasos' [Steps], of *Claros del bosque*, where we read:

> Brota el delirio al parecer sin límites, no sólo del corazón humano, sino de la vida toda y se aparece todavía con mayor presencia en el despertar de la tierra en primavera, y paradigmáticamente en plantas como la yedra, hermana de la llama, sucesivas madres que Dionisos necesitó para su nacimiento incompleto, inacabable. (Zambrano 1986a: 43)
>
> [Delirium emerges, seemingly unrestrained, not only from the human heart, but from all life and appears even more present in the awakening of the earth in spring, and paradigmatically in plants such as ivy, sister of the flame, the successive mothers Dionysus needed for his incomplete, endless birth.]

Claros del bosque is laconically dedicated: 'En memoria de Araceli' [In Memory of Araceli]. Araceli's birth had been a 'regalo del cielo', a godsend, as her family put it. She was born on 21 April, and María on the 22nd of the same month. For many of those who knew them in Spain, María and Araceli, or Araceli and María, were a single being composed of body and beauty (Araceli) and thought (María). After a dark episode in Paris, where Araceli was tortured by the Gestapo and her second husband arrested and sent to Spain to be executed, María decided never to separate from her sister again. Zambrano had also been married, in 1936, but in 1947 she and her husband were living apart, finalizing their divorce in 1953. As she told her friend, the writer Rosa Chacel: 'No tengo amor ninguno desde hace muchos años' [I have had no love for many years] (Zambrano 2014c: 98). These were the years when Zambrano developed a sort of pathological mysticism. In a text from 21 April 1990, where she refers to the Roman years and to the visit of Jaime Gil de Biedma, Zambrano recalls taking her young friend, the poet, to visit her current love at the end of the Via Appia. The object of her love was a statue.

Araceli was eventually buried in La Pièce with the epitaph: *Surge amica mea et veni* [Arise, my friend, and come]. Surely, María must have wanted the remains of her sister to rest alongside those of her mother, also named Araceli, in Paris. In the end the remains of all three of them were buried together under the same lighthearted epitaph that María had chosen for Araceli from the *Song of Songs* in the cemetery of Vélez-Málaga.

The first years of friendship between Valente and Zambrano were characterized by an intense intellectual exchange and by constant cross-references to the other in their respective work. In his 1971 book *Las palabras de la tribu* [The Words of the Tribe] Valente included an essay entitled 'El sueño creador' [The Creative Dream] in which he reviews two books recently published (in 1965) by Zambrano: *España, sueño y verdad* [Spain, Dream and Truth] and *El sueño creador*. Valente's essay had first appeared in the magazine *Ínsula* in September 1966. Together with another article written by José Luis L. Aranguren, it was, in fact, the first vindication of María Zambrano within Spanish territory.

In 1975 Zambrano published the article 'Miguel de Molinos, reaparecido' [The Reappearance of Miguel de Molinos], welcoming the recent publication of Molinos's *Guía espritual* [Spiritual Guide] edited by Valente. To the collaboration already mentioned, i.e. the revision and ordering of *Claros del bosque*, should be added her article 'El Temblor'[Trembling], dedicated to Rosalía de Castro. In 1981 Zambrano published in the journal *Quimera* the text 'La mirada originaria en la obra de José Ángel Valente' [The Primary Gaze in the Work of José Ángel Valente], in which she reviewed *Punto cero* (1980) [Point Zero], a collection of Valente's poetry from 1953 to 1979. Zambrano also quoted a few lines from Valente's poem 'Hoy andaba' [Walking Today] from *Breve son* in her re-edition of *El hombre y lo divino*, a book to which she added a final chapter, 'El libro de Job y el pájaro' [The Book of Job and the Bird]. There seems to be general agreement among critics that one of the reasons for the distancing between Valente and Zambrano was Valente's divorce from Emilia Palomo, his first wife from Seville, with whom he had four children and who had shared his important years in Oxford and Geneva. The story, told by Valente in a somewhat cryptic manner and without many concessions to the uninitiated reader, was published posthumously in 2014 with the title *Palais de justice* by Galaxia Gutenberg. It is a narrative arranged in fragments of great intensity, where memories of the family home become mixed with childhood memories, reminiscences of passionate romantic encounters and the icy coldness of the present situation, in room C of the courthouse where the process that would confirm the final separation of the couple is taking place. 'Escribir es como estar muerto y volver para ver los estragos del campo de batalla donde el propio cadáver yace [...] Lo más terrible es ser, al cabo, comido por un muerto' [Writing is like being dead and coming back to see the ravages of the battlefield where one's own body lies [...] The most terrible thing after all is to be eaten by someone dead] (Valente 2014: 95). Hence the identification of the narrator of *Palais de justice* with Orpheus, who is made to declare in a moment of protean exaltation in the text:

> *Orfeo sono io.* La oscura majestad del rodaballo, el plateado vientre del bonito, la luminosidad caudal del barbo, la ductilidad del salmonete, la corpórea densidad de la dorada, el pecho sacrificial del rape [...] la metálica piel de la caballa, la perplejidad total de los crustáceos, la supervivencia tenaz de la langosta, el color clausurado de la sepia, y los ojos del hielo resbalando por la amargura de la sal gloriosa. *Orfeo sono io.* (Valente 2014: 95)
>
> [*Orfeo sono io.* The dark majesty of the turbot, the silvery belly of the tuna, the luminous flow of the catfish, the ductility of the mullet, the corporeal density of the bream, the sacrificial chest of the monkfish [...] the metallic skin of the mackerel, the total bewilderment of the crustaceans, the tenacious survival of the lobster, the muted sepia colour of the cuttlefish, and the eyes of the ice slippery from the bitterness of the glorious salt. *Orfeo sono io.*]

It is as if the trial, the witnesses who testify and the choreography that surrounds it, have transformed him, even more, into an alien bewildered by being present at this strange ritual:

> Lo más terrible es ser, al cabo, comido por los muertos que no tienen memoria. Viste al mirarte en el espejo a alguien que tenía tu imagen y que no eras tú y que te sonreía mientras tú llorabas. Luego el espejo se llenó de sangre. Bebe, dijiste, y al mirar de nuevo viste en tu rostro el rostro de tu padre. (Valente 2014: 97)
>
> [All in all the most terrible thing is being eaten by the dead who have no memory. You saw in the mirror someone in your own image but who was not you and he smiled at you while you cried. Then the mirror filled with blood. Drink, you said, and looking up again you saw in your face the face of your father.]

These lines reveal the radical poet who years later would write *Paisaje con pájaros amarillos*, an elegy for his dead son. Orpheus in the realm of Thanatos. We recognize María Zambrano, never mentioned explicitly, in some passages of *Palais de justice*. Valente is baffled by the appearance at the scene of his friend, testifying on the opposite side. Valente experiences it as a descent into Hades, and yet, there would be an even worse descent, following the death of his son Antonio, who had been born in Oxford in 1958.

During this second descent Valente did not feel the presence or the support of his friend either. A brief note was sent by Zambrano on 23 August 1989: 'Con inmenso dolor he sabido el final de la vida tan prometedora y joven de tu hijo Antonio. PD. Te ruego trasmitas mi sentimiento a Emilia y a quien le acompañare en ese momento' [With great sorrow I have learned of the end of such a promising and young life, that of your son Antonio. P.S. Please pass on my condolences to Emilia and whoever is with her at this time]. This is the final piece of writing that Zambrano addressed to Valente, and it received no reply. Twelve days later, on 3 September, Valente noted in his diary:

> El 28 de junio murió Antonio. Yo llegué a Ginebra, desde Almería, en coche, el 30. Antonio fue incinerado el lunes 3, a las 2 de la tarde. El 4 de julio por la noche me trasladaron de urgencia al Hospital Cantonal. En las primerísimas horas del día 5, tuve un infarto. Estuve en el Cantonal tres semanas, cuatro en la clínica de la Lignière. Luego, me reincorporé al Palais, donde he estado dos semanas. Hace dos meses largos de su muerte. (Valente 2011: 258)

> [On 28 June Antonio died. I arrived in Geneva from Almería by car on the 30th. Antonio was cremated on Monday 3rd at 2 p.m. On the evening of the 4th, they admitted me as an emergency to the Cantonal Hospital. In the very early hours of the 5th I had a heart attack. I stayed at the Cantonal for three weeks, then four weeks at the clinic of Lignière. Afterwards I rejoined the Palais, where I have spent two weeks. It has been two long months since his death.]

María Zambrano died on 6 February 1991. Only three days later, her old friend published, in the pages of *ABC*, a devastating article, 'The Double Death of María Zambrano', where he writes:

> Aquí en el Jura estaba, aquí estuvo, la granja de las dos hermanas, el gran tilo sagrado de la entrada, el campo donde heráldica crecía la cicuta. Ahora ya están muertas las dos o desaparecidas, las dos hermanas que eran una sola. Araceli y María; María y Araceli. (Valente 2008: 1473)

> [It was here in the Jura, where once had been the farmhouse of the two sisters, the great sacred lime tree at the entrance, the field where hemlock grew heraldic. Now both are dead or disappeared, the two sisters who were one. Araceli and María; María and Araceli.]

He evokes the room full of fateful resonances, one of sinister needles and evil incantation. Of María, Valente finally says:

> No supo nunca cuál era el contenido del amor o la muerte. Retablo ciego el suyo. Jamás entró, por terror, al fondo oscuro de la humana experiencia. Ingresaba la hermana así, despacio, en los campos sin fin de la locura. (Valente 2008: 1475)

> [She never knew the content of love or death. Hers was a blind altarpiece. Out of fear, she never entered the dark recesses of human experience. Thus our sister was admitted, slowly, into the neverending lands of madness.]

Although the final outcome seems to have been so bitter and, by all appearances, unjust, Valente and Zambrano had so many things in common that for two decades they seemed to have developed their respective work along the same path: overlapping on mysticism, particularly on St John of the Cross and Miguel de Molinos, sharing an interest in the thought, spirituality, and poetry of East Asia, particularly Japan — in Zambrano's case through the direct influence of her cousin Miguel Pizarro, and in Valente's through his appreciation of the concise form of the haiku, the essence of Zen and Chinese thought. Yet at this point certain differences should also be noted. Valente's omission of the role that María Zambrano had played in his edition of the *Guía espiritual* by Miguel de Molinos is unfair. She is never cited and only in a longer text 'Ensayo sobre Miguel de Molinos' [Essay on Miguel de Molinos] is her name mentioned in a footnote on a tangential issue, namely the problematic relationship between mysticism and Christianity. It was Lezama Lima who reminded Valente, upon receiving *El Inocente* (1967–1970) [The Innocent] by post that Zambrano had already written about the *Guía*, although without explicitly mentioning Miguel de Molinos, in her article. Valente's book was dedicated to Calvert Casey 'In Memoriam', because, according to Valente, Molinos was the source of his friendship with Casey, his co-worker at UNESCO and a fellow reader of the *Guía espiritual*. None of the more than thirty instances that Valente refers to Molinos, is in relation to Zambrano, whereas he does, on the other hand, mention Antonio Machado and, particularly, Valle-Inclán. It is as if the book had been born directly from those intellectuals, recognized as masters, and not from his conversations with Zambrano. However, Zambrano's accounts reveal another side to the story, one not mentioned by Valente. In her text written in Geneva in 1980, 'Calvert Casey, el indefenso: entre el ser y la nada' [Calvert Casey, Defenceless: Between Being and Nothingness], Zambrano writes:

> 'María, qué himno védico a la nada,' me dijo, sí, me dijo, pues que me miró de frente, inclinado ya sobre la mesa donde depositó el pequeño volumen de *Guía espiritual* de Miguel de Molinos que yo le había prestado por tiempo ilimitado. Y como ya se iba, me lo trajo. No volvería a verlo más. (Zambrano 2014c: 601)

> ['María, what a Vedic hymn to nothingness,' he said, yes, he said that, as he faced me, already bent over the table where he had placed the small volume of *Guía espiritual* by Miguel de Molinos which I had lent him indefinitely. And as he was leaving, he was bringing it back. I would not see him again.]

Valente is present, though; and not only is he present, the conversation takes place in his home, on a Sunday afternoon. Valente had gone to pick up María and Araceli to eat at his home, with his family and with Casey. The latter did not attend the meal because his mother had just died, but he did arrive shortly after. 'No recuerdo que Casey me hablase de otra cosa que de la *Guía* de Molinos. En un libro mío había encontrado una referencia a Molinos que le despertó irresistiblemente el deseo de leerlo' [I do not remember Casey speaking to me about anything but Molinos's *Guía*. In a book of mine he had found a reference to Molinos that awakened an irresistible desire in him to read it] (Zambrano 2014c: 603). The book was none other than *El hombre y lo divino*, published by Zambrano in 1955, in which Molinos is mentioned in the chapter 'La última aparición de lo sagrado: la nada' [The Final Apparition of the Sacred: Nothingness]. It is therefore not surprising that Casey suggested that Zambrano should write a foreword to publicize the *Guía*. There is, moreover, no doubt regarding the 'Molinosism' of Zambrano from school age: after referring to the poor edition she had read, she concluded:

> Y, en las escasísimas hojas que, por cierto, saqué conmigo, con el nombre de la revista *Hora de España*, tenía escrito a mano y a lápiz un esquema del 'querer' o de la voluntad centrada en Molinos, como un suceso decisivo y no sobrepasado. Se conjugaba con San Juan de la Cruz, acerca del cual seguí ya en México escribiendo un ensayo publicado en *Sur* — diciembre del 39. (Zambrano 2014c: 604)

> [And in the very few pages which, incidentally, I took with me with the name of the journal *Hora de España*, I had handwritten in pencil, a sketch of the 'desire' or will centred on Molinos, as a decisive event that was never surpassed. It went well together with St John of the Cross, on whom I continued writing an essay in Mexico, published in *Sur* — December of 1939.]

No further comment is needed, since in 1939 José Ángel Valente was only ten years old.

There are, however, other connections, such as those linking poetic creation with music and silence. Similarly, 'the Word' is at the centre of the works of both. Zambrano writes:

> 'El Principio era el Verbo, y el Verbo era Luz, y la Luz era Vida, y el Verbo se hizo carne y habitó entre nosotros lleno de gracia y de verdad'. Ésta es la revelación que me ha sostenido a lo largo y a lo ancho de toda mi vida. (Zambrano 2014c: 619)

> ['In the beginning was the Word, and the Word was light, and the light was Life, and the Word became flesh and dwelt among us, full of grace and truth'. This is the revelation that has sustained me throughout my life.]

Yet this word is enshrined in music, is itself musical. Among the fragments María Zambrano read aloud in 1981 at Valente's request for a recording, intended for a public hearing in a series of events that took place in Madrid at the Colegio Mayor San Juan Evangelista, she refers to the Word in these terms:

> Y de ella sale, desde su silencioso palpitar, la música inesperada, por la cual la reconocemos; lamento a veces, llamada, la música inicial de lo indecible que no podrá nunca, aquí, ser dada en palabra. Mas sí con ella, la música inicial que se desvanece cuando la palabra aparece o reaparece, y que se queda en el aire, como su silencio, modelando su silencio, sosteniéndolo sobre un abismo. (Zambrano 2014c: 625)

> [And from it, from its silent pulse, springs unexpected music, by which we recognize it; sometimes I mourn that which is called the initial music of the unsayable that can never, here, be expressed in words. But it may be through that initial music, which fades away when the word appears or reappears, and which stays in the air, as its silence, modelling its silence, sustaining itself over an abyss].

She concludes: 'La música sostiene sobre el abismo a la palabra' [The music holds the word over the abyss].

Likewise for Valente, 'Los textos de *Tres lecciones de tinieblas* tienen su origen en la música. [...] En su forma musical, las lecciones reflejan la misma estructura'

[The texts of *Tres lecciones de tinieblas* are rooted in music [...] In their musical form, the lessons reflect the same structure] (Valente 1981: 3–4). This is the text of which Valente, as mentioned above, sent a complete typed copy to Zambrano. The following year she would receive a copy of the edition published by La Gaya Ciencia, which he dedicated to Zambrano 'en la antepalabra' [in the foreword] and which was illustrated by Baruj Salinas. Although Valente relates his *Tres lecciones* to the musical tradition, there is also a non-explicit connection with mysticism. In the *Corpus Aeropagiticum*, a tradition initiated by Saint Gregory of Nyssa (335–94), the 'third' stage, darkness (*la tiniebla*), corresponds to the mystical experience.

The idea of poetry as the source of language is also present in Paul Celan, an important figure in the work of Valente:

> El poema, en la medida en que es, en efecto, una forma de aparición del lenguaje, y por lo tanto de esencia dialógica, puede ser una botella arrojada al mar, abandonada a la esperanza — tantas veces frágil, por supuesto — de que cualquier día, en alguna parte, pueda ser recogida en una playa, en la playa del corazón tal vez. Los poemas, en ese sentido, están en camino: se dirigen a algo. ¿Hacia qué? Hacia algún lugar abierto que invocar, que ocupar, hacia un tú invocable, hacia una realidad que invocar. (Celan in Valente 1992a: 10)

> [The poem, insofar as it is, effectively, one form of linguistic manifestation, and therefore dialogic in essence, is like a message in a bottle, abandoned to hope — so often fragile, of course — that one day, somewhere, it may be found on a beach, on the beach of the heart, perhaps. The poems, in that sense, are on their way: they head towards something. Towards what? Towards somewhere open to be invoked, to be occupied, towards an other to be invoked, towards a reality to be invoked.]

As Ana Bundgaard has noted, the metaphor of the heart is also central to Zambrano's thought.

Poetry, according to Valente, is the experience of the 'interiority' of the Word. As José Jiménez explains:

> Es un proceso abierto de *descenso*, a través de tres ciclos o pruebas, al triple horizonte de la memoria: memoria personal, memoria colectiva y memoria del mundo o de la materia. El *telos*, la finalidad que la pone en movimiento es el amor, *eros*, en su también abierta infinitud, y que se desvela en el 'tercer y más radical descenso' de la palabra poética, el descenso a la memoria de la materia. (Jiménez 1996: 67)

> [It is an open process of *descent* through three cycles or tests, to the threefold horizon of memory: personal memory, collective memory and memory of the world or of matter. The *telos*, the purpose which sets it in motion is love, *eros*, in its open infinity, which is disclosed in the 'third and most radical descent' of the poetic word, the descent to the memory of matter.]

Valente writes:

> En él, la palabra no versa sobre la materia: es materia; no versa sobre el cuerpo: es cuerpo. La palabra, la materia, el cuerpo del amor, son una sola y misma cosa. La poesía estaría, en ese ciclo, regida por el primado absoluto de la infinitud del eros. (Valente 1988b: 19)

[In it, the word is not about matter: it is matter; it is not about the body, but it is the body. Word, matter, the body of love are one and the same thing. In this cycle, poetry would be ruled by the absolute primacy of Eros's infinity.]

Zambrano does not share Valente's conception and idea of the body: she was always close to Plotinus, an heir to, and militant of, a dualistic view. According to his disciple Porphyry, he did not hold the body in much esteem, seeing in it an obstacle to the union with God. Of course, Zambrano had a body and she suffered and lived it completely, but in her mature philosophy her thinking tends towards that of Plotinus.

There is, in Zambrano, either through direct influence of Plotinus, through mysticism, or through pure Platonism, a constant flight to immateriality. In a text preceding *El Preludio* [Prelude], a poem by Antoni Marí, translated from Catalan by Antonio Colinas and published in 1979, Zambrano asks '¿Por qué hay que decir? ¿por qué la palabra y no su silencio luminoso, con su propia materialidad? ¿por qué no la materia, ella, sin lo material?' [Why speak? Why the word and not its luminous silence, with its own materiality? Why not matter itself, without the material?] (Zambrano 2014c: 650). The word, subtle in its materiality, sonic material after all, moves towards the matter of silence; but there is still one more step, that of matter without the material. Is that possible? What matter is here being spoken of? Of the immateriality of sub-atomic particles or the ghostly life of the spectre? This does not appear to be Zambrano's idea, rather it is what is revealed in poetry. It appears always in the material, and with the material (papyrus, she says, the palm leaf, the barely smoothed pine bark), but transcends it. As she claims: 'No hay poesía sin revelación, y a su vez no hay revelación sin misterio donde, más que el lugar, importa la materia' [There is no poetry without revelation, and in turn there is no revelation without mystery where, rather than place, matter is of importance] (Zambrano 2014c: 650).

Plotinus, in *Ennead* IV, 8 (6), 'On the Descent of the Soul to the Body', reflects that:

> Many times, waking the body and returning to myself, leaving other things and entering myself, I see an extraordinary, marvelous beauty. Convinced, then, more than ever that I belong to the upper portion of beings, I renew the most eminent form of life and, identified with the divine and established within it, I perform that form of activity and I stand above all the rest of the intelligible. (Plotinus 2015: 161)

Valente does not share this 'disembodied' view of the spirit. He had already expressed this on several occasions but it was in the inaugural lecture of the academic year 1989–90 at the Instituto de Estética y Teoría de las Artes, where he takes on this subject. There, he attributes to Origen the idea of a 'disembodied spirit', which we see Zambrano taking from Plotinus. Valente vindicates carnality and, furthermore, sexuality as loci wherein to experience the divine. And he attributes the neo-Platonic link, within certain branches of Western Christianity, to an excision to which some forms of mystical experience, as well as other readings of the theological tradition, are equally opposed:

> Pero en otras ocasiones ('El misterio del cuerpo cristiano' en *La piedra y el centro*), nos hemos referido a la raíz escasamente cristiana de la concepción desencarnada que acaba por dominar las formas religiosas (y no religiosas) del pensamiento occidental, pero no las formas del pensamiento de la iglesia oriental o de la teología de los Padres griegos. (Valente 1990: 11)
>
> [But at other times ('The Mystery of the Christian Body' in *The Stone and the Centre*), we have referred to the hardly Christian roots of the disembodied conception which have ended up dominating the religious (and non-religious) forms of Western thought, but not the ways of thinking of the Eastern Church or the theology of the Greek Fathers.]

After a detailed survey of other traditions that clearly relate divine love to carnal desire or deny the difference between *eros* and *agape*, he concludes, quoting Lacan (*Écrits* and Book XX of *Le Seminaire*), that desire is the desire of desire, desire of the desire of the other. Not content, however, with a modern vision of the matter he refers to pseudo-Dionysius (*Divine Names*, IV, 13) to conclude:

> Dios también sale (éxtasis) de sí mismo cuando cautiva a todos los seres por el sortilegio de su amor y de su deseo [...] Del ser que reúne la belleza y el bien cabe decir que es objeto del deseo de eros y que él mismo es deseo de eros. (Valente 1990: 25)
>
> [God also transgresses beyond Himself (ecstasy) when He captivates all beings through the spell of his love and his desire [...] The being that brings together beauty and the good can be said to be the object of desire of eros and that he himself is the desire of eros.]

Nowadays, it is difficult to understand what is expressed in this thought. Modern Western experience, if such a generalization may be permitted, has from Romanticism on rigorously separated truth, good, and beauty. Since then beauty and all its negations have belonged to the new territory of 'aesthetics', with good and all its problems in their ethical or metaphysical versions relegated to the margins of philosophical reflection. And truth? When we are reminded that 'beauty is the splendour of truth', something of a lost paradise is evoked before us. This separation into disciplines has nothing to do with the wholeness of experience lived in poetic creation, with its narrowing of the categorical gap established by those modes of thinking that wishes to separate emotions and concepts. Certain forms of contemporary poetic experience seek, in their radicalism, to rescue an explicit link between poetic creation and mystical experience: the mystical, as attention to silence, as an attitude of listening, as an escape from, a limited condition, not as a dark practice linked to regressive forms; and not necessarily religious. That is to say, the possibility of a mysticism without transcendence. In this, Zambrano and Valente differ again. The former, whose work is a synthesis of religion, philosophy, and poetry never ceases to believe in transcendence, in the natural return of the soul to its place of origin, after passing the martyrdom of living in a body. For the later works of Valente such phantasmagoria is meaningless, and he strives to find the possible transcendence in immanence, such as the present sought in Zen, and the cessation of time in the haiku. Both writers, who shared so much, do, however, look with admiration and respect to each other in their understanding of friendship as a kind of Orphic union (Zambrano, Lezama, Valente) and know how to listen to the voice of dissent. María Zambrano was born in 1904 and Valente died in 2000. The life and work of both summarize some of the best that the twentieth century had to offer in Spain — a country that after a million had died in the Civil War lived divided between those who collaborated with the regime, the internal exiles, and those who, attentive to the reality of the country, lived in exile. María Zambrano experienced an imposed exile and Valente another, more or less chosen one. Their respective works read together are perhaps a necessary lesson for the younger generations, because both learned to live in extreme circumstances and found a response of ethical and political coherence from a position of incorruptible freedom, leaving behind a rigorous and exemplary body of work; work that, as the result of poetic and creative labour, takes us closer to a new truth and helps us in the discovery of new forms of beauty.

CHAPTER 5

Hope beyond Hope: The Motif of Ruins in María Zambrano and Luis Cernuda

Federico Bonaddio, King's College London

> This principle of ruin is nothing other than death: not the dying-properly but, and it is quite different, the end of the properly-dying. This end threatens and makes possible the *analysis* itself as a discourse of delimitation, of guaranteed dissociation, of the border or the determined closure.
>
> JACQUES DERRIDA, *Aporias*[1]

María Zambrano first discovered Luis Cernuda's poetry in 1928 at the age of twenty-four (Valender 1998: 166). All the evidence suggests that she admired the poet intensely, although the feeling seems not always to have been mutual (Berrocal 2011: 52–53). James Valender (1998: 168–69 & 180) and, after him, Alfonso Berrocal (2011: 53) note how the two diverged on certain matters of principle, both in terms of how each viewed the popular, which Zambrano along with many other Republican writers exalted during the years of the Spanish Civil War, but which Cernuda most definitely did not; and in terms of their views of love, which for Cernuda, however idealized it might appear in his work, did not possess the divine character that Zambrano intuited in it. Although Zambrano had been an advocate of the poet's work for some time, the two first met as late as 1934 or 1935, at a *tertulia* organized by Concha de Albornoz, daughter of the Republican minister Álvaro de Albornoz (Valender 1998: 165). They would also meet in Valencia in 1937 during the International Congress of Antifascist Writers and Artists held in that city, although most likely not during the sessions themselves since Cernuda seems not to have been much involved, but rather at the offices of *Hora de España*, a Republican magazine with which both writers were collaborating (167). Interestingly, Valender remarks on the fact that Zambrano's contributions to the magazine 'reflect a combative fervour that is notably absent from the poems Cernuda writes around the same time'.[2] At the end of the Civil War, Zambrano took refuge first in Mexico and then in Cuba where, apart from a two-year interval in Paris between 1946 and 1948, she resided until she left for Italy in 1953 (Valender 1998: 170, 172, 177). Despite the fact that for much of this time she was not in contact with Cernuda, Zambrano continued to promote his work along with that of other Spanish poets (1998: 170). Cernuda, for his part, left Spain for England in 1938 to give a series of lectures, his stay there eventually becoming, with the outcome of the Civil War, the beginning of his years of exile (Gómez Canseco 1993: 227). After spells in Glasgow, London, and Oxford, he left Great Britain in 1947 to take up a teaching post at Mount Holyoke College, a women's college in Massachusetts (1993: 227–28). Despite the presence of his good friend Concha de Albornoz, Cernuda soon became unhappy in New England and made a number of short trips to the warmer climes of Mexico, with a view to planning a permanent move to a Latin American country (Valender 1998: 172). It was no doubt this same restlessness that made the opportunity to visit Cuba towards the end of 1951 all the more attractive. There, after some thirteen years, he met up once more with Zambrano, according to whom his visits to her were almost daily for the duration of his stay (172–74). As Valender notes, professionally both writers would have had much to talk about: Zambrano was now at work on various projects which would come together in 1955 as *El hombre y lo divino* [Man and the Divine], while Cernuda, only a few years earlier in 1947, had published his collection *Como quien espera el alba* [Like Someone Waiting for the Dawn] in Buenos Aires (174). Whatever it is they talked about, this would prove to be their last encounter, although they did manage to correspond with one another occasionally in the years to come.

Existing scholarship, therefore, acknowledges the points of contact between Zambrano and Cernuda, in the way of meetings, collaborations, and written correspondence, as well as the divergences between them; but nothing to date has focused specifically on the coincidence represented by their recourse to the motif of ruins.[3] Cernuda produced two poems that refer directly to ruins: 'Las ruinas' [Ruins], written in England in 1941, which was included in the aforementioned *Como quien espera el alba*; and 'Otras ruinas' [Other Ruins], written later in New England in 1949. It is the first of these that interests us because of its focus on ancient ruins specifically.[4] This focus is shared by Zambrano's 1951 essay 'Una metáfora de la esperanza: Las Ruinas' [A Metaphor of Hope: Ruins], which was subsequently reworked and published under the title 'Las ruinas' [Ruins] in 1953 and then incorporated into *El hombre y lo divino*.[5] That both Cernuda and Zambrano used the motif of ruins is not in itself confirmation of a historical dialogue on the subject between the two, and it is not clear what, if anything, can be inferred from the dates of Cernuda's visit to Havana — November 1951 until February 1952 — or the time he spent there with Zambrano. It does, however, point to some common concerns between the writers and says something important about the nature of their respective world views, the distinction between which has already been alluded to in the references above to their views of the popular and, in particular, to their views of love. The very mention of ruins, of course, has resonance in the context of their mutual experience of exile and the devastation of war; and yet neither war nor exile is dealt with in any explicit sense in the texts in question. Instead, ruins are the starting point for an enquiry by each writer into the possibilities and limitations of human endeavour in face of the inevitability of ruination.

'Real ruins of different kinds,' writes Andreas Huyssen, 'function as screens on which modernity projects its asynchronous temporalities and its fear of and obsession with the passing of time' (2010: 19). Huyssen also recalls the metaphorical potential of ruins noted by Walter Benjamin, according to whom, as he puts it, 'allegories are, in the realm of thought, what ruins are in the realm of things' (19). Here Huyssen acknowledges both the material fact and imaginary function of ruins. While it has been suggested that Cernuda based his ruins, in 'Las ruinas', on his idea of Pompeii, perhaps more significant than this connection with physical reality is the very literal materiality of the ruins conjured up in the poem despite the many figurations it contains.[6] Figurative processes are recognized rather self-consciously in the allusion in the second stanza to the work of the dream in completing the image of ruins which are not wholly distinguishable in the hazy moonlight: 'Y en esta luz incierta las ruinas de mármol | Son construcciones bellas, musicales, | Que el sueño completó' [And in this uncertain light the marble ruins | are beautiful, musical constructions | finished by dreaming].[7] Otherwise, the scene of ruins amidst nature appears 'real', to echo Huyssen. Thus we find in the first stanza, 'hierba | Creciendo oscura y fuerte entre ruinas' [grass | Growing dark and thick amongst the ruins] (ll. 1–2) and 'bajo el viento | Las hojas en las ramas' [beneath the wind | The leaves on the branches] (ll. 4–5); in the second, 'Puro, de plata nebulosa, [...] | El agudo creciente de la luna' [Pure, of nebulous silver, [...] | The sharp crescent of the moon] (ll. 7–8); in the third, 'La avenida de tumbas y cipreses, y las calles | Llevando al corazón de la gran plaza | Abierta a un horizonte de colinas' [The avenue of tombs and cypress trees | Leading to the heart of the great square | Open to a horizon of hills] (ll. 14–16); in the fourth, 'Levanta ese titánico acueducto | Arcos rotos y secos por el valle agreste | Adonde el mirto crece con la anémona' [That titanic aqueduct raises | Broken and parched arches along the wild valley | Where myrtle grows amongst windflowers] (ll. 19–21) and 'el agua libre entre los juncos | pasa' [water freely amongst the reeds | flows] (ll. 22–23); in the fifth, 'tumbas' [tombs] and 'urnas' [urns] (l. 25); and in the sixth, 'piedras' [stones] (l. 32), 'columnas | En la plaza' [columns | In the square] (ll. 34–35), 'altares' [altars] (l. 36), and 'muros' [walls] (l. 37).

In the twelfth and final stanza of the poem, the speaker situates himself amidst all he has described: 'me reclino | A contemplar sereno el campo y las ruinas' [I lean back | To contemplate the countryside and ruins] (ll. 72–73). Were it not for his presence here and for his creative intervention throughout, human beings would be completely absent from the scene, and it is the very contrast between the presence of things conveyed so concretely — both natural and manmade — and the absence of human beings that is key to the speaker's message. All that is there and can still be seen is a constant reminder of what, in contrast, is long gone. Thus, leaves quiver on branches 'vagas | Como al roce de cuerpos invisibles' [faintly | As if touched by invisible bodies] (ll. 5–6). The tombs are 'vacías' [empty], the urns 'sin cenizas' [emptied of ashes] (l. 25), and their carved reliefs commemorate souls that have been consigned to 'la inmensa muerte anónima' [the immense anonymity of death] (l. 27). The speaker declares that everything on the site is the same 'aunque una sombra sea | De lo que fue hace siglos, mas sin gente' [even though a shadow | Of what it was centuries ago, but without people] (ll. 17–18); while in the sixth stanza, the sequence of verbs in the preterite and imperfect tenses recalls the inhabitants of the site and their acts, but also emphasizes their absence by relegating them to the past:

> Las piedras que los pies vivos rozaron
> En centurias atrás, aún permanecen
> Quietas en su lugar, y las columnas
> En la plaza, testigos de las luchas políticas,
> Y los altares donde sacrificaron y esperaron,
> Y los muros que el placer de los cuerpos recataban. (ll. 32–37)

> [The stones which living feet abraded | Centuries ago, remain yet | Still in their place, and the columns | In the square, witnesses of political battles, | And the altars where they made sacrifices and hoped, | And the walls which the pleasure of bodies hid.]

The point is made emphatically again in the next stanza which begins 'Tan sólo ellos no están' [Only they are not there] (l. 38). The absence of former inhabitants is echoed in the notion that silence seems to be awaiting 'la vuelta de sus vidas' [the return of their lives] (l. 39), and ultimately it is the probability that manmade things will outlive their creators that aggrieves the speaker:

> Mas los hombres, hechos de esa materia fragmentaria
> Con que se nutre el tiempo, aunque sean
> Aptos para crear lo que resiste al tiempo,
> Ellos en cuya mente lo eterno se concibe,
> Como en el fruto el hueso encierran muerte. (ll. 40–44)

> [But men, made of that fragmentary material | On which time nourishes itself, | Although able to create that which resists time, | Those in whose minds the eternal is conceivable, | Contain death as does a fruit its stone.]

The contemplation of ruins serves, as Bruton explains, 'to frame the poet's reflection on his life and art' (1984: 391). It is important that the frame should be realistic because it is the literal materiality of the scene that sets in relief the central dilemma for the speaker: humanity's corruptibility and the fleeting nature of existence. The comparison is stark: on the one hand, the ruins that have endured, along with Nature that is ever-present; on the other, the tangible absence of human beings fated to disappear. Of course, the ruins themselves have suffered the ravages of time and as such are an example of how that which is manmade is also destined to degrade and fade. In an apostrophe that spans three stanzas, the speaker addresses God, reproaching Him for having filled human beings with the impossible desire for immortality — a desire which also characterizes the work of poets: 'Oh Dios. Tú que nos has hecho | Para morir, ¿por qué nos infundiste | La sed de eternidad, que hace al poeta?' [Oh God. You who have made us | To die, why did you instil in us | The thirst for eternity, which makes a poet?] (ll. 45–47). The speaker then proceeds to deny the existence of God in his very address to Him:

> Mas tú no existes. Eres tan sólo el nombre
> Que da el hombre a su miedo y su impotencia,
> Y la vida sin ti es esto que parecen
> Estas mismas ruinas bellas en su abandono:
> Delirio de la luz ya sereno a la noche,
> Delirio acaso hermoso cuando es corto y es leve. (ll. 51–56)

> [But you do not exist. You are only the name | That man gives his fear and his impotence, | And life without you is just as appear to be | These same beautiful ruins in their abandon: | Delirium of the light now serene at night, | Delirium perchance beautiful when it is brief and slight.]

The absence which the ruins foregrounded before this moment of confrontation was specifically human. Now it is divine. The simile comparing life with the ruins is an exhortation to accept God's inexistence — His absence — just as we should accept the ephemeral nature of our own lives. It is an exhortation that is premised on the value of the here and now over and above any longing for eternal life or the fear that leads humanity to 'perseguir eternos dioses sordos' [pursue eternal deaf gods] (l. 64). 'Life [without God] is like the delirium provoked by the aesthetic experience of the ruins, beautiful and endurable as long as it lasts a few moments in time' (Enjuto Rangel 2010: 83). The logic is that by accepting the limits of its existence, humanity may allow itself to appreciate the beauty in an instant: 'Todo lo que es hermoso tiene su instante. | Importa como eterno gozar de nuestro instante' [All that is beautiful has its moment. | It is important to enjoy our moment as if it were eternal] (ll. 57–58).

With didactic purpose, the speaker affirms in the penultimate stanza that 'Esto es el hombre' [This is man]. This affirmation is repeated from the third stanza where it was implied that, as Cecilia Enjuto Rangel puts it, 'humanity is equal to its remains and its works' (2010: 79). By the poem's end, the speaker asks that we be inspired not dejected by this equation. Yet while the serene contemplation of the final stanza seems to convey calm acceptance rather than resignation, it is not easy to shrug off the pessimism underpinning the earlier moments of defiance, particularly from the perspective of the poet whose work, explains Enjuto Rangel, 'just like ruins, is determined by its concreteness, its body, and therefore [...] is always vulnerable to the passage of time and history' (82). The speaker claims that he is not envious of God, that 'El afán de llenar lo que es efímero | De eternidad' [The desire to fill all that is ephemeral | With eternity] (ll. 61–62) is no less valuable than His omnipotence; and yet the speaker cannot deny the simple fact that his 'obras humanas [...] no duran' [his human works [...] do not last] (l. 60). On the evidence of this poem, Enjuto Rangel is right when she suggests that 'Cernuda's position is not close to Huidobro's 'creacionismo' (82). For while the speaker asserts the value of the poet as creator, that value, rather than being augmented by the fact of working in a Godless world, seems instead to be diminished by it. Which is perhaps why his rousing *carpe diem* leads not to a declaration but a question: 'Tu vida, lo mismo que la flor, ¿es menos bella acaso | Porque crezca y se abre en brazos de la muerte?' [Your life, just like a flower, is it perchance less beautiful | Because it grows and blossoms in the arms of death?] (ll. 66–67). Despite the speaker's tone of defiance — or perhaps because of it — it is not as clear as it ought to be that the answer to this question is 'no'.

In 'Una metáfora de la esperanza: las ruinas', Zambrano includes personal, anecdotal information which is omitted from her subsequent essay, entitled simply 'Las ruinas'. It centres on the way in which her nanny, Alhama, would have her young charge look about her for consolation in moments of anxiety and difficulty. With the words 'Mira, niña' [Look, child], she would point María towards 'una nube o conjunción de nubes en el cielo, una mariposa dando vuelta en torno a la luz, algún insecto más menudo todavía' [a cloud or cloud formation in the sky, a butterfly circling the light, or some still smaller insect] (1996: 138). Alhama would say nothing more and, to begin with, the child did not know what to make of such things. In time, however, it dawned on Zambrano that what her nanny had been pointing out to her were natural metaphors which could help her give form and meaning to her obsessions: 'Transformar la pesadilla en metáfora' [Transform nightmare into metaphor] (138). Thus, when, many years later, on a visit to the Forum in Rome she recalled Alhama's words, the question that came to mind about the ruins before her was '¿Qué era aquello? ¿Quizá una metáfora?' [What was this? A metaphor perhaps?] (138).

Antiquity and an actual place, as in the case of Cernuda's poem, once again provide the starting point for considerations around the motif of ruins. Yet whereas the scene of ruins in Cernuda's poem provides a frame for the speaker's reflections on mortality, while the literal materiality of what remains serves as a stark reminder of what does not, namely humanity, Zambrano's ruins are more specifically a metaphorical device in which, importantly, the play between presence and absence emphasizes possibility rather than limits. As part of an intuitive process that manifests itself in the wisdom handed down by Alhama and accords with the philosophical method Zambrano called 'razón poética' [poetic reason], the metaphor of ruins gives form not only to the awareness of finitude but also to the inkling of transcendence.[8] For Zambrano, 'poetic reason' provided an alternative to the method of traditional philosophy which considered the impassive view a condition of thought and an indispensable requisite of philosophical practice. What philosophy seemed to ignore was revelation born of poetic engagement with the world and exemplified by Greek tragedy's deciphering of the most essential events of life and even of history — 'esa historia esencial de las entrañas' [that essential history of the human conscience] — which reveal themselves 'sin merma de su misterio' [without losing their mystery]; or by the intuitions of a poetic wisdom handed down through the centuries — a more humble, anonymous tradition rooted in popular, oral culture and regarded by Zambrano as the 'essence of our western culture' (1996: 137). 'Philosophy,' Zambrano insisted, '[had] till now not put this mysterious knowledge, this poetic revelation, to use' (137). This is clearly Alhama's form of knowledge. It is also the form Zambrano employs in her essay and it begins with the contemplation of ruins.

'En la percepción de la ruina,' writes Zambrano, 'sentimos algo que no está, un huésped ido: alguien se acaba de marchar cuando entramos, algo flota en el aire y algo ha quedado también' [In our perception of the ruin we sense something that is not there, a host who has gone: someone has just left as we enter, something hovers in the air and something has remained also] (1996: 138). As in Cernuda's poem, the ruin denotes absence; but whereas Cernuda places the emphasis on erosion, Zambrano, while acknowledging the process of decline, foregrounds the act of construction:

> Las ruinas son una categoría de la historia y hacen alusión a algo muy íntimo de nuestra vida. Son el abatimiento de esa acción que define al hombre entre todas: edificar, Edificar, haciendo historia. Es decir una doble edificación: arquitectónica e histórica. (Zambrano 1996: 138)
>
> [Ruins are a category of history and they allude to something very intimate in our life. They are the abatement of that action which amongst all others defines man: building, Building, making history. This is to say, a double construction: architectural and historic.]

Through building, Zambrano explains, man realizes his dreams, and at the root of his dreaming lies the hope which she understands as being the 'motor of history' (1996: 139). But rather than representing the destruction of this hope, Zambrano senses a ruin to be a place where it somehow survives. In fact, hope seems strangely more present in a ruin than it does in any building in its pre-ruinous state, structural integrity somehow obscuring the fact of a structure's inspiration. Zambrano's sensations lead her to ask how it is that absence can be something more tangible than presence. This leads her in turn to consider the nature of absence, which she divides into two categories: 'ausencia de algo que simplemente no está presente, pero que puede estarlo y lo estuvo alguna vez; es la falta de algo o de alguien que conocemos, cuya figura hemos podido contemplar íntegramente' [absence of something which is not present, but which can be and was at some time; it is the lack of something or someone we know, whose figure we have been able to contemplate entirely]; and another, 'ausencia pura, verdadera' [pure and true absence], 'aquella que jamás estuvo presente' [that which was never present] (140), that which characterizes the divine. Because our experience of a ruin is characterized by an absence that was never actually present for us, it begs the question, '¿no hace pensar que se trate de algo divino?' [Does it not make us think that we may be dealing with something divine?] (140). This idea seems to be supported by the fact that 'la ruina perfecta sea la de un templo. Y también el que toda ruina tenga algo de templo, de lugar sagrado. Lugar de perfecta contemplación' [the perfect ruin should be a temple. And also that every ruin should have something of the temple, of the sacred place, about it. The place of perfect contemplation] (140).

Zambrano elaborates on the idea of the ruin as sacred place in her second essay, 'Las ruinas'. The ruin is sacred:

> Porque encarna la ligazón inexorable de la vida con la muerte; el abatimiento de lo que el hombre orgullosamente ha edificado, vencido ya, y la supervivencia de aquello que no pudo alcanzar en la edificación: la realidad perenne de lo frustrado; la victoria del fracas. (Zambrano 2011d: 259)
>
> [Because it embodies the inexorable link between life and death; the abatement of what man has proudly built, now vanquished, and the survival of that which

he could not attain through building: the perennial reality of what is frustrated; the victory of failure.]

The paradoxical character of this explanation cannot be reduced to the simple point Zambrano also makes, namely that a ruin 'es solamente la traza de algo humano vencido y luego vencedor del paso del tiempo' [is only the trace of something human that is vanquished by and is victor over the passage of time] (2011d: 259). It can only be fully understood in the context of a more elastic notion of human beings' relationship to time and history; one that finds solace in the idea of a life-death cycle, but also recognizes its triumph. Indebted no doubt to the Romantic imaginaries of ruins, Zambrano's vision concedes that what once imposed itself on the natural world — whether of architectural or historic construction — will eventually cease to hold sway over nature. Yet the moment in which human works enter what she calls the 'enigmatic order of nature' (260) does not represent the end. For when what is human is returned to the earth, this integration with nature gives birth to 'la esperanza convertida en libertad: un soplo divino agente de la obra y su prisionero a la vez' [hope transformed into freedom: a divine breath that is at once the work's agent and prisoner] (260). Whereas Cernuda finds it difficult to see beyond the tragedy which is, as Zambrano puts it, authored by time (257) and chooses to focus instead on the work in hand, on the beauty in a moment, Zambrano is able to conceive of an impact for human beings that is transcendental and extends beyond the individual. Rather than a sign of limits, ruins for Zambrano become 'la imagen acabada del sueño que anida en lo más hondo de la vida humana, de todo hombre' [the finished image of the dream that nestles in the depths of human life] (260). For Zambrano the triumph for man resides in his knowledge that 'al final de sus padeceres algo suyo volverá a la tierra a proseguir inacabablemente el ciclo vida-muerte y que algo escapará liberándose y quedándose al mismo tiempo, que tal es la condición de lo divino' [once his suffering is over, something of his will return to the earth to continue endlessly the life-death cycle and that something will escape at once to free itself and remain, such is the condition of the divine] (260). It is its character as meeting-place between life and death — vegetation emerging from the rubble — that explains the sacred character of ruins and produces an inkling of the divine. In her earlier essay, Zambrano singles out ivy as a metaphor for life born of death, a symbol of 'el renacer incesante de la esperanza humana' [the endless rebirth of human hope] (1996: 140). In 'Las ruinas', Zambrano stresses that it is 'el abandono y la vida vegetal naciendo al par de la piedra y de la tierra que la rodea' [abandon and vegetable life being born on a par with the stone and the earth that surrounds it] (2011d: 260) that make a ruin a sacred place. What Zambrano sees in an overgrown ruin ('Mira, niña' [Look, child], Alhama would tell her) is a moment of reconciliation between the triumph of man over nature and its reverse. For the contemplator of ruins, the effect is cathartic, purifying — and here again the connection with tragedy. Thus 'la tragedia,' writes Zambrano in her earlier essay, 'brota de la esperanza en lucha exagerada con la fatal limitación del destino, de las circunstancias. La esperanza [...] queda libre y al descubierto ya, liberada de sus luchas, en las ruinas. Es la trascendencia de la esperanza' [And tragedy springs from the extreme conflict between hope and the fatal limitations of destiny, of circumstance. Hope [...] is now free and in the open, freed from its struggles, amidst the ruins. It is the transcendence of hope] (1996: 140).

Whereas an uneasy mix of defiance and resignation characterizes Cernuda's attachment to the contemplation of ruins and the beauty of the fleeting moment, Zambrano's vision is altogether more hopeful. As Carmen Revilla Guzmán explains, for Zambrano, 'safeguarding the place of hope is one of the tasks, if not the task, of thought' (1998: 16). In her idea of the ruin as metaphor, therefore, hope takes pride of place. In *Los bienaventurados*, first published a year before her death, Zambrano would devote a chapter to outlining 'Las raíces de la esperanza' [The roots of hope] (1991: 97–112). In it she would assert that hope gives meaning and continuity to life, to life's stories, to history. At the root of her philosophy, as Jorge Velázquez Delgado has pointed out, is the proposal to rescue history from the clutches of tragic time and conceive of it in more human terms as ethical time (2007: 209). For Zambrano what is important is not understanding man as being subject to history, but rather focusing on how he may fulfil his potential across time, 'abrirse un futuro promisorio para su realización como persona humana' [to open up a promising future to realize himself as a human being] (Velázquez Delgado 2007: 218). This requires a poetic view of time and history, one that counters the tragic, one where human beings learn from the past, from past errors; where, unshackled from sequential chronology and by making sense of the past, historical knowledge acquires contemporary relevance and past events are transformed into levers of freedom. For Zambrano, 'el tiempo real de la vida no es el que se hunde en la arena de los relojes, ni el que palidece en la memoria, sino el que contiene ese tesoro: las raíces de nuestra propia vida de hoy' [the real time in life is not that which sinks in the quicksand of clocks, nor that which pales in the memory, but that which contains this treasure: the roots of our very life today] (2011d: 256). She explains:

> Lo histórico es [...] la dimensión por la cual la vida humana es trágica, constitutivamente trágica. Ser persona es rescatar la esperanza venciendo, deshaciendo, la tragedia. La persona, la libertad, ha de afirmarse frente a la historia, receptáculo de la fatalidad. (Zambrano 2011d: 257)
>
> [The historical is [...] the dimensión by which human life is tragic, fundamentally tragic. To be a person is to rescue hope by vanquishing, undoing, the tragedy. A person, freedom, must affirm him or itself against history, the receptacle of doom.]

In his own contemplation of ruins, Cernuda was reminded of his mortality, of the human tragedy. For Zambrano, the ruin is also a place where hope and tragedy collide, but hope must, and will, win out in the end. 'La contemplación de las ruinas,' she admits, 'ha producido siempre una peculiar fascinación, sólo explicable si es que en ella se contiene algún secreto de la vida, de la tragedia que es vivir humanamente' [The contemplation of ruins has always given rise to a peculiar fascination, only explicable if in it is contained some secret of life, of the tragedy that is living humanly] (2011d: 257). Importantly, however, such contemplation also provides glimpses of real freedom because what the ruin represents is truly historic.

Not in the sense of something that is resurrected from the past — 'fantasma de su realidad' [the ghost of its reality] — but in the sense of facts that have survived along with the meaning that resides in the body of those facts. 'Las ruinas,' concludes Zambrano, 'son lo más viviente de la historia, pues sólo vive históricamente lo que ha sobrevivido a su destrucción, lo que ha quedado en ruinas' [ruins are the most living aspect of history, as the only thing that lives historically is that which has survived its own destruction, that which has been left in ruins] (257). And in our contemplation of ruins:

> Se aparece ante nosotros la perspectiva del tiempo, de un tiempo concreto, vivido, que se prolonga hasta nosotros y aún prosigue. La vida de las ruinas es indefinida y más que ningún otro espectáculo despierta en el ánimo de quien las contempla la impresión de una infinitud que se desarrolla en el tiempo. (Zambrano 2011d: 258)
>
> [There appears before us a view of time, of a concrete time, a lived time, that extends towards us and still beyond. The life of ruins is indefinite and more than any other spectacle awakens in the soul of whoever contemplates them the impression of an infinitude developing in time.]

As Zambrano states in *Los bienaventurados*, nothing is built without the intention that it should last forever; and this, for Zambrano, is a fundamental principle in the history of humanity as it moves, constantly, forward (1991b: 106).

Huyssen writes:

> In contrast to the optimism of Enlightenment thought, the modern imaginary of ruins remains conscious of the dark side of modernity, what Diderot described as the inevitable 'devastation of time' visible in ruins. It articulates the nightmare of the Enlightenment that all history might ultimately be overwhelmed by nature. (Huyssen 2010: 24)

His words seem to ring true in the case of Cernuda's 'Las ruinas'. Clearly, for Cernuda, as Enjuto Rangel puts it, 'ruins represent life without God, a city without its inhabitants' and 'there is anguish over death, embodied in the unalterable future of ruins' (2010: 83 & 85). Enjuto Rangel sees in Cernuda's poem a possible critique of social and cultural values, specifically a criticism of 'how the desire for eternity upholds both religious and aesthetic discourses' (86). The underlying pessimism of the poem may also relate to Cernuda's experience of war, to 'his state of mourning for the past and the future', to the traumas of exile (86). For Neil C. McKinlay, 'the tension between doubt and faith' in Cernuda's work is an element of 'his desperate struggle to come to terms emotionally and psychologically with his isolated existence in exile' (1999: 61). If Cernuda and, indeed, Zambrano were using the motif of ruins as a displaced working-through of this personal catastrophe, Zambrano's view of history as ethical time offers, in contrast to Cernuda, some hope of making sense of the traumatic event and of transforming it into a lever for freedom. As Antolín Sánchez Cuervo states in his treatment of the metamorphosis of exile in her work, the void of exile does not lead Zambrano towards nihilism or alienation (2010: 185–86). 'La esperanza,' argues Zambrano in *Los bienaventurados*, 'al proporcionar el sentido de la historia, de toda historia, construye la continuidad en la vida' [Hope, by providing the meaning of history, of all history, builds continuity into life] (1991: 106). It is perhaps ironic, at least in the context of our comparison with Cernuda, that in adopting her poetic approach, Zambrano was acknowledging the ability of poets to offer the vision for all humanity she sought in her own work. Yet despite the seemingly universal concerns of Cernuda's poem, it becomes apparent that he is unable to offer his reader any comfort in a common destiny or cause which might render him — as Zambrano thought poets could — 'no el sujeto de su pequeña vida particular, sino el sujeto de la vida humana, sin más' [not the subject of his own little life, but the subject of human life, just that] (2011d: 258). Cernuda's poem fits broadly into the 'poetics of disillusionment in twentieth-century Spanish literature' (Enjuto Rangel 2007: 146), and this despite, or perhaps because of, the defiance his speaker displays in facing down God and extolling the virtue of the moment, however brief. Zambrano, on the other hand, does not have divinity in her critical sights but instead the failure of individuals to see beyond the moment or themselves, which is the consequence of being shackled to sequential time. For McKinlay, Cernuda's 'expression of independence, of a desire to go forward on his own' equates to 'a solipsistic arrogance [...] which revalues the persona's open individuality to the exclusion of all else' (1999: 76). 'There is,' adds McKinlay in respect of Cernuda's poem, 'a desire to ignore death, to seize the day and recognize beauty for what it is' (76). What Zambrano does share with Cernuda is a belief in the value of human works; but rather than settle on their material limitations or on the moment, she looks for the eternal hope, the vision, the dreams, that made them and remake them. It is fitting that Zambrano's reflections on the metaphor of ruins in her first essay should end with an ethical interpretation of the words of another Spanish dreamer: 'Y si Calderón dijo "obrar bien que ni aun en sueños se pierde" cabría entenderlo pensando que de toda realidad lo único que queda será su sueño. Que el soñar bien ni aun muriendo se pierde' [And if Calderón said 'working well not even in dreams is lost', we should understand this by thinking that the only thing remaining of all reality will be the dream. That dreaming well is not lost even with our dying] (1996: 141). Ultimately, in Zambrano's work, it is a hope beyond hope that is laid bare, one that defies the end and, as Velázquez Delgado puts it, emphasizes 'the central role that Transcendence plays in the history of man' (2007: 212).

Notes to Chapter 5

1. Derrida 1993: 73–74.
2. Valender 1998: 167. All translations are my own unless otherwise stated.
3. On the points of contact between Zambrano and Cernuda, see Valender 1998: 165–97, and Berrocal 2011: 52–56.
4. 'Otras ruinas' is more clearly about the modern city, and among the titles the poet considered for his poem was 'Londres' [London]. By contrast, 'Las ruinas' was originally entitled 'Campos de soledad' [Fields of Solitude], the emphasis here being on existential concerns. See Enjuto Rangel 2007: 148, and 2010: 75–76. All references to 'Las ruinas' are Cernuda 1973: 282–84.
5. All references to 'Una metáfora de la esperanza: las ruinas', in *La Cuba secreta y otros ensayos*, are Zambrano 1996: 135–41. It was first published in *Lyceum*, 26 (1949), 7–11. References to 'Las

ruinas', in *El hombre y lo divino*, are Zambrano 2011d: 254–60]. It was originally published in Asomante, 1 (January to March 1953), 8–14. On the genealogy of Zambrano's 'Las ruinas', see Zambrano 2011d: 1256, n. 98.

6. For Cernuda's idea of Pompeii, see Enjuto Rangel 2010: 75–76.
7. Enjuto Rangel (2010: 79), suggests that the poem 'portrays itself as an act of imagination from the very beginning', and describes it as a 'dreamlike journey', 'a journey into the past', and 'a process of reconstruction'; while Kevin J. Bruton, who sees Coleridge's theory of the imagination as being a significant influence on Cernuda's work, explains that in the poem 'the imagination synthesizes various disparate elements, allowing easy movement from perception to abstract comment, from the visual to the visionary'. See Bruton 1984: 390.
8. On Zambrano's concept of 'razón poética', see Johnson 1996; and Pérez 1997.

CHAPTER 6

Poetry and Realization: Towards a Knowledge of the Poet's Place in María Zambrano

Alberto Santamaría, Universidad de Salamanca

The Question of the Poet's Place

In 1946 Martin Heidegger published his essay entitled 'What Are Poets For?' One year later, Witold Gombrowicz gave his well-known lecture *Against Poets*. The distance between them is important and irreconcilable. There is nothing to connect the German philosopher with the Polish writer. However, despite notable distances, there is a common murmur, a shared horizon. That horizon can be summed up as the question of the place of the poet in a society shaken by different tragedies caused by humankind itself. Heidegger begins his text with the line that provides the title for his work: '...and what are poets for in a destitute time?' This line is taken from the German poet Friedrich Hölderlin, and forms part of the poem 'Bread and Wine'. Heidegger felt a special interest in this poet inasmuch as he was a poet capable of guiding the vision of a people in search of a lost origin, of unveiling what has remained hidden after the flight of the gods. For Heidegger, in the midst of the ruins of Germany, poets are a necessary component in its rebuilding in that they could be the ones that prepare for the coming of the gods, whose absence has caused us to live in times of penury. This is how Heidegger answers the question posed in the title of his text: 'the time remains destitute not only because God is dead, but because mortals are hardly aware and capable even of their own mortality. Mortals have not yet come into ownership of their own nature' (Heidegger 2001: 94). What is more, the times are so bad that the human being 'can no longer discern the default of God as a default' (89). Thus, for Heidegger the poet was akin to a spiritual member of an expedition who descends into the abyss in search of a trace of the lost gods. In this sense, he considers that poets (where metaphysics and creation come together in a knot) are those who take risks, since they descend in search of being to illuminate the darkness in which mortals live.

On the other hand, one year later, we have *Against Poets* by Witold Gombrowicz. His position is diametrically opposed to that of Heidegger, and from the very beginning we read his response to Heidegger's worldview:

> The most serious difficulty on a personal and social level that a poet must face comes from the fact that, by considering himself superior, like a priest of poetry, he addresses his listeners from above; but his listeners do not always recognize his right to that superiority and do not want to listen from below. The more the number of people who question the value of the poems and are disrespectful to the cult, the more delicate and bordering on the ridiculous the poet's attitude becomes. (Gombrowicz 2006: 19)[1]

For this Polish writer the place that the poet held until then in the social order, at least as a spiritual reference, had to be revised and transformed. Gombrowicz considered that poetry had lost its meaning in the midst of the great tragedies of the twentieth century, which it had not been able to respond to. In this sense, his initial thesis is this: 'almost nobody likes verse, the world of poetry is fictitious and fake' (Gombrowicz 2006: 12). And he adds:

> [This thesis] will seem desperately childish; and yet, I confess that I do not like verse and that it bores me a little. What is interesting is that I am not at all ignorant when it comes to artistic matters nor am I lacking in poetic sensibility; and when poetry appears mixed with other cruder and more prosaic elements [...] I tremble like any other mortal. (Gombrowicz 2006: 16)

And he concludes his thesis thus: 'what my nature can hardly stand is the pharmaceutical and purified extract of poetry called 'pure poetry' and, above all, when it appears in verse' (Gombrowicz 2006: 13). Gombrowicz does not grant the poet a special place. His is, in effect, another way of addressing that generational concern with the position from which the poet speaks. According to Gombrowicz, this position should be situated between things and the rest of humanity, as just one more person seeking to communicate, and not the superior redemptive position in which Heidegger situates the poet, in respect of which he wrote: 'If we do not want culture to lose all of its relation to human beings, once in a while we should interrupt our laborious exercises to find out whether what we produce expresses us or not' (32). Here we have another way of responding: the only viable poetry is the one that tries to reconstruct the links between us, between human beings. This is its meaning, and the place that the poet should occupy.

These are two radically opposing positions, but they bring to the fore a real problematic in the middle of the post-war years: where is the poet to be located in the new society being built on the ruins of rationalism? In this context, some years later, we find Theodor Adorno. In 1951 we had the most well-known and misinterpreted statement that this philosopher ever made, endlessly taken out of context: 'to write poetry after Auschwitz is barbaric' (Adorno 1981: 28). Western culture's eagerness for reductionism and story-telling turned this statement into 'the impossibility of writing poetry after Auschwitz'. At no time did Adorno reject poetry, and what is more, one of his texts from that same time called 'On Lyric Poetry and Society' is a whole manifesto about the possibilities of the relation between poetry and society. In any case, what Adorno is referring to is that it is not possible to go on writing poetry with the same cultural mentality that existed prior to Auschwitz. He develops this idea in the following way in *Negative Dialectics*:

> Whoever pleads for the maintenance of the radically culpable and shabby culture becomes its accomplice while the man who says no to culture is directly furthering the barbarism which our culture showed itself to be. Not even silence gets us out of this circle. (Adorno 2005: 367)

This entrapment in a vicious circle that Adorno's words reveal again re-enacts the greater problem hounding all these authors. What is the poet's place? In contrast to the salvational place where Heidegger locates the poet, or the peripheral space that Gombrowicz appoints for them, Adorno looks on the poet as a trapped subject.

This is just a small sample of a much larger problem that could be the basis for more extensive research. The amount of texts that refer to the place of poets and poetry is endless. However, just from these examples it is easy to understand that the matter can be read as follows: how can we write poetry *now*? If instead of philosophers we turn to the poets themselves, we find even greater radicalism (but also anguish). Without going further afield, T. S. Eliot, just after the United States entered the Second World War in 1942, wrote, as cited by Helen Gardner:

> In the midst of what is going on now, it is hard, when you sit down at a desk, to feel confident that morning after morning spent fiddling with words and rhythms is a justified activity — especially as there is never any certainty that the whole thing won't have to be scrapped. (Gardner 1978: 21)

The situation that emerges from reflecting on 'writing-now' involves asking oneself not 'what is writing?' (something fairly inane and out of context), but rather posing a question of more complexity: what to write? Or better, why write? This is what Wallace Stevens, that same year, 1942, called the 'pressure of reality'. Stevens defines it as a violence that affects everything alive and that obliges the poet to live in a perpetual balance between language and now, between the word and reality. In 1942 Stevens was to speak of a 'new Romanticism' to explain his place. In regard to the poet of the Romantic now he wrote the following:

> He happens to be one who still dwells in an ivory tower but who insists that life would be intolerable except for the fact that one has, from the top, such an exceptional view of the public dump and the advertising signs of Snider's Catsup, Ivory Soap and Chevrolet Cars; he is the hermit who dwells alone with the sun and moon, but insists on taking a rotten newspaper. (Stevens 1990: 214)

This brief summary, in which we have tried to approach distant positions, leads us to think that within the time-frame in question, 1933 to 1951, the issue of writing poetry in a world in the midst of full change becomes a fundamental one, at least for the intellectuals of that time.

Following the Traces of Poetry and Philosophy in María Zambrano

It is against this background that I would like to read María Zambrano, who can be perfectly located in this space of generational concern with the place of the poet and poetry. Very early on, in 1934, Zambrano began to contemplate this problem. In the text entitled 'Por qué se escribe' she broaches the radical question of why one writes. The title is interesting. She does not ask 'Why write?' or 'Why writing?', but rather 'Why does one write?' The reflexive *se* in the passive construction used in Spanish is radically impersonal on one hand, but on the other it serves to highlight the deeper problem: one writes with a purpose. At the beginning of the article she points out that:

> Escribir es defender la soledad en la que se está; es una acción que brota desde un aislamiento efectivo, pero de un aislamiento comunicable, en que, precisamente, por la lejanía de toda cosa concreta se hace posible un descubrimiento de relaciones entre ellas. (Zambrano 2004b: 35)
>
> [To write is to defend the solitude in which one finds oneself; it is an action that arises from effective isolation, but a communicable isolation in which, precisely because of the remoteness of all concrete things, it is possible to discover the relations between them.]

Writing would imply, on one hand, an isolation, a withdrawing, or a descent into the depths, and on the other, an opening, that is, a showing of the path traced by writing. In this sense, Zambrano was to opt for a 'communicable solitude' or a 'shared solitude' that would be present throughout her entire philosophical trajectory. This is the reading that Zambrano chose in 1934. Thus we read: 'El escritor sale de su soledad a comunicar el secreto. Luego ya no es el secreto mismo conocido por él lo que le colma, puesto que necesita comunicarle' [The writer comes out of his solitude to communicate a secret. So then it is no longer the secret itself that fulfils him, because he needs to communicate it]; and further on she adds, 'Como quien lanza una bomba, el escritor arroja fuera de sí, de su mundo y por tanto, de su ambiente controlable, el secreto hallado' [Just like someone throwing a bomb, the writer tosses the discovered secret out of himself, out of his world and thus out of the context he controls] (Zambrano 2004b: 39). Given all of this, for Zambrano, in 1934, to write is *escribirse*, to write oneself, to make visible a secret that is only possible through language, in search of a 'spiritual community' (43). Five years later, in 1939, she focuses on a more complex problem: why write poetry and what is its place in relation to philosophy? Many events took place during this five-year interval on both the personal and political level. Imbued with a manifest awareness of defeat, in exile in 1939, she published two books in which the problem of the place of poetry is central: *Poesía y pensamiento en la vida española* [Poetry and Thought in Spanish Life] and *Filosofía y poesía* [Philosophy and Poetry]. Both of these are books which, despite differences in style and content, reflect a common and generational concern about what place poetry and the poet's voice should occupy. The first book concludes with a declaration of intent: 'La continuidad de España se ha expresado por la poesía, sin que nadie pueda ya impedirlo, pero se ha expresado igualmente por la sangre. Y la sangre también tiene su universalidad. Mas sin la palabra no sería comprendida' [The continuity of Spain has been expressed through poetry, and now no one can impede it, but it has also been expressed through blood. And blood also has its universality. But without the word it would not be understood] (Zambrano 2015: 656). After these closing words, if we look at *Filosofía y poesía,* we can understand perfectly how her perspective fits in easily with a European context in which this issue is a central one. Poetry is not only a question of the poet as subject but, more importantly, the product of a new sensitive reality, a new sensitive community within a common consciousness of defeat. That is the mission of the poet in a period of defeat and permanent crisis: to make of poetry a new place for accessing hidden reality. She herself describes this book, *Filosofía y poesía,* as written 'después de la derrota' [after the defeat] (Zambrano 2015: 684), and in which defeat and the search for a new sensitive space for the subject becomes central. It is a book that is not easy to synthesize or summarize. What we can say is that in Zambrano there is an awareness of a failure, a concept that can help us to attain a general understanding of all her work. This failure is experienced in the successive distances that she describes: the word and language, the sacred and the divine, poetry and philosophy, etc.

Within this context of distances, language is the indication of humankind's failure to reveal its own being to itself. However, within this failure, poetry can open roads that philosophy has denied itself. Thus, Zambrano's objective is to point out how poetry can (and should) be the path through which humankind can uncover the centre, the being, the core, the starting point that supports everything, as she says:

> Poesía y pensamiento se nos aparecen como dos formas insuficientes, y se nos antojan dos mitades del hombre: el filósofo y el poeta. No se encuentra el hombre entero en la filosofía; no se encuentra la totalidad de lo humano en la poesía. En la poesía encontramos directamente al hombre concreto, individual. En la filosofía, al hombre en su historia universal, en su querer ser. La poesía es encuentro, don, hallazgo por la gracia. La filosofía busca, requerimiento guiado por un método. (Zambrano 2015: 687)
>
> [Poetry and thought appear to us as two insufficient forms, and call to mind the two halves of man: the philosopher and the poet. The whole man cannot be found in philosophy; the whole of what is human cannot be found in poetry. In poetry we find the specific, individual man directly. In philosophy we find man in his universal history, in what man desires to be. Poetry is encounter, gift, discovery through grace. Philosophy seeks, it is a petition guided by a method.]

It is in this context that Zambrano discovers that poetry also entails a form of knowledge, that all thought carries within it a poetic component. Nonetheless, going beyond an idea of fusion of genres, poetry-philosophy (in fact a Romantic project), it is more accurate to say that her objective is different: to open the way to a new historical sensibility within which a writing will emerge to reveal the centre, the being, the place from which everything comes. Poetic reason would thus have the purpose of unveiling a new sensibility. In the context of European thought mentioned above, Zambrano's contribution follows this path, making her position highly original.[2]

On the one hand, when speaking of poetic reason we must consider that Zambrano was not trying to carry out a detailed analysis of the historical links between poetry and philosophy. But on the other hand, neither was she aiming for a quantitative analysis of how much thought or poetry there should be, as if poetic reason were something like a chemical product composed of two different liquids.

Instead, her intention was to open up through language the possibility of a new sensibility that would allow a thought removed from rigid systems to emerge. In this way, poetry and thought would turn into movable and variable pieces serving the word and opening up a different historical sensibility which would have the poet (or the act of making poetry) at its centre. This is a thought that Zambrano borrowed from Ortega y Gasset but then developed further.

Before focusing on a topic such as the relation between poetry and thought, Zambrano had noted the question in the book *Horizonte del liberalismo* [The Horizon of Liberalism]. There, when referring to the view of a Europe in crisis, she points out that only a change in sensibility could open up new historical possibilities. She writes:

> Y es que cuando el mundo está en crisis y el horizonte que la inteligencia otea aparece ennegrecido de inminentes peligros; cuando la razón estéril se retira, reseca de luchar sin resultado y la sensibilidad quebrada sólo recoge el fragmento, el detalle, nos queda sólo una vía de esperanza: el sentimiento, el amor, que, repitiendo el milagro, vuelva a crear el mundo. (Zambrano 2015: 104)

> [And so it is that when the world is in crisis and the horizon that our intelligence can glimpse appears blackened by imminent danger, when sterile reason withdraws, dried up from fighting unsuccessfully, and a broken sensibility can merely gather fragments, details, we are left with only one path of hope: feeling — love — which, repeating the miracle, again creates the world.]

This final text of *Horizonte del liberalismo* (normally dissociated from books such as *Filosofía y poesía*) acquires strength if we link it with her entire subsequent trajectory. This first book contains, albeit only in seed form, her commitment to overcoming defeat by means of the creation of a new sensibility that emerges from individual experience but tries to surpass that same experience. And for Zambrano, a short time later, it was the poet who possessed this way of glimpsing that new sensibility understood as an act of newly creating the world.

However, before continuing we must posit the following question: which poet is Zambrano talking about? As Ana Bundgaard so pertinently writes:

> This 'poet' that Zambrano refers to in her writings addressing the relations between philosophy and poetry is an ideal and anachronistic abstraction, somewhat like a metaphor, we could say, that designates the subject who is the creator of a future metaphysics that would have to surpass and reform from the roots up classical metaphysics, modern metaphysics, and the metaphysics contemporary with Zambrano herself. Thus in Zambrano the figure of the poet, the antipode of the philosopher, refers both to herself, as the creator of a new method of apprehending reality, the ratio-poetic, and to those initiates who manage to follow her in her own thought. The 'poet' then, will be the 'new' philosopher who is able to overcome the 'violence' of classical metaphysics and the voluntarist 'spirit' of modern metaphysics. (Bundgaard 2000: 216)

We can see from a close reading that the poet Zambrano speaks of, rather than being a concrete subject, rooted in a certain place, is the personification of a different sensibility; it is a possibility, even an allegory. However, at the same time, we cannot forget that Zambrano had and would have certain names in mind while writing. It is on this border between possibility and reality that Zambrano's poet sits.

Poetry, then, is that place from which it is possible to glimpse a territory that designates another place. Cioran was able to see it: 'everything in María Zambrano leads into something else, everything entails her *other* place, everything' (Cioran 1981: 100). This is where the sense of poetry and the poet can be found. The poet does not ask, does not begin with an interrogation, since any question presupposes a separation, an impossible unity. Zambrano herself wrote that 'la filosofía se inicia del modo más antipoético por una pregunta. La poesía lo hará siempre por una respuesta a una pregunta no formulada. [...] Toda pregunta indica la pérdida de una intimidad o el extinguirse de una adoración' [philosophy begins in a most unpoetic way by means of a question. Poetry will always begin with an answer to an unformulated question. [...] Every question indicates the loss of an intimacy or the extinguishing of an adoration] (Zambrano 2007a: 100). Put simply, it is for this reason that poetry for Zambrano is directly linked to sacred language. This idea recurs in several places in her writings. The sacred is understood as the area that points to the possibility that things exist, 'la nada que precedió a la creación' [the nothingness that preceded creation] (Zambrano 1989c: 123). In *El hombre y lo divino* [Man and the Divine] she points out that 'la realidad es lo sagrado y sólo lo sagrado la tiene y la otorga' [reality is what is sacred and only the sacred has it and grants it] (Zambrano 2014b: 114). The sacred is thus understood as the originary vacuum that defines a lost unity, a unity that has nothing to do with the disciplinary or hierarchical order of organized religions. The unity found in this originary centre is a unity that brings together what is disparate, and that is the source of its sacredness, a unity where everything remains connected. An everything in which the diverse comes together, flows together, in the sense that it flows in harmony. It would be an act of awakening, that moment of sudden lucidity, in which the centre, the unity, would be revealed to us. This is undoubtedly a Romantic type of thinking, but if we look more closely, it may perhaps be a view that came from Spinoza's thought, as well as from the mystic tradition. Zambrano considers that no theme can live separated from the rest, that everything is a fragment of an order, of an orbit continuously travelled around and which would only show itself whole if its centre were made manifest.

The poet, then, understood as the bearer and the creator of a new sensibility, should be the one to open up the mystery since the mystery cannot be defined as a function of rational concepts but rather is only approachable and comprehensible through poetic knowledge which diverges from the path of discursive reason. For this reason she states that 'poesía tendrá o buscará tener [...] algo de este lenguaje sagrado autónomo y querrá realizar algo anterior al pensamiento y que el pensamiento, cuando se da a correr discursivamente tan solo y sólo, no podrá cumplir' [poetry will have, or will seek to have [...] something of this autonomous sacred language and will wish to realize something prior to thought, and that thought, when running only discursively and alone, will not be able to comply] (Zambrano 2012a: 68). But how do we escape this discursive reason? How do we touch this mystery that dwells in us and links us to the centre?

Path, Time, Memory

It is indeed the poetic word that, according to Zambrano, invites us to descend into the dark areas, the gloom, in a kind of counter-platonic journey in which instead of leaving the cave and coming into the light, we seek to go down to the depths, to the Hades of the soul in search of that lost unity. She speaks about this in a text written in 1944 entitled 'La destrucción de las formas' [The Destruction of Forms]:

> Todo da a entender que busca algo dejado atrás y que quiere adentrarse en algún secreto lugar, como si buscara la placenta de donde saliera un día, para ser de nuevo engendrado. Abandona el mundo donde tenía que ser hombre entero, y sostener una idealidad; se muestra reacio a vivir a la luz del día, que es la luz de la razón, de esa razón que puso orden una vez en la realidad pavorosa. Busca el lugar oscuro, la caverna de donde saliera para en ella hundirse de momento. (Zambrano 2012a: 29)[3]

> [Everything implies that [the poet] is seeking something left behind and that he wants to get inside some secret place, as if he were searching for the placenta he once came out of, in order to be newly engendered. He abandons the world in which he had to be a whole man, and uphold an ideality; he appears reluctant to live in the light of day, which is the light of reason, of that reason that once brought order to frightful reality. He seeks the dark place, the cavern he came out of, in which to plunge himself momentarily.]

It is within this framework that Zambrano tries to unravel the risk of walking towards these infernos, which years later she would describe in the book *Claros del bosque* [Clearings]. That risk has to do with the necessary view that the place of the poet/poem is a place without time. The first step along this path towards what we call a new sensibility would be to liberate oneself from time as we understand it, that is, time which subjugates us according to its own political or work-related functions, upheld by the normalized discourse of routine. Freeing oneself from time would be something that would come from the hand of the poet, understood as an allegory of the creative act. Indeed, the descent and awakening that the poet undergoes through language is a descent that involves the fracture of the whole causal concept of time. Atemporality is key to Zambrano's ratio-poetic schema. She writes, 'poesía no es sino la huella de esa forma de lenguaje que es propia de otro tiempo y de otra vida' [poetry is nothing but the trace of that form of language that is proper to another time and another life] (Zambrano 2007a: 72). Another time and another life that point in reality towards that sacred space that the poet seeks. She adds, 'porque este desorden era el fragmento de lo sagrado, la huella preciosa a descifrar. Y esta palabra activa está al comienzo del lenguaje. Después el tiempo se introdujo escindiéndola' [because this disorder was the fragment of the sacred, the precious trace to decipher. And this active word is at the beginning of language. Then time came in and split it] (72). The idea of time that we usually have involves a disciplinary, almost military, impulse, which makes it impossible for us to become aware of the failure that that time implies. This failure entails the impossibility of observing the truth, the impossibility of a being understood as the sacred core from which everything comes. Poetry thus moves closer to memory with the idea of recapturing that lost reality. The poet is one who reminds us of the origin through language. The word of the poet is different from normal words in that the poet's word is charged with a different time, it is a word that has escaped the military discipline of the dictionary. That is why Zambrano writes, 'todos los poemas verdaderos de la poesía serían rememoraciones, intentos de captura, no por la razón, sino por la memoria' [all the true poems of poetry would be recallings, attempts at capture, not through reason, but through memory] (73), and going further, 'la poesía se acerca a esta realización del tiempo perdido' [poetry approaches this realization of lost time] (74). We shall return to the concept of 'realization', which seems of capital importance in understanding Zambrano's project. For now we shall focus on the connection between atemporality and memory. In *Notas de un método* [Notes on a Method] she writes:

> El recordar viene así a ser siempre un desnacerse el sujeto para ir a recoger lo que nació en él y en torno suyo y viéndolo, devolverlo, si le es posible, a la nada, o para rescatarlo de su oscuridad inicial y prestarle ocasión de que renazca de otro modo ya en el campo de la vision. (Zambrano 1989c: 81)

> [Remembering thus always ends up being an unbirthing of the subject so that he can gather up what was born in him and around him and by seeing it, return it, if he can, to nothingness, or to rescue it from its initial darkness and give it a chance to be reborn in another way, this time in the field of vision.]

The problem resides in the moment at which memory yields its place to consciousness, which orders the past like a closed discourse. In this sense, Zambrano distinguishes between remembering and going over the past. Both are exclusive exercises since they refer to different times. For Zambrano the poet turns remembering into the possibility of bringing to the present and to the language of the poem a past that attempts to make transparent the experience of the journey and of the origin. The poet remembers in order to undo time, not with the idea of causally linking together a story. The poet is the irreconcilable enemy of historicism. The poet extracts the past from memory in order to illuminate it, to make it live. This is the case of poets able to open up spaces to a new sensibility, such as Rimbaud or García Lorca. Zambrano describes it thus:

> El remitirse enteramente a la conciencia, tal como lo viene haciendo, y cada vez con mayor furia, el hombre occidental, impone la ley del tiempo de la conciencia pasado, presente, porvenir —; tiempo sucesivo, discursivo, que constriñe el original ímpetu en busca de algo perdido, de la memoria, y lo encamina a recorrer simplemente el pasado. Un recorrer el pasado aplanándolo, como preparación del discurrir del pensamiento racional. (Zambrano 1989c: 83)

> [Abiding wholly by consciousness, as Western man has been doing, and with ever more fury, imposes the law of the time of consciousness — past, present, and future; successive, discursive time, which constrains the original impetus in search of something lost, of memory, and sets it simply on a path around the past. A path around the past that flattens it down, in preparation for the discourse of rational thought.]

Rationalism has caused memory to be 'destituida de su función originaria rescatadora' [dismissed from its originary rescuing function] (Zambrano 1989c: 83), that is to say, 'la condición humana impone inexorablemente un tiempo objetivado correspondiente a la sociedad, al estado y especialmente al estado moderno' [the human condition inexorably imposes an objectified time that corresponds to society, the state, and especially the modern state] (83). In contrast, memory becomes like a process whose objective is to penetrate into what has been lived and that we have allowed to get away, something similar to what the Italian philosopher, Palo Virno, calls 'potential plots': 'When a certain thing happens, besides perceiving reality, we also apprehend its potential plot' (Virno 2003: 25–26). Perhaps it is this impulse that lies hidden behind Zambrano's idea. This is precisely what she observes in Federico García Lorca, of whom she says: 'La poesía [...] fue encontrando el cauce de esta potencia del soñar y, con él, su fluir, por haberle dado al sueño su tiempo propio. La oscura, quieta atemporalidad se convierte entonces en manantial' [poetry [...] was gradually finding the course of this power of dreaming and, with it, its flow, by having given dream its own time. The dark, motionless atemporality then becomes a flowing spring] (Zambrano 2007a: 167–68). In *El sueño creador* [Creative Dreaming] she develops this in more depth. There we read: 'Al ser mirados los sueños desde su forma y no desde su contenido, como es habitual, se descubre la atemporalidad como su *a priori*, que los separa del estado de vigilia' [Since the dreams are looked at for their form and not for their content, as is customary, atemporality is discovered as their a priori, which separates them from the waking state] (Zambrano 1986b: 48). Poetry, memory, dream, atemporality — all of these form a path that Zambrano considers essential for opening up a space that is always shown to us as closed: the being, the core. This opening, this new visibility, will be offered to us by a kind of illumination, like a lightning bolt that lights up a part of reality in the middle of a dark night. She herself wonders about this experience: '¿No sucede, no me habrá sucedido a mí [...] que lo que está escondido pueda aparecer en forma fulminante, hasta en forma de rayo?' [Doesn't it happen, as it happened to me [...] that what is hidden can appear suddenly, even in the form of a lightning bolt?] (Zambrano 2012a: 83). It is this experience of illumination that Zambrano attempts to describe to us and that we find narrated in different ways at this same time. For example, in 1945, Jean Cocteau wrote:

> In the space of a lightning bolt we *see* a dog, a horse-drawn carriage, a house, for the first time. Everything special they offer, of madness, ridiculousness, beauty, overwhelms us. Immediately afterwards, habit erases this powerful image. We pet the dog, stop the carriage, live in the house. We no longer see them. This, then, is the role of poetry. It unveils with all the strength of the word. It shows us naked, under the light that shakes off the dimness, the surprising things that surround us and that our senses register mechanically. (Rosset 1974: 51)

We find similar words in Paul Valéry or in Walter Benjamin. The need for this new experience forms part of the search for a new sensibility that attempts to create a world from within the awareness of defeat. Poetry will be the hand that guides us in this; poetry or the poetic word that acts a mediator and that we should also read as an allegory of a larger act of realization.

That noted, we may consider, by way of synthesis, that for Zambrano poetry is something like a magical spell inasmuch as it mediates with the inexpressible. In *De la aurora* [On Dawn] she writes that 'la palabra [...] es revelación' [the word [...] is revelation] (Zambrano 1986c: 123). But decades earlier she had expressed it thus: 'El arte comenzó por ser un modo de ocultamiento y de contacto con lo no-humano, con lo tangible sagrado, adorno y máscara: máscara con sentido mágico' [Art began by being a way of concealing and contacting the non-human, with the sacred tangible, ornament and mask: mask with a magic meaning] (Zambrano 2012a: 30). Words understood, then, as masks that are carriers of a poetic possibility; words able to penetrate the thickness and reach the centre and speak of it.[4] In this way words, certain words, can make something appear; they can reveal. Like a magical spell, words conceal that power of access to the non-visible. The poetic word in this sense reveals another space that the poet listens to and brings to us. Zambrano is aware of this drift and writes: 'La poesía pretende ser un conjuro para descubrir esa realidad cuya huella enmarañada se encuentra en la angustia que precede a la creación' [Poetry tries to be a spell for discovering that reality whose entangled trace can be found in the anguish that precedes creation] (Zambrano 2007a: 66). And this is precisely the task of the modern poet, who, in the midst of an experience of defeat and anguish, must recover that word. Thus, the modern poet tends to 'apegarse al inicial delirio y el retrotraerse a las palabras como invocación y conjuro' [become attached to the initial delirium and go back to words as invocation and spell] (Zambrano 2012a: 72).

The Concept of 'Realization' in María Zambrano as the Basis of 'Poetic Reason'

In everything we have seen so far there is an underlying premise that Zambrano neither hides, not makes explicit. That premise tells us that her project to create a new common sensibility is based on the fact that it is necessary to be aware of a series of dichotomies: sleep-wakefulness, light-shadows, sacred-divine, etc. All of them, though different, preserve the form of a distance. Distance can be read in many ways, but in Zambrano it seems to be a matter of a distance whose trajectory not only demands risk but also necessarily involves the awareness of a defeat, of a failure. This centre, this unity, will only be attainable as a glimpse, nothing more. Of these distances there is one in particular to highlight, that which separates the word as grammatical exercise imposed as a norm and the word understood as a place able to pull free from that tyranny. Zambrano, indeed, points towards a difference between word and language, the former showing itself as a rupture, as dissent, and the latter offered as consensus, as a word secured on a fixed horizon and established by some regulatory class.

How can that word which seeks to distance itself from the word understood as the syntax of thought or discursive reasoning be read from the point of view of a concept that usually goes unnoticed: the concept of 'realization'. This is a key concept in understanding the opening-up of what is closed. Zambrano writes: 'Y así, encontramos que la acción del lenguaje sagrado se ejerce ante todo en abrir un espacio, un verdadero "espacio vital" antes cerrado' [And thus we find that the action of sacred language is practised above all in opening up a space, a true 'vital space' that before was closed off] (Zambrano 2012a: 70). The poet has to open that space with the purpose of generating a new place within which a new sensibility can emerge, and this he does through 'realization'.

'Realization' is the process by which, starting from a creative perspective, thought and poetry can be connected. Although in the extensive bibliography of Zambrano we do not find works that address this matter directly or in any depth, the term 'realization' is not used casually by the author. She is a writer so careful in her use of language that it is impossible to think that this word slipped into her writings involuntarily.

That said, it is possible to understand the concept of the creative act in María Zambrano as realization, as shall be demonstrated. 'Realizing' indicates a transition, an act typical of the creative subject that moves from the light to the darkness (in a clear movement of descent). In the poet's return to those infernos he or she attempts to reveal, that is, to realize that experience in writing until it becomes transmissible:

> Toda poesía tendrá siempre mucho de ese lenguaje sagrado, primero; realizará algo anterior al pensamiento, y que el pensamiento no podrá él solo cumplir cuando no se verifique. [...] Las palabras se juntan en formas que hace abrirse un espacio antes inaccessible. (Zambrano 2007a: 65)

> [All poetry will always have much of that sacred language, first; it will realize something prior to thought and that thought alone will not be able to fulfil when not verified. [...] Words are joined in ways that open up a hitherto inaccessible space.]

This concept of realization was not at all alien to María Zambrano. Indeed, it was one of the concepts used at many different times by her teacher Ortega y Gasset, to refer to, among other things, artistic process and activity.

In 1910, in the text 'Adán en el paraíso' [Adam in Paradise], Ortega wrote the following: 'Cézanne used to have at the tip of his tongue a word of enormous aesthetic transcendence: *to realize*. According to him, this word contains the alpha and the omega of the artist's role. To *realize*, that is, to convert into a thing something that in itself is not a thing' (Ortega y Gasset 2004–2010: VII, 69). For Ortega this word contains the nucleus of all artistic possibilities. We can imagine that Zambrano took it from here, from Ortega's thought, to amplify it, and above all, to take it further than her teacher did. Ortega considers the mission of the artist to reside in a process that involves a dual movement: on the one hand, to 'de-realize', that is, to move away from or break with reality understood as a closed and rational form, and on the other, once this breaking away has been carried out, to come back to realize, that is, to reveal a new and 'pure' artistic experience. Ortega applies this schema in different texts and if we look closely, this is the schema that María Zambrano was to develop, although with different intentions.

According to Ortega, Cézanne aimed to overcome the prevalent realism of his time. Under the label of 'realization' he returned to the ideal of the coexistence of the creative spirit and the powers of the real world. In the same text, Ortega points out some of the key elements: 'Reality is the reality of the painting, not that of the thing itself. [...] Art has to take nature to pieces in order to articulate the aesthetic form' (Ortega y Gasset 2004–2010: VII, 70). Thus, for Ortega, to realize 'will not be to copy a thing, but rather to copy the totality of things' (70). In art there is a need to point to that consciousness that realizes, which, as Ortega clearly underscores, asks itself not *how* to paint or write but more radically, *what* to paint or write. For Ortega, to realize entails creation in the full sense, in which the realizing subject does so according to his or her own inner schemata.

Four years later, in 'Ensayo de estética a manera de prólogo' [Aesthetic Essay in the Manner of a Prologue] Ortega was to write the following:

> Art is essentially IRREALIZATION. Within the aesthetic sphere, there may arise occasions on which to classify the different trends into idealist and realist, but always with the ineluctable supposition that the essence of art lies in the creation of a new objectivity born from a prior break with and annihilation of real objects. (Ortega y Gasset 2004–2010: I, 678)

For Ortega, to realize entails de-realizing, and in this sense metaphor is an essential weapon, given that the new poet confronts a new situation: 'Before, metaphor was poured over reality, like a decoration, an appliqué, or a rain cape. Now, the opposite occurs; one endeavours to eliminate the extra-poetic or real support, and it is a matter of realizing the metaphor, of turning it into the poetic *res*' (Ortega y Gasset 2004–2010: III, 867). In *The Dehumanization of Art* he was to state:

> If now, instead of letting ourselves go in this direction of the proposal, we turn it on its head and, turning our back on so-called reality, we take the ideas as they are — mere subjective schemata — and we make them live as such, with their angular, frail, but transparent and pure profile — in short, if we set ourselves deliberately to realize the ideas, we will have dehumanized, de-realized, them. Because they are, in effect, unreality. To make them live in their very unreality is, shall we say, to realize the unreal inasmuch as it is unreal. Here we are not going from the mind to the world, but vice-versa, we give plasticity, we objectify, we worldify the schemata, the internal and the subjective. (Ortega y Gasset 2004–2010: III, 868)

As we can see from this brief review, Ortega highlights the concept of realization as a key element in the new art or what he himself called the 'new sensibility'. Realizing, then, is understood as a process of opening up or discovery of that which had remained outside the limits of discursive reason and where metaphor is able to offer a path or road to the appearance of that which is hidden. The differences between these two philosophers are important; nonetheless, the process or structure they use to support their ideas is strikingly similar. If we read Zambrano closely we see how this concept, realization, always appears in her texts linked to the process of the creation of a new world, as Ortega pointed out.

Zambrano wrote that poetry 'se acerca a esta realización del tiempo perdido' [approaches that *realization* of lost time] (2007a: 74); and that 'toda historia, la de España y la de cualquier otro lugar, sea en último término poesía, creación, *realización total*' [all history, that of Spain and of any other place, in the last instance is poetry, creation, *total realization*] (2015: 186); and at another time, in a text about García Lorca, she added, 'sólo siendo vivido [el sueño], trascendiéndose creadoramente-poéticamente, se *realiza*' [only if [the dream] is lived, creatively-poetically, is it *realized*] (2007a: 177). For our author, poetry is pure realization, that is, the creation of a new world. In other words, the opening-up of a lost reality.

But even earlier, in *Los intelectuales en el drama de España* [Intellectuals in the Drama of Spain], we see the proximity of Ortega's thought, which she then takes down a different road. When speaking of mystical literature, she writes:

> El místico ha realizado toda una revolución; se hace otro, se ha enajenado por entero; ha realizado la más fecunda destrucción, que es la destrucción de sí mismo, para que en este desierto, en este vacío, venga a habitar por entero otro; ha puesto en suspenso su propia existencia para que este otro se resuelva a existir en él. (Zambrano 2015: 289)

> [The mystic has carried out (realized) a whole revolution; he becomes another, he has been completely alienated; he has realized the most fertile destruction, which is the destruction of himself, so that in this desert, in this vacuum, another can come and inhabit it; he has suspended his own existence so that this other can resolve to exist in him.]

Where Ortega located the new art, Zambrano radicalizes the process and points towards mysticism, towards the poet through whom the revolution will take place. However, it would be in *Filosofía y poesía* [Philosophy and Poetry] where this reflection on the concept of realization as creation is observed in greater detail. There we read:

> Así, el poeta en su poema crea una unidad con la palabra, esa palabras que tratan de apresar lo más tenue, lo más alado, lo más distinto de cada cosa, de cada instante. El poema es ya la unidad no oculta, sino presente; la unidad realizada, diríamos encarnada. (Zambrano 2015: 694)

> [Thus, the poet in his poem creates a unity with the word, those words that try to capture what is most tenuous, what is most aerial, what is most different of each thing, of each instant. The poem is now the unity that is no longer concealed, but present; the realized unity, the incarnate unity, we could say.]

Here the poem is understood as a realized unity. When the poem is realized, it causes a glimmer, a flash of light that lets the reality hidden from us through the fault of discursive reason to show itself. To realize is to make be seen, to awaken. And this is a clear advance on Ortega's idea of realization which only served as a path to aesthetic enjoyment, to play. In this way Zambrano took Ortega's concept, as well as its operational structure, and applied it to her own project, that of poetic reason. The influence that she receives from Ortega and transforms is equally observable when referring to time. In contrast to the logos, in contrast to temporality and syntax, Zambrano chooses 'lo que se realiza y desrealiza en el tiempo' [what is realized and unrealized in time] (2015: 713). And in this same book she even highlights the work of two 'realizers' who could also be present in Ortega's thought: Valéry and Baudelaire. 'Y la razón de que esto ocurra es precisamente que el poeta se afirma en su poesía. Baudelaire, Valéry son realizadores y definidores, al par, de la "poesía pura"' [And the reason why this occurs is precisely because the poet affirms himself in his poetry. Both Baudelaire and Valéry are realizers and definers of 'pure poetry'] (2015: 745).

For Zambrano the concept of realization is not only understood as a way of generating *style* (as Ortega seems to emphasize) but rather as a way of making the journey or descent into the infernos. To realize (in the sense of poetic reason) is to make visible an experience and at the same time the possibility of generating a common sensibility. We read: 'El poeta se basta con hacer poesía para existir; es la forma más pura de realización de la esencia humana' [Poetry is all the poet needs to exist; it is the purest form of realizing the human essence] (2015: 745). And she adds: 'Y tan es así, que el poeta tiene ya su ética en la realización de su poesía' [So much so, that the poet already has his ethics in the realization of his poetry] (746). Realizing, in Zambrano's sense of the word, in short, points to a radical awareness of creation. Realizing is the form in which the poet descends into hell and returns in order to reveal an experience or make it visible, the experience of the sacred word, unpronounced. The poet descends into his past, crosses through his memory, liberates himself from time. 'La poesía busca realizar la inocencia, transformarla en vida y conciencia; en palabra, en eternidad' [Poetry seeks to realize innocence, to transform it into life and consciousness; into word, into eternity] (756). In other words, we may conclude that Zambrano's project implies a 'sueño que aspira a realizarse por virtud de la palabra poética' [dream that aspires to become realized by virtue of the poetic word] (746).

Notes to Chapter 6

1. All translations are my own unless otherwise stated.
2. At this point it is interesting to consider the possible influence of Heidegger on this aspect of Zambrano's thought. The connections may seem obvious at first: to think the unthinkable, opening up poetry as territory for reclamation of a new way of thinking, etc. Nonetheless, the distances have to do with the *finality*. In Heidegger we cannot leave to one side (and this is perhaps why Zambrano does not cite him much, as Ana Bundgaard points out) the fact that a National-Socialist impulse was at work in him. Poetry is the poetry of the German people, a desire to search for that legacy of the originary Greek in the poetry of Hölderlin, for example. As Philippe Lacoue-Labarthe (2002) points out, in Heidegger there is a marked nationalist aesthetic beating beneath his search for that originary poetry. Heidegger's Greek fantasy is linked to his desire to see in Hölderlin's poetry the originary rebirth of a culture that was capable of unveiling being. It is true that Heidegger repudiated Hitler's racism in 1934 (not in 1933), but he did so because he understood that the essence of Germany did not reside in biology or race but in a kind of originary gift. He makes this clear in his *Introduction to Metaphysics*: 'What is peddled about nowadays as the philosophy of National Socialism, but which has not the least to do with the inner truth and greatness of this movement [namely, the encounter between global technology and modern humanity] is fishing in these troubled waters of "values" and "totalities"' (Heidegger 2000: 213). Heidegger is trying to find that inner truth of National Socialism which deep down is going in search of an origin, a being, whose purpose is to legitimize domination. In this project, Hölderlin's poetry plays a key role for Heidegger. Poets, as we saw at the beginning, are meant to descend in order to offer mortals the road to a coming god. Therefore, although superficially Heidegger appeared to have an influence on Zambrano, this influence becomes vague and then fails as soon as their ideas on art and poetry

are confronted with the historical and political horizons from which their respective works were written.
3. This image can also be found in *Filosofía y poesía*: 'No sólo se conforma [el poeta] con las sombras de la pared cavernaria, sino que, sobrepasando su condena, crea sombras nuevas, y llega hasta a hablar de ellas y con ellas. Traiciona la razón usando su vehículo, la palabra, para dejar que por ella hablen las sombras, para hacer de ellas la forma del delirio' [Not only is [the poet] satisfied with the shadows on the cavern wall, but, overcoming his imprisonment, he creates new shadows and even speaks of them and with them. He betrays reason by using his vehicle, the word, to let the shadows speak through it, to make of them the form of delirium] (Zambrano 2015: 703).
4. In this sense the mask is not meant to be ornamental or contemplative, but rather an instrument of mediation. It will be later that the mask loses its originary sense and is transformed into an object of ludic contemplation. According to Zambrano, this art that she points to under the form of the mask (*máscara*) is understood as an instrument (but not in the technical sense) by which to enter into contact with types of realities that can only be accessed in this way, that is, by participating in their form. The mask is used as an other and to enter into another reality. However, 'no se trata de un conocimiento, sino de una *posesión*, de una apropiación de *algo* que el encontrarlo sea dejar que entre en nosotros o entrar nosotros en ello. Alimentarse y ofrecerse en alimento. La máscara es instrumento de trato con lo sagrado, y lo sagrado devora y es devorado' [it is not a matter of knowledge, but rather of *possession*, of an appropriation of *something* whose discovery means letting it into us or our entering into it. Feeding oneself and offering oneself as food. The mask is an instrument for dealing with the sacred, and the sacred devours and is devoured] (Zambrano 2012a: 30).

PART II

Identity and Representation

CHAPTER 7

Melancholy and Loss in María Zambrano's Journals

Goretti Ramírez, Concordia University

The ramifications of melancholy in Europe's cultural history are long and sinuous. It is possible to follow its trajectory from ancient Greece to the present day and find its manifestations across a spectrum of disciplines comprising astrology, medicine, philosophy, literature, art, history, psychology, and psychiatry, among others. Melancholy has thus been defined from diverse angles that, although contradictory at times, generally agree that the melancholic state is characterized by painful, permanent introspection. The cause of said state has been attributed to equally diverse circumstances. Based on observations by critics such as Jonathan Flatley (2008: 1) and Julia Kristeva (1989a: 6–8), for instance, melancholy can be due to an astrological conjunction (the influence of Saturn), a physiological disturbance (as in melancholia, an excess of black bile in the body's humours), a religious sin (acedia or indolence), or, in specific cases, an inability to overcome loss (of a loved one who has died, a primal figure from childhood, the poet's source word, or a historical juncture, to name but some).

For some contemporary critics, Jonathan Flatley and Sanja Bahun included, melancholy is an integral part of modernity. Indeed, European modernity favours the development of historical and philosophical frameworks that are particularly fertile for melancholic introspection, especially in the period arching from the second half of the nineteenth century to the end of the tumultuous twentieth century. The astrological, physiological, and religious causes of the melancholic state continue to be relevant in this period, but they receive less attention. In contrast, intense consideration is given to the examination and revision of the notion of loss, which has been historically bound to the origin of melancholy. In this sense, European modernity can be regarded as the expression of a melancholic world in more global facets, such as the crisis of the philosophy of history (Walter Benjamin), depression resulting from the breaking of significant links with the world (Julia Kristeva), or, on a more abstract plane, the disillusion that predominates in a world that failed to fulfil the promises of the project of the Enlightenment (Flatley 2008: 31).

In this context, it is striking to note the absence of studies about the thought of María Zambrano (1904–1991) within the context of Europe's cultural history of melancholy and, in particular, that of Spain. Certainly, a number of existing critical studies suggest a possible path to embark on. Thus, for example, María Zambrano's thought has been interpreted as the shipwreck of an initially more unified philosophical entity (Moreno Sanz 2008); as the philosophy of a modern world in crisis (Bundgaard 2000); as an attempt to recover a lost word (Valente 1978); or, on the plane of the empirical author's experience, as a reflection whose maturity is determined by her sister Araceli's death and the loss of Spain after exile. Nevertheless, despite the above considerations and even more recent ones (Gómez Blesa, in Zambrano 2015a; Moraga 2012), the growing literature on María Zambrano still lacks an inclusive study that locates and evaluates all such manifestations within the more comprehensive, unified framework of the cultural history of melancholy in Europe and Spain. Within said parameters, Zambranian thought functions as a suggestive catalyst that receives, transforms, and delivers this fertile cultural history.

As a first approach to the major task of locating and evaluating María Zambrano's thought within the framework of the cultural history of melancholy, this study proposes the reading of a limited, yet relevant textual corpus: her personal journals, written between 1928 and 1990, which remained unpublished almost in their entirety until 2014. María Zambrano's journals enable the identification and analysis of multiple manifestations of the painful, permanent introspection that has been constant in the description of melancholy across the centuries. The working hypothesis guiding this study is that Zambranian melancholic introspection ultimately responds to modernity's privileged vision of melancholy as a reaction to loss. In more concrete terms, in addition to establishing the recurrence of annotations about the loss of everyday objects and elements, it is possible to divide the melancholic lament in María Zambrano's journals into two groups of loss: the loss of loved ones; and the loss of meaning in an individual life, resulting from vital ruptures and discontinuities connected to the loss of meaning in the equally fractured history of modern Europe. In both cases, Zambranian thought suggests a critique of the solipsism inherent in melancholy as highlighted by critics such as Sigmund Freud and Julia Kristeva. Conversely, it is also more closely aligned with the communitarian sense and engagement in history that a critic such as Walter Benjamin sees as characteristic of melancholy. Starting from the analysis of María Zambrano's journals, melancholy reveals itself as a defining tool for an unexplored reading of her thought.

Melancholy: Introspection and Loss

The cultural history of melancholy in Europe runs across seemingly disparate centuries and disciplines: from ancient Greece to the present day, from the sciences to the humanities. Despite its diverse manifestations, attempted descriptions generally converge in presenting the melancholic as someone characterized by a state of painful, permanent introspection. However, although it is a paralyzing, abysmal mental state, since Aristotle it has been observed that the suffering of the melancholic temperament is also a creative constant among prominent figures in philosophy, politics, literature, and art (Flatley 2008: 1). María Zambrano is conscious of such a circumstance and observes that 'de cara a la plenitud siempre puede estar la melancolía. Esta mezcla paradójica de plenitud y melancolía es lo propio del héroe romántico' [in the face of plenitude, there can always be melancholy. This paradoxical mixture of plenitude and melancholy is a key characteristic of the romantic hero] (1933: 146).

The aetiology of the melancholic condition has changed throughout the centuries. Based on observations by critics such as Jonathan Flatley (2008: 1) and Julia Kristeva (1989a: 6–8), its underlying causes can be classified into four general, at times overlapping, categories: astrological, physiological, religious, and affective (a loss). Astrology, among others, is explored in the foundational *Saturn and Melancholy: Studies in the History of Natural Philosophy, Religion, and Art* (1964) by Raymond Klibansky, Erwin Panofsky, and Fritz Saxl. The volume analyzes the belief that the melancholic is born under the sign of the stern planet Saturn. The description of astrological influence on the sombre state of mind of the melancholic had been gathered by, for example, Marsilio Ficino (1433–1499) in his *Three Books on Life* (1489) and by Albrecht Dürer (1471–1528) in his engraving *Melencolia I* (1514). In contrast to the sense of cosmic destiny implied by astrological causes, physiological causes are imposed by a disturbance of bodily health that can (at least in theory) be healed — an excess of black bile, one of four elements comprising the system of humours underlying Hippocrates's synthesis of ancient Greek medical knowledge. A third category, acedia or indolence, posits a disease as well. The cause of melancholy is religious, a disease of the spirit considered sinful within Christian moral parameters, as it implies the introspection of a subject who has retreated from the world created by God.

The rise in the examination of the three causes of melancholy (astrology, physiology, and religion) took place mainly before modern times, though several cases can be found in the modern world. In the case of Spain, for example, they are present in intellectual contemporaries of María Zambrano such as Guillermo Díaz Plaja (1918–2012), who alludes to 'humor negro' [black humour] (1975: 27) in his *Tratado de las melancolías españolas* (1975) [Treatise of Spanish Melancholies]. Similarly, María Teresa León (1903–1988) describes how the protagonist of *Memory of Melancholy* (1970) 'se llenó de bilis hasta el borde' [became filled to the brim with bile] (1977: 80), while on a more allusive plane, Rosa Chacel (1898–1994) — who shares María Zambrano's interest in subjective introspection through confessional writing — chose the title *Saturnal* (1972) for one of her books of essays. All cases refer to a tendency that has gradually been overtaken by the consideration of loss as the principal cause of melancholy.

In contrast to this move away from an interest in the astrological, physiological, and religious causes of melancholy, modern times mainly explore the idea that the melancholic state is caused by loss. In his foundational 'Mourning and Melancholia' (1917), Sigmund Freud adopts a psychological approach to outline a number of the most influential principles in the consideration of loss as the root of melancholy: 'a profoundly painful depression, a loss of interest in the outside world, the loss of the ability to love, the inhibition of any kind of performance and a reduction in the sense of the self' (2005: 204). Mourning entails a further step, for it does not imply the internalization of loss leading to 'the disorder of self-esteem' (204), but rather, in a particularly relevant way, 'overcomes the loss of the object' (214). In the same vein as Freudian psychoanalysis of loss, Julia Kristeva delves into the affective and linguistic ambivalences of melancholy, which she connects with the black sun of modern depression and, more generally, with narcissism (1989a: 3–13).

Within this framework, the analysis of introspection found in autobiographical writing is particularly productive for the interpretation of literary and philosophical representations of melancholy. In the case of Spain, there is Gregorio Marañón (1887–1960), whom María Zambrano sees not as 'un médico a secas' [just a doctor], but as 'un conocedor, un pensador' [an expert, a thinker] (2014c: 735). He examines introspection in his diary *Amiel: un estudio sobre la timidez* (1933) [Amiel: A Study of Shyness], whose concerns are similar to those expressed in 'Sobre la melancolía involutiva' (1932) [On Reactionary Melancholia] published during the same period. However, although both Freud and Kristeva focus mainly on an analysis of melancholy as an introspective state, their critical approaches allude to the possibility of considering loss within a more collective socio-historical or epistemological framework. Indeed, Freud refers to a broader framework formed by 'the reaction to the loss of a beloved person, or an abstraction taking the place of the person, such as fatherland, freedom, an ideal and so on' (2005: 203). Melancholy can thus be considered as the reaction to not only individual and concrete loss, but also abstract or philosophical loss.

In this emphasis on the notion of loss, melancholy results from a state of introspection inherent in European modernity itself. In this sense, a number of contemporary scholars of melancholy highlight the close link between individual melancholy and losses resulting from the abrupt changes produced by modernity in all dimensions of social and historical life. Jonathan Flatley points at changes caused by industrialization to the traditional concepts of work, family, social organization, transport, migration, and technologies of war and destruction in general (2008: 30), as well as the depressive state experienced by the modern subject upon confirming that 'the utopian promises of modernity [...] are never fulfilled' (31). At the centre of this modern crisis of loss lies a sense of discontinuity and fragmentation derived from a constant barrage of what is new (Fritzsche 2011: 117; Gibson 2011: 102–03). In this way, in contrast to the traditional idea that the melancholic's isolation from the world is depressive and solipsistic, melancholy can paradoxically imply an interest in the world (Flatley 2008: 1–2) — a concern shared by María Zambrano, as her post-exile thought emerged, to a large extent, as a creative introspection intending to overcome the losses Europe had suffered after the wars and the failed promises of modernity: 'Ha desaparecido el mundo, pero el sentir que nos enraíza en él, no' [The world has disappeared, but the feeling that roots us in it has not] (2000a: 21).

Lastly, it is crucial to highlight the thought of Walter Benjamin (1892–1940) and its relevance within the parameters of modern melancholy as a reaction to loss. Three elements yield a particularly productive analysis. First, texts such as 'The Paris of the Second Empire in Baudelaire' (1938), 'Central Park' (1939), 'On Some Motifs in Baudelaire' (1940), and 'N [On the Theory of Knowledge, Theory of Progress]', among others, highlight the sense of inexorable change and destruction in the modern world. Such a circumstance is connected to a second element, exposed in works such as 'On the Concept of History' (1940): history, in its inexorable advance into the future, has left a number of minor fragments from the past that must be recovered and interpreted. Third, the analysis of *Trauerspiel* in *The Origin of German Tragic Drama* (1928) stresses the connection with the world fostered by melancholy and mourning: 'Mourning is the state of mind in which feeling revives the empty world in the form of a mask, and derives an enigmatic satisfaction in contemplating it' (1998: 139).

María Zambrano's Journals

María Zambrano's *oeuvre* represents a crucial episode in Europe's cultural history of melancholy and, in particular, in Spanish culture of the twentieth century. Since the publication of his 'Del conocimiento pasivo o saber de quietud' [Of Passive Knowledge or the Wisdom of Stillness'] in 1978, the poet and critic José Ángel Valente notes the importance of the notion of loss in understanding María Zambrano's thought, particularly when he underlines her search for the lost word. Nonetheless, this dimension of her work has rarely been the subject of critical study, although a number of studies in recent literature have suggested isolated points for possible exploration. Among them, Ana Bundgaard, in *Más allá de la filosofía: sobre el pensamiento filosófico-místico de María Zambrano* (2000), identifies the experience of modern crisis as one of the foundations of Zambrano's reflection on the 'proceso de destrucción y desintegración de lo humano' [process of destruction and disintegration of the human] (Bundgaard 2000: 258). Similarly, starting with the subtitle of his work *El logos oscuro: tragedia, mística y filosofía en María Zambrano. El eje de 'El hombre y lo divino', los inéditos y los restos de un naufragio* (2008), Jesús Moreno Sanz takes up the idea that María Zambrano's work is given to the reader as if it were the debris of a shipwreck. In the same book he points out that what is lost is central to the nucleus of her thought: 'Es, pues, "la ausencia", como un *algo* que se ha ido irremediablemente en la cultura europea, lo que propulsa este pensar y la raíz misma de la *razón poética*' [It is, therefore, 'absence', as a *something* that has irretrievably departed from European culture, that propels this thinking and the very root of *poetic reason*] (Moreno Sanz 2008: 74). In the same vein, Pablo Moraga's doctoral thesis 'El género de la guía en María Zambrano' includes a few, yet explicit pages regarding the role of melancholy in Zambranian thought (2012: 69–81). In a more recent example, Mercedes Gómez Blesa places Zambrano's *Pensamiento y poesía en la vida española* (1939) within a Spanish tradition of melancholy (Zambrano 2015: 527 & 541).

As outlined in the recent literature, therefore, the advancement of a more global interpretation of the contribution of María Zambrano's thought to the cultural history of melancholy, and vice versa, namely the traces left by the cultural heritage of melancholy on María Zambrano's thought, is necessary. An analysis of her journals opens an avenue for highly productive critical analysis to delineate and briefly introduce the project. Although they remained unpublished almost in their entirety until 2014, María Zambrano's journals constitute a corpus of texts of paramount importance: they traverse her entire intellectual trajectory from 1928 to 1990, thus enabling the observation of how a number of her philosophical and vital concerns evolved, including the various dimensions of melancholy. In particular, they offer numerous displays of the two main concepts linked to modern melancholy: introspection and loss.

The introspective character of María Zambrano's journals is determined by the very nature of the journal, which, according to Alan Girard, is intimately connected to the development of modern subjectivity (1963: xi). Jean Rousset (1983) observes that, even in cases where a journal has an external interlocutor or when published, it has no other recipient than the writer herself. In 'El diario de otro' (1989) [The Other's Journals], one of her last reflections about her work, María Zambrano considers that her journals have served as a point of departure from which to develop more elaborate thoughts for later publication:

> Nada había allí que diese brillo a los llamados escondrijos del alma y menos todavía a ilusorios secretos íntimos. No había nada que revelar. La única revelación, la mía, es que yo tenía que trabajar y trabajar a partir de mis cuadernos, pues para eso eran. (Zambrano 2014c: 776)
>
> [There was nothing in there that would shine a light on the so-called secret places of the soul, and even less on illusory intimate secrets. There was nothing to reveal. The only revelation, mine, was that I had to work and work from my notebooks. That's what they were for.]

However, María Zambrano's journals clearly show as well the self-referential nature of modern journals, as they contain fragments of intimate reflections that may prove hermetic even for the expert reader. Next to fragments that gather reflections on positive life experiences, it is thus possible to find numerous examples that chart the chronological development of a subject in a state of painful, permanent — and, in fact, abysmal — introspection. From a note dated 28 December, c. 1933, she laments that 'la nada se agiganta en torno, alrededor, me gana' [the void becomes gigantic on all sides, all around, overcomes me] (2014c: 219), in an awareness of failure that intensifies on 31 December 1948, with a characterization of her own life as having 'ya devenida, ya desvelado su enigma en el dolor y en el fracaso de cuanto de ella esperaba' [already occurred, already revealed its enigma in the pain and failure of everything I expected from it] (320). On 19 November 1960, she notes down a sensation of 'hundimiento que no me atrevo a decir "máximo", por si llegan aún otros más hondos' [sinking I do not dare to call 'deepest', in case even deeper ones arrive] (435). Similarly, on 24 July 1973, she records feeling 'muy desolada y llena de dolor' [devastated and filled with pain] (514). In her last journal entry, dated 8 November 1990, she comments on the risk of succumbing to 'la vana esperanza' [false hope] (799).

The reasons that lead to such a painful and permanent introspection are diverse. Ultimately, they are linked with a feeling of solitude that, as demonstrated by Roberta Johnson (2013), traverses the entire Zambranian trajectory. Within the more global framework of the cultural history of melancholy, where various reasons have been examined for the melancholic state of mind (mainly astrological, physiological, religious, or affective), this facet of the journals corresponds to the idea that melancholy emerges as a reaction to loss. Entries from late 1933 read: 'Nada de lo que se hace, de lo que se gana, queda prendido al ser para siempre, incorporado al mundo de lo que es [...]. Sombras, huecos, ausencia; ausencia siempre. Sé de las cosas por el hueco que dejan' [Nothing that one does, that one gains, remains attached to one's being forever, incorporated into the world to which it belongs [...]. Shadows, gaps, absence; always absence. I know of things because of the gaps they leave behind] (2014c: 217–20). Within the parameters of this consideration of melancholy that has predominated in modern times, María Zambrano's journals introduce reflections on different types of loss. In addition to recurring references to the loss of objects and everyday objects, the melancholic lament in these journals can be articulated in two groups of losses: the loss of loved ones (people and a cat) who have died, leading to a stage of mourning; and the loss of meaning in an individual life that seems discontinuous and broken, a loss that is ultimately connected to the loss of meaning in the equally fractured history of modern Europe.

Albeit in a subtle, sporadic way, throughout the years, María Zambrano's journals gradually develop the notion that life is generally marked by a succession of different types of losses: 'estoy sujeta a la privación y al despojo' [I am subject to hardship and loss] (2014c: 436), reads an entry from 30 January 1961. A significant case is the lost key, mentioned in outlines for her project 'El umbral' [The Threshold] of 22 April 1954: 'Se me ha perdido la llave... Pero yo tenía, creo, una llave. Si la recobrara, estoy seguro de poder responder a esas preguntas [...]. Yo he perdido el pensamiento' [I have lost the key... But I had, I think, a key. If I were to find it, I am sure I would be able to answer those questions [...]. I have lost the thought] (354–55). The loss of that key, which appears in dreams but is impossible to reach, becomes the point of departure for a reflection on the fleeting nature of life and thought dated 29 May 1955:

> No es que la llave que se me aparece así, distante, esté realmente separada de mí por ese centímetro. Es que no coexiste conmigo, está en otra esfera. Por eso cuando la fui a tocar se desvaneció, o bien me desperté. Es que no estaba en mi tiempo ni en mi espacio.
> Lo fugitivo es la coincidencia de lo que no está en nuestra esfera existencial. ¿Y qué hay en nuestra vida de no fugitivo?
> Hasta el conocimiento es *fugitivo*.
> ¿Qué es lo nuestro? (Zambrano 2014c: 383)
>
> [It's not that the key appearing to me in this way, distant, is truly separated from me by that centimetre. It does not coexist with me, it is in another sphere. That is why when I went to touch it, it vanished, or I woke up. It was not in my time or in my space.
> What is fugitive is the coincidence of what is not in our existential sphere.

And what is in our life that is not fugitive?
Even knowledge is *fugitive*.
What is ours?]

In this sense, the impossibility of recovering what has been lost proves to be a revealing experience in apprehending the ultimate meaning of existence and philosophy. The same experience repeats itself in other moments in which a dialectic develops between what is possessed in the present and what has been possessed and later lost (perhaps unknowingly) in the past: 'Ese billete del cual me han dado la vuelta, y sólo entonces supe que yo había dado el billete antes' [That note from which they gave me change, and only then did I realize I had handed over the note before] (2014c: 386); a flower offered in dreams 'como si me tuviese que dar cuenta de que era mía o algo de mí' [as if I had to realize that it was mine or something of me] (426); or a silver cross with diamonds at a store in Rome, 'Traía el dinero, pero ¿cómo entrar a comprarla? Me entristecí porque no veo cómo pueda ser mía, llegar a mi poder' [I had the money with me, but could I walk in and buy it? I was saddened because I can't see how it could be mine, come into my possession] (436–37). In addition to the loss of those everyday objects, an entry from 21 July 1954 reports the disappearance of her cat Zampuico on the streets of Rome, an event that brings both María Zambrano and her sister Araceli 'al borde de la locura' [to the edge of madness] (362).

In the context of this life marked by successive losses, annotations regarding the death of beloved persons and a cat comprise a first revealing group. María Zambrano's journals gather melancholic laments for the death of loved ones: her father Blas Zambrano in 1938 (252–53); her mother Araceli Alarcón in 1946, but evoked in 1974 (548); Bianquina, her cat, in 1960 (435); her sister Araceli Zambrano in 1972 (499); Alfonso Costafreda in 1974 (546); and Rafael Dieste in 1981 (630). Such an impulse also develops in other texts in which she evokes and pays homage to teachers and friends who have died, mainly in separate articles more elaborate than her journal entries: Manuel Azaña, José Bergamín, Julián Besteiro, Rosa Chacel, Miguel Hernández, José Herrera Petere, Antonio Machado, Gregorio Marañón, José Ortega y Gasset, and Miguel de Unamuno, amongst others.

Entries about the deaths of her father and sister, beyond fostering access to circumstances in which María Zambrano the empirical author faces bereavement, offer a particularly productive critical analysis within the framework of melancholy. The melancholic note about the loss of the father recreates a situation in which the daughter takes her father's pen after his death and, recalling what his hand was like, details the qualities of strength, knowledge, honesty, and cordiality of the paternal figure. Zambranian thought thus defends the importance of something it will refer to as the 'principio sagrado de la paternidad' [sacred principle of paternity] (1987a: 143), two years later, in 'El freudismo, testimonio del hombre actual' (1940). Indeed, in its criticism of Freud's thinking, the 1940 text points at the gravity of denying being 'ligado y obligado' [bound and obliged] (143) with regard to the paternal figure:

El 'freudismo' al deshacer la idea del padre y, más que la idea, la trascendencia de la paternidad, no hace sino completar la obra de todas las demás teorías que han ido cortando los hilos que mantenían al hombre enlazado con sus principios, supeditado a sus orígenes [...]. Y al ser así, ¿no será que al dejar de ser hijos dejemos también de ser hombres? (Zambrano 1987a: 147–48)

['Freudianism', by undoing the idea of the father and, beyond the idea, the transcendence of paternity, basically completes the work of all the other theories that have cut the threads that kept human beings connected to their beginnings, subordinated to their origins [...]. And, for that matter, could it be that when we stop being sons and daughters, we also stop being human beings?]

Mourning Blas Zambrano thus implies not only a step towards overcoming melancholy, but also an indication of the necessity in human life to maintain its sacred and, ultimately, religious bonds. That is, melancholic introspection not as a solipsistic retreat from the world, but as a state that enables a connection with something higher. Mourning the dead is necessary, and it is carried out by the ritual of taking the father's pen (2014c: 252–53), dedicating a book to the mother (548), or paying for the burial of the sister (585). The pain after the death of Bianquina the cat (435) is located within the same necessity of mourning in order to recover the human sense of community. Mourning animals in the modern world can indeed be interpreted as opposition to the Cartesian and Darwinist dehumanizing effect that prevents recognition of the other (Schiesari 2011: 224). In this sense, it is similarly inscribed within the criticism of rationalist and individualist philosophy that suffuses all of Zambranian thought.

Entries dedicated to the mourning of her sister Araceli cover aspects such as joy or consolation upon understanding that she 'ha muerto para seguir viviendo' [has died in order to keep on living] (2014c: 499), the memory of her stay at the clinic (500–01), and reflections on limits between life and death on a day she finds herself 'muy desolada y llena de dolor por la partida y por la ausencia de Araceli' [deeply devastated and filled with pain by Araceli's departure and absence] (514). Mourning manifests as well in the expression of a feeling of guilt at not having previously understood the sacred meaning of her sister's life:

> Y ésa mi culpa [...].
> Y de ahí mi falta de constancia en el amor, en la dulzura indispensable, en la ternura, de ahí... todo este desastre [...].
> Pido perdón.
> Perdón, perdón.
> A ella, a Giovanni, a Araceli, a mis padres. (Zambrano 2014c: 500)

> [And that is my offence [...].
> Hence my lack of resolve in love, in the indispensable gentleness, in tenderness, hence... all of this disaster [...].
> I ask for forgiveness.
> Forgive me, forgive me.
> I ask her, Giovanni, Araceli, my parents.]

This mourning, again, enables a contrast between Freud's thinking, who observes that the melancholic shows feelings of guilt and self-blame, an implication that blame towards the lost object (person) has been internalized by the ego through a process of introjection (2005: 207–08). In María Zambrano's journals, in contrast, self-blame occurs within the most intense manifestation of a 'inspiración de la hermana' [sister's inspiration] (2014c: 511). The recognition of the bond with the absent one then brings about the beginning of a new creative phase of life during which the 'itinerario verdadero de *Notas de un método*' [true itinerary of *Notas de un método*] (513) and the inspiration for the Islamic writings (514) are created, in an echo of that which is expressed in *La confesión, género literario y método* (1943): 'La vida deja de ser pesadilla cuando se ha restablecido el vínculo filial, cuando hemos encontrado al Padre, pero también a los hermanos' (2011a: 64) ('Life ceases to be a nightmare when the filial bond is re-established, when we find our Father, but also our brothers', Zambrano and Chacel 2015: 37). In the same vein, the death of Bianquina the cat in 1960 had already brought about the beginning of 'una nueva fase' [a new phase] (2014c: 435).

The second group of losses in Zambranian journals is comprised of references to losses that go beyond the individual and point towards collective losses in European and Spanish history in the twentieth century. The life of María Zambrano, the empirical author, was subject to constant ruptures, especially after an exile in which — as noted on 3 February 1940, one of her first journal entries after her departure from Spain in 1939 — she considers herself a 'survivor' (2014c: 259): 'yo ya he saltado y más de una vez' [I have already leaped, and more than once] (415), she later reflects in an entry dated 9–10 January 1957. In that mode of 'vivir el tiempo discontinuamente, como a saltos' [living time discontinuously, as if by leaps] in a life marked by losses (2011d: 401) the 'saber de experiencia' [knowledge from experience] starts to blossom (2014c: 677): it is a discontinuous, experiential knowledge that challenges 'tiempo sucesivo, discursivo que constriñe el original ímpetu en busca de algo perdido de la memoria' [successive, discursive time that constrains the original impulse in search of something that has been lost from memory] (1987c: 121). Journal entries thus leave records of the discontinuity in an individual life whose ultimate meaning, in principle, may seem lost.

The fractured discourse in María Zambrano's journals becomes an effective strategy to reflect upon the equally discontinuous character of modern melancholic discourse, which laments the loss of continuity in the meaning of the world. According to Sanja Bahun, the sensation of void and lost roots of the modern subject leads to strategies such as 'the obsessive partitioning of the text' (2014: 32), parataxis (66), ellipsis (66) and 'gaps [which] serve as performative embodiments of the melancholic hole that both promises the return of lost objects and precludes their reappearance; and thus as a good analogue for some irretrievables of received history' (199). These journals can thus be read as a materialization of the Zambranian ruins, as they give testimony of a destruction that is simultaneously individual and collective:

> Y así, las ruinas nos darían el punto de identidad entre el vivir personal –entre la personal historia– y la historia. Persona es lo que ha sobrevivido a la destrucción de todo en su vida y aún deja entrever que, de su propia vida, un sentido superior a los hechos les hace cobrar significación y conformarse en una imagen. (Zambrano 2011d: 257)

[And thus, the ruins would give us the point of identity between a personal life –between the personal history– and history. Person is what has survived the destruction of everything in their life and still allows a glimpse that, from their own life, a higher meaning makes facts gain significance and makes them take shape into an image.]

To refer to this interweaving of the individual with the historical, María Zambrano coins the term 'personal historia universal' [universal personal history] (2014c: 273) in a speech given on 18 July 1945, in which she develops an intention summarized in one sentence in her journals from *c.* late May, 1947: 'Transformar la propia vida en historia' [To transform one's own life into history] (284).

The journals thus converge with the conception of a melancholic modernity of the twentieth century that laments the ruptures and losses produced in the collective history due to wars, industrialization, and the constant irruption of what is new (Flatley 2008: 30; Fritzsche 2011: 117; Gibson 2011: 102–03). This concern clearly inscribes María Zambrano's thought within the context of twentieth-century European philosophy, according to a conception of history present in books by María Zambrano such as *La agonía de Europa* (1945): 'Las últimas creaciones europeas se caracterizaban por ser obras en que se ejecutaba una destrucción, en que se verificaba un perdimiento [...]. Nada íntegro, nada entero' [The latest European creations were characterized by being works in which a destruction was carried out, in which a loss was verified [...]. Nothing whole, nothing complete] (2000a: 32).

The correspondence between the personal and the historical in María Zambrano's journals is once again in dialogue with the reflections about melancholy that can be derived from Walter Benjamin's writings. As Jonathan Flatley points out, melancholy in Walter Benjamin 'is no longer a personal problem requiring cure or catharsis, but is evidence of the historicity of one's subjectivity, indeed the very substance of that historicity' (2008: 3). On the other hand, in addition to reflections on the rupture implied by the irruption of the new in modernity (developed mainly in texts about Baudelaire and the modern city), 'On the Concept of History' (1940) draws attention to the need for history to recover the heterogeneous remains that, as ruins, it has gradually lost in its inexorable and lineal advance towards the future: 'nothing that ever happened should be regarded as lost to history' (Benjamin 2003: 390). On 8 February 1957, at a moment in which Zambranian journals consist of a succession of annotations and outlines with no apparent development, the possibility of preserving what has been outlined (instead of allowing it to be lost) reveals a direction for the future: 'Una nueva idea: dejar estas cuartillas como testimonio del hacerse de una, del proceso de creación en el pensamiento' [A new idea: to leave these pages as testimony of an idea in the making, of the process of creation in thought] (Zambrano 2014c: 419).

Walter Benjamin sets forth an idea of particular interest for the interpretation of that ultimate *raison d'être* for María Zambrano's journals. With regard to the angel of history, who looks towards what has been lost with the gaze of a melancholic, but is impelled to leap into the future, Benjamin expounds:

> His face is turned toward the past [...]. The angel would like to stay, awaken the dead, and make whole what has been smashed. But a storm is blowing from

Paradise and has got caught in his wings [...]. This storm drives him irresistibly into the future, to which his back is turned, while the pile of debris before him grows toward the sky. What we call *progress* is this storm (Benjamin 2003: 392).

In María Zambrano's journals, the melancholic lament for what has been lost leads to a situation similar to that of the angel of history. In an entry from 28 December, *c.* 1933, the individual loss of God refers to a greater loss in a life divided between the past and the future:

> Si he perdido a Dios, ¿cómo entonces no acabo de irme, ya que siempre estoy yéndome, mas sin acabar? [...] la vida misma es en su esencia forzosidad de huir, perentoria fuga, incontenida ansia. Si me detengo un momento, mi vida rebota hacia atrás, lanzada como iba hacia adelante, rebota y se hace recuerdo, inmersión en el pasado [...]. Todo es en nuestra vida proceso inacabado, frustrado mejor [...] ¿podré decir, podremos decir que hemos perdido de veras, de veras, a Dios? No, no pierdo a lo único que puede perderme, a lo único que puedo perderme si no gano, en quietud, a la nada. (Zambrano 2014c: 219–20)

> [If I have lost God, how is it that I haven't left already, since I am always leaving, but without putting an end to it? [...] life itself is in its essence a compulsion to flee, peremptory flight, uncontained yearning. If I stop for a moment, my life bounces back, from being launched forward, it bounces and becomes memory, immersion in the past [...]. Everything in our life is unfinished process, failed, rather [...] could I say, could we say that we have truly, truly lost God? No, I am not losing the only thing that can lose me, the only thing I can lose if I don't overcome, in stillness, the void.]

As it happens with the impulse for spiritualization that can be deduced from the loss of loved ones who die, the experience of loss here enables once again the transcendence into another ontological and epistemological state. It corresponds to an impulse to transcend into the divine and religious that equally characterizes the ruins in *El hombre y lo divino*:

> Algo alcanza la categoría de ruina cuando su derrumbe material sirve de soporte a un sentido que se extiende triunfador; supervivencia, no ya de lo que fue, sino de lo que no alcanzó a ser [...]. De toda ruina emana algo divino. (Zambrano 2011d: 258–59)

> [Something reaches the category of ruin when its material collapse serves to support a sense that extends triumphantly; survival, no longer of what it had been, but of what it could not be [...]. Something divine emanates from every ruin.]

Melancholic introspection after loss, far from always entailing a retreat from the world, tends towards a more immediate vital, historical consideration of reality. For instance, the introspection contained in the first journal entry, on 29 June 1930, expresses it thus:

> Los valores propios son de uno porque en uno mismo están, porque dentro de sí uno los ha encontrado, pero no por otra cosa. Entonces, ¿qué inconveniente que vuelvan a la vida que los creó y nos los dio? Pero da mucho miedo quedarse vacío y mejor es, vida, que me lleves en ti, que me absorbas. (Zambrano 2014c: 199)

[One's own values belong to oneself because they live in one's self, because one has found them within one's self and not for any other reason. Then, why should they not return to the life that created and gave them to us? But it is frightening to be left empty and it is better for you, life, to take me within you, for you to absorb me.]

More relevant, fragments related to the loss of God from *c.* December 1933-January 1934 end with drawings that include the words *pathos* and *apatheia* (which, in some senses are in dialogue with the melancholic acedia) and a declaration of attachment to the world:

Hoy se inicia tras el fragmentarismo pasado. (Hubo una vez un mundo y se disolvió en análisis.) Hoy nos toca construir, montar otra vez el mundo, aglutinar la sociedad [...] nuestra raíz vuelve a hundirse en la vida profunda y cambiante y firme a la vez, y no en la transparente y estéril razón [...]. Que la política sea, la nuestra, no carcasa vacía, sorda al rumor de la vida, sino antena receptora de las ideas [...]. Afirmamos la vida; [...] afirmamos el individuo y sus derechos. (Zambrano 2014c: 223)

[Today begins after the fragmentalism of the past. (Once there was a world and it dissolved into analysis.) Today we must build, to assemble the world again, agglutinate society [...] our root buries itself again deep into life, at once changing and firm, and not into transparent, sterile reason [...]. Let politics be our politics, not an empty shell, deaf to life's murmurs, but an antenna receiving ideas [...]. We affirm life; [...] we affirm individuals and their rights.]

The introspection of Zambranian melancholy does not lead thus to the depressive, narcissistic state of the melancholic that Freud and Kristeva point to, but in an interest in the world as observed by Jonathan Flatley in the modern melancholic (2008: 1–2). Here Zambranian melancholy remains intimately connected with Walter Benjamin's thought, for whom melancholy 'betrays the world for the sake of knowledge', while 'mourning' occurs out of loyalty to the things of that very world (Benjamin 1998: 157). Similarly, melancholy and mourning enable a connection with the world in the *Trauerspiel*: 'Mourning is the state of mind in which feeling revives the empty world in the form of a mask, and derives an enigmatic satisfaction in contemplating it' (139).

Towards a Reading of María Zambrano's Melancholic Work

The analysis of María Zambrano's journals within the framework of the cultural history of melancholy opens up a new perspective from which to understand the modernity of her thought. The representation of melancholic introspection inscribes her thinking within the idea privileged by modernity of melancholy as a reaction to an experience of loss. In addition to numerous references to lost everyday objects and elements, her melancholic lament is articulated within two groups of losses: the loss of loved ones, which causes a process of mourning that leads to the recovery of the connection with the sacred or the divine; and the loss of meaning in an individual life subject to ruptures and discontinuities, leading to a collective loss of meaning in the equally fractured modern European history. In both cases, María

Zambrano's journals suggest a criticism of the solipsism inherent in melancholy maintained by thinkers such as Sigmund Freud and Julia Kristeva, and approaches instead a more communitarian sense and an interest in the world and history found in the notion of melancholy as set forth by thinkers such as Walter Benjamin.

The preceding analysis of María Zambrano's journals offers a contribution for future studies to interpret the significance of melancholy in her work overall. Possibilities for critical exploration worth noting include at least two. On the one hand, Zambrano's melancholic introspection, far from plunging into Ortega y Gasset's self-absorption or Freud's narcissism, points instead toward a notion of being defined by its connection to the other and that which is other. Melancholy thus enables access to another dimension of criticism of rationalist individualism developed by Zambrano throughout her entire body of work, in a gradual deepening into communitarian sense as an integral part of being human. As Roberta Johnson points out, Zambrano's thought attempts to overcome Sartre's dichotomy between the *en soi* (amorphous, inaccessible being) and the *pour soi* (being in the world) (Johnson 2015: 178) and, in dialogue with Unamuno's thought, it seeks 'a place for the emotions in explaining human life' (179). Could the intimate discourse of Zambranian melancholy also be a space from which to consider the fractures between self and other? 'La confesión solamente se verifica con la esperanza de que lo que no es uno mismo aparezca [...]. Todo el que hace una confesión es en espera de recobrar algún paraíso perdido' (Zambrano 2011a: 52 & 58) ('Confession is only substantiated with the hope that what is not one's self might appear [...]. Anyone who makes a confession is hoping to recover some lost paradise', Zambrano and Chacel 2015: 27 & 32), María Zambrano observes in *La confesión: género literario y método* (1943).

On the other hand, the melancholic lament in these journals enables an appreciation and refinement of the axial character of what is lost and what is absent for an interpretation of Zambranian thought. In particular, most of the literature expounding on the nature of poetry and art in Zambranian thought has stressed the importance granted to the connection with the world. However, this aspect remains as of yet unconnected to melancholy in all its dimensions and details. For example, *Filosofía y poesía* (1939) highlights the melancholy of the poet (2015: 756), who maintains a bond with the world, in contrast with the philosopher, who lives separated from that same world. It is 'melancolía, lenta fiebre, angustia y hasta agonía' [melancholy, slow fever, anguish and even agony] for matter which likewise defines the poet in a text such as 'Pablo Neruda o el amor a la materia' (1938) (2015: 259), as well as the artist in 'Apuntes sobre el tiempo y la poesía' (1942) [Notes on Time and Poetry]: 'El arte parece ser el empeño por descifrar o perseguir una forma perdida de existencia' [Art seems to be a commitment to decipher or pursue a lost form of existence] (2004b: 45). The Zambranian poet and the artist are defined, in sum, by their melancholy.

Similarly, the sense of loss in the same melancholic lament is crucial for understanding works such as *Pensamiento y poesía en la vida española* (1939) [Thought and Poetry in Spanish Life], which express 'la melancolía inmensa de vivir entre fantasmas, sombras y espejismos' [the immense melancholy of living among ghosts, shadows, and mirages] (2015: 565) which European rationalist philosophy attempted to escape, in contrast with the poetic acceptance of melancholy in Spanish thought. In *Pensamiento y poesía en la vida española,* that melancholy is connected to a way of experiencing temporality and, to a great extent, to reflections on the loss of the empire. As Ricardo Krauel demonstrates, the consideration of melancholy and mourning of what is lost proves to be crucial when interpreting the Spanish crisis at the political and historical juncture between the nineteenth and twentieth centuries (2013: 83–123). Could this dimension of Zambranian melancholy also be a dialogue with the imperial thinking of the so-called 'Generation of '98'? 'Cuando se dice que algo está ausente es para afirmarlo, aunque sea en negativo' [One says something is absent in order to affirm it, albeit in the negative] (1988c: 7), María Zambrano sentences in 'Ausencia y presencia' (1988) [Absence and Presence].

CHAPTER 8

La tumba de Antígona: Psychoanalysis and Feminism

Xon de Ros, University of Oxford

> My sorrow is the hidden face of my philosophy, her mute sister.
> JULIA KRISTEVA, *Tales of Love*[1]

In 1943 the Falangist journal *Escorial* included an essay entitled 'Antígona y el tirano o la inteligencia en la política' [Antigone and the Tyrant or Political Intelligence] written by the classicist Antonio Tovar whose edition of Sophocles's *Antigone* had been published a year earlier.[2] In the article Tovar follows Hegel's reading of the play which acknowledges the validity of both the instinctive right of the family ties represented by Antigone and the rational right of the state embodied by Creon. While for Hegel it is the absoluteness of the claim of each of these forces that leads to the tragedy, Tovar's sympathy is clearly for Creon's 'revolutionary reason' against Antigone's appeal to the equalizing laws of Hades, identifying her voice with superstition and the irrational. The gender alignment is unequivocal: 'Lo más varonil que hay es la razón revolucionaria, como, por el contrario, la tradición, el respeto a las normas irracionales, la piedad, es lo más femenino' [Revolutionary reason is the epitome of masculinity whereas tradition, respect for irrational norms, piety, are that of femininity] (1960: 24). Tovar's reading departs from Sophocles's text where Creon is portrayed as an unjust, misogynist ruler whose failure to integrate family rights within the political sphere results in tragedy. Sophocles's partiality for Antigone is attributed by Tovar to the democratic ethos of the ancient Greek *polis* which he describes as 'religiosa, matriarcal, supersticiosa, tradicional, mítica, hereditaria, oscura' [religious, matriarchal, superstitious, traditional, mythical, hereditary, obscure] (19). For the secular totalitarian ideology of the early Falange, the political heroine of non-violent civil disobedience represents a hysterical reactionary, a slave to ancestral obscurantist forces and a deranged individual. Tovar remarks that 'varias veces en la tragedia la heroína cruza la escena como alucinada, con una firmeza extraña, hablando cosas que ya no son de este mundo, con obsesiones maternales, preocupada por su virginidad, con que no dejaba descendencia' [several times in the tragedy the heroine crosses the stage as if stunned, with a strange determination, talking of things that are no longer of this world, obsessing about maternity, worried about her virginity, about not leaving any offspring] (26).

It is unsettling to detect echoes of Tovar's condemnation, this time from the other end of the political spectrum, directed at the Spanish philosopher María Zambrano. The critic Jonathan Mayhew deplores the influence of her 'poetic irrationalism' on late modernist poets such as José Ángel Valente and some unnamed 'younger women poets' for fostering pre-logical forms of knowledge and 'a regression to womb-like origins' (2012: 77). Mayhew traces Zambrano's poetic mysticism back to the tradition of Spanish mystics, equating her to a number of her contemporaries such as Unamuno, Antonio Machado, Juan Ramón Jiménez, and García Lorca, setting this mysticism in opposition to 'teleologies of linear progress' and 'secular forms of modernity' represented by the 'decisively philo-Germanic José Ortega y Gasset, who emphasized Enlightenment transparency and rationality' (78).[3] While any assessment of Zambrano's work turns inevitably on her relation to Ortega, under whose aegis she started her career and to whom she explicitly refers on several occasions, her formulation of a 'razón poética' [poetic reason] represents a distinctive departure from her mentor's *raciovitalismo* [vitalist reason]. Moreover, according to Mayhew, her critique of rationalism is inflected by a politics of national essentialism which links her 'razón poética' to Lorca's concept of 'duende' and Unamuno's 'intrahistoria', all rooted in 'forms of thought resistant to modernity' (2012: 98). The critic doesn't consider, though, the gender politics which are also fundamental for an understanding of Zambrano's phenomenology.

Most commentators of Zambrano's work feel compelled to note her distance from feminism, without pointing out exactly in what ways this is so or which feminist positions she takes issue with. While there is a general acknowledgement that her work shows a concern with women's consciousness, much of the critical discussion around her gender ideology reveals attitudes to feminism which seem to be out-of-date or misconstrued, self-contradictory, and occasionally openly hostile.[4] In any case, the exceptionality of her status as a female intellectual is in itself a feminist statement and the reasons adduced should not necessarily disqualify her work from feminist analysis. Those are variously based on the fact that the dialogue sustained throughout her work is mostly with male philosophers and rarely includes women writers, that she adopts the universal subject position marked as male, and that her declarations with regard to her own stance vis-à-vis feminism have at times been unambiguous.[5] In fact these attitudes can equally apply to the French philosopher Julia Kristeva and certainly in her case that has not hindered her inclusion in and contribution to feminist debate.[6]

Zambrano shares with Kristeva a fascination with 'madness, holiness and poetry', in particular with their transgressive potential regarding binary oppositions.[7] Arguably, Kristeva's vision of the liberation of the subject which entails, just as for Zambrano, superseding sexual difference may be problematic for a feminist agenda. From this perspective we can understand statements such as Clare E. Nimmo's that 'any attempt to infiltrate Zambrano into the ranks of European feminist thinkers is set to fail, and critics of her work have shown a degree of judiciousness by side-stepping the feminist question' (1997: 893). Despite her caveat, Nimmo goes on to establish a correspondence between Zambrano's concept of 'razón poética' and Hélène Cixous's theorization of a female aesthetic predicated on metaphorical thinking and poetic writing, both formulated as utopian potentialities. While the lack of gender specificity in Zambrano's formulation distinguishes it from Cixous's theories, her own poetics can be associated with Cixous's conception of 'écriture féminine' in her 1976 essay 'The Laugh of the Medusa'. But perhaps a closer connection can be established with Luce Irigaray with whom Zambrano shares an interest in images of women in Greek mythology which they turn into metaphors to interrogate woman's position in the patriarchal order. Among these, Athena becomes for both a mouthpiece for masculine values. A motherless daughter who conceals her femininity and rejects sexuality and motherhood, she also represents science and philosophical knowledge in the Greek pantheon. Zambrano reproaches Athena for her collusion with an order that dictates her own containment and suppression:

> Te admiran los hombres que hacen las leyes, los que fabrican las razones, te dejas engañar bobalicona por todos los Creones que vengan. [...] Virgen impotente. Torre de frío cristal, los hombres pasan sobre ti siempre, y tú, sin enterarte, escondida aurora que no luce, [...] Pobre niña obligada a saber, vete, nada puedes. Escondida en la luz de tu Padre, tímida. Aurora, ¡algún día serás rescatada! (Zambrano 2012b: 273–74)[8]
>
> [You are admired by the men who write the laws and fashion rationality. Silly fool, you let all kinds of Creons deceive you. [...] Impotent virgin. Tower of cold crystal, men keep passing you over without you even noticing, like a hidden dawn without brightness, [...] You, poor child forced into learning, go away, you are powerless. Hidden under your father's light, timid. Oh Dawn, one day you will be rescued!][9]

But it is the character of Antigone that receives most extensive treatment in their work. Like Irigaray, Zambrano also offers an indirect commentary on Hegel's interpretation of Sophocles's tragedy. Whereas for Irigaray, Antigone is 'still a production of a culture that has been written by men alone' (1993: 119) from which she must be released, in Zambrano's portrayal she is a figure of rebellion and resistance who achieves a degree of agency over her fate, even though the extent of her release from patriarchal proscription is still left unclear.

The re-working of the myth occupies a central position in Zambrano's work, starting with the essay dedicated to her sister Araceli, 'Delirio de Antígona' [Antigone's Delirium], written during her early exile in Paris and published in 1948 in Havana (2012b: 239–51). Antigone reappears in Zambrano's memoirs and later in her play *La tumba de Antígona* [Antigone's Tomb] written in 1967, as well as in fragments and references scattered elsewhere in her work. The first section of 'Delirio de Antígona' introduces the character and offers a commentary on her predicament along the lines of Hegel's interpretation. Antigone is presented as a pre-pubescent girl whose behaviour is dictated by an unconscious intuition of her ethical duty. As in Hegel's model, Antigone is defined by her self-abnegation and compassion within the sphere of the family: she was the guide to her blind father through his exile and she dies after performing funerary duties for her dead brother. As a punishment for contravening Creon's interdiction of giving burial to a traitor, she is condemned to be buried alive. Thus Antigone's compulsion to rescue and restore the dignity of her lineage ends in her own entombment. She represents the Hegelian figure of femininity that 'has her substantial vocation in the family, and her ethical disposition is to be imbued with family piety' (Hegel 2008: 169).[10] By asserting ties of blood over those of the political authority, she has stepped out of the sphere of the family becoming in the process a victim of the State. She is guilty as it were of two charges by transgressing both the public law and the conventions of gender.

However, Zambrano argues against Antigone's subsequent suicide in Sophocles's text apparently following Hegel's account which overlooks Antigone's death. In contrast with feminist readings which see in Antigone's eventual suicide a gesture of defiance against patriarchal domination (see Kristeva 2010: 221), for Zambrano, Antigone's self-destructive action is incongruous with the nature of a character guided by feeling and intuition and whose consciousness is still embryonic. Moreover, with her suicide the familial bond would be reasserted, repeating the fate of her mother and linking her destiny to the destructive passion that ruined other members of her family, leading to incest, parricide, and fratricide. Instead, in Zambrano's version, Antigone's desire is not acted upon but expressed in a delirium which occupies the second part of the essay with a monologue in which she conveys her sexual longings and her desperation at seeing herself abandoned. By remaining alive Antigone breaks with the destiny dictated by her bloodline and through reflection she achieves an individual self-consciousness. Her stance, however, is problematized by the repeated association of her discourse with the idea of delirium.[11]

The term delirium is given prominence in the title of Zambrano's memoir *Delirio y destino* [Delirium and Destiny], written in 1952, which includes a series of five individual narratives or 'delirios' that constitute the second of the two parts into which the book is divided. The first part ends with a passage in which the figure of Antigone is evoked in relation to Zambrano's own sister Araceli, establishing a correspondence between the two:

> La había llamado Antígona, durante todo este tiempo en que el destino las había separado apartándola a ella del lugar de la tragedia, mientras su hermana — Antígona — la arrostraba. Comenzó a llamarla así en su angustia, Antígona porque, inocente, soportaba la historia; porque habiendo nacido para el amor la estaba devorando la piedad. (Zambrano 1989b: 249)

> [She had called her Antigone during the whole time in which fate had separated them, moving her away from the site of the tragedy while her sister — Antigone — faced up to it. She started calling her Antigone out of anxiety, because despite her innocence she carried history on her shoulders; because despite having been born for love she was being devoured by piety.]

Under the title 'La hermana' [The Sister], the passage refers to the sisters' reunion in 1946 in Paris, where Araceli had been tortured by the Gestapo, a traumatic experience which would leave deep psychological scars in her psyche making her dependent till her death in 1972 on her older sister. When the latter arrived in Paris she also found that their mother had died shortly before and in a letter to a friend she recalls, 'Llegué a ver sólo a mi hermana enferma para siempre' [I only managed to see my sister, now ill for life] (in Ortega Muñoz 2006: 86). After Araceli's death, in a letter to Lezama Lima, Zambrano refers to her sister's last days suffering from a 'doble depresión delirante' [a delirious double depression] and concludes, lamenting her powerlessness regarding her sister's condition, 'yo soy la derrotada por no habérselo sabido, podido curar ¡cuánta impotencia!' [I'm the one defeated because I didn't, I couldn't cure her. What helplessness!] (1996: 225). Obviously Zambrano is not referring here to the thrombophlebitis that killed her sister but to the underlying long illness that afflicted her for at least the last twenty-five years of her life. Moreover, her sister was not the only member of her family suffering from mental illness, their father Blas Zambrano had also been prey to bouts of acute depression with suicidal tendencies — later, in one of her diaries, she would recall the extreme anxiety she experienced as a child fearing for his life (Ortega Muñoz 2006: 41).

It is interesting at this point to consider the character of Aracoeli in Elsa Morante's eponymous novel of 1982 which is allegedly based on Araceli Zambrano, with whom she was acquainted from the time of the sisters' stay in Rome in the 1950s. In Morante's novel Aracoeli is a Spanish woman displaced from her country because of the Civil War, estranged from her own life and psychologically disturbed after a series of traumas, whose erratic behaviour haunts her uncomprehending son. After her death he travels from their exile in Italy to her birthplace in the province of Almería in southern Spain in an attempt to come to terms with her past and recover his own sanity. The journey is portrayed as a descent or regression to a pre-Oedipal state from which he is able to reconnect imaginatively with his mother and, in the process, reconcile himself with the figure of his absent father. Elisa Martínez Garrido (2009) demonstrates the influence of Zambrano's philosophy on Morante's work, highlighting among other things, the interweaving of the biographical — Zambrano's mother was also called Araceli and she was originally from a village in Almería — and the historical, in the upheavals in Europe from 1936 to 1975, which form the background to Morante's novel and have devastating consequences for both the individual and the collective psyche. This movement from the individual to the collective is one of the characteristics of Zambrano's philosophical meditations, and Morante's case is yet another among many instances of the seminal role played by Zambrano among contemporary writers, an influence which remains largely unacknowledged.

While the context of the myth of Antigone is a fratricidal war, the connection with the Spanish Civil War and Republican exile is made explicit in *Delirio y destino*, and is also underlined in the prologue to *La tumba de Antígona*, where the association between the figure of Antigone and the idea of delirium is once again re-stated. At the time of her sister's death in the psychiatric hospital of Bel-Air in Geneva, Zambrano was working on a text entitled 'El delirio: El dios oscuro' [Delirium: The Dark God], later included in her book *Claros del bosque*, where she identifies delirium with a sort of Dionysian possession characterized by its perfomative expression:

> La comunicación es su don. Y antes de que ese don se establezca hay que ser poseído por él, esencia que se trasfunde en un mínimo de sustancia y aun sin ella, por la danza, por la mímica, de la que nace el teatro; por la representación que no es invención, ni pretende suplir a verdad alguna; por la representación de lo que es y que sólo así se da a conocer, no en conceptos, sino en presencia y figura; en máscara que es historia. (Zambrano 1986a: 43)
>
> [Communication is its gift. Before the gift is bestowed one needs to be possessed by it, an essence that is transmitted with minimal signs or even with none at all, through dance, through mime from which theatre is born; through a representation which is neither invention nor has any claims on truth; by self-representation, not as a concept but as presence or form; through the mask which is history.]

During her exile delirium becomes a keyword in Zambrano's lexicon and its use in our post-Freudian world has specific connotations. It describes a psycho-pathological symptom identified with irrationality and hysteria, and marked as feminine. The long-standing cultural association of women and nervous disorders was highlighted by Gregorio Marañón in his discussion on the aetiology of hysteria where he appreciatively quotes from the eighteenth-century scholar Benito Jerónimo Feijóo: 'en el útero femenino está sin duda escondido el Proteo de las enfermedades' [the female womb undoubtedly holds the Proteus of all illnesses] (Marañón 1967–1973: v, 348). Identified with the womb, hysteria became known as the female malady in nineteenth-century medical discourse (see Showalter 2007). It does not seem coincidental that some of the deliriums included in Zambrano's memoirs are narratives of female desire which is portrayed as both enigmatic and imperious. Two of them are stories of madwomen, one explicitly entitled 'La loca' [The Mad Woman] reads like a case study of psychosis in which a detached observer describes a woman's erratic behaviour and also records the uncomprehending attitude of those around her for whom her madness approaches sainthood. Ironically, one of the madwoman's obsessions is with a bacchanalian image of a woman dancing that suggests the sexual origin of hysteria as postulated by Freud, in a case said to be the founding moment for psychoanalysis.[12]

We can reasonably assume that Zambrano's knowledge of Freud's work was extensive, not only spurred by her experience with a family history of mental disorders, but also because the impact of Freud's ideas among the Spanish intellectual circles of the 1920s and 1930s had been widespread and the debate over psychoanalysis was conducted to a large extent outside the medical community (Glick 1982). The diffusion of Freudian theory championed by Ortega with the translation of Freud's complete works and the publication of reviews and articles in both *Revista de Occidente* and *El Sol* had a palpable influence on the artistic community. From plays such as Sánchez Mejías's *La sinrazón*, and Antonio and Manuel Machado's *Las adelfas*, both of 1928, to Dalí's Surrealist paintings and Buñuel's film *Le Chien Andalou* (1929), a vogue of Freudianism was also perceptible among the poets of 1927.

It is possible that Zambrano's self-reproach regarding her sister's illness in the letter to Lezama quoted above — 'por no habérselo sabido, podido curar' — is an indication that her frustration was not entirely due to a lack of knowledge or unwillingness to act upon it. By identifying her sister with Sophocles's heroine, Zambrano tacitly places herself in the role of Antigone's sister Ismene, whose attitude to Antigone's predicament can easily be transferred to that of the analyst in the psychoanalytical situation. In the same letter to Lezama Lima, Zambrano mentions her old friend Gustavo Pittaluga, a haematologist with a keen interest in psychiatry who had publicly declared his objection to the central role of sexuality in psychoanalysis (Glick 1982: 543) — a view also shared by Zambrano in the article she published in 1940 on the subject, with the title 'El freudismo, testimonio del hombre actual' [Freudianism, a Testimonial of Contemporary Man]. There Zambrano criticized the centrality of the libido in Freud's theory of the psyche, seeing it as the symptom of an era fixated on immanence, which has lost its sense of direction. Over the forces of *eros*, she invokes the primacy of *agape* identified with Christian charity, as an enabling, redemptive form of love (1987a: 118).[13]

Roberta Johnson (1997) relates Ismene's role of 'empathetic witness' and 'judicious spectator' to the ethical stance implied in Zambrano's concept of the 'razón poética', focusing on its social dimension.[14] But it is not only at the level of social critique that the character operates. While the relation of the individual to the social is a central concern in Zambrano's philosophy, her invocation of female figures such as Antigone and Ismene also reveals an interest in the specific position granted to women in the discourse — an aspect that Johnson notes but does not explore in her article. At least in Zambrano's re-working of the Antigone myth, the speaking subject is clearly marked as feminine. The character of Ismene, often eliminated in versions of the tragedy, was used by Sophocles to articulate questions on the role of women in civil society and in politics. Throughout the play she upholds the status quo. She initially refuses to help bury Polynices out of caution but in view of Antigone's punishment she feels moved to join her out of sisterly solidarity, although her offer is rejected by Antigone. In both cases, Ismene's actions remain within the conventions of womanhood, first colluding with male political authority and then yielding to the principle of 'family piety'. Unsurprisingly Tovar has only contempt for this character with which he concludes his essay, underscoring once again the gender bias of his argument:

> La vulgar, modesta y débil Ismene, la hermana de la heroína, que no se decide a seguirla, y que luego, en un arranque muy de persona débil, la quiere sustituir en el holocausto [...] Ismene acata por igual unas normas y otras, y vive como la gran masa de los humanos, encogida, temerosa, sumisa, sujeta por toda clase de temores y respetos. (Tovar 1960: 31)
>
> [The common, modest, and weak Ismene, the heroine's sister, who hesitates to follow her, and eventually in an impulse typical of a weak person, would like to take her place in the holocaust [...] Ismene complies with every norm and lives like most humans, constrained, timorous, submissive, subject to all kinds of fears and pieties.]

The psychic duality represented by the two sisters, already suggested in Sophocles's text, is internalized in Zambrano's version, marking a departure from her precursors.[15] While Antigone expresses her wish for Ismene to live her own life, rejecting the sacrificial role for her sister, she also insists on their mutual bond: '[Ismene] es la única de nosotros que tendrá su propia vida. Y por lo demás, ella está siempre conmigo; irá conmigo donde yo vaya' [Ismene is the only one of us who will live her own life. In any case, she is always with me; she will go with me everywhere I go] (2012b: 216).[16] The sense of intimate connection between Antigone and Ismene is a reflection of Zambrano's attachment to her sister.[17] This self-affirmation through interconnection with others represents, according to Julia Kristeva, one of the distinctive features of the feminine genius, at a remove from the solipsistic ethos of the masculine model (2004: 498–99). Another characteristic that Kristeva associates with feminine creativity is an emphasis on the temporality of birth and rebirth, a conception of time concerned with renewal and new beginnings. This is in turn related to the temporality of psychoanalysis conceived as a 'perpetual rebirth of the subject: beyond biological destiny and the weight of family' (502). This concern with rebirth is paramount in Zambrano's play *La tumba de Antígona*, which also dramatizes the series of splittings that re-enact the process of individuation postulated in traditional psychoanalysis.[18] Taking its cue from Kristeva's dictum, 'Psychoanalysis is also a way of reading texts' (in Kristeva 1996: 187), the following attempt to explore the play from a psychoanalytical perspective will reveal the extent of Zambrano's insight into the psychic life which anticipates more recent formulations. The density of allusion and conceptual complexity of her prose requires a solid philosophical grasp as well as an engagement with the web of cross-references to other texts by the author, but here I will try to focus as much as possible on the play itself.

La tumba de Antígona concerns itself with one episode which is significantly absent in Sophocles: the night Antigone spends in the funeral chamber, entombed before her death. Throughout the twelve short scenes that comprise the play she appears in this enclosure where she reflects on her predicament while summoning and being visited by the familial ghosts of her past. Antigone's long monologue, which includes several instances of internal and dramatic dialogue can be interpreted in relation to Freud's talking cure in which the subject reveals her psychic interiority by dwelling on its formative experiences.[19] Kristeva calls Antigone a 'heroine of self-analysis' (2010: 19), and we find in Zambrano's play a conception of subjectivity which strongly resonates within a Kristevan psychoanalytical framework. Building on Lacan's reworking of Freud's theory of the psyche, as well as drawing from object-relation theories derived from Melanie Klein, Kristeva's emphasis on a mode of signification related to the maternal, her view of a feminine symbolic and the dynamics of abjection in the constitution of the speaking subject, are distinctive traits which find a correspondence in Zambrano's play.[20]

In the first monologue Antigone expresses her sense of alienation, despair, and dejection at her predicament. Her recriminations are directed at the sunlight which filters through a crack in the wall and in its movement becomes not only a reminder of temporality and finitude within the otherwise suspended time of the grave, but it also exacerbates her experience of exile which she extends to include her past existence. A psycho-social dimension along gender lines is conveyed in the contrasting images of the sun and the dawn — one which places woman outside intellectual discourse, as Antigone's remonstration with the sun for having been denied the word seems to suggest. Her position as outcast is underlined with recourse to insisting on spatial references: 'estoy fuera, afuera' [I'm outside, out there] (177). Kristeva reminds us of Hegel's use of the sun metaphor as an affirmation of man as a reasoning being at home in the State (1984: 35),[21] and in one of her early essays the image of the sun appears as a symbol of the paternal law locked in an Oedipal struggle with the poet.[22] But here Antigone's reproach is also extended to the more comforting if enigmatic glare of dawn whose luminous appearance she welcomes, even though it heralds the sun and remains silent and unresponsive to her plea. In psychoanalysis the precedence of dawn would correspond to the pre-symbolic dimension, linked to the unconscious and related to the maternal, thereby marked as feminine. For Kristeva, both the symbolic and pre-symbolic, even if sequential in terms of subject formation are nevertheless inextricably linked, and Zambrano's image which conflates the two successive phenomena in their common luminous quality is an apt correlate.

In the second scene, the sepulchral chamber, now in total darkness, prompts Antigone's imaginary regression to a pre-symbolic stage: 'como si estuviera naciendo en esta tumba [...] Iré a nacer aquí, ahora. Como si no hubiese ni tan siquiera comenzado a revolverme en el vientre de mi madre' [as if I was being born in this grave [...] I'll be born here, now. As if I had not yet begun to move in my mother's womb] (180). Her statement 'no siento nada' [I feel nothing] (181) suggests the death of the self, linking the two moments of conception and extinction.

More pointedly, Antigone's references to intrauterine life recall Kristeva's notion of the semiotic *chora*, which is replicated in the womb-like enclosure of the play's crypt, and Antigone's self-perception as an embryo or larva reinforces the primordial context.[23]

Borrowed from Plato's *Timæus* where the term *chora* is used in reference to the origins of the universe, denoting a space conceived as nourishing and maternal, in Kristeva's psychoanalytic idiolect *chora* refers to the stage of primary narcissism dominated by the mother's body where the infant experiences the first impressions of space (1984: 25–30, 239).[24] The infant's tactile communication with the mother is suggested in Antigone's touching and caressing the walls of the tomb, and her reference to the music emanating from this space is akin to what Kristeva describes as a pre-verbal perception of the maternal language. The fusion between mother and infant is enacted in Antigone's depersonalization: 'Sombra de mi vida, sombra mía [...] ¿Porqué veo esta sombra? ¿es la mía?' [Shadow of my life, my own shadow [...] why do I see this shadow? Is it my own?] (181).

In the play, the initial stage of non-differentiation is followed by a series of instances of separation involving the identification with and detachment from familial figures, as we witness Antigone working through the process of individuation, described by Kristeva as 'a kaleidoscope of ego images that build the foundation for the subject of enunciation' (1995: 104). In 'El sueño de la hermana' [The Sister's Dream], the intimate relationship with her sister Ismene is predicated upon regression and replication: 'nosotras no sabíamos y sabíamos, sentíamos nuestro secreto, el de nosotras solas, solitas.' [we didn't know and we knew; we experienced our secret, our very own secret, ours alone] (183). Their tacit complicity recalls Kristeva's description of a female bond with the maternal: 'women doubtless reproduce among themselves the strange gamut of forgotten body relations with their mothers. Complicity in the unspoken, connivance of the inexpressible' (1987: 257). Arguably, this identification with the mother comes at an extra cost for the female subject as the socially and culturally devalued status of women within the symbolic induces an internalized sense of marginalization, where desire is denied and instead *pietas* is reasserted, a virtue related to kinship values and the cult of the dead represented by Antigone in Sophocles's narrative. In Zambrano's play, however, Antigone's emphatic claim: 'tengo voz, tengo voz' [I have my voice, my voice] (185) suggests a distinction between language and voice, the latter, like dawn, precedes signification. This dichotomy between word and voice reappears in the play's concluding act.

The precariousness of the self in the first stages of individuation is conveyed in the tension provoked in the text by the idea of demarcations, and the transgressive crossing of boundaries: 'Yo pasé la raya y la traspasé, la volví a pasar y a repasar, yendo y viniendo a la tierra prohibida' [I crossed the line and went beyond, crossed it again and again, going back and forth to the forbidden land] (183). This increasing motility leads to a rupture in the narrative with a vision of spilt blood, suggesting a breaking of the boundaries between the body's outside and inside. Even if within the logic of the original narrative the blood belongs to Antigone's brother, blood is a bodily fluid symbolically associated with the maternal which carries a threat of excess and lack of containment. The process of washing it away and having it re-absorbed by nature which symbolizes the fertility identified with the mother, corresponds to what Kristeva describes as abjection. The threatening presence of this invasive and overflowing fantasy is counteracted with an allusion to the enforced subterranean exile of Persephone and, by implication, to her wrathful mother, Demeter. Despite the reassuring estrangement between mother and daughter enacted in the myth, here, upon returning to the consciousness of her present state, Antigone expresses her impotence to release the hold of the maternal figured in the spilled blood and the distress involved in the process of abjection: 'Pero mi historia es sangrienta. Toda la historia está hecha con sangre, toda la historia es de sangre, y las lágrimas no se ven. El llanto es como el agua, lava y no deja rastro' [But my history is full of blood. All history is made out of blood, all history is of blood, and tears cannot be seen. Tears are like water that washes without leaving any trace] (186). Eventually, the maternal loss is internalized by the subject, even if, according to Kristeva, abjection cannot be completely washed away. The persistence of this memory within the psyche finds an image in the motif of the 'cantarillo de agua' [the little water jug] that the young Antigone carries with her, adopting the form of a mobile receptacle which functions as a figurative embodiment of what Kristeva calls the 'semiotic disposition' (1984: 25).

The figure of Oedipus, Antigone's father, who is also her brother, too weak to effect a separation from the semiotic, suggests a crisis in the paternal function. He appears in the guise of a narcissistic depressive wrapped in his own melancholia, whose self-absorption prevents him from acknowledging anything other than his own self, seeing in his daughter a projection of his own ego, addressing her as 'mi razón', 'mi pensamiento', 'mi promesa', 'mi palabra sin error' [my reason; my thought; my promise; my true word], suggesting a relation of dependency, both physical and psychological. In an interplay of fluid identities, Antigone replaces Jocasta as Oedipus's companion. This scene is followed by the appearance of another figuration of the mother in the form of the wet-nurse and storyteller, who embodies the socializing function of the maternal, as postulated by Kristeva. She facilitates the introduction of the subject to language opening up the system of binary structures necessary for individuation, first established between the two sisters and then extending to dualities such as dirty/clean, inside/outside. Later on in the play, Antigone refers to binary oppositions in relation to the incest interdiction, under the figurative aegis of the Sun, a symbol of the Law of the Father:

> Porque todo lo que desciende del Sol es doble: luz y sombra; día y noche; sueño y vigilia; hermanos que viven uno de la muerte del otro. Hermano y esposo que no pueden juntarse y ser uno solo. Amor dividido. (231).
>
> [Because all that comes from the Sun is double; light and shadow; day and night; sleep and wakefulness; brothers who live one from the other's death. Brother and husband who cannot be reunited and become one. Divided love.]

In the scene entitled 'Sombra de la madre' [The Mother's Shadow], Antigone invokes her biological mother with some ambivalence. As in Sophocles's tragedy the name of Jocasta is never mentioned in Zambrano's play, but her figure is repeatedly invoked, generating a reaction in her daughter which oscillates between identification and rivalry. In the dialogue with Oedipus, Antigone had reacted against the idea of Jocasta's sexuality, rejecting her image as her father's lover in favour of her role as mother. Here Jocasta is first evoked as blocking the entrance to the symbolic by negating the place of the father and displaying a narcissistic possessiveness towards the daughter. But she is subsequently celebrated as a life-giver as Antigone exhorts her to leave her company and integrate with an idealized archaic figure of a Universal Mother assimilated to nature. Later on, the reference to the 'bocas oscuras que se abren en la tierra como las de una madre ávida' [dark mouths opening in the earth like that of an avid mother] (229) reinstates the idea of the abject projected on the mother. Jocasta's imagined departure marks the move into the process of separation from the sphere of the maternal highlighted by Antigone's statement: 'sigo estando *aquí todavía*' [I'm *still here*] (201, my emphasis). At the same time, through a process of identification and incorporation Antigone assimilates her mother's role as generative source: 'La sombra de mi madre entró en mí, y yo, doncella, he sentido el peso de ser madre' [my mother's shadow entered me and, though still a virgin, I have felt the weight of being a mother] (201). Incidentally, the idea of delirium, associated with Antigone, is also connected to the mother in Polinices's description of Jocasta as 'la madre enloquecida, hablando sola por las galerías, los patios, por los rincones, delirando' [the deranged mother, speaking to herself in corridors, patios, corners, delirious] (212).

In the last scene dedicated to female imagos, the Harpy stands at the threshold of the semiotic and the symbolic, whose interpenetration is expressed in a riddle: 'La Ley del Amor es muy distinta de la Ley del Terror y ni siquiera se puede decir que sean todo lo contrario' [Love's law is very different from terror's law yet it cannot be said that they are utterly opposed] (203). The Harpy introduces the issue of sexual difference and her craftiness is reminiscent of the mythological figure of Metis mentioned by Kristeva in *Tales of Love* where she is presented as 'a wily agent of the symbolic within the maternal continent' (1987: 73). Kristeva does not dwell on this myth in which Metis was swallowed by Zeus while pregnant with Athena, the goddess of philosophy and weaving, who was subsequently born from his forehead.[25] In Zambrano's play the Harpy, described by Antigone as 'la Diosa de las Razones disfrazada' [The Goddess of Reasons in disguise] (206), is also a weaver (*tejedora*) and therefore associated with the mythological female upholder of patriarchy.

From this point on, we enter the masculine sphere of the symbolic, with a series of male visitors: starting with Antigone's brothers, then her fiancé, and finally her uncle Creón. The dialogue with the two brothers revolves around the possibility of a just society and the relation of the individual to the community. The imagery is suffused with references to death and strife, and the insistence on the past tense reinforces the sense of a present inhabited by the past in an atmosphere of mourning. The passage highlights the centrality of the notion of paternity for the constitution of a unified subject and by extension a unified state, which imposes a split in the distribution of power along gender lines, within the family and society at large. Antigone's feeble vindication of Jocasta is received with protestations about her disruptive and dissociative behaviour. From a psychoanalytical perspective the two brothers represent two different models of subjectivity: the Oedipal and the Narcissistic, ruled by paternal law and maternal authority respectively (see Beardsworth 2005). Etéocles, dominated by the superego, embodies the agency of the father, upholding his law and keen on religious ritual. Polinices represents the rebellious son identified with the lost maternal territory which has become a nostalgic ideal pursued in the name of an originary unity. He is now reduced to what Kristeva describes as a 'dweller in the imaginary realm' (1989a: 61). Both positions are antagonistic and ultimately irreconcilable. As with Hemón, who joins them in pleading with Antigone to abandon her tomb, they seek in her their own reflection, a signifier for their desires. With the arrival of Creón, Antigone's initial frustration has turned into defiance: 'Pues no es la condena, es la ley que la engendra, lo que mi alma rechaza' [yet it is not the sentence that my soul rejects but the law which enforces it] (224). Refusing to rejoin the world of the living Antigone is transformed into a rebellious Persephone.

In her final soliloquy Antigone asserts her estrangement and her self-excluded position, invoking the image of Venus and thus reinstating the correlation between the feminine and exile. In a similar vein, drawing on Hegel's description of Antigone as 'the eternal irony of the community', Kristeva suggests a feminine form of subjectivity defined by dissidence: 'a sort of separate vigilance that keeps groups from closing up, from becoming homogeneous and so oppressive. That is, I see the role of women as a sort of vigilance, strangeness, as always to be on guard and contestatory' (1996: 45). This role, Kristeva concedes, can be construed as hysterical. However, whereas for some feminists hysteria can be considered a site of feminine empowerment (Irigaray 1985: 214–26), it is a position in which the subject is bound up with both the maternal power and the authority of the father but unable to identify satisfactorily with either parent, and therefore potentially self-annihilating, as reflected in Antigone's predicament. In her essay 'Psychoanalysis and the Polis', Kristeva refers to delirium as a discourse related to dreams and the unconscious operating through condensation and displacement where the speaking subject identifies with a place of alterity resistant to meaning (Kristeva and Waller 1982): a position identified with Antigone in the play's denouement.

Kristeva's application of delirium to psychoanalytic hermeneutics sheds some light on the enigmatic conclusion of Zambrano's play, when two unknown figures ('desconocidos') enter the stage. The first stranger wants to lift Antigone from her tomb, a psychic space marked by distress and longing: 'de estos lugares de encierro saco a alguien que gime, a que cuente su historia en voz alta. Porque los que claman han de ser oídos. Y vistos' [from these places of confinement I rescue grieving individuals so that they can tell their story aloud. Because those who cry should be heard. And be seen] (234). Unlike previous visitors, this character upholds an ethics of listening which Kristeva opposes to 'the militant ethics resting on a deceitful discourse' (1996: 173).[26]

The first stranger defers to the second and more enigmatic 'desconocido' who introduces the idea of resurrection with an allusion to the Emmaus apparition: '¿no me reconoces porque vengo de este modo?' [is it because of how I look that you cannot recognize me?] (233), and indeed he is the one able to release Antigone from the maternal shelter of the tomb. In an earlier version of the play, this character is described also through a Biblical allusion, as a redeeming figure:

> Que viene a redimir a la madre, no a aniquilarla, el que bajará hasta el centro mismo de la tiniebla, donde cielo y tierra se confunden, para repartir el amor. El que está al mismo tiempo arriba en lo alto y abajo en la oscuridad, en la tierra. (226, n. 76)[27]
>
> [The one who comes to redeem the mother, not to destroy her, the one who will descend to the very heart of darkness, where the earth meets the sky, to share out love. The one who stands at the same time above and below in the darkness, in the earth.]

His position in the play — he claims to have been there all along standing by the door — suggests that of a mediator between the semiotic and the symbolic realms, postulated by Kristeva in the figure of the 'imaginary father' (1987: 33–48),[28] which she associates with a type of psychoanalytical practice based on empathetic transference, where the analyst 'neither judges nor calculates but attempts to untangle and reconstruct' (1989a: 206). In contrast to the dissociative impulse articulated around the Oedipal conflict, this third party unifies the maternal semiotic and the paternal symbolic in a 'harmonious blend' facilitating the subject's socialization.[29]

The final exchange between the two strangers revolves around the idea of epiphany conveyed through the allusion to the Pentecostal experience. While the first stranger expresses a strong emotional attachment to the figure of Antigone, the second stranger recommends a degree of distance and worldly detachment, which should unleash the generative power of language in a stream of words: 'La oirás más claramente de lejos, aunque estés sumergido en otros asuntos [...] Y esas palabras que se aglomeran ahora en tu garganta, saldrán sin que lo notes. Su voz desatará tu lengua' [You will hear her more clearly from a distance, even if you are immersed in other business [...] And those words that now block your throat, will flow effortlessly. Her voice will unleash your tongue] (236).

Araceli Zambrano is one of the two dedicatees of *La tumba de Antígona*, the other is Laurette Séjourné, a French archaeologist known to the Zambrano sisters — a double dedication in which the play's concerns are encrypted. If psychoanalysis provides an access to a feminine inflected subjectivity, associated with the unconscious and incarnated by Antigone, *La tumba de Antígona* is a testimonial of the creative power this approach can unleash in the writer or cultural analyst represented by the first stranger, and ultimately by Zambrano as author. In 'Delirio de Antígona', the protagonist is internalized and presented as the hidden side of our personality, a symbol of alterity within identity: 'La tumba de Antígona es nuestra propia conciencia oscurecida. Antígona está enterrada viva en nosotros, en cada uno de nosotros' [Antigone's tomb is our own darkened conscience. Antigone is buried in us, in every one of us] (2012b: 247). This conception is closely related to Kristeva's image of the stranger within oneself, which the ethics of psychoanalysis re-integrates within the subject, implying a politics founded on the 'consciousness of its unconscious', as a way towards the recognition and acceptance of the other, the foreigner, and those excluded from the *polis* (1991: 192). The allusions to psychoanalysis in *La tumba de Antígona* reveal that for Zambrano, just as for Kristeva, psychoanalysis represents 'the discourse of the intellectual life, if the intellectual life is also characterized by this uneasiness and a constant questioning of meanings, heritages, doctrines, and appearances' (Kristeva 1996: 197). It provides an inroad into the rich generative semiotic unconscious, a painful journey illustrated in Antigone's delirium, but also a source of poetic discourse and artistic creation.

In the play's final scene, the female exile from the *polis* has become an existential exile. Her deliverance may suggest a rebirth of the subject. And yet, Antigone's uncertainty and her disconnected, incoherent speech — 'Ah, sí. ¿Dónde? ¿Adónde? Sí, Amor. Amor, tierra prometida' [Ah, yes. Where? Where to? Yes, Love. Love, the promised land] (236) — casts doubts on the possibility of social and political action, suggesting instead that Antigone's rebellion may ultimately lead to the disintegration of the self. The ambiguity is left unresolved. We can conclude with Elaine Showalter that 'hysterics should be classed not with feminist heroines, but with deviants and marginals who actually reinforce the social structure by their preordained place on the margin' (1993: 332). Or alternatively, we can celebrate Antigone's articulate hysteria as a 'specifically feminine pathology that speaks to and against patriarchy' (Showalter 1993: 286). In any case Zambrano's reclaiming of delirium suggests her engagement with a feminist practice which appropriates hysteria as a 'subversive discourse, a practice of representation, and a woman's language' (Devereux 2014: 34).³⁰

As we have seen, there is a striking correspondence between Zambrano and Kristeva in their understanding of the human psyche. Their writings show a similar concern with the disruptive effects of the unconscious in language and life, and by implication, with those dimensions — affects, emotions, sensations — which are associated with the feminine. Both are exiles in a foreign land, not only geographically but also as women philosophers, challenging the marginal position granted to women intellectuals in history. Arguably from the point of view of a positivist rationality the relationship between interpretation and transformation is problematic, even if the analysis has the potential of cutting through political discourse, acting as a corrective. Moreover, as one of Kristeva's critics points out: 'the clinical implications of the semiotic or abjection have never been spelled out by Kristeva herself' (Macey 2006: 47). Exile was linked to Zambrano's own biography, and so was the close experience of mental disorder. Whereas for Kristeva it is women's psyche that turns them into exiles, for Zambrano, whose Antigone is ultimately identified with her sister Araceli, women are primarily the victims of history.³¹

Notes to Chapter 8

1. Kristeva 1987: 14.
2. Tovar 1960: 15–31; like Zambrano, Tovar had been a student of the philosopher Xavier Zubiri, but unlike her he would join the Falangist party and became one of the advocates of the Francoist regime (later to defect together with other Christian liberals such as Dionisio Ridruejo).
3. It is rather baffling to read that one of the charges Mayhew raises against Unamuno, García Lorca, Zambrano, and Valente is that 'none of these four writers is seriously attracted to Marxist thought' (2012: 93), which at the very least in the case of Unamuno is incorrect.
4. For Jesús Moreno Sanz, Zambrano's views on gender in 1933 represent her position throughout her career, setting her work against any feminist interpretation (2003: 75 & 442); see also Virginia Trueba Mira in her introduction to *La Tumba de Antígona*: 'No se trata de feminismo — Zambrano nunca se definió como *feminista* y en cuanto a su reflexión sobre las mujeres no dejó de mostrar ambigüedades y emitir juicios en ocasiones muy discutibles' [It is not feminism — Zambrano never defined herself as a feminist and her reflections about women were always ambiguous and at times very objectionable] (Zambrano 2012b: 98).
5. 'No soy feminista, pero no he podido abdicar de pensar, aunque pareciera imposible; no he podido abdicar ante lo imposible' [I am not a feminist, but I could not give up thinking, even if it seemed impossible; I could not give up when faced with the impossible], from an interview in 1989, quoted in Nimmo 1997: 893.
6. For a critique of Kristeva's stance towards feminism see Elizabeth Grosz (1989: 63–69).
7. See Julia Kristeva *La traversée des signes* (1976), cited in Grosz 1989: 97.
8. This passage is in one of the drafts of *La tumba de Antígona* later discarded, where Athena appears as one of the characters; in the same edition, see also p. 272, n. 4; cf. Zambrano, 'De los dioses griegos' in *El hombre y lo divino* (1955). Zambrano must have felt the painful experience of having been abandoned by her own 'daylight gods' during her exile. The precarious existence of the two sisters in the 1950s and 1960s is described in the correspondence with her friends Rosa Chacel and Reyna Rivas (see Zambrano 1992c, and Zambrano and Rivas 2004). Jesús Moreno Sanz's anthology *La razón en la sombra* (2003) only includes the dialogue of Antigone with Creon and her address to the Sun, out of the twelve acts which include a dialogue with her sister,

her mother, a wet-nurse, the night, and the Harpy, suggesting that perhaps it may not only be 'reason' that is 'in the shadow' here.
9. All translations are my own unless otherwise stated.
10. In addition, Hegel claims that 'women are capable of education, but they are not made for activities which demand a universal faculty such as the more advanced sciences, philosophy, and certain forms of artistic production' (2008: 169).
11. Beatriz Caballero Rodríguez (2008) offers an illuminating account of the complexity and semantic range that the concept of delirium acquires in Zambrano's *oeuvre*, where the term comes to denote a transformative liberating process of catharsis. This conception is problematized by the association of delirium with the clinical disorder of hysteria historically associated with femininity. The re-articulation of hysteria's symptoms with feminism in the late twentieth-century has been condemned by critics such as Elaine Showalter (1993), who see this gesture as ideologically counter-productive.
12. 'Envuelta en unos velos rojo fuego como llamas y tenía los cabellos entrelazados con racimos de uvas negras y unos pámpanos que le caían por el cuello' [wrapped up in fire red veils like flames, with the hair entwined with bunches of black grapes and some vine tendrils around her neck] (Zambrano 1989b: 261).
13. 'El amor en el mundo cristiano tiene la virtud de redimir, no al que lo siente, como en Platón, sino al que lo recibe. Desciende a quien no lo espera, a quien no lo merece, vence al rebelde. Es la victoria cristiana en la que no existe el vencido' [Love in the Christian world is redemptive, not for the one who feels it, as in Plato, but for the recipient. It descends upon the one who does not expect it, does not deserve it, overcoming the rebellious one. It is the Christian victory in which there are no vanquished] (Zambrano 1987a: 118), 'El freudismo, testimonio del hombre actual', first published in *La Verónica* (Havana, 1940) and later included in *Hacia un saber sobre el alma* (1987a).
14. For Roberta Johnson 'Ismene/María Zambrano is an individual with a social conscience who finds in literature the means to channel the emotions toward social ends that encompass the possibility of a better future' (1997: 194); Johnson relates 'razón poética' to Adorno's 'subjective reason' and Nussbaum's 'poetic justice', and it could be equally related to Kristeva's discourse of love, figured in the relation with the 'imaginary father' which is discussed here.
15. George Steiner (1984: 144) notes how Ismene is often absent in accounts of the myth, citing Euripides, Seneca, Racine, and the commentaries of Kierkegaard and Hegel.
16. Antigone's message to Ismene is eloquent: 'Que viva por mí, que viva lo que a mí me fue negado: que sea esposa, madre, amor. Que envejezca dulcemente, que muera cuando le llegue la hora. Que me sienta llegar con la violeta inmortal, en cada mes de abril, cuando las dos nacimos' [Let her live for me, let her have what was denied to me: to be a wife, a mother, love. Let her grow old sweetly and die when her time comes. Let her feel my presence, together with the immortal violet, every April, the month of both our birthdates] (Zambrano 2012b: 222; all quotations in the text are from this edition); the two Zambrano sisters, Maria and Araceli, were born in April.
17. Zambrano in a letter to Agustín Andreu (17 October 1985): 'Araceli y yo, nuestro secreto es que somos la misma' [Our secret, Araceli's and mine, is that we are both the same one] (Zambrano 2002: 107).
18. The connection with Lacan is suggested by Erminia Macola and Adone Brandalise: 'parece que la autora tenga presentes los pasajes esenciales de la teoría psicoanalítica a pesar de las reservas que tiene sobre esta' [it looks as if the author has in mind all the essential stages of the psychoanalytical theory despite her reservations about it] (Macola and Brandalise 2004: 100).
19. Freud's pre-Oedipal and post-Oedipal stages in the developmental constitution of subjectivity correspond in Lacan's terminology to the imaginary and the symbolic, and in Kristeva's to the semiotic and the symbolic. For each of these theorists the transitional moment is the Oedipus complex, the mirror phase and the 'thetic break' respectively. For a glossary of psychoanalytical terminology see Grosz 1989: xiv-xxiii.
20. Abjection in Kristeva's lexicon describes the rejection of what is other than oneself in the process of self-differentiation and it is associated with the maternal semiotic. It is close to Freud's 'return of the repressed' in that it is never overcome but haunts the subject's consciousness.

21. See also Kristeva 1989a: 28–30, where the Oedipal conflict is seen in terms of the struggle of the poet and the image of the sun.
22. In Lacan's lexicon, adopted by Kristeva, the symbolic refers to the social and signifying order governing culture, to the post-Oedipal position the subject must occupy in order to be a subject, hence the expression 'law of the father' to describe this domain.
23. For a discussion of the concept see the chapter 'Semiotic Chora: Ordering the Drives', in *Revolution in Poetic Language*' (Kristeva 1984: 25–30).
24. Kristeva evokes this experience on the occasion of her own pregnancy: 'I have only spatial memory. No time at all. [...] Almost no sight — a shadow that darkens, soaks me up or vanishes amid flashes' (1987: 256).
25. See the reference to Metis's daughter in connection to women's writers in Nikolchina 1991: 40.
26. 'DESCONOCIDO PRIMERO: [...] Pero escúchame. DESCONOCIDO SEGUNDO: Te escucho. DESCONOCIDO PRIMERO: No; no es así como tendrías que escucharme. Tendrías que darme aliento. Tendrías que darme la palabra' [1st Stranger: But listen to me. 2nd Stranger: I'm listening. 1st Stranger: No, this is not how you should listen to me. You should encourage me. You should grant me the word] (235).
27. This loving figure was anticipated in Zambrano's essay on Freud, where she refers to the crisis in 'el principio sagrado de la paternidad' [the sacred principle of paternity] (1987a: 119). This paternal function represents the integration of Socratic reason and Christianity ('El Padre de la Religión y la Razón griega', 1987a: 123). Thomas Mermall (1976: 56) sees in Zambrano's essay a critique of the erosion of the power of patriarchal symbolism. However, Zambrano's appeal to a paternal symbolism should not be confused with a vindication of patriarchal values, nor necessarily to be related to a biological father or even a male subject. Instead, this figure is conceived as a site of primary identification: 'es la experiencia primera de la vida, el encuentro original y decisivo, de donde parte todo lo demas' [it is the first experience of life, the original and decisive encounter, from which all the rest derives] (1987a: 120), recalling the notion of the imaginary father theorized by Kristeva in *Tales of Love* (1987), a relation that precedes the Oedipal triangle and binds the individual to higher accomplishments of civilization, embodying a form of love that combines the qualities of both mother and father.
28. See also Kelly Oliver's argument that 'The imaginary father provides the support necessary to allow the child to move into the Symbolic. This is a move from the mother's body to the mother's desire through the mother's love' (1991: 55, 44).
29. According to Kristeva; 'It is imperative that this father in individual prehistory be capable of playing his part as Oedipal father in symbolic Law, for it is on the basis of that harmonious blending of the two facets of fatherhood that the abstract and arbitrary signs of communication may be fortunate enough to be tied to the affective meaning of prehistorical identifications, and the dead language of the depressive person can arrive at a live meaning in the bond with others' (1987: 23–24), see also Beardsworth 2001.
30. Devereux 2014: 19–45, offers a critical discussion of the reclaiming of hysteria as a cultural condition by Second Wave feminism in the 1970s and 1980s, which in some ways reflects Zambrano's stance.
31. 'Delirio nacido de la herida de la humillación del hombre [*sic*] bajo la historia' [delirium born from the wound of man's humiliation], 'Delirio, esperanza y razón'(1959), (Zambrano 1996: 170); *cf.* Kristeva's claim: 'A woman is trapped within the frontiers of her body and even of her species, and consequently always feels exiled both by the general clichés that make up common consensus and by the very powers of generalization intrinsic to language' (1986: 296).

CHAPTER 9

Metaphor in María Zambrano: Theory and Practice

Roberta Johnson, University of Kansas and UCLA

In 1944 María Zambrano published her article 'La metáfora del corazón' [The Metaphor of the Heart] in the Cuban journal *Orígenes*. In that essay she developed a corporal theory of metaphor, usually considered a rhetorical (linguistic) trope. Her definition and use of metaphor is intimately bound up with her central philosophical notion of 'razón poética' [poetic reason] — 'otros modos de conocimiento' [other modes of knowing] (Zambrano 1987c: 4). The heart is linked to blood, which 'como el vino, embriaga. [...] Es metáfora en suma de comunión, es un culto dionisiaco, de embriaguez vital, en el que se transfunde una vida divina a quien la bebe; metáfora de una sed infinita, una sed por esencia inextinguible' [like wine, intoxicates. [...] It is, finally, the metaphor of communion; it is the Dionysian cult of vital inebriation that infuses a divine life into whoever drinks it — metaphor of an infinite thirst inextinguishable in its essence] (7). Zambrano's theorizing about metaphor in the mid-1940s was prescient. The post-structuralists took up the cause thirty years later in the 1970s (see especially Fredric Jameson, Samuel Levine, and Jacques Derrida). And Zambrano in some respects followed in the footsteps of her professor José Ortega y Gasset who also theorized metaphor. In fact Zambrano could be considered a bridge between Ortega y Gasset on the subject and post-phenomenologists such as Maurice Merleau-Ponty, if not necessarily the post-structuralists. In Ortega''s 'Las dos grandes metáforas' [Two Great Metaphors] of 1924, he states that 'La metáfora es un instrumento mental imprescindible, es una forma del pensamiento científico' [Metaphor is a necessary mental instrument; it is a form of scientific thought] (1966: 387), and that 'Metáfora es transposición de nombre' [Metaphor is the transposition of names] (389). Zambrano flies full in the face of her professor on this issue as she does on many other matters (see Pérez 1999). If for Ortega metaphor is a mental instrument, Zambrano approaches the metaphor of the heart as corporeal and as a source of emotional, not scientific, knowledge. Ortega also states in his essay on two metaphors that in saying 'fondo del alma' [depths of the soul] (390), 'depths' 'nos significa ciertos fenómenos espirituales ajenos al espacio y a lo corpóreo, donde no hay superficies ni fondos' [means certain spiritual phenomena that are outside space and the corporeal where there are neither surfaces nor depths] and that it is 'un medio esencial de intelección' [an essential medium of intellection] (390). In the first part of this essay, I will explore some of Zambrano's ideas on metaphor in the context of her opposition to Ortega and in light of some post-phenomenological ideas.[1] In the second half of the article, I analyze Zambrano's use of metaphor as a philosophical tool in her two published works on Antigone — 'Delirio de Antígone' and *La tumba de Antígona*.

For Ortega, 'la metáfora es un procedimiento intelectual por cuyo medio conseguimos aprehender lo que se halla más lejos de nuestra potencia conceptual' [metaphor is an intellectual procedure by means of which we grasp what is far from our conceptual power] (391). Employing a hunting metaphor, Ortega defines metaphor as our 'brazo intelectivo' [intellectual arm], 'la caña de pescar o el fusil' [fishing pole or shotgun] (391). Continuing his emphasis on the conceptual nature of metaphor, Ortega avers that metaphor arose from man's need to acquire 'cierto dominio mínimo sobre las cosas corporales. Las ideas sensibles de los cuerpos concretos fueron las primeras en fijarse y convertirse en hábitos' [a certain minimal dominion over corporal things. The sense ideas of concrete bodies were the first to become fixed habits] (394). He goes on to point out that the spirit or psyche or whatever one wishes to call the constellation of conscious phenomena is always seen as fused with the body, and if we want to think of it as separate, we have tended to embody it. Ortega gives primacy to consciousness in this procedure, as the:

> Objeto que va incluso en todos los demás que está en ellos como su parte e ingrediente, de la misma manera que el hilo rojo va trenzado en todos los cables de la Real Marina inglesa. Este objeto universal, ubicuo, omnipresente que dondequiera se halle otro objeto hace su inevitable presentación, es lo que llamamos conciencia. (Ortega y Gasset 1996: 396)

> [Object that even goes with all the others and is in them as a part or ingredient, in the same way that the red thread is interwoven into all the ropes of the English Royal Navy. We call consciousness this universal, ubiquitous, omnipresent object that makes its inevitable presentation wherever an object is found.][2]

Ortega further remarks that consciousness is exceptionally difficult to describe; thus metaphor is essential to positing the relationship between the subject and object. Language intervenes between subjects and objects, a concept that brings Ortega into the orbit of the post-structuralists, who argued that there is no reality outside language (or better said, brings the post-structuralists into Ortega's orbit).

In Ortega's view, the main categories of life (morality, politics, art) 'viene[n] a descansar sobre el menudo cuerpo aéreo de una metáfora' [come to rest on the tiny airy body of a metaphor] (396–97). Ortega presages Zambrano's corporal view of metaphor when he notes that when we are forced to think that A is B, we get seasick. He continues by noting that the mind has no extension, no colour, or resistance, and yet it can comprehend a mountain that is made of bluish and reddish granite, so the two seem incompatible, a contradiction: 'El hecho de la conciencia nos obliga a pensar que dos términos completamente distintos son, a la vez, uno y mismo' [The fact of consciousness obliges us to think that two completely different terms are, at the same time, one and the same] (397). Thus it is necessary to understand how things are in consciousness. Ortega sets out two historical positions on reality: 1) the ancient Greeks' notion that realism arises when we consider that both consciousness and the thing it perceives (the mountain, for example) are things among other things; and 2) idealism, which holds that things do not come from outside the consciousness but rather are contained in it as ideas under the maxim that 'Conciencia es creación' [Consciousness is creation] (400). Ortega does not choose sides between the ancient view of objects in the world having a presence outside the consciousness before and after consciousness grasps them and the modern view that things only exist in consciousness — Fichte's 'el Yo es todo' [the I is everything] (400). Ortega draws closer to Heidegger who postulated that 'Things are defined in the world by "what comes between" [...] by difference' (in White 1977: 46).

In her attempt to overcome consciousness as the centre of being as it had been since Descartes and as it continued to be up through Husserl, Heidegger, the early Ortega, and Sartre, Zambrano is perhaps most in tune with Merleau-Ponty who understood that in order to perceive, we have to be involved in the world we perceive. Our body is an object among objects, and it is also what sees and touches these objects.[3] Merleau-Ponty further asserts that:

> Physical nature in man is not subordinated to a vital principle, the organism does not conspire to actualize an idea, and the mental is not a motor principle *in* the body; but what we call nature is already consciousness of nature, what we call life is already consciousness of life and what we call mental is still an object vis-à-vis consciousness. Never, while establishing the ideality of the physical form, that of the organism, and that of the 'mental', and *precisely because we did it*, we could not simply superimpose these three orders; not being a new substance, each of them had to be conceived as a retaking and a 'new' structuration of the preceding one. (Merleau-Ponty 1963: 184)

For Merleau-Ponty the body is fundamental to knowledge of the world:

> The body is no longer merely *an object in the world*, under the purview of a separated spirit. It is on the side of the subject; it is our *point of view on the world*, the place where the spirit takes on a certain physical and historical situation. As Descartes once said profoundly, the soul is not merely in the body like a pilot in his ship; it is wholly intermingled with the body. The body, in turn, is wholly animated, and all its functions contribute to the perception of objects — activity long considered by philosophy to be pure knowledge.
>
> We grasp external space through our bodily situation. A 'corporeal or postural schema' gives us at every moment a global, practical, and implicit notion of the relation between our body and things, or our hold on them. (Merleau-Ponty 1964: 5)

Zambrano's rendering of the Antigone figure, as we shall see below, admirably captures the corporeal nature of being and knowledge. Antigone is the embodiment of the heart (passions) metaphor.

If for Ortega, metaphor has a scientific function, Zambrano opines that:

> No sólo de pan vive el hombre, es decir no sólo de ciencia y técnica. También podría decirse que no sólo de filosofía, pero tal cosa al hablar de las metáforas

> no tiene sentido, porque la filosofía más pura se ha desenvuelto en el espacio trazado por una metáfora, la de la visión y la luz inteligible. (Zambrano 1987c: 3)

> [Man does not live by bread alone — in other words science and technology. One could also say not only by philosophy, but when one speaks of metaphors such a thing has no meaning, because philosophy has developed in a space marked out by metaphor — vision and intelligible light.]

If Ortega's two metaphors both refer to the intellect — one to the exterior of the mind and the other to its interior — Zambrano divides the metaphorical in another way:

> Al lado de la gran metáfora de la 'luz intelectual' ha vivido otra de destino bien diferente: su continuidad no parece haberse mantenido, de tal manera que hemos de echar mano de otra metáfora: la del río cuyas aguas se esconden absorbidas por el tiempo para luego reaparecer; nada más parecido a la arena que se traga el agua que el paso del tiempo que, a veces, parece encubrir muchas cosas que han muerto y que prosiguen su vida secretamente, casi clandestinamente, con una continuidad que podríamos llamar infrahistoria. (Zambrano 1987c: 4)

> [Alongside the great metaphor of 'intellectual light', there has been another with a very different destiny. Its continuity does not seem to have been maintained, so I will employ another metaphor — that of the river whose waters are hidden, absorbed by time, only to reappear. There is nothing more like the sand that the water swallows up than the water, which with the passage of time, seems to cover up many things that have died and that continues its life secretly, almost clandestinely, with a continuity that we could call infrahistory.][4]

Zambrano continues by observing that this water often does not rise to the visible surface, but remains hidden in folklore. The heart is, according to Zambrano, one of the metaphors that has been relegated to folklore. While the metaphor of the heart as a vehicle for knowledge has its origins as far back as Aristotle, it came to historical recognition in the romanticisms of the Middle Ages and of the early nineteenth century. In Zambrano's literary works that focus on Antigone, Antigone — buried alive in a cave, but receiving visits from other characters in her story — epitomizes the inside/outside nature of the heart, as Zambrano understands it.

Zambrano draws a parallel between the heart and blood metaphors, and especially points out the spatial aspect of the heart metaphor:

> Es grande, es como un espacio que dentro de la persona se abre para dar acogida a ciertas realidades. Lugar donde se albergan los sentimientos inextricables, que saltan por encima de los juicios y de lo que puede explicarse. Es ancho y es también profundo, tiene un fondo de donde salen las grandes resoluciones, las grandes verdades que son certidumbres. (Zambrano 1987c: 8)

> [It is large; it is like a space, which opens up within the person in order to take in certain realities. It is where inextricable sentiments that are beyond judgments lodge. It is wide, and it is also deep. It is the fount from which all great resolutions arise, the great truths that are certainties.]

The heart has weight, and Zambrano points out that the Spanish word *pesadumbre* [weighty sorrow] conveys this feature. According to Zambrano, *pesadumbre* always emanates from the heart (as in English we say 'with a heavy heart' of actions we have taken or will take that cause us pain). Ultimately, Zambrano endows the heart with the same metaphorical language — light — that tradition has assigned to the intellect, the mind: 'Y es luz que ilumina para salir de imposibles dificultades, luz suave que da consuelo' [And it is light that illuminates in order to get out of impossible difficulties, light that consoles] (1987c: 8).[5] (As we will see, in *La tumba de Antigone*, Zambrano maintains the separation between heart and intellect via darkness and light metaphors, respectively.) For Zambrano, the heart is the noblest locus of all the viscera, because it has space. We are reminded of Gaston Bachelard's analysis of different kinds of space as metaphors for human feelings:

> The two extreme realities of cottage and manor, [...] take into account our need for retreat and expansion, for simplicity and magnificence. [...] we read the landscape in the glass nucleus. We no longer look at it while looking through it. This nucleizing nucleus is a world in itself: The miniature deploys to the dimensions of a universe. (Bachelard 1964: 65 and 157)

Bachelard analyzes the poetic images of immensity as expressions of intimate space, and he arrives at such a concept of immensity by carrying the phenomenology of perception to the realm of the imagination: 'In other words, since immense is not an object, a phenomenology of immense would refer us directly to our imaginary consciousness. In analyzing images of immensity, we would realize within ourselves the pure being of pure imagination' (1964: 184). Bachelard concludes that the perception of immensity has its origin in solitary contemplation: 'Immensity is within ourselves'. And we project this immensity into the world in the dialectics of quiet perception. Bachelard's notion of an '*inner immensity* that gives their real meaning to certain expressions concerning the visible world' (185) is pertinent to Zambrano's recourse to images of expansiveness in contemplation.

Doors are the freest passage-way to and from the interior and exterior. 'For the door', says Bachelard, 'is an entire cosmos of the Half-open. In fact, it is one of its primal images, the very origin of a day dream that accumulates desires and temptations: the temptation to open up the ultimate depths of being' (222). Bachelard interprets poetic images representing dialectical interior-exterior space as illustrative of man's nature:

> In that region where being *wants* to be both visible and hidden, the movements of opening and closing are so numerous, so frequently inverted, and so charged with hesitation, that we could conclude on the following formula: man is a half-open being. (Bachelard 1964: 222)

But he wonders, after explaining several authors' use of the door image, 'onto what, toward what, do doors open? Do they open for the world of men, or for the world of solitude?' Bachelard, quoting Ramón Gómez de la Serna, concludes that 'Doors that open on the countryside seem to confer freedom behind the world's back' (1964: 224). The images of doors, windows, and balconies seem to have significance for Zambrano's view of the way man perceives the world in an interior-exterior (I non-I) dialectic.

Evoking the complexities metaphors acquire, Zambrano applies some of these principles to her analysis of the heart metaphor. According to Zambrano, the heart is a dark cavity, a hermetic place that occasionally opens up:

> Este abrirse es su mayor nobleza, la acción más heroica e inesperada de una entraña que parece al pronto no ser otra cosa que vibración, sentir puramente pasivo. Signo de generosidad porque indica que aquello que primariamente es sólo pasividad — acusación — se transforma en activo [...] Suprema acción de algo que sin dejar de ser interioridad la ofrece en un gesto que parece podría anularla, pero que sólo la eleva. Se ofrece por ser interioridad y para seguirlo siendo. Y esto: interioridad que se ofrece para seguir siendo interioridad, sin anularla, es la definición de la intimidad. (Zambrano 1987c: 9)

> [This opening-up is its greatest nobility, the most heroic and unexpected action in an entrail that at first does not seem to be anything other than vibration, a purely passive feeling. It is a sign of generosity because it indicates that that which is primarily passive — an accusation — becomes active. [...] Supreme action on the part of something that without ceasing to be interiority offers it in a gesture which could annul it, but only elevates it. It offers itself because it is interiority and in order to continue being interiority. An interiority that offers itself in order to continue being interiority, without annulling it is the definition of intimacy.]

The heart's secret is that it can open up without losing its interiority, without ceasing to be 'cavidad, interioridad que brinda o que era su fuerza y su tesoro, sin convertirse en superficie' [cavity, interiority that offered or that was its force and its treasure, without becoming surface] (Zambrano 1987c: 10). The heart offers itself not in order to leave itself but rather to make what is outside it enter into it, because the heart is an open interiority, an active passivity. However, the other viscera must participate in this opening-up in some way, because '[s]i tal participación no sucediese, el corazón podría tener una vida independiente y solitaria, como la llega a tener el pensamiento' [if there were not this participation, the heart would have an independent, solitary life, like the intellect does] (10). Significantly, Zambrano believes that the heart cannot live independently:

> Pues vida es esta incapacidad de desligarse un órgano de otro, un elemento de otro; esta imposibilidad de disociación que es tan arriesgada porque al no haber separación, cuando llega es fatalmente la muerte. Incapacidad de liberación, de vivir independiente y por sí mismo, que es la forma de la libertad del pensamiento, que logra así su superioridad, pero sin heroísmo, porque nunca arriesga ni padece, porque al liberarse de la vida nada tiene que temer de la muerte. (Zambrano 1987c: 10)

> [Because life is this inability to disconnect one organ from another, one element from another; the impossibility of disassociation that is so risky because when there is no separation, when it comes it is fatally death. Incapability of liberation, to live independently and for oneself, which is the form of liberty of thought, which in that way achieves its superiority, but without heroism, because it never took risks or suffered, because upon liberating itself from life nothing has to fear death.]

Zambrano ends her essay revisiting the spatial nature of the heart and the fact that it is interior, a space that it is not able to enjoy, since it is the intellect that enjoys space, because it 'anda suelto y libre por él' [goes around loose and free in it] (1987c: 11). Open space is the dominion of the intellect; the heart is deepness, profundity: 'Lo profundo es una llamada amorosa. Por eso, toda sima atrae' [The depths are an amorous call. For this reason, all abysses attract] (12).[6]

As Virigina Trueba notes, the light metaphor is perhaps the most pervasive in Zambrano's prose, a lesson she may have learned at the knee of Federico García Lorca. In her introduction to her anthology of García Lorca's poetry compiled in 1937 in Chile, Zambrano states that:

> Cualquier albañil de Triana o de Albaicín, analfabeto inclusive, pero que lleva en sus ojos el sentido de las proporciones, del color y de la figura y sin darle importancia, de modo espontáneo, pinta la fachada de su casa del color justo para que armonice con la luz que recibe, con las casas que tiene al lado, con el árbol que le da sombra y realiza así una verdadera creación continuadora de la tradición artística de tantos siglos. (Zambrano 1937: 12)

> [Even if he is illiterate, any stone mason from Triana or Albaicín carries within his eyes a sense of proportion and colour and shape without even recognizing it; it a spontaneous way he paints the facade of a house with just the right colour so that it harmonizes with the light it receives with the contiguous houses, with the tree that gives it light and in that way achieves a true creation that continues in the artistic tradition of so many centuries.]

Zambrano especially points to the visceral, metaphoric nature of Andalusian speech, which she finds in García Lorca, and which, although unacknowledged by her, forms the basis of her own language. Zambrano gives a phenomenological explanation for the way in which native Andalusians use language:

> El andaluz crea cuando habla; si se le pregunta a cualquier campesino, qué es aquel árbol, p. ej., nunca responderá de la misma manera. Su respuesta será casi siempre metafórica, pero la imagen será distinta, hallada sin esfuerzo, porque según su presentimiento el árbol será distinto. Porque su definición del árbol está en función de su vida en aquel instante. (Zambrano 1937: 12)

> [The Andalusian creates when he speaks; if you ask any peasant, what is that tree, for example, he never responds in the same way. His answer will almost always be metaphorical, but the image will be different, found effortlessly, because his sense of the tree will be different. Because his definition of the tree arises from his life at that moment.]

This metaphorical/phenomenological approach to language is also Zambrano's own, and one cannot help but understand that she includes herself in her interpretation of Andalusian speech (Zambrano was born and lived the first years of her life in Vélez-Málaga in Andalusia).

Zambrano's employment of metaphorical language is most intense in her literary-philosophical works, *La tumba de Antígone* [Antigone's Tomb], *Delirio y destino* [Delirium and Destiny], and her most literary philosophical work, *Claros del bosque* [Clearings in the Woods], which is cemented in one continuous metaphor — the clearing in the woods. Virginia Trueba writes of the 'tejido de imágenes' [the weave of images] (Zambrano 2012b: 69) on which Zambrano's thought rests, relating this strategy to the author's interest in painting. Just as Zambrano noted the linguistic variations in Andalusian peasant speech according to the way the speaker was perceiving reality on any particular occasion, Trueba notes that Zambrano's 'denso lecho de imágenes [...] de una riqueza inmensa, las cuales actúan de modo distinto dependiendo de los contextos en que aparecen' [dense bed of images [...] of an immense richness, that act in a different way depending on the contexts in which they appear] (Zambrano 2012b: 69–70). Trueba also observes: 'Muchas de las imágenes zambranianas presentan [...] una dificultad: al provenir de los arquetipos de lo imaginario, impiden diferenciar con claridad las que actúan a modo de símbolo y las que lo hacen como metáfora' [Many of Zambrano's images present [...] a difficulty: for the origin of the archetypes of the imagination, it is difficult to distinguish clearly between those that act as a symbol and those that act as a metaphor] (Zambrano 2012b: 70). Here I am not attempting to distinguish between symbol and metaphor, as I suppose that all metaphors create meanings that could be considered symbolic.

We know that Zambrano wrote poetry in her youth, and a few examples of it survive.[7] This poetic drive undergirds some of her basic philosophical concepts, such as consciousness, and perhaps takes some of the sting out of the notion of consciousness, which so disturbed Ortega that he eventually eliminated the notion from his epistemology. In Zambrano's 'Delirio de Antígone' [Antigone's Delirium], published in the Cuban journal *Orígenes*, the first paragraph develops the notion of consciousness via a continuous metaphor. We are told that Antigone is a:

> Símbolo perfecto de la virginidad que ni siquiera ha reparado en sí misma. Misterio de la virginidad en toda la plenitud; y por ello, de la conciencia en estado virginal. La conciencia virgen alumbra y se dirige a lo que no es ella misma, a lo que no es tampoco el sujeto a quien pertenece. Raro momento de perfección humana, pues el hombre, sale de su sueño para entrar en la conciencia a través de una falta, de un crimen. Conciencia es despertar del sueño de la vida; pues vivir debe ser originalmente hundido en el sueño sin saber alguno acerca de las diferencias entre las cosas; diferencia que se da sobre la primera, aquella abismal entre nosotros y la realidad que nos rodea.
>
> Y una vez que los humanos despiertan de su ensueño a la conciencia, inmediatamente vuelven la luz que ella arroja, sobre sí mismos, caen en la cuenta de sí y lo que nombramos *yo* toma cuerpo y lo que es peor, peso, Y así, nuestro propio ser viene a interferirse en la luz, destello de la luz original que es la conciencia. Y se pierde la conciencia pura, original. La Filosofía ha hecho siempre el máximo esfuerzo para devolvernos a la luz original a través de una larga historia, ahondando la conciencia o bien devolviéndola, reintegrándola a su punto de origen, a lo divino. (Zambrano 1995b: 66–67)

> [Perfect symbol of the virginity that has not even taken notice of itself. The mystery of virginity in all its plenitude: and for that reason, of consciousness in its virginal state. Virgin consciousness illuminates and directs itself toward what is not itself and what is not the subject to which it belongs either. It is a rare moment of human perfection, since man comes out of his dream in order to enter into consciousness through a fault, by means of a crime. Consciousness is an awakening from the dream of life; living originally means to remain in the dream without knowing anything about the differences between things;

differences found in the first abyss between us and the reality that surrounds us. Once humans awaken to consciousness from their dream, they immediately turn the light of consciousness upon themselves, and they see themselves and what we call *I* takes shape and what is worse, weight. And thus our own being comes to interfere in the original light, flash of original light that is consciousness. And the pure, original consciousness gets lost. Throughout history, philosophy has always made the maximum effort to return us to the original light through its long history, probing consciousness or rather returning it, reintegrating it into its point of origin, in the Divine way.]

Zambrano achieves a conceptual frame in the use of the term 'symbol' as a metaphor for Antigone. Not only is Antigone a symbol, she is a 'perfect symbol of virginity' — virgin in both her physical and conscious being. Thus Antigone's vital state becomes a metaphor for Zambrano's notion of the way in which consciousness functions in its pre-conscious 'pure and original' state and its fully conscious state. The use of the 'light' completes the metaphor for the workings of consciousness. 'Light' appears four times in the passage — the 'virgin consciousness illuminates and directs itself toward what it is not'; once the human being awakens to consciousness from the primal dream, he/she turns its light upon him or herself, and the self takes on shape and weight, and this light obliterates pure, original consciousness, which philosophy attempts to recover. It is hard to imagine such a complex philosophical concept being explained so efficiently without the light metaphor. Zambrano completes the thought with more metaphorical language: 'Para la perfecta virginidad del alma y de la conciencia, sólo tienen los hombres preparada una celda donde se consume lentamente o una hoguera, fuego que se lleva para sí lo que en realidad le pertenece' [For the perfect virginity of the soul and of consciousness, people have only prepared a cell or a bonfire where they are slowly consumed, a fire that carries away what in fact belongs to it] (1995b: 67). If light is the metaphor for the awakening of consciousness, fire is the metaphor Zambrano elects to represent the destructive force of that consciousness toward the pre-conscious state, once it has been surpassed by full consciousness. Full consciousness is the equivalent of hell, also suggested by the fire metaphor. Then, comparing Antigone to Persephone — Spring — who was kidnapped by the god of fire, Antigone becomes 'la primavera de la conciencia humana, la pureza de la conciencia' who will return over and over again to 'alumbrar el mundo' [shed light on the world] (1995b: 68):

> Claridad que ilumina abismos últimos, llama que nunca se volvió sobre sí sino para consumir el leve cuerpo; por eso ardió lenta sin arrebato. Luz alada que desde las sombras asoma, claridad nacida del abismo como pálido verdor de la primavera, y entre la verde pelusa una flor azulada, una roja, amoratada amapola que los hombres no deben rozar: gritos incontenibles del delirio. (Zambrano 1995b: 70–71)
>
> [Clarity that illuminates ultimate abysses, flame that never turned upon itself except to consume the slight body; for that reason it burned slowly without fury. Winged light that peeped out from the shadows, clarity born of the abyss like the pale green of spring, and among the green fuzz a bluish flower, a red, bruised poppy that men should not touch: uncontrollable shouts of delirium.][8]

Ultimately, for Zambrano, Antígone is a 'personaje poético' [poetic personage] (1995b: 71).

In *La tumba de Antígona* (1967), a play or set of dialogues and Zambrano's most developed work on Antigone, Zambrano greatly extends the light/consciousness (reason) metaphor as it contrasts with allusions to darkness/emotions. In this work, Antigone allies herself with the cave and darkness (she refuses to leave when Creon grants her freedom), while the men in her life — Creon, Oedipus, Haemon, Eteocles, and Polynices — attempt to bring her out of the cave into the light (of full consciousness). She resists until two strangers arrive in the final section of the work to take her away, but they do not answer her question as to where they will be going. The play ends with Antigone's own answer to her interrogative: 'Sí, Amor. Amor, tierra prometida' [Yes, Love. Love, the promised land] (2012b: 236). Importantly, in an alternate ending that Virginia Trueba has found in the archives at the Zambrano Foundation, Antigone accepts the 'male' reason she seems to reject in the final published version: 'La luz está viva en mí y no me quema. El germen de la luz' [Light lives inside me and does not burn me. It is the root of light] (2012b: 236, n. 100).

The entire work is woven together with strategically placed light and fire metaphors, which are firmly established in the 'Prólogo':

> Parece que la condición sea ésta de haber de descender a los abismos para ascender, atravesando todas las regiones donde el amor es el elemento, por así decir, de la trascendencia humana; primeramente fecundo, seguidamente, si persiste, creador. Creador de vida, de luz, de conciencia.
> Pues que el amor y su ritual viaje a los *ínferos* es quien alumbra el nacimiento de la conciencia. (Zambrano 2012b: 150)

[It would seem that the condition is that of having to descend to the abyss in order to ascend, crossing through all the regions where love is the element, so to say, of human transcendence; firstly fecund, and then, if it persists, creative. Creator of life, of light, of consciousness. Love and its ritual journey to the lower reaches lights the birth of consciousness.]

Here more explicitly than in 'Delirio de Antígona', 'light' is the metaphor for consciousness:

> Como si ella [Antigone] fuera una Perséfone sin esposo que ha obtenido únicamente una estación: una primavera que no puede ser reiterada. El mundo propiamente terrestre donde ha nacido, en el laberinto unas entrañas como sierpes; en el laberinto de la guerra civil y de la tiranía subsiguiente, es decir: en el doble laberinto de la familia y de la historia. Y al realizar ella su sacrificio con la lucidez que le descubre la Nueva Ley, que es también la más remota y sagrada, la Ley sin más, llega hasta allí donde una humana sociedad exista. Su pureza se hace claridad y aun sustancia misma de humana conciencia en estado naciente. Es una figura de la aurora de la conciencia. (Zambrano 2012b: 151–52)

[As though she were a Persephone without a husband who had only been granted one season: a spring that cannot be reiterated. The terrestrial world where the labyrinth of the entrails was born like snakes: in the labyrinth of civil war and the resultant tyranny — that is to say, the double labyrinth of family and history. And upon carrying out her sacrifice with the lucidity she discovered in the New Law, which is the most remote and sacred, simply the Law reaches there where a human society exists. Its purity becomes clarity and even a substance itself of human consciousness in its nascent state. She is a figure of the dawn of consciousness.]

Ninguna víctima de sacrificio pues, y más aún si está movida por el amor, puede dejar de pasar por los infiernos. Ello sucede así, diríamos, ya en esta tierra, donde, sin abandonarla, el dado al amor ha de pasar por todo: por los infiernos de la soledad, del delirio, por el fuego, para acabar dando esa luz que sólo en el corazón se enciende. Parece que la condición sea ésta de haber de descender a los abismos para ascender, atravesando todas las regiones donde el amor es elemento, por así decir, de la trascendencia humana; primeramente fecundo, seguidamente, si persiste, creador. Creador de vida, de luz, de conciencia. Pues que el amor y su ritual viaje a los *ínferos* alumbra el nacimiento de la conciencia. Antígona lo muestra [...]. Su pureza se hace claridad y aun sustancia misma de humana conciencia en estado naciente. Es una figura de la aurora de la conciencia. (Zambrano 2012b: 149–52)

[No sacrificial victim, and even more so if moved by love, can avoid going through Hell. It is that way in this world for the one who is given over to love must go through everything: through the Hell of solitude, of delirium, through fire, in order to end up giving that light that can only be turned on in the heart. It would seem that the condition is that of having to descend into the abyss in order to ascend, crossing through all the regions where love is the element, so to say, of human transcendence; firstly fecund, and then, if it persists, creative. Creator of life, of light, of consciousness. Love and its ritual journey to the lower reaches lights the birth of consciousness. Antigone demonstrates it. [...]. Her purity becomes clarity and even the substance itself of human consciousness in a nascent state. She is the figure of the dawn of consciousness.]

Mas Antígona, aurora de la humana conciencia, no la tuvo tan siquiera de su sacrificio. (Zambrano 2012b: 164)

[But Antigone, dawn of human consciousness, was not even aware of her sacrifice.]

Here in these three quotations, Zambrano brings together the whole of human experience — consciousness, the body, the emotions, society, and history. Zambrano invests the Antigone figure with existence in all its facets, including the impossibility of human consciousness to grasp existence's complexity ('Antigone [...] was not even aware of her sacrifice'). Zambrano's achievement in her version of the Antigone story is summed up in this passage in which Antigone is pure being, experiencing life — being in the world — through consciousness and emotion.

A few pages later Zambrano reiterates the light/consciousness metaphor with reference to Antigone:

La conciencia en ella refleja un rayo de luz a la que enteramente se remite, sin sufrir por un instante la tentación de querer verse a sí misma. Camina a tientas en la luz como si no fuese, como suelen, los mortales, acompañada de su sombra movediza, y precedida de su imagen. (Zambrano 2012b: 164)

[Her consciousness reflects a ray of light to which she commits herself completely without suffering for a moment the temptation to see herself. She walks gropingly in the light as though she were not accompanied, as mortals usually are, by her moving shadow, and preceded by its image.]

And here Zambrano foreshadows what will be her major metaphor in her last important book *Claros del bosque*:

> El tiempo que se les debe, que coincide con el tiempo que los humanos necesitan para recibir esa revelación, claros que se abren en el bosque de la historia.
> Ya que el bosque, dicho sea de paso, se configura más que por los senderos que se pierden, por los claros que en su espesura se abren, aljibes de claridad y de silencio. (Zambrano 2012b: 166)

> [The time that is owed that coincides with the time that humans need in order to receive this revelation, clearings that open up in the woods of history. Since the forest, I note in passing, is configured more than by the paths that get lost in it, by the clearings that open in its thickness, wells of clarity and silence.]

Thus, the clearing in the woods is that moment when consciousness captures (perceives) a phenomenon. Again, as in *La tumba de Antígona*, Zambrano captures the fullness, the completeness of experience.

In Zambrano's interpretation of it, Antigone's tomb, then, is the ante-chamber of human consciousness. It is the liminal, auroral time and space between raw sensory perception and intellection — a kind of pre-consciousness, of the kind Merleau-Ponty wrote about. Zambrano notes in her prologue to *La tumba de Antígona* that:

> Antígona en su tumba es una presencia. En la vida común la persona, en el mejor de los casos, llega a hacer esa su máscara un tanto transparente y al par animada, pues que no hay que olvidar que de luz de vida estamos tratando. Mas en la vida de una persona humana, por dada que sea a la luz, hay siempre una oscuridad y en ella algo que se esconde; la persona resiste a la luz en los mejores casos tanto como la busca. [...]
> Y así, la persona nunca está del todo presente ni para su propia conciencia, y a veces para ella menos aún que para la de ajenos ojos. (Zambrano 2012b: 172)

> [Antigone in her tomb is a presence. In the common life of the person, in the best case scenario, he/she manages to make his/her mask somewhat transparent and at the same time animated, since we should not forget that we are talking about the light of life. Yet in the life of a human person, however much this light may be present, there is always a darkness and something is hidden in it; in the optimal case, the person resists the light as much as he/she looks for it. [...] And thus the person is never completely present even for his/her own consciousness, and sometimes less so than for the consciousness of others.]

The light metaphor guides the viewer or reader through the philosophical problem of situating Antigone's representation of the auroral consciousness. Each character that enters Antigone's tomb and dialogues with her is identified by the density of the metaphors of his/her speech. And this poetic weight, as we have seen throughout this essay, carries philosophical weight. Antigone, who utters soliloquies at the beginning and ending of the work, speaks in an idiom only lightly seasoned with a metaphorical language that enhances her extreme situation — imprisoned in a cave and left to die for having attempted to bury her dead brother against the specific orders of the tyrant Creon. The first part of her soliloquy focuses on light imagery, especially the sun, which Antigone had always sought out, waiting for the Sun to speak; the Sun is the logos (intellect) and the word: 'Tu palabra, luz, sin que yo la entienda, dámela, luz que no me dejas' [Your word, light, without my understanding it, give it to me, light that does not leave me] (2012b: 177). In the second part of her initial speech titled 'La noche' [Night], Antigone further assesses the meaning of her entombment:

> La desgracia golpeó con su martillo mis sienes hasta pulirlas como el interior de una caracola [...] Nunca estuve desnuda; mi piel fue deshojada por este parásito. Un día me vi de repente y me dio sobresalto. ¿Era yo esa larva sin cuerpo [...]? [...] No, tumba mía, [...] [n]o voy a estrellar contra ti mi cabeza [...] Una cuna eres; un nido. Mi casa. [...] Pero yo, mientras muero, quiero oírte a ti, mi tumba, [...] blanca como la boca del alba. (Zambrano 2012b: 178–79)

> [Misfortune beat on my temples with its hammer until it polished them like the interior of a conch shell. [...] I was never naked; my skin was peeled off by this parasite. One day I suddenly saw myself, and I was frightened. Was I that larva without a body [...]? [...] No, my tomb, I am not going to beat my head against you. [...] You are a crib; a nest. My house. [...] But while I die, I want to hear you, my tomb, white like the mouth of the dawn.]

Zambrano seems to agree with Merleau-Ponty that perception is primary amongst human experiences, as the predominance of light would suggest.

In the next section, Antigone's sister Ismene dreams, and clarity dawns after the night; they are not enclosed in the tomb: 'y una grande claridad se derramaba dentro, y una luz blanca afuera, que no era en verdad afuera, sino un lugar abierto que seguía' [and a great clarity streamed in, and a white light outside that was not really outside but an open place that continued] (2012b: 182). In this section, as well as the first, Zambrano distinguishes between the light of the sun, which is too strong and the softer auroral light — the full intellectual consciousness and the dawning consciousness. Oedipus's section is by far the most metaphorically charged. The father's importance to the story, as the one who unleashed all the misfortune that befalls his family for having killed his father and married his mother, is conveyed in the poetic flight that his section represents. Oedipus describes himself as ivy that wanted to climb and Antigone as 'rosa a la luz más allá de la vergüenza. Eras tú mi cumplimiento, tú mi corona' [rose in the light beyond shame. You were my complement, you my crown] (189). Antigone was born of his thought; she was his reason. Oedipus continues that he was only a cloud, a soft, warm cloud, carried along by the wind. He did not have 'una brizna de razón' [a blade of reason] (189). Antigone was 'mi palabra sin error. [...] el espejo donde un hombre puede mirarse' [my word without error. [...] the mirror in which a man can look at himself] (189). Further he is 'como un sueño' [like a dream] (189): 'Yo era apenas el despertar de una luciérnaga, el parpadear de una llama, un poco de aliento, un palpitar de un corazón pálido. Yo no era casi nada. Era casi, era apenas, y tuve que ser eso: un hombre' [I was scarcely the awakening of a firefly, the blinking of a flame, a little bit of breath, a beating of a pale heart. I was hardly anything at all. I was almost; I was scarcely, and I had to be this — a man] (189). The densely metaphoric language continues throughout the passage as Oedipus defines himself in relation to Antigone:

'tuve que seguir como una nube de esas que se quedan olvidadas después de una tormenta, cuando ya brilla el Sol. [...] Estaba yo hecho de olvido. Un hombre o un dios acaso' [I had to go on like one of those clouds that is left behind after a storm when the sun has come out. [...] I was made of forgetfulness. A man or perhaps a god] (190). Oedipus repeats his cloudlike condition, accompanied in his exile by Antigone 'como un cordero y me alegrabas en mi destierro' [like a lamb and you made me happy in my exile] (190). Toward the end of the section, Antigone engages in a rare case of metaphoric wordplay: 'Y ahora me han dado tierra, aunque estoy enterrada' [And now they have given me land, although I am buried] (190).

Two following sections — encounters between Antigone and her nursemaid and then her mother — focus on the light metaphor. The nursemaid's speech is replete with sensory references — seeing, hearing — that do not become light or intellect. Antigone is left in her tomb, which she remarks is her loom:

> Me dejas sola con mi memoria, como la araña. A ella le sirve para hacer su tela. Esta tumba es mi telar. No saldré de ella, no se me abrirá hasta que yo acabe, hasta que yo haya acabado mi tela. (Zambrano 2012b: 195–96)

> [Like the spider, you leave me alone with my memory. That is her web. This tomb is my loom. I will not leave it; nor will it open up for me until I finish, until I have finished my web.]

The mother is a shadow that does not have light in her entrails, but she is the fertile ground in which light can grow:

> No tiene la Madre entrañas de luz, aunque algún día de algún modo alguna haya de tenerlas. Hasta ahora todas han sido por dentro oscuras también, como tú. Pero dan algo, algo vivo a la luz. Dan vida a la luz, Eso. Y eso tú, madre nuestra, lo hiciste. (Zambrano 2012b: 200)

> [The Mother has no entrails of light, although some day in some way she may have them. Until now they have all been dark inside, like you. But they have something, something alive in the light. They give life by the light. That. And that you, our mother, you achieved it.]

The harpy, by contrast, is identified metaphorically as a spider, a reasoner: 'la Diosa de las Razones disfrazada. La araña del cerebro' [the disguised Goddess of Reason. The brain's spider] (2012b: 206).

Moving further toward light and reason is the section with Antigone's brothers Eteocles and Polynices on hard, tough metaphorical language (as opposed to Oedipus's nature metaphors — a cloud, a rose, a lamb) 'la destrucción de la Patria, su caída' [the destruction of the Fatherland, its fall] (209), 'le ofrecen como exvoto un corazón de piedra' [their offering is a heart of stone] (209), 'Todo se vuelve pesado bajo los vencedores, todo se convierte en culpa, en losa de sepulcro. Todos vienen a ser sepultados vivos, los que han seguido vivos, los que no se han vuelto, tal como ellos decretan, de piedra' [Everything becomes heavy under the conquerers; everything becomes guilt, a gravestone. All those who have continued alive, those that have not become, as they decree, made of stone become buried alive] (209). Thus we are prepared to understand the violet metaphor for 'the vanquished Second

Spanish Republic' when Antigone mentions 'aquella violeta que se me cayó de las manos una tarde que cogía flores' [that violet that fell from my hands one afternoon when I was gathering wildflowers] (210), the Republican flag being distinguished by its bottom purple band. In the culminating moment of the scene, in a metaphorical statement, Eteocles declares himself to have been the Fatherland: 'Yo era la Patria. Yo la Patria' [I was the Fatherland. I the Fatherland] (211). Antigone briefly identifies herself with 'light' (reason): 'Cada gota de esa luz de ésta que venís a beber ahora ya muertos, cuesta sangre. [...] Mi sangre fue, todavía más que la vuestra, sacrificada: a ese poco de saber, a esa brizna de luz' [Each drop of light, that light that you have come to drink as dead men, costs blood. [...] My blood was, even more than yours, sacrificed to this small bit of knowledge, to this small blade of light] (214). There are few metaphors in the section with Haemon that follows. Antigone points out that she is 'la ceniza de aquella muchacha. Me deshojé' [the ashes of that girl. I lost my leaves] (218), to which Haemon responds that she is 'más blanca que nunca, luz de tu propia luz' [whiter than ever, light of her own light] (218). He also indicates that she is being born (surely alluding to the fact that she is growing into consciousness). Creon and then Antigone have the final speeches. Creon says to Antigone that the Sun is waning and that she should regard it, but she answers, 'Ese Sol no es ya el mío' [That Sun is no longer mine] (223). Antigone will remain at the dawn of consciousness without entering fully into rational consciousness, represented by the Sun. Her final speech confirms her position:

> Oh Sol: estás todavía aquí como un reproche, como remordimiento que se arrastra, como una insidia. Ya sé que te veo por última vez, Sol de la Tierra, y que cuando te vayas, mis ojos, estos de la tierra, dejarán de ver, pues que no se abrieron solos, tú los abriste como una herida. Esa herida de la luz en el rostro de los mortales. Sé que yéndote tú, Sol, se cerrarán estas llagas [...] Allí donde nunca llegó la luz del Sol que nos alumbra. Sí, una luz sin ocaso en el centro de la eterna noche.
>
> Aún luces, aún me hieres con tu reverberar; estoy todavía viva: veo, respiro y toco y, como nadie me llama, no sé si podría oír. (Zambrano 2012b: 226)
>
> [Oh, Sun: you are still here, like a reproach, like remorse that drags like a snare. I know that I am seeing you for the last time, Sun of the Earth, and when you leave, these earthly eyes will cease to see, given that they did not open alone; you opened them like a wound. This wound of light in the face of mortals. I know that with your departure, Sun, these wounds will heal. [...] There where the Sun's light that lights us never reached. Yes, a light with no sunset in the centre of the eternal night. You are still shining and you hurt me with your reverberating; I am still here alive: I see, I breathe, and I touch, and, since no one calls me, I do not know if I can hear.]

Once again, Antigone is associated with raw sensory perception rather than full intellection. In her final soliloquy, her speech becomes increasingly metaphorical as she reflects upon her condition as an exile:

> Náufragos que la tempestad arroja a una playa como un desecho, que es a la vez un tesoro. [...] algo que solamente tiene el que ha sido arrancado de raíz [...] crecemos como las plantas, como los árboles. (Zambrano 2012b: 227–28)

[Shipwrecked persons that the storm throws up on the beach like debris that is also a treasure. [...] something that only he who has been pulled up by the roots possesses [...] we grow like plants, like trees.]

Y ese tiempo inacabable y renaciente, como el Mar. [...] Hay que subir siempre. Eso es el destierro, una cuesta, aunque sea en el desierto. Esa cuesta que sube siempre y, por ancho que sea el espacio a la vista, es siempre estrecha. Y hay que mirar, claro, a todas partes, atender a todo como un centinela en el último confín de la tierra conocida. (Zambrano 2012b: 227–28)

[And this endless and renewable time, like the Sea. [...] One has to continue to climb. That is exile, a hill, although it is in a desert. That slope that keeps going up and, however wide the space may be to the sight, it is always narrow. And, of course, one has to look around everywhere, attend to everything like a sentinel at the end of the known world.]

Antigone's culminating soliloquy ends with a number of references to the dawning light: 'Íbamos andando a la claridad de las estrellas, hacia el alba, hacia el alba siempre' [We were walking toward the light of the stars, toward the dawn, always toward the dawn] (2012b: 229). Antigone is coming into her conscious state; it is in this pre-conscious state that the *desconocidos* (unknown persons) arrive in the final scene to lead her to she knows not where, leaving her at the dawn of full consciousness, a state in which the full light of reason has not obliterated the passions and other forms of reason — like that of the heart — unlike the blinding sunlight of eighteenth-century Enlightenment reason.

Notes to Chapter 9

1. Chantal Maillard (1992) argues that Zambrano's philosophical method 'la razón poética' is itself metaphorical and that Zambrano's ontology is likewise metaphorical. My purpose here is not to revisit these notions but to discuss Zambrano's philosophy of metaphor and explore some of her specific uses of the trope in her prose.
2. All translations are my own unless otherwise stated.
3. Edmund Husserl and Jean-Paul Sartre asserted that consciousness can overrule the body and its immediate contact with things.
4. This statement resonates with Unamuno's and Azorín's notions of *intrahistoria*.
5. Virginia Trueba observes: 'Para Zambrano, el corazón es asimismo el centro, en tanto constituye el órgano con capacidad de mediación, de distribución del *logos* por las entrañas, el lugar donde "aquí" y "allí" se identifican. En el texto 'La metáfora del corazón' de *Hacia un saber sobre el alma* (1950), habla Zambrano del corazón del siguiente modo, deslizando la metáfora hacia el símbolo: "[...] lo primero que sentimos en la vida del corazón es su condición de oscura cavidad, de recinto hermético; víscera; entraña. El corazón es el símbolo y representación máxima de todas las entrañas de la vida, la entraña donde todas encuentran su unidad definitiva, y su nobleza. Se puede y la expresión popular bien lo sabe, tener entrañas y no tener corazón" (Zambrano, 2001, 65). Tener corazón supone que la herida no se desangre del todo. La "herida": imagen asimismo zambraniana. Herida es la de Antígona, pero también la de la aurora, la cual tiene que violentarse en el seno de la noche para llegar a la luz' [For Zambrano, the heart is also the centre in that it is the organ with the capacity for mediation between the logos and the entrails, the place where 'here' and 'there' are identified. In 'La metáfora del corazón' [The Metaphor of the Heart] in *Hacia un saber sobre el alma* 1950 [*Towards a Knowledge of the Soul*], Zambrano writes of the heart in the following manner: moving the metaphor toward a symbol: '[...] the first thing that we feel in the life of the heart is its condition as a dark cavity, a hermetic place, the entrail where everyone

finds his/her unity and nobility. One can, and the popular expression knows it well, have guts and not have heart' (Zambrano, 2001, 65). To have heart means that the wound is not fatal. The 'wound' is also a Zambranian image. Antigone has a wound, but it is of the dawn, which has to break through the breast of night in order to arrive at the light] (Zambrano 2012b: 74).

6. Merleau-Ponty understands the relationship between language and the body in a similar way: 'By these words, the "primacy of perception", we mean that the experience of perception is our presence at the moment when things, truths, values are constituted for us; that perception is a nascent *logos*; that it teaches us, outside all dogmatism, the true conditions of objectivity itself; that it summons us to the tasks of knowledge and action. It is not a question of reducing human knowledge to sensation, but of assisting at the birth of this knowledge, to make it as sensible, to recover the consciousness of rationality. This experience of rationality is lost when we take it for granted as self-evident, but is, on the contrary, rediscovered when it is made to appear against the back ground of non-human nature' (1964: 25).

7. For example, 'Árbol', published in *Nostromo: nave cultural del siglo XXI* (Guadalajara, Mexico), 19 (6 March 1994), 12.

8. See my article on María Zambrano's 'Delirio de Antígona' (Johnson 2016) for an explanation of the colour symbolism here that replicates the colours of the flag of the Second Spanish Republic. A sentence in the following paragraph allies Antígone via metaphor with the vanquished Republic: 'Y así Antígona se irá transformando; era como una azulada, flor, de ese azul puro, dulce y violento, de virginidad creadora. [...] se convierte en una ortiga gris y áspera, no tiene sino la sed imposible ya de satisfacer' [And so Antigone became transformed; she was like a bluish flower, of this pure, sweet and violent blue, of a creative virginity. [...] was converted into a grey and rough thistle left with only the now impossible to satisfy thirst] (Zambrano 1995b: 71).

CHAPTER 10

About Painting and Dialectical Images of María Zambrano

Elide Pittarello, Università Ca' Foscari Venezia

In the beginning María Zambrano invents images, her main device for thinking. She colonizes ideas with the senses producing mimetic hybrids between psyche and soma. Her images revitalize the abstractions of metaphysics with the paradigm of an embodied view. Zambrano's metaphors are well-known, they are her way of expressing figuratively revelations through a gaze which rejects 'la tiranía del concepto, que somete la libertad con el cebo del conocimiento' [the tyranny of the concept, which constrains freedom with the bait of knowledge] (Zambrano 1986c: 35).[1] The gaze implies the urgency of knowing (Zambrano 1989c: 126), but by which means? The logos has reached its conceptual limits, and it is necessary to overcome it by also changing the linguistic legacy of idealism. Metaphors are an experimental enterprise; they do not exist in a dictionary, they are constructed in speech (Ricoeur 1975: 125). To quote Aristotle, they put real things under one's eyes, they visualize existing relationships in the material world (Ricoeur 1975: 61). Being a process, metaphors generate a semantic sketch with no conceptual referents; they presuppose a movement from a familiar referential field to an unknown one in order to develop a semantic intention. Thus metaphors are the dynamic result of an 'ontological vehemence' that articulates a new kind of linguistic information through semantic skills (Ricoeur 1975: 379).

All Zambrano's interpretations of paintings are visions of visions, the application of her philosophy to a branch of visual arts. In her paradigm, paintings are not mere representations, i.e. mimetic portions of 'reality' in the wider sense of the term. They are appearances, which she does not separate from the creative process and its effect or dissemination. Once more she applies to them 'poetic reason', an oxymoron that involves dialectical investigations but without synthesis. It is open to what is irrational and ineffable, vital but not based on history (Bundgaard 2005: 74). Avoiding the opposition between subject and object, Zambrano attends to the swing between the two. On the one hand, she does not isolate any artist from his work (there is no woman among her favourite painters). On the other hand, she plays the role of a living viewer who enhances her own experience, without regard to the linguistic approach of the art historian. Zambrano's attitude, which links thoughts and perceptions, gives rise to a personal hermeneutics of painting. After coming back to Spain, Zambrano decided to collect some of her texts on this subject in a book, *Algunos lugares de la pintura* [Some Places of Painting]. The title itself is a key to her original practice of contemplation. In her 'Introduction' she declares: 'La pintura es una presencia constante, existe para mí, ha existido siempre, como un lugar privilegiado donde detener la mirada. Lugares privilegiados, algunos, donde la semilla esencial del arte se da con abundancia e intensidad' [Painting is a constant presence, it exists for me, it has always existed as a privileged place where my gaze can rest. In certain privileged places the essential seed of art is given with abundance and intensity] (Zambrano 2012a: 12).

The first article, 'Nostalgia de la tierra' [Longing for Land], was published in 1933 in Madrid, when Zambrano was an enthusiastic supporter of the Second Republic's revolutionary reforms. The last was composed in the same city after an exile of nearly half a century, when Spain had become a democratic monarchy. The title, 'Aparición de Santos Alonso' [Appearance of Santos Alonso], is metaphorical. It refers to the light or knowledge that had come out from the darkness, the metaphysical origin of every being, but also a real condition of her writing. In fact, Zambrano ends the manuscript not only putting the place and the date, but also the exact time of night: Madrid, one thirty a.m., 2nd February 1989 (Zambrano 2012a: 178). Maybe due to her age, such unusually precise chronological details authenticate the endurance of her love for painting. At that period she was selecting the articles to be published in *Algunos lugares de la pintura*, with the assistance of Amalia Iglesias (Zambrano 1989a; Iglesias 2004), and *Notas de un método* [Notes on a Method] (1989c). She would die two years after.

María Zambrano and the Iconic Turn

There is no doubt that the debate on different theories of the image in the last two decades helps to approach Zambrano's hermeneutics of painting with new critical tools. Gottfried Boehm underlines that the problems concerning research on images, with their non-verbal expression, go beyond philosophical orientation, traditionally rooted in *logos* (2009: 40–41). But, after Nietzsche, we are aware that conceptual language also has metaphorical origins (Blumenberg 1998) and metaphors have become a suitable device to provide the structural model of images. Because of their visual interactions and referential contrasts, metaphors remove the conventional coherence of discourse. With their semantic incompleteness, they open the linguistic meaning to echoes, allusions, emotional evocations (Boehm 2009: 56–57). The visible discontinuity of language is a pillar of Zambrano's philosophy based on metaphors, as she wrote: 'Nada es solamente lo que es' [Nothing is merely what it is] (1989c: 119). In metaphors she finds simultaneous functions that compensate for the sensual deficits of conceptual knowledge:

> No se trata [...] en la metáfora de una identificación ni de una atribución, sino de otra forma de enlace y unidad. Porque no se trata de una relación 'lógica' sino de una relación más aparente y a la vez más profunda; de una relación que llega a ser intercambiable entre formas, colores, a veces hasta perfumes, y el alma oculta que los produce.
> Mas la vida de la metáfora no queda ahí, en lo que inicialmente es, en lo que inicialmente se presenta. Ciertas grandes privilegiadas metáforas, como la de

la luz, como la del corazón, como la del fuego, han penetrado en los más altos planos del pensamiento abstracto y allí se han instalado, podríamos decir que permanentemente, ricas de significaciones, inagotables de sentido. (Zambrano 1989c: 120)

[Metaphor is not a matter of identification or attribution, but a link, a unity of another kind. Because it is not a matter of a 'logical' relationship but of one which is more apparent and at the same time deeper; a relationship thanks to which shapes, colours, sometimes perfumes, and the hidden soul that produces them, become interchangeable. But the life of metaphor does not stop there, with what it initially is, what initially appears. Certain great, privileged metaphors, such as light, heart, fire have penetrated the highest levels of abstract thought and settled there, we could say as if permanently, rich in significance, inexhaustible in meaning.]

Gottfried Boehm extends the semantic contrast that characterizes metaphors to images, which he defines in terms of unities of meaning due to the 'iconic difference'. This is a visual and logical power inscribed in the material world with transcendent significations. Far from being copies, images are representations that make visible the process of existence between a surface and its interior. In this sense the iconic difference builds up a productive tension (2009: 57–59). It is a plausible proposal for approaching Zambrano's concept of metaphor, that she so originally exploited in all her books. From the perspective of the iconic difference, what she wrote about painting achieves an unsuspected relevance.

There is no evolution in Zambrano's phenomenological practice of standing in front of paintings, but some texts she wrote on this subject are more explicit than others. In 'España y su pintura' [Spain and its Painting], written in Rome in 1960, she declares that painting is an agreement between light and shadow and that vision produces a revelation of what human beings are always seeking, i.e. knowledge (Zambrano 2012a: 51). In 'Sueño y destino de la pintura' [Dream and Destiny in Painting], the draft of which was written in the early sixties, she states that paintings, even when perfectly finished, are never static, they never stop making themselves. Exchanging a concept for an image, she transforms painting's stillness into incessant movement, expressed by metaphors such as these: 'Van como en un río, transcurren, pasan, suceden' [They move like in a river, they flow, pass, happen] (63). Thus she classifies painting as an intimate occurrence in human subjects, but disregards both the traditional role of the artist and of the spectator: '[la obra] muestra un suceso que le ha sucedido a alguien y que le sucede a quien lo mira' [A painting shows an event that has happened to someone and that happens to whoever looks at it] (63).

This approach, so heterodox if related to traditional art history, presents phenomenological analogies with contemporary debates on the image. Devoid of metaphysical implications, in his anthropology of images Hans Belting highlights the importance of the *medium* and of the *body*. The first is seen as 'the agent by which images are transmitted', the second points out 'either the performing or the perceiving body on which images depend' (2005: 302). In Belting's view both of them are significant in the energetic circuit of images:

Images are neither on the wall (or on a screen) nor in the head alone. They do not *exist* by themselves, but they *happen*; they take place whether they are moving images (where this is obvious) or not. They happen via transmission and perception. (Belting 2005: 302–03)

The interaction of mental and physical images is crucial to obtain a better focus on Zambrano's hermeneutics of painting. In fact, Belting illustrates them as 'the two sides of the same coin. The ambivalence of endogenous images and exogenous images, which interact on many different levels, is inherent in the image practice of humanity' (2005: 304). Having a body, María Zambrano realizes images of her own by animating the painted images. She attributes to them the possibility of assuming vital existence.

Close to Ramón Gaya, Painter and Writer

Born in Murcia in 1910, Ramón Gaya was an enthusiastic participant in the project of the so-called 'People's Museum', a branch of the Pedagogical Missions of the Second Republic (Tejada Minguez 2011: 61). He was one of the three painters who made copies of some famous paintings in the Prado that were to be exhibited in countryside villages. He was also very active as a lecturer and travelled many times around Spain to introduce those paintings to uncultivated people (Gaya 2006: 372–77; Dennis 2011: 15–26). This utopian commitment made him yet more familiar, if possible, with the Prado's masterpieces that he used to contemplate and that he missed so much during his exile in Mexico, from 1940 to 1952. There he began to paint homages to Velázquez and Titian, to Murillo and Rembrandt among others: it was his way of dealing with the physical, cultural, and emotional distance from his country and, in a wider sense, from European painting, the main cause of his homesickness.

While he was living in Mexico, Gaya collected many photographic reproductions of the artworks he had admired and also of those he had never seen in person. Thus he refined his ghost practice of painting. Instead of making copies, when he paid tribute to his favourite painters he opened a vital dialogue with them, adding small objects from his everyday life to his pictorial reinterpretations of the reproductions of the originals. A glass of water, a book, some flowers or fruits, a majolica cup, or a mirror resting on a bare console: things such as these set the domestic scenery in which his homages — generally partial sketches of the chosen paintings — take place. Thus the painter hosted all his favourite memories in a domestic interior marked by traces of his own life. José Muñoz Millanes observes that in his homages Gaya evokes every artist as if he were a guest. It is a style of his own, as he feels painting is alive and physically present (2011: 163). In an essay written in 1945, 'Homenaje a Velázquez' [Homage to Velazquez], Gaya declares his radical refutation of the history of art, which can be summarized in two crucial statements. The first one is: 'la obra de arte no es, como se supone, eterna, sino presente, incesantemente presente, viva sin descanso' [the artwork is not, as one believes, eternal, but present, incessantly present, living without pause] (1999: 50). The second one is: 'el arte es un vacío, un sitio, un lugar al que se asoma el hombre, no para comprender las cosas y comprenderse, sino para sentirse, es decir, casi para ignorarse' [art is a void, a site, a place that man faces not to understand things and understand himself, but to feel himself, that is, almost to ignore himself] (1999: 52). Gaya's homages are the practice of his unorthodox aesthetic. They make real a deliberate art of the anachronism according to Walter Benjamin's definition, elaborated by Georges Didi-Huberman: a combination of unconscious feelings and semiotic competences (2000: 40). It was always like that. Far from marking a crisis of the exiled artist, who would have recreated works according to the European tradition (Murcia Serrano 2011: 92), the homages that Gaya made in Mexico inaugurate an artistic and sentimental education based on the refusal of history and chronological time (Trapiello 2000: 23). He painted homages throughout his life out of the need to remind himself and everybody else that his cherished painters were constantly close to him, part of his life (Dennis 2010: 230).

According to Boehm's theory, which incorporates the thoughts of both Merleau-Ponty and Lacan on the gaze, vision, and desire, this attitude is an extreme manifestation of the iconic difference and its transcendent possibilities. In Gaya's Mexican production, the use of printed reproductions intensifies the actualization of memory through a montage of dialectical images, and, according to Walter Benjamin's definition, 'image is that wherein what has been comes together in a flash with the now to form a constellation. In other words: image is dialectic at a standstill' (1999a: [N3, 1] 463). This constellation refers to the heterogeneous fragments of the past which one remembers. It is especially true in Gaya's artwork, which is a very personal case of hybridization or medial transposition (Rajewski 2005: 51) before the postmodern use of intermedia (Bolter and Grusing 1999). Gaya uses printed reproductions as one source, among others, for his own paintings. Even if a photographed object testifies to what Roland Barthes summarized in the formula 'That-has-been' (1981: 77), the image produced by an analogical camera is a trace of the instantaneous contact with the referent. It emanates from a lost reality in a temporal and spatial distance. Because of this material connection, a photograph is above all a Peircean index (Dubois 1983) that in Gaya's painting works like a dialectical image. In his case the trace of this medium seems to be close to Didi-Huberman's definition of the footprint: 'something that tells us both of the *contact* (the foot sinking into the sand) and the *loss* (the absence of the foot in its footprint)' (2008: 18).[2]

In the gap between resemblance and reminiscence, Gaya, like Zambrano, feels painting to be an art of revelation. Before being a painter he is a spectator who never considers his figurative art a mimetic process, an aesthetic representation of the visible world. What he tries to bring to light is the sacred nature of reality. This becomes especially clear to him the first time he went to Venice, in July 1952. After seeing Giovanni Bellini's paintings he writes in his diary that he believes in 'la sustancia y el ... *sentimiento* de la pintura, de una pintura sola y única' [the substance and ... *feeling* of painting, of a unique total painting]. He adds that he believes also in painting's movement, 'en ... su paso, en su ir, subterráneamente, pasando' [in ... its transition, in its subterranean passage] (1994: 36). Reflecting on painting, Gaya uses a metaphorical language similar to that of Zambrano's philosophy. In Venice, after seeing all of Tintoretto's works, he concludes that Venetian painting is not a school or a new pictorial concept or manner, but 'una ... reaparición de lo pictórico perenne, fijo, original, originario' '[a ... *reappearance* of the perennial picture, the fixed, original, primeval one]. Venice does not invent painting: it simply lets it sprout, and surface. The creative genius of Venetian painters consists in feeling the secret, hidden presence of painting and letting it *appear* by itself, that is all (1994: 37). These metaphysical ideas, including the definition of Venetian painting as 'un lugar, una atmósfera propicia, un criadero, un vivero' [a place, a favourable atmosphere, a breeding place, a nursery] (1994: 38) precede some of Zambrano's lucubrations on the same subject. After staying some months in Paris, when Gaya travelled to Venice for the second time, in January 1953, he wrote in his diary that he had returned not to study Venetian painting, but to do 'nothing'. He had no purpose other than 'sentirme estar aquí, como inmerso en el agua de la pintura, de la pintura *única*' [to feel myself staying here, as if I were submerged in the water of painting, the *unique* painting] (1994: 75). Three days after his arrival, he adds: 'Creo que me encuentro, casi sin querer, aquí en Venecia, y no en Florencia o Roma, porque Venecia es *un lugar* de pintura, *un suelo* suyo, un pedazo de *tierra firme* suya' [I think I am almost by chance here in Venice, and not in Florence or Rome, because Venice is *a place* of painting, *a ground* of its own, its own piece of terra firma]. Venice as '*a place* of painting' makes him understand that during the thirteen years of his exile in Mexico he had felt 'como desterrado, y no ya de mi país, o de Europa, sino de esa otra patria subterránea, más substancial, que viene a ser, para un pintor, la Pintura' [as if banished, and not from just my country, or from Europe, but from that other underground, more substantial country that is painting for a painter] (1994: 75). Does Zambrano's title *Some Places of Painting* come from Gaya's Venetian notes? In June of the same year he went back to Mexico, exactly when she left Havana and moved to Rome. They had known each other since the time of the Republic. In 1956, Gaya too decided to live in the Italian capital, and they met frequently and shared common friends, but their relationship was discontinuous (Zambrano 2014c: 98, 107). In 1960, the painter went back to Madrid for the first time since 1939 and published *El sentimiento de la pintura* [The Feeling of Painting], including several statements from his diaries, such as those quoted above. The essay was published both in Spain and in Italy (Gaya 1960a & b).

Pedro Chacón's scholarly edition of *Algunos lugares de la pintura* has made us aware of the dates of composition and publication of every text that Zambrano collected in her 1989 book. So it is possible to verify that the first time she conceived painting as a flow or transit was in Rome, in 1959, when Gaya finished his essay. In her article 'Mitos y fantasmas: la pintura' [Myths and Ghosts: Painting] (2012a: 44), Zambrano defines painting as 'un extraño fluir que permanece, un río temporal que se queda; no una forma de estar, sino del pasar' [a strange flowing which persists, a temporal river which remains, not a way of staying, but of passing away]. Previously she had never used those kinds of metaphors for painting. For instance, in the two texts she dedicated to the Mexican neo-Cubist artist Juan Soriano, written in Rome in 1954 and 1956 (Zambrano 2012a: 145–58), the prevalent metaphors are linked to the book she was preparing at that time, *Los sueños y el tiempo* [Dreams and Time].

No wonder that in the essay 'La pintura en Ramón Gaya' [Painting in Ramón Gaya], published by Zambrano in 1960, we find cross-references to their respective works:

> Según dice Ramón Gaya en su ensayo *El sentimiento de la pintura*, la pintura viene del agua, descubrimiento que hizo un día en Venecia. [...] Y así, en su visión de la pintura en los canales de Venecia, Ramón Gaya vio espejada su propia pintura o la pintura tal como a él había llegado. (Zambrano 2012a: 140)

> [As Gaya says in his essay *El sentimiento de la pintura*, painting comes from the water, he made this discovery one day in Venice. [...] And so, through his vision of painting in the canals of Venice, Ramón Gaya saw his own painting mirrored or painting as it had come to him.]

The philosopher's mystical way of thinking bestows a sense of the sacred on Gaya's subjects such as the Baptism of Christ, the Passion, the figure of Mary Magdalene and the homages. In particular, asserting that painting, like any art, is 'a realized dream' (Zambrano 2012a: 141), the philosopher extends the domain of her 'poetic reason', though she does not mention it in this text. The new term she introduces to comprehend the phenomenological process of visual artworks is 'purity', another dynamic metaphor because 'en ella, por ella, a través de ella, está sucediendo algo [in it, for it, through it, something is happening] (143).

This is her dialectical approach to Gaya's revelations or appearances. Standing in front of his paintings, Zambrano stresses her transcendent role as a viewer affected by a powerful astonishment. Suspending one's certitudes and sense of identity, astonishment is the paradoxical condition of unpredictable discoveries (Gargani 1986: 5–25). Similar to a shock, for Zambrano the astonishment caused by Gaya's paintings actualizes an absence, a fragment of a truth never seen before. It happens by means of a presence which is a symbolic trace of the whole: 'es lo que aparece: lo que va apareciendo como un suceso que no acaba, en una especie de fluir que es como ser. En la aparición, fluir y ser, suceder y proseguir están unidos' [it is what appears: what is appearing as an event that has no end, in a kind of flow that is like being. In what appears, to flow and to be, to happen and to go on, are joined together] (Zambrano 2012a: 138). Years after, in *Notas de un método*, the philosopher defines this emotion: 'El asombro es pasmo, el pasmo que se da cuando se vislumbra algo insólito, pero que es aún más puro y fecundo cuando se produce ante algo de sobra conocido y que de repente se presenta como nunca visto' [The astonishment is amazement, it happens when something unusual is seen, but it is even more pure and fruitful when it comes to something well-known and suddenly presents itself as never having been seen] (Zambrano 1989c: 99). Gaya's paintings have on her the effect of a return to metaphysical origins. Through astonishment she is able to reach a peaceful state of contemplation. To her, it means the act of seeing into the depths of the other side of the real and transforming painting into a living experience (Zambrano 2012a: 139).

While reason awakes and senses are alert, the contemplated images start to show their power or energy, both to the painter and the spectator. They feel passive in the sense that they are involved in the reality of the senses and give themselves up as in a sacrificial offering. In fact, both of them use the same metaphor, the 'wound': a familiar term in Zambrano's philosophy. So they conceive the vision of painting as a human stigma (Gaya 1999: 34; Zambrano 2012a: 141). Gaya does not consider himself an artist but a creator, i.e. somebody who obeys painting-nature as its humble vassal, as 'a servant of the pictorial feeling' (Gaya 1999: 26). And Zambrano writes that he has received the 'stigmata' of painting (Zambrano 2012a: 137). This attitude, even if indebted to esoteric beliefs, is close to the challenges posed to traditional visual art studies by the 'iconic turn', which emphasizes the phenomenological reception of paintings as if they were present, offering 'not just a surface, but a *face* that faces the beholder' (Mitchell 1996: 72).

Through Gaya's paintings, Zambrano enlarges the semantic paradigm of flowing and its synonyms. Generally applied to the multiplicity of time, she includes Gaya's artworks in her sensual thought as fragments of life or natural phenomena, like the painter himself. To refer to the origin of painting they have in common another metaphor, the image of an obscure cave and its metamorphosis as a female incarnation. This is a milestone in Zambrano's philosophy. Nevertheless, in this text, she only says that Gaya's painting is 'la manifestación de una interioridad, la revelación de algo oscuro' [the manifestation of an inner life, the revelation of something obscure] (Zambrano 2012a: 138), while the painter explicitly refers to the mystical centre as 'a cave', as a 'womb', and also as 'el manantial antiguo, femenino, tibio, húmedo, materno, de la pintura' [the ancient, female, warm, wet, motherly source of painting] (Gaya 1999: 27, 19, & 24).

After writing on Gaya's art, Zambrano's gaze will be marked with reciprocity and movement. The act of seeing some paintings implies not only being seen by them and being subjected to them, but also perceiving them as dynamic events of life which move continuously. For instance, 'En la pintura de Baruj Salinas' [In the Painting of Baruj Salinas], written in 1981, there are intra-textual quotations from the article she dedicated to Gaya in 1960. Besides mentioning 'purity' again, the philosopher starts saying that the artworks of this Cuban neo-Cubist painter lead the spectator to a desire for their source, they keep him or her in motion. Looking at them means to feel oneself 'ante algo que viene de alguna parte y va a alguna parte, que transita ante un suceso ante todo, en verdad con un acontecimiento en vez de con algo fijo que ya está ahí a la vista' [facing something that comes from somewhere and goes to somewhere, something that first of all is in transit, something that is a real event, that is really happening instead of being fixed, already there under one's eyes] (Zambrano 2012a: 172). She feels that Salinas's artworks call both the creator (in Gaya's semantics) and the spectator 'para que la pintura, el pensamiento pictórico suceda, se verifique, al modo de un universo que se hace' [so that painting, pictorial thinking happens, becomes manifest, like a universe which is creating itself] (174). It is like the ambiguous character of 'poetic reason', partially submerged. For instance, among the metaphors of her paradigm, ignorance is represented as 'el abismo viviente del otro lado' [the living abysm of the other side]

(Zambrano 1989c: 130). For this philosopher such a dynamic and risky relationship gives birth to every human discovery and creation, always incomplete.

In Front of *The Tempest* by Giorgione

The article 'El enigmático pintor Giorgione' [The Enigmatic Painter Giorgione], written in Madrid in 1987, is a brilliant demonstration of how deeply the philosopher developed her mystical hermeneutics of painting, becoming close to the contemporary debate on the visual image.[3] Once more she focuses her attention on her emotional involvement as a spectator, but what critics have generally observed in her interpretation of *The Tempest* (*La Tempesta*) relates more to her ideas on painting than to her peculiar reception of Giorgione's famous work. There is no doubt that it concerns a non-conventional way of looking at this Renaissance painting, which still troubles many art historians after half a millennium. Salvatore Settis, who collected a great number of heterogeneous interpretations in his classic monograph on *The Tempest*, assumes that the painting could be an early example of 'non-subject' (1978: 17). Thirty years later Augusto Gentili, complaining about the lack of verifiable information about Giorgione, gives a sharper definition of the painting, naming it the '*Pseudo-Tempest*' (2008: 109). And Enrico Maria Dal Pozzolo adds: 'Countless are the words that have been written on *La Tempesta*, and nearly every time with the confidence of having finally unearthed its hidden key to interpretation. The scene is so enigmatic as to have defied the skill of many of its viewers' (2009: 242). So Zambrano's point of view does not contradict any canon. It is a matter of fact that she applies her philosophy to this work and to painting in general, leaving aside the orthodox exegesis of art history (Murcia Serrano 2009: 203, 293). Nevertheless, this kind of approach is not a breaking of any critical code of visual art any more. In the frame of the contemporary debate on image, it has become a pertinent issue: an original contribution among many others and a milestone in Zambrano's personal relationship with painting.

In her case, the unreachable or perhaps lost meaning of *The Tempest* is a perfect opportunity to talk about the physical and metaphysical experience of standing in front of a beloved artwork, to keep it in mind for the rest of her life. Zambrano does not remember when her devotion to it began. This painting has become a permanent reference in her experience, as she declares in the introduction:

> De los cuadros y de la pintura que el destino me ha dado a ver al recorrer diversos museos, se ha destacado siempre para mí el cuadro, visto en la Academia de Venecia, de Giorgione, *La Tempesta*. Hay allí otros cuadros ¡tantos!, pero *La Tempesta* tiene algo que ha fijado en mi memoria, mi atención, que me ha acompañado, que parece que sea algo así como un espíritu, un ánima más bien, pues el espíritu no se pinta sino que hace pintar, muy veneciano, típicamente veneciano. (Zambrano 2012a: 85)

> [Among the artworks and the painting that destiny let me see when I visited several museums, one has always stood out for me. It is the painting I saw in the Accademia in Venice, *The Tempest* by Giorgione. There are many other paintings! But *The Tempest* has something that fixed it in my memory, in my

attention. It has accompanied me — it seems to be something like a spirit, a soul rather, for spirit is not to be painted, rather it makes itself be painted in a Venetian way, a typical Venetian way.]

In this autobiographical premise, 'soul' is a crucial term. For instance, we find a useful definition, among many others, in *Hacia un saber sobre el alma* [Towards a Knowledge of the Soul]: 'Entre el *yo* y el fuera de la naturaleza se interpone lo que llamamos alma' [Between the self and the outside of nature mediates what we call soul] (Zambrano 2004b: 33). Soul, for Zambrano, is a topological image, it has its own space or landscape. Opposed to the dominant knowledge of reason, the comprehensive knowledge of soul is 'un decir poético del cosmos, de la naturaleza, como no dominable' [a poetic discourse upon the cosmos, upon nature, as though uncontrollable] (25). She remembers some Romantic metaphors that linked knowledge of the soul to the inclemency of the weather. Their revelations appeared in the fury of a storm, illuminated by lightning, the spark, the electric shock (25, 26, 27). But this is not Zambrano's condition. To interpret the scene painted by Giorgione she chooses a glass pane as a metaphorical device, an image of the soul: 'Transparente es algo que decimos en alabanza de un cristal, por ejemplo de una cosa que es el medio para dejar pasar otra' [We say transparent in praise of a glass, for instance of a thing by means of which something else passes through] (33). Besides, in the Accademia *The Tempest* is now protected by actual glass. But the one Zambrano evokes is an imaginary, transparent filter that reduces the rational power of her gaze. The presence of the soul/glass activates a double, topological configuration: from one side she, the viewer, applies her transcendent vision; from the other side the painting, visible but untouchable, produces its dynamic effects. The soul/glass inserts a phenomenological border. Under the effect of the painting, Zambrano disarticulates it in order to host other images, the latent ones she will montage in a personal combination. Didi-Huberman, basing his theory on dialectical image, states that a montage is a way of exposing the truth by means of a disarticulation which replaces the explanation (2013: 85). It is interesting to notice that Zambrano, looking through the soul/glass, defines a more impersonal strategy of enunciation:

> Es una distancia, una cierta indiferencia, como si el cuadro estuviese visto a través de un cristal y no se le pudiera tocar, en el que ni siquiera una mujer desnuda, bella y joven, tampoco despierta el deseo de tocarla. Ella está en sí misma y parece indiferente a todo lo que la rodea. Enfrente, más acá del puente, y como en una pasarela, pasa un caballero que tampoco se cuida de la mujer; nadie se cuida de nada. Él está en sí mismo o en otro. Ella se diría que está en la naturaleza, donde cada cosa es lo que es, y sin ocuparse de todo lo demás. Está ensimismada, pero no en su espíritu, no en alguna cosa distinta de ella misma, sino ensimismada y perdida al mismo tiempo, inaccesible. ¿Quién podría, ni en sueños, acercarse a ella? Es, pues, la naturaleza, a mi modo de ver, la que se nos presenta así. (Zambrano 2012a: 85)
>
> [It is a distance, a certain indifference, as if the painting were seen through a glass and it were not possible to touch it, a painting where not even a naked woman, beautiful and young, gives rise to the desire to touch her. She is self-

absorbed and seems indifferent to whatever is around her. In front of her, on this side of the bridge and as in a gangway, a knight is passing by and he too takes no heed of the woman. Nobody takes heed of anything. He is self-absorbed or absorbed in another. One could say that she is in a state of nature, where everything is what it is and without care for all the rest. She is self-absorbed but not in her spirit, not in something different from herself. At the same time she is self-absorbed and lost, inaccessible. Who could approach her even in dreams? From my point of view, then, nature is what is presenting herself to us.]

The presence of the soul/glass awakes the tangible quality of the gaze, i.e. the palpable element of sight. In Maurice Merleau-Ponty's phenomenological ontology there is a chasm between the visible and the tangible. It concerns the flesh, the body of beings: 'the flesh we are speaking of is not matter. It is the coiling over of the visible upon the seeing body, of the tangible upon the touching body' (1968: 146). From this moment on, she, the viewer, leaves aside the knight and focuses her attention only on the young woman who is nursing her baby. Through her motherhood she incarnates nature. It is the first step to disassembling Giorgione's painting by means of Zambrano's metaphysical vision, her method of facing any subject (Prezzo 2006: 22–23). With few metonymies — that are the proper way of naming what is beyond the limit of any evidence (Trías 1999: 68) — the philosopher inserts another heuristic device: the dream. Nevertheless she discards it immediately, and adds that *The Tempest* 'is not a dreamt painting' (Zambrano 2012a: 85). This statement makes sense if we remember what dream means in her philosophy: an intermediate knowledge that rescues what the conscience forgets or casts down in an atemporal and concealed state: 'El que duerme se ha retirado del lugar de la visión: ha dejado de ver. No comparece ante la realidad y en tanto que no comparece ha dejado también de ser visible: no está presente' [The one who sleeps has withdrawn from the place of vision: he has stopped seeing. He does not appear before reality and while he does not appear he has also stopped being visible: he is not present] (Zambrano 1992a: 24–25). But she, the viewer, is awake and stares at the work of art, complaining about the lack of reciprocity between her and nature, that naked and impassive mother who does not need anything or anybody. That self-absorbed female figure monopolizes Zambrano's interest completely. The painted woman is an example of the image-symptom which arouses one or more anachronisms (Didi-Huberman 2000: 40). In front of the maternal image, she, the viewer, perceives her inadequacy, her abysmal distance from nature. In this way, to quote Didi-Huberman, the unavoidable modality of the visible works: 'when to see is to feel that something inescapably breaks away from us. In other words: when to see is to lose' (1992: 14).[4]

Close to the approach of the 'iconic turn', in *El sueño creador* [The Creative Dream] the philosopher says that 'el ver al modo humano es inseparable del ser visto' [seeing in the human way is inseparable from being seen] (Zambrano 1986b: 38). What she is losing here is the transcendent chasm, her vital contact with the sacred. Deconstructing *The Tempest*, she reveals something which is both tacit and familiar, the traditional relationship between nature and birth deriving from Greek naturalism. To her, the young mother is the powerful and eternal *natura mater* who covers all phenomena or sensory appearances, the *physis* in motion that casts things into shapes. No wonder that Zambrano also ascribes to this representation the 'star', 'water', 'fire', and even the self-portrait of Giorgione, representing himself in the biblical role of David. The painted mother, nursing her baby, is a dialectical image which is interpreted without any attention to the semiotic approach of the art historians. It is a vision in which only the viewer's latencies come into existence.

One can see the portrait evoked by Zambrano not in Venice but in the Herzog Anton Ulrich-Museum of Braunschweig in Germany: it is a fragment of a lost painting (Gentili 1999: 35). But the philosopher does not justify her semantic detour, thinking of another painting, physically far from Venice, and linking it to *La Tempesta*. It is the effect of the dialectical image, the latent connection that comes out. Through this unexpected and recalled image, which only shows the face and the right shoulder of a young man, Zambrano appeals to the ghost of Giorgione. Then, with a further imaginary displacement, she compares this portrait with the self-portrait of Velázquez in *Las Meninas*. Assembling heterogeneities, at this point Zambrano cuts the Gordian knot of her exegesis — she estimates the cryptic meaning of *The Tempest* by including another painting with a different subject, a Venus, physically far from Venice too:

> Giorgione no se autorretrata como pintor; se da a ver como si David fuera también un río, como si fuera, tratándose de música, una canción. Entonces, ¿por qué se entretiene — diríamos entre comillas — en pintar un acontecimiento que no acontece?, ¿dónde ocurre esta tormenta, acaso sobre la ciudad? Está demasiado cercana para que no importe a los que huyen de ella — y aquí no huye nadie — o se esconden para proteger al niño que esta mujer desnuda lleva en sus brazos. ¿Qué clase de tormenta es esta? Este es el enigma principal del cuadro: un acontecimiento que no acontece o que no amenaza, un fuego que no devora, una lluvia que no empapa, un rayo que no va a caer y, si cae, es como si no cayese. ¿Qué clase de acontecimiento es este que sucede igual que con la Venus, que se deja ver, pero que no sabe si la ven o no? (Zambrano 2012a: 86)

> [Giorgione does not portray himself as a painter; he shows himself as if David were also a river, as if — being music — he were a song. Then why does he entertain himself — we would say between quotation marks — painting an event which does not happen? Where does this storm happen, perhaps above the town? It is too nearby to those who are fleeing from it — and here nobody is fleeing — as they take no heed of it; or to those who are in hiding to protect the baby that this naked woman is carrying in her arms. What kind of storm is it? This is the chief enigma of the painting: an event that does not happen or does not threaten, a fire that does not devour, a rain that does not soak, a lightening that is not going to strike, and if it strikes, it is rather as if it does not strike. What kind of event is this? This happens equally with the painting of Venus. She lets them see her, but she does not know if they see her or not.]

The image-symptom produces a new anachronism, the inclusion of a Venus. As Giorgione is the painter, Zambrano is probably thinking of the *Sleeping Venus*, an unfinished painting on which Titian worked (Pignatti and Pedrocco 1999: 75–77), which hangs in Dresden, in the Gemäldegalerie Alte Meister. In the foreground this painting shows the goddess lying down, naked, peacefully asleep. Her eyes are closed, she does not see whoever sees (and desires) her. Evoking this image, Zambrano reacts in the same way she did with Giorgione's self-portrait. She omits as usual any discursive details, her thought takes trajectories unguessed-at before. She updates the mythological time of the pagan gods, as she sees in *The Tempest* 'algo muy griego que ha quedado depositado, no se sabe por qué' [something very Greek which has been settled in Venice, one has no idea why] (Zambrano 2012a: 87). Perhaps, like the Venus, it is a matter of those pagan gods:

> En cierto modo, son dioses que no han nacido humanamente, dioses que están ahí, tal vez por nacer. No se sabe si estos dioses, tan poco o nada cristianos, se enteran o no. Esta falta de conciencia — iba a decir de irresponsabilidad, de respuesta de sentimiento — causa estupor. Son simplemente dioses. ¿Para quién, por qué lo son? ¿Por qué sí? No hay respuesta, es un enigma. (Zambrano 2012a: 87)

> [Somehow they are gods who were not born in a human way, gods who are there, perhaps they are about to be born. One does not know whether these gods, hardly or not at all Christian, are aware or not of it. This lack of awareness — I would say of responsibility, of a reaction to feeling — causes astonishment. They are simply gods. For whom? Why are they like that? Because it is so? There is no answer, it is an enigma.]

It is useful to remember that, in the philosopher's opinion, the Greek gods represent a metaphorical way of dealing with the *physis*, as human beings feel different and unequal when they compare themselves to it. These gods are the image of an archetypal attitude, due to the human need to stay in front of something, under something (Zambrano 1993: 30–31). Once again she, the viewer, comes back to that border with the sacred and to the event that does not occur or act in the painting. The so-called tempest is a phenomenon that does not alter or destroy the landscape, it does not scare the natural beings which apparently seem free of sensations and feelings. The painted image does not show the violence of a storm, but the demonstration of its power, i.e. the possibility of not bursting forth. It is the concept of power that Giorgio Agamben applies to his interpretation of the famous statement 'I would prefer not', by Melville's *Bartleby, the Scrivener*. In this context, the experience of the true power is not only the possibility of acting, but also the possibility of not to do or think anything (1989: 59). The storm that does not happen in any place rouses in the viewer a productive anxiety. First she assumes there is no correspondence between what the painting shows and its title: 'Es la tormenta en sí misma, es el ser de la tormenta, pero este su ser es estallar, amenazar. El enigma prosigue insoluble, pues' [It is the storm itself, the being of the storm, but this being means to burst, to threaten, to frighten. So the enigma remains insoluble] (Zambrano 2012a: 87). This is the reason why the painting, once seen, is unforgettable. She insists that *The Tempest* is 'una imagen que no llega a actuar. Es la falta de acción, es un ser, pero no una acción, no actúa' [an image that fails to act. It is the lack of action — it is a being, but not an action; it does not act] (88). So many repetitions of the same paradox are the linguistic symptom of a deep, emotional involvement. The dialectical image of *The Tempest* cannot help producing connections in the spectator, who withholds a coherent conclusion to her interpretation. The one who makes a montage does not care for an exhaustive result (Didi-Huberman 2013: 99) and, according to this perspective, Zambrano brings her text to an autobiographical end.

In *Notas de un método*, she defines image as a hidden and condensed knowledge that needs a retrospective and sensual gaze. In other words, another human configuration where mind and body join to seek out what has been lost or forgotten. The goal of such an image is another image, something like an 'embryonic labyrinth' (Zambrano 1989c: 88). With this metaphor, the philosopher increases the peculiarity of her interpretation of Giorgione's painting. Years after having seen it in Venice, when she was living in exile, the text she wrote in Madrid almost at the end of her life is a reminiscence. No wonder that she finally extends her hermeneutics of the work of art to the town of Venice and to the Veneto region. She declares that both of them share the same indifference, both of them are like the prodigy seen in *The Tempest*. She also adds that she feels unafraid of Venice, although:

> Es un laberinto y donde de un momento a otro se puede caer. [...] Venecia, toda Venecia, es para mí un enigma que se deja ver, un laberinto que se aparece y que no hay que esforzarse por buscar, porque si se lo busca no se encuentra jamás. (Zambrano 2012a: 88)

> [It is a labyrinth where one can fall down from one moment to the next. [...] To me Venice, the whole of Venice, is an enigma that lets itself be seen, a labyrinth that appears and that one should not strive to find, because if one looks for it, one never finds it.]

Representing Venice as a labyrinth seems obvious, but not in Zambrano's philosophy, as she switches a commonplace into one of her existential images. It is the seamless visual representation of her erratic search for the unattainable origin and of her homesick peregrinations across two continents, far from Spain. In this sense she never left her labyrinth and Venice is only a variation of it, the one suggested by *The Tempest* with a deified and distant nature. There is an emotional displacement from the painting to the town that hosts it in the Accademia. The denied gaze of the young mother incarnates a broken relationship, a banishment.

In a chapter of *Los bienaventurados* [The Blessed], dedicated to 'El exiliado' [The Exiled], Zambrano recalls the interlaced link between vision and human existence. To her, the metaphysical experience of exile means the deprivation of the gods' gaze and a subsequent uprooting and loneliness [Zambrano 1991a: 32]. But she also talks in similar terms when she refers to the real experience of exile, to the loss of one's identity after feeling abandoned (31–32). Nevertheless exile was a painful but inalienable acquaintance, as she explains in an article published in the newspaper *ABC*, on 28 August 1989. She was back in Spain, but her exile had become a metaphorical country, as painting had been for Ramón Gaya: 'El exilio ha sido como mi patria, o como una dimensión de una patria desconocida, pero que, una vez que se conoce, es irrenunciable' [Exile has been like my homeland, or like a dimension of an unknown country, but which once known, cannot be renounced] (Zambrano 1995a: 14). In her exile she finds 'algo sacro, algo inefable' [something sacred, something ineffable] (14), the same qualities she applies to Giorgione, to

The Tempest, and to Venice, where she inscribes her unrequited longing. At the end they are an emotional backdrop to her autobiography, a striking case of dialectical image-making.

María Zambrano wrote this article when she was eighty-three years old. To discover other latencies in her texts on painting we would need to change the structure of *Algunos lugares de la pintura*. The book follows the conventional timeline of art history, starting with the old masters and ending with contemporary artists. By choosing not to highlight the dates at which single texts were composed, the author has left her own vicissitudes in the dark.

Notes to Chapter 10

1. All translations are my own unless otherwise stated.
2. 'Quelque chose qui nous dit aussi bien le *contact* (le pied qui s'enfonce dans la sable) que la *perte* (l'absence du pied dans son empreinte)'.
3. This section about Giorgione is a shorter and redrafted version of a previous article of mine (Pittarello 2014), less contextualized in the framework of the iconic turn and in the intertextual relationships of Zambrano's articles.
4. 'Quand voir, c'est sentir que quelque chose inéluctablement nous échappe, autrement dit: quand voir, c'est perdre'.

CHAPTER 11

The Ethics of Exile and Memory in Zambrano

Daniela Omlor, University of Oxford

For María Zambrano exile was not an abstract concept but a constant for most of her life. Crossing the Pyrenees on 25 January 1939 marked the beginning of an exile that would last for more than forty years, until her return to Spain in November 1984 not long before her death in 1991. Indeed, not least because of her exile did Zambrano consider the Civil War as a threshold that divided her life into a clear before and after. Zambrano came to truly embody the idea of 'España peregrina' [a wandering Spain], living a restless life and precarious and peripatetic existence in many countries, including Cuba, France, Italy, and Mexico, which she herself would call 'peregrinación entre las entrañas esparcidas de una historia trágica' [peregrination between the dispersed entrails of a tragic history] (1991a: 32).[1] Upon her return to Spain, Zambrano wrote 'Amo mi exilio' [I love my exile] (2009: 65), but, of course, things were not that simple, even though she already foregrounds exile in her family history:

> Sus padres habían sido ya 'exiliados' en Castilla donde nadie de la familia había vivido, porque nadie había vivido 'sin tierras'. Y había crecido así, sintiendo el destierro, y el que había perdido el lazo con la tierra y con la pequeña historia familiar que ha quedado remota, cosa de fábula, de 'otros tiempos'; cuando se ha perdido 'la fábula', ¿qué queda sino el pensamiento? Sí, desde la raíz de su vida la filosofía había sido 'a falta de otra cosa', la única manera, la solución única de vivir sin esas cosas, sin traicionarlas, de obedecer en esta libertad que deja el no ser nadie en parte alguna, de ser 'uno más'. (Zambrano 2014c: 1006–07)

> [Her parents had already been 'exiled' from Castile where no one of the family had lived, because no one had lived 'without their land'. And she had grown up like that, feeling exile, and that she had lost the link with the land and the small family history which had remained remote, a tale, of 'other times', when the tale is lost, what remains if not thought? Yes, from the beginning of her life, philosophy had been 'for lack of other things', the only way, the only solution to living without these things, without betraying them, to obey with the freedom that being no one anywhere gives, the freedom of being 'one among many'.][2]

In her autobiography there is a sense then that Zambrano fashions exile into a destiny that occurs in several stages, which can be traced back to the very origin of her family. As the first step towards 'destierro' [uprootedness] the tangible attachment to a specific place, the 'tierra' [land] is lost, due to geographical distance, then the 'fábula' [tale] of the family, that is to say not the legal records, but those family stories, which are only transmitted orally from generation to generation without being preserved in written documents.[3] Philosophy is the only foothold available on the descent to complete freedom in exile which goes hand in hand with being nobody, nobody in particular.

Regardless of the many material and physical hardships that exile entailed, Zambrano was more interested in describing the immaterial losses to which the state of exile inevitably led. Focusing mainly on *Delirio y destino* [Delirium and Destiny], Zambrano's intellectual autobiography, and *Los bienaventurados* [The Blessed], her most systematic account of exile, this chapter sets out to explore the dialectics of exile's existential and ethical condition.[4] In spite of her personal experience, as Ortega Allué points out (1998: 438), Zambrano came to see exile primarily as a universal category that could be used for thinking through other experiences. In many ways, this is a typically Zambranian approach given that rather than striving for categorical separation, a common thread that runs through Zambrano's work is the desire to leave behind binary opposition by reimaging former separates in a fusion that can bring opposites together without eradicating their differences.

For Zambrano the exile is not a migrant but a perpetual wanderer. The exile takes on a different role from that of the refugee, who, in Zambrano's eyes, is welcomed lovingly by his hosts, enabling him to fill the hole that the absence of the fatherland has left behind. Even the 'desterrado' [uprooted] is only a step further towards exile:[5]

> El encontrarse en el destierro no hace sentir el exilio, sino ante todo la expulsión. Y luego, luego, la insalvable distancia y la incierta presencia física del país perdido. Y aquí empieza el exilio, el sentirse ya al borde del exilio. (Zambrano 1991a: 32)
>
> [Finding oneself uprooted does not make one feel exile, but above all expulsion. And then, later, the irrecoverable distance and uncertain physical presence of the lost country. That is where exile begins, the feeling of already being on the brink of exile.]

As will become clear, it is the ethical dimension that for Zambrano warrants the definition of exile.[6] Expulsion is a biblical term but, historically, this lexical choice also harks back to the expulsion of the Jews and Moors after the Spanish Reconquista. The first stage of exile then is that of being an outcast, quite literally. The outcast experiences his being outside of space not as the encounter with an alternative place but as an encounter with the void, which signifies the lack of belonging: 'Al exiliado le dejaron sin nada, al borde de la historia, solo en la vida y sin lugar, sin lugar propio' [The exile is left with nothing, at the edge of history, alone in life and without a place, his own place] (Zambrano 2014a: 10). Due to the geographical distance every presence recalls the absence of the lost home and the new state of non-belonging and uprootedness.

The difficulty inherent in exilic existence is that it is founded on negation, on that which it is not. The dialectics between absence and presence mean that exile is epitomized by in-betweenness. This non-belonging extends beyond geographical displacement to incorporate a temporal uprootedness. In fact, Zambrano compares the state of exile to the souls in purgatory (2014a: 11), neither really here nor there. The suspension of both death and life can be seen not only as complete stasis, but also as an existence outside of time. Exile acts as a traumatic interruption of both life and death. Hence the exile's self-identification with the role of survivor, neither devoured by history, nor indifferent to it. Many of these symptoms also echo those commonly found in trauma, most importantly, the idea that as a survivor the exile has already confronted death without having completely succumbed to it, thereby inhabiting a grey zone:

> En el abandono sólo lo propio de que se está desposeído aparece, sólo lo que no se puede llegar a ser como ser propio. Lo propio es solamente en tanto que negación, imposibilidad. Imposibilidad de vivir que, cuando se cae en la cuenta, es imposibilidad de morir. El filo entre la vida y la muerte que igualmente se rechazan. Sostenerse en ese filo es la primera exigencia que al exiliado se le presenta como ineludible. (Zambrano 1991a: 32)
>
> [In abandonment only that which is one's own and of which one has been dispossessed appears, only that which one cannot become as a being of one's own. That which is one's own is only so that it is negation, impossibility. The impossibility to live, which, when one becomes aware of it, is the impossibility to die. The tightrope between life and death, both of which are rejected. To maintain balance on that tightrope is the first unavoidable demand with which the exile is confronted.]

Zambrano seems to imply that the exile has to walk this tightrope without fully embracing one side or the other. He ought to embrace liminality and a twilight existence above all.[7] In addition to being an apt description of the exile's non-belonging, in-betweenness as the 'umbral' [threshold], the moment she associated with sacrifice, can lead to new forms of knowledge and being (2014c: 1007). The threshold has to be crossed to reach the unknown and that is why it symbolizes the initiation in knowledge. Strictly speaking, 'la aurora' [dawn], a key concept in Zambrano's epistemology, fulfils a similar function and is equally located in-between; it signals the end of the night and the beginning of the day, but it is neither fully one nor the other. This in-between location is then the springboard for launching an enquiry into all that hitherto has been taken for granted, including one's own being.

In addition to temporal and spatial dislocation, the exile loses himself and forcibly becomes other: 'Y es que anda fuera de sí al andar sin patria ni casa' [And he who goes through life without fatherland or home finds himself outside himself] (1991a: 33). Exile makes it impossible to hold on to an old identity and necessitates a new negotiation of the self with its own history. Partly the difficulty of incorporating exile into one's life story is due to the fact that one's survival itself is what constitutes the trauma, having faced death and been spared, a phenomenon described by Zambrano in *Delirium and Destiny*:

> Y era como sentirse otra vez en vías de nacer a través de aquella agonía inédita. ¡Cuántas había atravesado ya! Vivir era eso: morir de muertes distintas antes de

> morir de la manera única, total, que la resume todas, agonizar también, pasar entre la vida y la muerte, ser rechazado de la vida de múltiples maneras sin que por eso la muerte abra sus puertas. 'Vivir muriendo'. (Zambrano 2014c: 1053)
>
> [And it was like experiencing birth all over again through that unknown agony. How many had she already lived through! Living was this: to die different deaths before dying in the only way possible, the one all-encompassing way that they all lead up to, to agonize as well, pass from life to death, be rejected by life in different ways without therefore death opening its doors. 'To be one of the living dead'.]

Being in exile means being one of the living dead, constant suffering, but it is also included in the list of other traumatic experiences that Zambrano underwent such as the loss of loved ones and her fragile health which many times saw her come very close to death.[8] The acceptance of this state of being, however, is the first step towards a revelatory process which will result in complete transformation.[9]

While such immense suffering might make one think that one is cursed, a more positive interpretation would be that one has been chosen. A similar dynamic can be seen in the discussion of the figure of Job later in this essay. Zambrano herself is reminded of the *homo sacer* when she dwells on the changes endured by exiles:

> Eran ya diferentes. Tuvieron esa revelación: no eran iguales a los demás, ya no eran ciudadanos de ningún país, eran... exiliados, desterrados, refugiados... algo diferente que suscitaría aquello que provocaban en la Edad Media algunos seres 'sagrados': respeto, simpatía, piedad, horror, repulsión, atracción, en fin... eso, algo diferente. Vencidos que no han muerto, que no han tenido la discreción de morirse, supervivientes. (Zambrano 2014c: 1052)
>
> [They were already different. They had that revelation: they were not like the others, they were no longer citizens of any country, they were... exiles, uprooted, refugees... something different that would arouse that which some 'sacred' beings in the Middle Ages provoked: respect, sympathy, pity, horror, repulsion, attraction, in brief... just that, something different. Defeated but not dead, those defeated who did not have the decency to die, survivors.]

What singles them out is their very act of survival, which is deemed a failure, a 'rejection' by death. Again, this is a very typical reaction to historical trauma.[10] The original concept of the *homo sacer* posits him already in a liminal position as both hallowed and cursed.[11] Anybody could kill a *homo sacer* but he could not be sacrificed in a ritual, he was thus both dead and alive and a societal outcast. The exile carries the burden of having been chosen in such a way forever. That is also why exile cannot simply be abandoned or redeemed through a geographical return. As an experience of the liminal, on the edge of life and death, the exile has to foresee the incomprehension he will receive from those not affected by this condition. Implied is also the view of the non-exiles that the exiles should have had 'the decency to die' and that in some ways the exiles are shameful living reminders of the others' failings. At the same time, exiles are forever linked to those who perished and cannot cut off this connection to death and the dead. Due to all of these issues, Zambrano considers that exile in many ways also constitutes an experience that cannot directly be spoken, although it is vital that it should be told.

In order for the exile to move forward, it is essential that he recognize his losses as unrecoverable and that he come to terms with the impossibility of a return and the undoing of exile. Only when this has been accepted can exile become the absolute freedom described earlier. Ultimately, the extremity of the situation also brings about the potential for renewal. Zambrano seems to equate exile with a sacrifice because it implies a conscious process of undoing, of leaving behind all possessions and giving over to an alternative existence. In fact, from a psychological vantage point this attitude could also be considered a defence mechanism, by ridding oneself of all material worth, and perhaps also of emotional attachment, one no longer needs to fear the incidence of loss itself. Notwithstanding this, it also chimes with Zambrano's attraction to mysticism, given that it can be interpreted as a process of purification. This purification leads to an understanding of oneself outside of the realm of history, as the following quotation illustrates. Rather than falling victim to history, the purified, dispossessed exile is able to overcome history and get in touch with 'intrahistoria':[12]

> Mientras que en el desconocido no hay pasión, a fuerza tal vez de la aceptación no de las circunstancias ni de su situación en medio de ellas, sino de su orfandad. Y de eso que le caracteriza más que nada: no tener lugar en el mundo, ni geográfico, ni social, ni político, ni — lo que decide en extremo para que salga de él ese desconocido — ontológico. No ser nadie, ni un mendigo: no ser nada. Ser tan solo lo que no puede dejarse ni perderse, y en el exiliado más que en nadie. Haberlo dejado todo para seguir manteniéndose en el punto sin apoyo ninguno, el perderse en el fondo de la historia, de la suya también, para encontrarse un día, en un sólo instante, sobrenadándolas todas. La historia se le ha hecho como agua que no lo sostiene ciertamente. Por el contrario, por no sostenerse en la historia se le ha hecho agua nada amenazadora. No es ya piélago, ni menos océano que pide siempre ser surcado, es más bien agua a punto de ser tragada. (Zambrano 1991a: 36)

> [Whereas in the stranger there is no passion, perhaps by force of the acceptance not of the circumstances nor of his situation among these circumstances, but of his being orphaned. And that is what characterizes him more than anything: to not have a place in the world, to not have a geographical, social, political, nor ontological place — the latter is extremely decisive for the stranger to emerge. To be no one, not even a beggar: to be nothing. To be only that which cannot be left behind or lost, and in the exile more than in anyone. To have left behind everything in order to keep oneself in that position without any support, to lose oneself at the bottom of history, of one's own history as well, to find oneself one day, in one unique moment, swimming above all of them. History for him has become like water that does not keep him fully afloat. On the contrary, due to not keeping afloat on the sea of history it has turned into a body of water that is not threatening at all. It is no longer open sea, and even less an ocean, that always demands to be ploughed through, it is more like water at the point of being swallowed.]

Exile and memory are intrinsically intertwined, because memory is a means of accessing that which remains outside official history. Zambrano vindicates the importance of the exiles' memories as that counterpart to official records to the extent that the exiles become saviours through memory: 'Somos memoria,

memoria que rescata' [We are memory, memory which saves] (2014a: 11). Elsewhere Zambrano accords memory a fundamental role that lends continuity to life and each person.[13] For Zambrano memory is not an unconscious process but an active contemplation of life, which condenses the essence of experience so that unity may be created and memory may acquire a timeless, eternal quality. She uses the example of the golden barge to reinforce the belief that individual memory serves to give an account of one's life at the end of it, so that this individual account may be reconciled with the memory of the universe.[14] While memory is thus seen by her as subjective it is also collective, functioning in a similar way to Jung's collective unconscious. Individual memory feeds into collective memory and the memory of the exiles can thus be shared by all. In the case of exile this two-way relationship becomes particularly important, as Mari Paz Balibrea argues:

> The status held by Republican exile within Spanish history and historiography is richly paradoxical: it is both central and residual; it has been dismissed and ignored by many and yet, its absence is structurally indispensable to any understanding of dictatorial *and* democratic Spain. There is arguably no more resilient ghost haunting actually-existing Spanish (post)modernity than that of Republican exile. (Balibrea 2005: 3)

After her return, Zambrano became increasingly aware of this:

> Es siempre y para todo pueblo, imprescindible una imagen del pasado inmediato, como examen de los propios errores y espejismos. El presente es siempre fragmento, torso incompleto. El pasado inmediato completa esa imagen mutilada, la dibuja más entera e inteligible. (Zambrano 2009: 66)

> [An image of the immediate past is always and for every people, indispensable as an examination of one's own errors and mirages. The present is always a fragment, an incomplete torso. The immediate past completes this mutilated image, depicts it more fully and intelligibly.]

There is a sense in which Zambrano admonishes against the dangers of forgetting. Her reference to the present as a mutilated body also implies that memories of the past can have a curative function, the wound, the trauma, can be healed, even if the scar remains visible. In addition, memory is important because it is connected to the soul. In her description of a soul filled with too many images that it is holding on to, Zambrano seems to provide something akin to a definition of trauma:

> Cuando se tienen demasiadas imágenes guardadas en el alma — memoria — y la conciencia no las atiende porque las sabe orgullosamente hechura suya, se produce una escisión en la persona, una vida por partida doble; que es esterilidad, incapacidad de crear no ya obras de arte ni 'obra' alguna, sino incapacidad de crear lo más 'elemental' que la vida humana necesita: el espacio de una convivencia. (Zambrano 2014c: 986)

> [When too many images are preserved in the soul — memory — and consciousness does not attend to them, because it is proud knowing that they are of its own making, an excision takes place in the person, a life of two halves, which is sterility, incapacity to create, not even works of art but not any 'work', incapacity to create the most 'elementary' thing that human life needs: a space for coexistence.]

Although Zambrano refers here to the capacity of the imagination to conjure up its own images — all images are of the past (2014c: 985) — there is also an understanding that these images are not being processed, as only active employment of reason, 'conciencia', can transform them into 'historia' (986). Like traumatic stagnation the accumulation of images thus leads to the impossibility of functioning normally. The splitting of the self that Zambrano refers to could also be interpreted under the heading of trauma, since a common symptom of an ongoing traumatization consists of the inability to incorporate the traumatic experience into one's life story, which means that it is common for sufferers of trauma to speak of different selves before and after the trauma.[15] So, even though Zambrano was not keen on Freudian psychology there is some overlap in her understanding of the interactions of exile and memory with common definitions of trauma, both on the individual and the collective level. Ultimately, the exile for Zambrano is also a survivor who can be saved by memory. On the collective level, the memory of the exile also has a corrective and restorative function, completing the picture of the past and making up for lacunae. Most importantly, memory constitutes the link between the exile as survivor and those who perished. The relationship between them is one of mutual dependency, wherein the dead rely on the survivors so as to not completely cease to live by being handed over to oblivion, whereas the survivors are only anchored in life through the roots provided to them by the dead and the very memory of their death: 'La vida se nos ha escindido; los supervivientes tenemos las raíces desnudas; vosotros los muertos, sois las raíces; sólo raíces hundidas en la tierra y en el olvido' [Our life has become divided; we survivors have had our roots laid bare, you, the dead, are our roots, only roots buried in earth and in oblivion] (232).

Finally, memory is an important tool in accessing the new existence that the process of purification entails. Memory comes into play once more because it is decisive for finding a complete reality, which transcends mere appearances:

> San Agustín, al ir a buscar la unidad, siente que ya la tiene de antes, que la recuerda. Para la vida, conocer es siempre recordar y toda ignorancia aparece en forma de olvido. Tal vez, porque la memoria sea la manera de conocimiento más cercano a la vida, la que le traiga la verdad en la forma en que pueda ser consumida por ella, como apropiación temporal. La 'reminiscencia' de que Platón nos habla, puede ser producto de la nostalgia de la realidad presentida, nostalgia de lo que no se tiene ni se muestra. Nostalgia de una vida en unidad. La memoria será la sede de este conocimiento, de este encuentro con la realidad total, porque ya entonces en ella, no habrá recuerdo ni olvido, sólo presencia. (Zambrano 1988a: 24–25)

> [St Augustine senses that he already has some grasp of it, that he remembers it from before. For life, knowing is always remembering, and all ignorance appears as a form of amnesia. Perhaps because memory is the kind of knowledge closest to life, delivering truth in the form in which life can consume it, as a temporal appropriation. The 'reminiscence' of which Plato speaks may be the product of longing for what cannot be grasped or shown. Longing for a life of oneness. So memory would be the seat of that knowledge, of this encounter with total reality, because then in reality there would be neither remembering nor forgetting, only presence.] (Zambrano and Chacel 2015: 29)

Again, Zambrano's expression is characteristically dense, but memory is seen as a form of acquiring a better understanding of reality by Zambrano that is not limited to its surface appearance. It is only the temporal coexistence of different realities which affords a complete picture of reality. Of course, Zambrano's statement also echoes Plato's idea that at birth memory is wiped from the human soul but that the soul can recover its prior knowledge during the course of a life. Both Plato's and Zambrano's view comprise the idea that memory is also testament to that which is absent, it includes both what is remembered but also what is forgotten. By definition, however, one does not know what one has forgotten even if one is aware of the fact that one has forgotten something. In this feeling the origin of nostalgia can be found. Nostalgia is of course the yearning for a place but Zambrano adds in its description the longing for a lost time when there existed a 'life in oneness'. Now, while this refers to a prelapsarian existence or Platonic world of ideas, it is also a common feature in exile. Geographical displacement in exile acts as a constant trigger for memory given that the distance and difference evoke the 'país perdido' [lost country] (1991a: 32) through juxtaposition. The longer exile continues the more this nostalgia is combined with the yearning for a bygone time that cannot be recovered as the exile also becomes aware of his spatial dislocation.

Zambrano is, of course, not the first to see a link between exile and memory. As is well-known, Judaism in particular upholds the memory of exile as a lesson to be remembered for the future. Obviously, exile as banishment is one of the oldest forms of punishment. After all, Adam and Eve were cast out of paradise for a transgression, paying the price for their acquisition of knowledge. The critic Nancy E. Berg lists 'the forced *wanderings* of Cain, and the *dispersal* of the builders of the Tower of Babel' as two other instances of Jewish exile in *Genesis*, stating that:

> These biblical stories reflect the progression toward noncommunicability in exile from the interspecial communication between Eve and the serpent to the creation of different languages at Babel. [...] Exile here is of universal nature: forced separation from home, continual rootlessness and the impossibility of communication. (Berg 1996: 9).

The memory of the Fall and other biblical diasporas such as that of the Jews in Egypt colour Zambrano's own view of exile and have left a mark on her understanding of it and the losses that it provokes, given that she conceives of it not merely as a condition of existence but accords it an ethical dimension that also goes beyond the purely existential. That is to say that all of humanity is in exile notwithstanding their actual circumstances due to a spiritual loss that they carry with them through existence. At the same time, it is significant that the thirst for knowledge brought about the Fall in the first instance. The tree of knowledge symbolizes the prevalence of reason; in order to return to the prelapsarian state humans have to acknowledge that reason is not the be all and end all, this is where Zambrano's notion of 'poetic reason' comes in useful, as it admits the impossibility of a return, but advocates a fusion of reason and intuition. In *Filosofía y poesía* Zambrano lays the foundations for poetic reason by discussing the juxtaposition of the two values that philosophy and poetry stand for and ways in which they could come together. In this work she also refers to the exile from Eden and explains how poetry maintains the connection to this foundational moment:

> La poesía manifiesta lo que el hombre es, sin que le haya sucedido nada, nada fuera de lo que le sucedió en el primer acto desconocido del drama en el cual comenzó el hombre, cayendo desde ese lugar irreconquistado que está antes del comienzo de la vida, y que se ha llamado de maneras diferentes. Maneras diferentes que tienen de común el aludir a algo, a un lugar, a un tiempo fuera del tiempo, en que el hombre fue otra cosa que hombre. Un lugar y un tiempo que el hombre no puede precisar en su memoria, porque entonces no había memoria, pero que no puede olvidar, porque tampoco había olvido. Algo que se ha quedado como pura presencia bajo el tiempo y que cuando se actualiza, es éxtasis, encanto. (Zambrano 2013: 99)

> [Poetry shows what mankind is, without anything having happened to it, nothing apart from the first unknown act in the drama in which man started out, falling from that unreconquered place which is before the beginning of life and which has been called different names. Different names which have in common the allusion to something, a place, to a time outside time in which man was another thing than man. A place and a time which man cannot determine in his memory, because then there was no memory, but which he cannot forget either, because there was no forgetting then either. Something which remained as pure presence beneath time and which when it is realized, is ecstasy, enchantment.]

As in Jewish experience the emphasis seems to have shifted from a particular sacred space to a particular time (Berg 1996: 10). Interestingly, Zambrano points out that memory only came into being as a result of this primordial exile, which made it necessary. Indeed, human existence as we know it is predicated on exile. Poetry and memory remind us of the first exile but also make exile meaningful, thus it can be utilized and turned into something alive with 'poetic reason', into ecstasy. The actual state of being in exile makes us also more aware of the universal exile undergone by humanity. While full recovery is impossible, as pre-exilic existence can only be gleaned, there is hope for redemption.

Another more unusual biblical cipher for exile is Job, who is a recurrent figure in Zambrano's thinking, particularly from the first decades of her exile.[16] At first glance, Job does not have much in common with the figure of the exile, as Jung writes:

> Without further ado Job is robbed of his herds, his servants are slaughtered, his sons and daughters are killed by a whirlwind, and he himself is smitten with sickness and brought to the brink of the grave. To rob him of peace altogether, his wife and his old friends are let loose against him, all of whom say the wrong things. His justified complaint finds no hearing with the judge who is so much praised for his justice. Job's right is refused in order that Satan be not disturbed in his play. (Jung 2002: 15)

Of course, Job's plight shares some similarities with that of the exile, as he lives in complete abandonment and loneliness, and most fundamentally there is no reason why he should be thus punished. This irrationality could be proof that Job has been deserted by his God whilst also pointing to the unfathomability of divine reasoning. Yet Job does not lose faith, nor blame God, instead he curses his own birth. In his profound loneliness all that is left to him is to voice his pain, but therein Zambrano also sees something profoundly human: 'Su primera forma de expresión es un clamor; un delirio de exasperación en que irrumpe la necesidad largamente contenida. Es la queja con la que Job inaugura la historia del hombre' [His first form of expression is a cry; a delirium of exasperation into which necessity, contained for a long time, erupts. It is the outcry with which Job inaugurates the history of mankind] (2014b: 197). Zambrano's dense prose here underlines two key ideas: firstly, that the history of humanity is a history of suffering; and secondly, the necessity to communicate one's anguish, the delirium. Job becomes the human per se because he does not suffer in silence. In spite of his suffering, Job maintains his spiritual connection and upholds his belief. Suffering then also becomes a sign of being chosen. Although Zambrano does not formally set out to detail her sorrow and make her own confession, in a sense this is exactly what she is doing by reinscribing the experience of exile into the history of Spain. The confessional mode is also necessitated because exiles have been cast into oblivion, as Zambrano tellingly states elsewhere: 'Todos los que han hecho el relato de su vida en tono de confesión parten de un momento, en que vivían de espaldas a la realidad, en que vivían olvidados'(1988a: 24) ('Anyone who has narrated the story of his life in a confessional tone begins with a moment in which he was living with his back turned on reality, buried in oblivion', Zambrano and Chacel 2015: 19).

In a similar vein, Zambrano writes that in a world governed by reason alone, where time rules supreme, man is exiled from the universe. The experience of exile is a way of gaining knowledge for her, not through rational means, but through what she calls a 'revelation'. As we shall see, she establishes a firm link between exile and revelation in *Los bienaventurados*. Zambrano equates the validity of a revelation for the acquisition of knowledge to that of a logical proof:

> La evidencia es el nombre filosófico de algo que en la mística se llama revelación. Es la presencia indudable de una realidad; una aparición. Mas, la realidad es de tal manera, que produce una huella o modificación en quien la recibe. (Zambrano 1988a: 43)
>
> [Certainty is the philosophical name for something that in mysticism is called revelation. It is the unquestionable presence of a reality, an appearance. But reality is such that it produces a trace or change in the person receiving it.] (Zambrano and Chacel 2015: 42)

Revelation is thus on an equal footing with other empirical methods of epistemology. Yet the difference is that revelation leads inevitably to change. Moreover, revelations as a phenomenological form of acquiring knowledge are also inextricably linked to lived life: 'Es en el ser y desde el ser como se reciben revelaciones' [It is in being and from being that revelations are received] (1991a: 30). We can trace the influence of Heidegger's notion of *Dasein* in this statement which emphasizes existence as a cornerstone of gaining knowledge. On the other hand, Ortega Allué points out that analysis of the experience is as important as the experience itself:

> Qué sea el exilio no puede conocerse sólo a través de la vivencia del exilio. Vivenciar algo nos ocurre de continuo en la existencia; pero nosotros no nos conformamos sólo con vivir. Necesitamos interpretar lo que vivimos, llenar los vacíos de nuestra historia personal y percibir bajo el caos de los acontecimientos, un *sentido*, una razón. (Ortega Allué 1998: 438)
>
> [What exile might be cannot only be known through the experience of exile. Experiencing an event is a continual occurrence of existence, but we should not resign ourselves merely to living. We need to interpret what we live, fill the voids of our personal history and perceive beneath the chaos of events, a *meaning*, a reason.]

Of course, this is precisely what Zambrano is doing in her writing. Although Zambrano claims that she does not consider revelation in its purely religious sense, it is above all through suffering that revelations come about and that we come into being: 'Voy siendo en virtud de lo que veo y padezco y no de lo que razono y pienso' [I come into being by virtue of what I see and suffer and not what I reason and think] (1991a: 31). Exile as a form of suffering can be a means of coming into being.

The first step of dispossession is the same for Job and the exile; neither willingly sheds their belongings. However, this step then becomes an example to follow:

> Apto para servir como paso en una iniciación, si se lograba que el iniciado pasase por donde Job pasó: por la desposesión completa que sólo le dejó vida y vigilia para asistir a sus males. Extrañados de todos, dice el 'a todos me he vuelto extraño' y era tan sólo el reflejo de la extrañeidad mayor de todas las posibles, y que a todas las hacía posibles. Se encontró Job extraño de su Dios, no de Dios, como un hombre moderno diría, no de Dios como un moderno nombra a esta ya más que realidad, idea de Dios. (Zambrano 2014b: 344)
>
> [Apt to serve as a step in an initiation, if it could be achieved that the initiated passed through what Job experienced: through a complete dispossession which only left him with life and vigil to help with his wrongs. Alienated from all, he says 'I have become alien to all' and it was only the reflection of the greatest strangeness of all possible ones, and one that makes them all possible. Job found himself a stranger to his God, not to God, as modern man would say, not to God as a modern man would name this already more than reality, the idea of God.]

Job's suffering is seen as an initiation and in many ways runs parallel to that of the exile, who also ends up being an outcast. Job undergoes the most extreme exile by becoming a stranger to *his* God rather than God, who has given his life meaning up until then. Everything he knew to be and to be true has been shattered. Nonetheless, once everything has been taken from him, he cannot simply go back and make undone what has happened in Zambrano's interpretation:

> No quería revestirse, volver a poseer, volver a esa su feliz vida cuya sustancia precaria ahora se le revelaba. Job no ansiaba que se le restituyera esa vida: nacimiento impuro, días contados, felicidad perdediza. Le dolía más que las llagas y que los hijos perdidos, el quedarse así, tal como al perdérselo todo se le revelaba, conociéndose como larva; como criatura apenas nacida, sin posible acabamiento. (Zambrano 2014b: 347)

> [He did not want to cover up, to possess again, return to his happy life whose precarious substance was now revealed to him. Job did not yearn for the restoration of that life: impure birth, counted days, fleeting happiness. More than the wounds and his children what pained him was the being left as such, in the way that losing everything had revealed to him, recognizing himself as a worm, as a creature barely born, without a possible end.]

Exile like Job's trials is thus also a tool for self-exploration and a stripping-away of everything. It is not loss itself that is painful but the realization that anything else was just futile and temporary, the recognition of one's bare existence becomes a truth that is difficult to bear. The reduction to physical life also makes it evident that material gains are only temporary. The description of Job then recalls very concretely the state of the exile on his path to purified knowledge. It should therefore have become evident that a comparison of the two is not only not too far-fetched, but, in fact, fruitful for thinking through Zambrano's ideas concerning exile.

Even though Zambrano's writings about exile may appear far and few between in the voluminous body that is her work, and in spite of the scarcity of direct references to them, exile and memory are fundamental concepts in Zambrano's thinking. Only a parallel reading of exile in conjunction with other texts not outwardly referring to exile allows for a full understanding of this issue. Zambrano's ideas on exile may often appear hermetic and difficult to disentangle, but this presentation mirrors the difficult realities that the exile experiences. What Zambrano was interested in, after all, was salvaging experiential wisdom from the all-encompassing realm of history, so that individual suffering would not remain in vain.[17] This desire is also driven by and runs in parallel to the discovery Job makes in his suffering:

> Es la esperanza que en realidad le movió a quejarse, pues sin la menor esperanza de ser escuchada, la queja no se produciría. Hasta el simple ¡ay! cuenta con un interlocutor posible. El lenguaje, aun el más irracional, el llanto mismo, nace ante un posible oyente que lo recoja. (Zambrano 1988a: 20)

> [It is hope that in truth stirred Job to complain, for without any hope at all of being heard, the complaint would not have been produced. Even the simple sigh counts on a possible interlocutor. Language, even the most irrational, lamentation itself, is born in the presence of a possible listener to receive it.] (Zambrano and Chacel 2015: 25)

Notes to Chapter 11

1. The phrase 'La España peregrina' comes from the title of a literary journal published in Mexico in 1940 by Republican exiles and edited by José Bergamín.
2. All translations are my own unless otherwise stated.
3. The English translation loses the etymological connection that persists in Spanish between 'uprootedness' (*destierro*) and 'land' (*tierra*).
4. Roberta Johnson calls *Delirio y destino* 'the closest thing to a novel that she wrote, and it is also an autobiography or memoir' (Zambrano 1999: 215).
5. See note 3 about the translation of 'desterrado'.
6. Zambrano's view of the exile resonates with the definition of the nomad by Rosi Braidotti, who

distinguishes the nomad from the migrant and the exile, defining the nomad as follows: 'The nomad does not stand for homelessness or compulsive displacement: it is rather a figuration for the kind of subject who has relinquished all idea, desire, or nostalgia for fixity. It expresses the desire for an identity made of transitions, successive shift, and coordinated changes without an essential unity. The nomadic subject, however, is not altogether devoid of unity: his mode is one of definite, seasonal patterns of movement through rather fixed routes. It is cohesion engendered by repetition, cyclical moves, rhythmic displacements. In this respect, I shall take the nomad as the prototype of the "man or woman of ideas" (Spender 1982); as Deleuze put it, the point of being an intellectual nomad is about crossing boundaries, about the act of going, regardless of the destination' (2011: 57–58).

7. The similarity between the exile and Antigone, a figure frequently contemplated by Zambrano in her exile, is striking, given that having been buried alive Antigone inhabits the same in-between zone between life and death as the exile. In *La confesión: género literario*, Zambrano compares the *poètes maudits* to Antigone in their solitude and anguish: 'Son muertos vivos, enterrados en una sepultura que, invisible, les aísla de los vivientes' (1988a: 67) [They are the living dead, buried in an invisible tomb, isolated from the living] (Zambrano and Chacel 2015: 59).

8. Her description of the living dead elsewhere shares a number of aspects with that of the exile: 'Los muertos vivos [...] los que andan errantes sin lugar donde posarse' (1988a: 69) ('The living dead, wanderers with no place to lay their heads', Zambrano and Chacel 2015: 62).

9. The following description strictly speaking refers to Kierkegaard, but retains its validity in this context: 'Esta manera de vivir, considerándose a sí mismo como muerto vivo, como actor de obras póstumas, era la única solución tal vez, para el hombre que había perdido el sitio de esas realidades que sin embargo le llenaban. Y era la manera de ir abriendo paso al que querían ser, a su unidad de seres humanos. Muertos vivos; hombres subterráneos cuya tarea agobiante es la de apropiarse una realidad extraña, extrayendo de ella su propio ser, pues lo que parece ser lo trágico de la tragedia es la falta de sujeto, de algo que quede exento y libre del destino y de las pasiones' (Zambrano 1988a: 71) [That manner of living, considering oneself as the living dead, as the protagonist of posthumous works, was the only solution, perhaps, for the man who had misplaced those realities with which nonetheless he was imbued. And it was the way to advance toward what the living dead wanted to be, toward their oneness as human beings. The all-consuming task of the living dead, of underground men, is to appropriate an alien reality, extracting from it their own being, for apparently the tragic element of tragedy is the absence of a subject, of something that remains exempt and free from destiny or the passions] (Zambrano and Chacel 2015: 63).

10. One of the topoi of Holocaust literature maintains that the most worthy and pure perished and that the survivors therefore do not represent the most noble, given that the pure souls could not survive in the barbaric environment of the concentration camps.

11. It is interesting to note that Zambrano thereby aligns herself with Giorgio Agamben's thoughts, as he traces the figure of the *homo sacer* through history all the way to Auschwitz. *Homo sacer* is a Roman legal category that paradoxically encompasses someone who has been deprived of their legal and social rights for a transgression and can therefore be killed with impunity. However, at the same time, he cannot be sacrificed to the Gods during a religious ritual. Agamben discusses this figure in detail in *Homo Sacer: Sovereign Power and Bare Life*.

12. 'Intrahistoria' is a concept developed by Unamuno that posits an unchanging eternal 'intrahistory' beneath the moving waves of history. Interestingly, Zambrano resorts to similar sea imagery.

13. Zambrano comments on the importance of memory in the article 'La barca de oro: Introducción a la memoria'.

14. Her article takes the discovery of a golden boat in the Cheops pyramids as the point of departure.

15. Cathy Caruth defines trauma as 'the breach in the mind's experience of time, self, and the world [...] [Trauma] is always the story of a wound that cries out, that addresses us in the attempt to tell us of a reality or truth that is not otherwise available' (1996: 4).

16. Although 'El libro de Job y el pájaro' was only added to the second edition of *El hombre y lo divino* and first published in 1969 as an article in *Papeles de Son Armadans*, references to Job predate this important addition.
17. 'Pues la historia parece devorarnos con la misma insaciable e indiferente avidez de los ídolos más remotos. Avidez insaciable porque es indiferente. El hombre está siendo reducido, allanado en su condición a simple número, degradado bajo la categoría de la cantidad' [History appears to devour us with the same insatiable and indifferent avidness of the most remote idols. Insatiable avidness because it is indifferent. Man is being reduced, made the same, in his condition of being a mere number, degraded by the category of quantity] (Zambrano 2014b: 108).

CHAPTER 12

María Zambrano: Philosophy, Literature, and Democracy

Francis Lough, University of Birmingham

Born in 1904, María Zambrano spent the first thirty years of her life in a Spain which was experiencing a cultural boom and at the same time a social and political climate which was becoming increasingly intense and violent. José-Carlos Mainer has famously described the first decades of the twentieth century in Spain as a 'Silver Age' in a deliberate attempt to draw a comparison with the great Golden Age of the sixteenth and seventeenth centuries (Mainer 1975). Zambrano spent most of her formative years in Segovia and Madrid, the cultural capital of Spain at the time, and was strongly influenced by her father Blas José Zambrano García (Moreno Sanz 1996: 48), a teacher and firm believer in education and the need to modernize Spanish society and politics. Blas Zambrano was a close friend of the poet Antonio Machado, who had studied philosophy and was attracted in particular by the ideas of Henri Bergson whose classes he attended in Paris in 1910–1911 (Johnston 2002: 169–71).[1] Machado would become a key influence on María Zambrano who was also an avid reader of Miguel de Unamuno, professor of philosophy at the University of Salamanca and author of many important novels in addition to his celebrated *Del sentimiento trágico de la vida* [The Tragic Sense of Life].[2] In 1921, Zambrano enrolled for a degree in philosophy at the Central University in Madrid where she studied under Xavier Zubiri and José Ortega y Gasset before going on to teach philosophy there in the years 1931–1939.

Zambrano began her education and professional career as a philosopher in the tumultuous years of the dictatorship of Primo de Rivera (1921–1930), the Second Spanish Republic (1931–1936) and the Spanish Civil War (1936–1939). After the war and the establishment of a new dictatorship under Francisco Franco, Zambrano, like hundreds of thousands of other Republican sympathizers, was forced into exile and only returned to Spain in 1984, nine years after Franco's death. It has often been commented that the experience of exile became fundamental to the very development of her philosophy and her political thought (see, for example, Di Pierro 2010: 73–74).[3] One of the consequences of this impact on her thought, however, is that to some degree the foundations of her early writings which brought together philosophy, the arts, and politics were weakened and inevitably lost as a result of that same experience. The key strand in the development of Zambrano's thought in exile is the emergence of a concept of 'poetic reason' which for many becomes increasingly difficult to fully understand because her ideas take shape in a highly poetic language in which form reflects content. This is Zambrano's main contribution to twentieth-century philosophy which inevitably, and rightly, has come to dominate many of the critical studies of her work. Nonetheless, prioritizing this area of her thought easily overshadows those other areas which sought to engage with more tangible problems relating to politics and the arts. This essay explores the intimate relation in Zambrano's thought between philosophy, politics, and literature as they developed in her early works and before the impact of her exile began to make its mark. What this shows is that, as a young philosopher, Zambrano was beginning to address some of the major themes in philosophy at the time, and in particular the meaning of democracy at a deeper level than the question of the politics of the day, and that many of her ideas continue to have relevance for our thinking on such issues, as indicated by the work of theorists in more recent times.[4]

Zambrano's formative years were lived in a period in which not only were philosophy and the arts in Europe undergoing a fundamental shift but, by the late 1920s and early 1930s, many artists and writers were looking for ways of fusing art and politics in a reversal of the elitism which had dominated much of the 1920s as exemplified by the writings of Ortega y Gasset, Spain's most important philosopher of the time and author of *La deshumanización del arte* (1925) [The Dehumanization of Art and Ideas about the Novel] and *La rebelión de las masas* (1930) [The Revolt of the Masses]. The importance of Ortega y Gasset in Zambrano's early development is significant but more so is her intellectual estrangement from him from the early 1930s, at the very beginning of her career as a philosopher, because he believed she was in danger of becoming too mystical or being side-tracked by literature (Revilla Guzmán 2012: 6). While Zambrano would always remain faithful to Ortega, it was clear that from the outset she was determined to follow her own path. This is what has made her voice unique in the context of Spanish philosophy at the time, and one which continues to resonate today.

The end of the twentieth century and the beginning of the twenty-first have been characterized by many turns in critical and theoretical debates in the humanities which have sought to re-evaluate and redefine the different spaces within which the arts operate. There has been, for instance, an aesthetic turn which is characterized by two inevitably overlapping areas of interest — aesthetic practice and the role of the arts in society (e.g. Levine 2007, Clark 2000, Carey 1992, Carey 2005, and Melzer and others 1999), on the one hand, and, on the other, aesthetic theory, metaphysics, and epistemology, and the deeper question of the very nature of democracy itself as an aesthetic experience (e.g. Eagleton 1990, Rancière 2009, Rancière 2010, Docherty 2006, and Hirschkop 1999). It is this second approach which is of most interest in relation to Zambrano. At the same time, there has been an affective turn (see, for example, Clough 2008, Massumi 1996, and Seigworth and Gregg 2010). One thing both turns have in common is the reconsideration of the value of lived experience in contrast to traditional modes of thought founded on abstract reason. Equally, both turns put the spotlight on the role of the arts, and particularly literature, and their importance for how we come to understand the world in which we live.

The aesthetic turn marks a particular shift of attention in theory and criticism but it is not itself radically new, as 'anyone who inspects the history of European philosophy since the enlightenment must be struck by the curiously high priority assigned by it to aesthetic questions' (Eagleton 1990: 1). At the beginning of the twentieth century this interest in art and aesthetics took a particular turn as a consequence of what many regarded as a time of crisis in Western culture and civilization associated with modernity. Edmund Husserl, one of the key exponents of this idea at the time, remarked in 1936 that 'the European nations are sick; Europe itself, it is said, is in crisis' (Husserl 1970: 270). The 'crisis of European existence' (299), he argued, began with philosophy and spread to the world of science calling into question the very meaning of cultural life and of humanity in Europe (12). Husserl saw as the root cause of the crisis the failure of a rational culture [which] 'lies not in the essence of rationalism itself but solely in its being rendered superficial, in its entanglement in "naturalism" and "objectivism"' (299), a situation in which everything, including the world of the spirit, is reduced to mere facts (6);[5] in other words, there emerged 'the threat of the instrumentalization of reason and the reification of social relations, in which the concrete identities of individuals are effaced by the powers of abstract, universal reason' (Cascardi 1999: 176).

Both Husserl and Zambrano saw the crisis of their time as the consequence of 'a departure from a natural attitude' in western philosophy (Gingerich 2009: 200) and sought a new form of understanding or reason which would represent a radical departure from centuries of traditional modes of thought. But while Husserl argued from within phenomenology for a return to a 'genuine rationality' in which the spirit is not in or alongside nature — rather, nature is itself drawn into the spiritual sphere (Husserl 1970: 297–98) — María Zambrano would argue for a return to what she saw as a new form of understanding which involves a re-evaluation of a pre-Platonic attitude when 'poetry and philosophy once were part of a unity, a single attitude toward the world' (Gingerich 2009: 200). It is important to stress here that Zambrano was recovering this idea to re-insert it into the modern context and was not advocating a naïve return to some golden age. This is the key foundation for her development of 'poetic reason' which, in *Los intelectuales en el drama de España* [Intellectuals and the Drama of Spain], she justified on the grounds that what she refers to as rational thought, reason, or scientific thought 'anula la heterogeneidad del ser, es decir, la realidad inmediata, sensible, que el poeta ama y de la que no puede ni quiere desprenderse' [annuls the heterogeneity of being, that is the immediate reality of the senses which is loved by the poet and from which he cannot nor does not want to detach himself] (2015: 193), citing Antonio Machado for whom 'poesía y razón se completan y requieren una a otra' [poetry and reason complete and require each other] (193). Zambrano's approach here is fundamentally modern as was that of Walter Benjamin who, according to Thomas Docherty, recognized the importance of 'the contest between, on the one hand, the material *content* of a lived experience, transient if intense, and, on the other hand, the abstract and unreal ideality of the *form* that such an experience assumes when it is construed in terms of a "monument of unaging intellect"', noting that the 'absolute prioritization of the latter is to be contested' (Docherty 2006: 63). Like the aesthetic turn at the end of the twentieth century, this attack on Western culture's over-confidence in the powers of reason or belief in reason as a source of absolute truth was in itself not new — Isaiah Berlin traced the history of what he termed the 'counter-enlightenment' to the late eighteenth century (Berlin 1980: 1–24) — but became ever more widespread as the twentieth century progressed. Solutions to the crisis did not mean, as Husserl noted, abandoning reason but recovering other aspects of human existence identified with nature, spirit, or life, those subjective elements which Platonic and neo-Platonic idealism had relegated to a poor second place.

Spanish writers and thinkers at the beginning of the twentieth century, María Zambrano amongst them, were just as concerned as their neighbours with the crisis in Europe and European thought, but they were also deeply preoccupied with a specific crisis of national identity in their own country (Balfour 1996). This crisis of identity came to the fore when Spain, once a great imperial nation, lost the last of its colonies in South and Central America in 1898 and the question of Spanishness, or what it meant to be Spanish, dominated the minds of key thinkers and writers. Two factors combined to make the Spanish context and Zambrano's response to it quite unique. The first was the complex relationship the domestic crisis was deemed to have with the wider European crisis. As is well-known, the political and economic decline of Spain in the seventeenth and eighteenth centuries, together with the resistance to the Reformation which was taking place in the rest of Europe, led to the country being marginalized until the time of the Peninsular War (1807–1814) which brought many British and French soldiers to the country and opened the way for the Romantic construction of Spain as an exotic land which would be epitomized in Prosper Mérimée's *Carmen* (1845), and Bizet's opera which was first performed in 1875 (Álvarez Junco 1996: 93–94). By the mid-nineteenth century, both Spaniards and non-Spaniards believed that 'there was such a thing as a Spanish identity, a Spanish character, a Spanish "soul" or "essence", with very definitive traits' (95). The idea of Spain as a site of difference was fundamental in the works of many Spanish writers at the end of the nineteenth century and beginning of the twentieth. As Stephen Gingerich has argued, for example, both Miguel de Unamuno and José Ortega y Gasset, two key influences on Zambrano's thinking, were representative of a Spanish 'tradition of privileging its own experience and perspective [...] in a way that connects it with some human experiences that are considered universal' such that 'reflections upon Spain and its place in the world do not focus on Spanish particularity so much as on what in the Spaniard transcends Spanishness' (Gingerich 2009: 197). Consequently, while many Spaniards throughout the nineteenth and early twentieth centuries had argued for modernization by means of a Europeanization of their country, part of the solution to the wider crisis would now be the 'Spanishization' of Europe. The influence of such thinking on Zambrano is clear. Her concept of 'poetic reason', for example, is premised on the bringing together of philosophy and poetry which she equated with a union of Western and Eastern cultures: 'Zambrano explains that philosophy was the one extreme of "classical culture," the one that took over and produced the West. The other extreme, poetry, she associates with the East, with yogis [...] Spanish culture is not merely poetic, but it possesses "poetic cognition." That is to say, it is not at one extreme with Europe at the other, but somewhere between the two extremes of West and East' (204). Spain, for Zambrano, then provided the balance between two radically different cultures each associated with the two interlocking strands of abstract reason and lived experience as conceived subjectively. As such, Spain was the site of the very same unity of philosophy and poetry to be found in Greek thinkers before Plato.

The second factor was Zambrano's own analysis of the political crisis of the 1930s in Spain and, later, writing in exile in 1939, the failure of the Second Republic to establish a functioning democratic state. Throughout the late 1920s and the period of the Republic, many Spanish intellectuals, like those in other Western countries, were moved to abandon their avant-garde elitism of previous years and to put their intellectual efforts and works in the service of the people. Their efforts, which were reflected in a wide-spread desire on the part of writers to fuse with the people (Lough 2002: 5–11), is the material manifestation of Zambrano's answer to the failure of rational thought and so of intellectuals generally. In *Los intelectuales en el drama de España* she was quite explicit in her belief that the solution to the crisis in Europe was for man to change, 'a que el *hombre vaya siendo otro*, a que las facetas inéditas de la hombría, las zonas no usadas de la humanidad, vayan apareciendo' [so that *man might become other*, and the unknown facets of 'hombría', the unused parts of humanity, might appear] (2015: 149), a project which could not be delivered by reason alone but required intuition.[6] The crucial point for Zambrano was that such a transformation — or revolution as she called it — could only take place as the result of some momentous event. The qualities required for this transformation were to be found in the Spanish people who, as a result of their country's centuries of isolation, had not been influenced by the idealist culture of the rest of Europe; the momentous event was the Spanish Civil War:

> España es el lugar de tal parto dolorísimo. Por su infinita energía en potencia, por su virginidad de pueblo apenas empleado en empresas dignas de su poder y por su profunda indocilidad a la cultura idealista europea, tenía que ser y es España [...] Es ahora el pueblo quien [...] se alumbra un nuevo hombre, una nueva realidad *que antes no había* [...] Ante esa *visión* del entrañable fondo humano que muestra el pueblo español en su lucha, todos los viejos proyectos idealistas aprovechados por el fascismo mistificador se desvanecerán. (Zambrano 2015: 149–50)[7]

> [Spain is where that most painful delivery will take place. It had to be Spain, given its potentially infinite energy, the virginity of its people who have rarely been employed in tasks worthy of their power and the deep refusal of idealist European culture [...] It is now the Spanish 'pueblo' that [...] will give birth to a new man, a new reality *which did not exist before* [...] Faced with this *vision* of the profound human depths the Spanish 'pueblo' is showing in its struggle, all

> the old idealist projects which have been abused by a mystifying fascism will
> fade away.]⁸

It is easy to dismiss this notion of the universal nature of the Spanish character and the myth of the 'pueblo', the Spanish people, as the repository of all that was good in the Spanish character or soul and as the source not only of the salvation of Spain but also of the solution to the crisis of European culture and thought, by seeing it as, on the one hand, a mis-placed national pride and, on the other, typical of the colourful rhetoric used by the Republican side during the Spanish Civil War. However, Zambrano herself was aware of the transient nature of the historical context and in *Los intelectuales en el drama de España*, for example, raised the explicit question of what would remain of the new relationship established between intellectuals and the people in the future. Writing with the conviction that the Republic and the 'pueblo' would be victorious, her answer was that new forms of art would appear but that, from that point on art and intelligence, the people and the state would be inseparable (2015: 170).⁹ By the same token, therefore, it can be argued that her responses to the political events of her time should not obscure the general principles and premises which lie behind some of her ideas. In other words, it is worth asking what remains of Zambrano's fundamental ideas when such nationalistic references are stripped away. This opens up a space for the re-evaluation of Zambrano's early thinking on democracy, and its relationship to philosophy and literature which can be better understood in the context of more recent critical debates. It is notable that, although a philosopher by training, Zambrano's first book is titled *Horizonte del Liberalismo* (1930) and that many of the essays in her second book, *Los intelectuales en el drama de España* (1937), along with other essays from the time, take literary figures as their subject.

When preparations were being made in Spain for the introduction of a democratic Republic in 1930 the Spanish political class was not fully prepared for the task. The period known as the Restoration (1875–1921) which had brought peace to Spain after more than sixty years of political turmoil — between 1814 and 1877 there were thirty-seven military uprisings (Beevor 2006: 8) — did so at a cost. The two main parties, Conservative and Liberal, simply agreed to share power by taking turns in office. In 1921, as peace was once again threatened, Primo de Rivera staged another military coup and remained in power as dictator for the rest of the decade until both his position and that of the monarchy were no longer tenable. So, by 1930 Spain had a political class with no real experience of how to conduct politics (Graham 1996: 135). Years later María Zambrano herself would reflect on this situation stating that:

> There was a lack of political training which is one of the most serious forms of damage such a situation can produce in a country. A generation had been denied access to seats in Parliament, had been given no opportunity to measure its strengths and ideas against 'reality'. (Zambrano 1999: 149–50)

Given this context and Zambrano's philosophical training, it is perhaps hardly surprising that her thoughts on liberalism and democracy in *Horizonte del liberalismo* did not extend to practical questions of citizenship and government. Her initial interest lay in more abstract considerations of the key relationship between the individual and society which were to be understood in the context of the crisis of rational thought. For Zambrano, politics, ethics, and metaphysics are all directly linked:

> La política, como la ética, es (si no consecuencia), rama o planta, quizá, que supone un suelo y un sostén, que no podrá ser, en último término, más que la metafísica, o sus sustitutivos en las desdichadas épocas en que se le ha negado. (Zambrano 2015: 71)
>
> [Politics, like ethics is (if not the consequence) the branch or plant, perhaps, which requires some ground or support which, in the final analysis, can be nothing other than metaphysics or its substitutes in those unhappy periods when it has been denied.]

Zambrano argues against the dominance of reason in *Horizonte del liberalismo* in her insistence that 'la vida está por encima de la razón' [life is above reason], the latter being associated with idealism which sees things as mere shadows of ideas (2015: 74), a clear indication of the anti-Platonic foundation on which much of her philosophy is built. Zambrano rejects all rational systems of thought or belief which dream of drying up 'el inmenso mar de la realidad con la cantarilla de la inteligencia' [the immense sea of reality in the little pitcher of intelligence] (74), or which, as she suggests elsewhere, pretend to have access to all the answers and are associated with notions of permanence, absolutism, or dogma — 'el dogmatismo, que consiste en creerlo todo revelado' [dogmatism, which consists of believing that everything has been revealed] (67). For Zambrano, life was fluid and characterized by change: 'todo lo humano pasa, fluye, muere' [everything human passes, flows, dies] (65); 'en lo humano todo cambia. La Historia es fluencia, muerte, renacimiento, transformación; magnífico sentido que el siglo XIX llevó hasta la quieta historia animal y vegetal; también las especies cambian' [everything human changes. History is flow, death, rebirth, transformation; a magnificent awareness that the nineteenth century brought to bear on even the still history of the animal and vegetable kingdoms; species also change] (70). And so politics, which operates in the realm of human rather than natural creation, must also be about constant movement and change. Conservative politics is associated with dogmatic thinking and stasis in which nothing new is possible (68). Revolution, on the other hand, is conceived of as a dynamic process (70) more in tune with man's nature. However, when Zambrano speaks of revolution she is not referring simply to the political sphere in a narrow sense.[10] A revolutionary is one who 'cree ante todo en la vida, presenta la intuición frente a la razón, la realidad siempre renovada frente a las inmóviles ideas' [believes first and foremost in life, who places intuition before reason, a constantly re-newed reality before static ideas] (74–75), while history 'no es sino un diálogo, bastante dramático, por cierto, entre el hombre y el Universo. Gracias al hombre hay diálogo, dualidad. Él es siempre *el otro* en la naturaleza' [is no more than a rather dramatic dialogue between man and the Universe. Thanks to man there is dialogue, duality. Man is always *the other* in nature] (59). Man here is conceived of as both the individual with his own sense of self and the freedom that entails and the individual as part of a community (79). Zambrano's ideas here can be seen as an early expression of ideas which have been subject to a more detailed formulation by Docherty for whom culture 'names the possibility of a transformation, a change in our ordinariness that is occasioned by aesthetics or art. The name we give to that change is history: our historical becoming and our becoming historical', and democracy:

> Like culture, is not a constant, not a state of affairs, not a political mode of being [...] Democracy we might say, is the condition of our becoming human; and a democracy that finds its episodic roots in the event we call cultural is the condition of our becoming humanly and socially historical. (Docherty 2006: xiii)

Politics for Zambrano, then, is 'reforma, creación, revolución siempre' [reform, creation, revolution always] (2015: 58). It is the action of engaging creatively in life with the aim of promoting change and therefore constitutes the most human of all activities (58). The challenge for the individual and society is to achieve a balance between the interests of the individual's ontological and social being. According to Zambrano, this was a challenge open to but not met by nineteenth-century liberalism. The idea of progress which dominated and shaped much of the nineteenth century had the positive consequence of making man believe that change, or evolution, was part of his essence. It may have derived from a rationalist discourse, but it gave man in the nineteenth century 'el ingenuo gozo de haber derribado las barreras, de haberse evadido de una cárcel, y pensó que la historia empezaba' [the naive pleasure of having torn down the barriers, of having escaped from a prison, and thinking that history was beginning. Humanity felt itself a child or, more than that, newly born] (76). Zambrano did not develop her ideas beyond such brief statements, but her conceptualization of the challenge faced by nineteenth-century liberals in relation to infancy, pleasure, and the beginning of history finds an echo in Docherty's more recent reading of Agamben. On the one hand, Docherty identifies:

> A crisis in that form of thinking — which we can call 'modernity' — that sees its goal or task as the regulation of the relations between the relative claims of the particular and the general, the individual and the universal, the idiosyncratic or idiomatic and the law. (Docherty 2006: 94)

On the other, he argues that:

> The question of autonomy is [...] how can we get a genuine history started; or (the better formulation here), what is the infancy of the present? How can a human subject or subjects initiate an event that is not always already given by the pure linearity of happenings that prefigure and determine it, thereby foreclosing its possibilities and limiting its intrinsic freedom? Agamben offers an answer: for everyone there is an immediate and available experience on which a new concept to time could be founded. This is an experience so essential to human beings that an ancient Western myth makes it humankind's original home: it is pleasure. (Docherty 2006: 102)

The failure of nineteenth-century liberalism, according to Zambrano, lay in the failure to equate progress in science with an equivalent development in morality and politics (2015: 76–77). This was manifest in a conflict between the promotion of the individual rights of man and the development of a liberal capitalist economy which, in reference to the famous slogan of the French Revolution, paid more heed to questions of liberty than equality and fraternity. Progress in a capitalist economy, therefore, was only made possible by the enslavement of some for the benefit of others (80–81). In Spain, this was evident in that the two main parties, Liberals and Conservatives, who agreed to share power during the Restoration (1875–1921) represented:

> An oligarchic system which by its very nature, conserving important remnants of the *ancien regime*, obstructed and delayed the birth of a modern nation-state. [...] They were not modern political formations but groups of notables and professional politicians who guaranteed the political supremacy of the financial landowning oligarchies of the country. (Romero Salvadó 1996: 119)

Zambrano, as did many others, believed that the task of the Second Republic was the creation of a new economic and political model which would allow for the creation of a new state as the expression of a new man. The defence of the *pueblo* and the democratic ideals of the Republic in the Spanish Civil War, she argued, offered the best hope for change in Europe, and for the emergence of this new man precisely because Spain had never fully developed a liberal capitalist economy. The strength of Zambrano's nationalistic sentiment in this regard is in part a reflection of the fact that this was written in 1937, in the middle of the Civil War, and in the full knowledge that the Western democracies would not come to the aid of the Republic whilst Hitler and Mussolini provided material support to Franco and the Nationalist side.

The immediate object of Zambrano's attack at this point is fascist ideology which she associates with out-dated and life-less words and concepts (2015: 147–48). Against the threat of fascism, she envisions a 'communist' state, to be understood, as is her idea of revolution, in the broadest possible sense; by communism, she means a state based on the idea of community as opposed to the narrow political sense associated with the Soviet state under Stalin in the 1930s. Underlying this political context, however, the vision of a new man is associated with a reality which has never existed before precisely because it merges reason with lived experience. It is around the notion of lived experience that Zambrano brings together her nationalist sentiment, politics, poetry, and metaphysics. To begin with she identifies the people of Spain as the repository of the real Spain which has survived untouched by an official, bureaucratic Spain. Then, she associates Spanish intellectuals and writers with the people. Consequently, when she emphasizes the importance of 'the immediate reality of the senses loved by the poet' she is referring to an aspect of reality which has remained hidden but alive in Spain, and which is accessible through intuition, or poetic rather than rational thought, which has come to the fore in the specific, political context of the Spanish Civil War and the defence of the democratic Republic. The re-incorporation of intuition or poetic thought into our understanding of human life presents a challenge to rationalist discourse and opens up the way for the creation of a new man and a new world, defined as 'communist' in its broadest sense.

The core of Zambrano's thinking here is the connection between poetry, or more precisely *poiēsis*, and love which, in a social context, manifests itself as a belief in co-existence. *Poiēsis* here is best understood as a pre-Socratic concept which, according to Alexander Di Pippo, Heidegger came to understand as 'not merely a [*sic*] expression of subjectivity [but as] a constitutive feature of Da-sein's Being-in-the-world' and as 'the basis for the kinship between the poet and philosopher' (Di Pippo 2000: 44–45). Zambrano describes different aspects of reality as poetic. For example, in her essay 'La guerra, de Antonio Machado' [*The War* by Antonio Machado], first published in 1937, she begins by suggesting that perhaps 'toda historia [...] sea en ultimo término poesía, creación' [all history [...] is, in the final analysis, poetry, creation] (2015: 186), and then declares that the poet's word is an allusion to and testifies to the destiny of a people: 'es la mejor unidad de poesía con la acción, o como se dice, con la política' [it is the best unity of poetry with action, or as one might say, with politics] (188). In the essay 'La reforma del entendimiento español' [The Reform of Understanding in Spain], she also draws a connection between philosophy and the state which begins in ancient Greece, because Platonic and Aristotelian systems of thought have as part of their essence 'la idea sistemática de la convivencia, la sistematización, objetivización de las relaciones humanas en el Estado' [the systematic idea of human co-existence, the systematization and objectification of human relations in the State] and this has continued until the present day (209–10). In Spain, she argues, in previous centuries 'se paraliza nuestro pensamiento al mismo tiempo que se petrifica el Estado' [our thought is paralyzed at the same time as the State becomes petrified] (209). The consequence of this for Spain was the 'petrification of Spanish life' and the 'slow and very sad dismemberment of a society' (211–12).

Zambrano's analysis of Spain's history reveals that the decline of the state leads to a stagnation in which philosophical thought and a re-organization of the state become impossible leaving *poiēsis* to find refuge in literature (213–14, 216) such that the Spanish novel 'desde Cervantes a Galdós, pasando por la picaresca, nos trae el verdadero alimento intelectual del español' [from Cervantes to Galdós, passing through the picaresque, brings us the true intellectual food of the Spaniard] (214); the novel represents 'para los españoles lo que la Filosofía para Europa' [for Spaniards what Philosophy was for Europe] (213). The realms of fiction, therefore, became the repository of man at his best, of a new form of co-existence increasingly distant from European idealism. It is in the creations of Cervantes and Galdós, in particular their key protagonists, the eponymous Don Quixote, Galdós's Fortunata in *Fortunata and Jacinta* (1887), and Benigna, Nina, and the moor Mordejai in *Misericordia* (1897), that the ideals of co-existence and fraternity survive. Don Quixote's idealism, whatever his madness, is linked to belief in a 'profunda, esencial convivencia; allí donde está su voluntad, allí está el *otro*, el hombre igual a él, su hermano, por quien hace y arremete contra todo' [deep, essential co-existence; wherever his will is, there is to be found the *other*, the man who is his equal, his brother, for whom he does everything and attacks everything] (215). Fortunata is considered to be the nineteenth-century equivalent of Don Quixote, almost his twin (218); their essence is embodied in the defenders of the Republic during the Spanish Civil War (220). *Misericordia* is a key text for Zambrano because the characters can be associated with her idea of the Spanish nation and the prioritizing of life as the bedrock of the community. Benigna and Mordejai represent life and poetry, respectively, and the unity of Christianity and Islam, West and East, the two cultures which, as noted above, shaped Spain's identity. The relationship between Benigna and Mordejai stands for the possibility of co-existence when their beliefs 'are truly lived' (252). Nina, for her part, is described as 'la fuerza inagotable de la vida transformándolo todo en vida' [the inexhaustible force of life which transforms everything into life] (253). She represents the essence of mercy or compassion, the 'misericordia' of the title, and as such the idea of co-existence based on a recognition of the rights of the other which are fundamental to democracy. This recognition, importantly, derives from a feeling of love rather than any sense of duty and so finds a parallel in Todd May's discussion of the ethics of equality in Jacques Rancière and in particular the ethical character of a democratic community:

> The concepts of sharing and trust do not lend themselves to an entirely cognitive approach. Sharing and trust are based not on reason — at least not solely — but also on an affective bond that eludes the formal morality of a Kantian (or even utilitarian) approach. (May 2007: 32)

In essence, for Zambrano, the novels of Galdós are about the triumph of life over the power of ideas, and so they offer a perfect representation of the essence of Spain which she believed the Republican side were trying to make a political reality as part of the construction of a new man.

The vitality of life and the idea of co-existence which Zambrano found in these Spanish novels are more directly expressed as the quality of love in her comments on the poetry of Antonio Machado in which she found the coming together of reason and poetry. As Janet Pérez has noted, Machado 'incarnates for Zambrano the ideal fusion of poet and philosopher' (1999: 60). Indeed, it was in her essay, '*La guerra* de Antonio Machado' that Zambrano first used the term 'poetic reason' (2015: 193). In this regard, however, Machado is not unique. Just as the idea of Spain as a fusion of cultures which represents thought and poetry is not in itself new, it is the political reality being created which is new, Zambrano saw Machado as part of a tradition which includes Parmenides and Pythagoras, Dante (in whom philosophy is expressed as theology) and Baudelaire, and, in Spain, the fifteenth-century poet Jorge Manrique. What Zambrano finds in the poetry of Machado are 'misterios hondos en que juegan muerte y amor' [deep mysteries where death and love play], a sense of life which owes something to Heidegger (191–92), and specifically:

> Razones de amor porque cumplen una función amorosa, de reintegrar a unidad los trozos de un mundo vacío; amor que va creando orden, la ley, amor que crea la objetividad en su más alta forma [...] Amor infinito hacia la realidad que le mueve a reintegrar en su poesía toda la íntima sustancia que la abstracción diaria le ha restado. (Zambrano 2015: 192)

> [Reasons for love because they fulfil a loving function of reintegrating into a

unity the bits of an empty world; love which creates order, the law; love which creates objectivity in its highest form [...] Infinite love towards reality which moves him to re-integrate in his poetry all of the intimate substance which everyday abstraction has taken from it.]

All of this needs to be understood in terms of a recovery of 'the sensible', which is required for the transformation of man and his world, and man's true being or 'hombría'.[11] As Zambrano noted in *Intelectuales en el drama de España*, intelligence driven by reason has not been able to provide 'una intuición del hombre, *un proyecto de hombría* que no fuese proyecto pensado' [an intuition of man, *a plan for 'hombría'* that was not the product of thought] (2015: 149).

In the political context of the Spanish Civil War, *hombría* is equated with the unity of the people and constitutes the rationale for the fight against the Nationalist forces and fascism (2015: 193–94). Spain becomes the site of a potential transformation towards a human rather than capitalist or bourgeois economic liberalism (2015: 103) which entails the individual accepting his social condition and, therefore, the existence and rights of 'the other' — realigning equality and fraternity with liberty. Self-interest needs to be balanced with tolerance, 'saber que existe "lo otro"; amar lo contrario, que es lo humano [knowing that 'otherness' exists; loving our opposite which is what makes us human] (62). The trope of love as a social bond was common in the 1930s as a way of expressing the political desire on the part of intellectuals to fuse with the working classes in Spain and beyond (Lough 2002: 7–10; Kermode 1989: 25, 40). Zambrano uses it to bridge the gap between the social and the ontological to refer both to the sense of brotherhood she associates with the democratic ideals of the Republic and to all of humanity in the struggle to create a new man and new society. In this regard, she is very much in tune with Husserl who declared that 'to be human at all is essentially to be a human being in a socially and generatively united civilization' (1970: 15). It also possibly prefigures, although in a much simpler manner, Agamben's later notion of a 'being-towards-love' which 'stems from the possibility of "loving without a cause"', the basis of a singularity which 'renounces the false dilemma that requires that knowledge choose between the ineffability of the individual and the intelligibility of the universal' (Docherty 2006: 97–98).

Throughout the 1930s, then, Zambrano was driven by the idea of transformation in both the philosophical and social spheres as the key to resolving the crises of Western thought and Western culture which she equated with the political struggle to defend the Second Spanish Republic. She formed part of an emerging tradition in European thought which attacked traditional instrumental reason (and its inherent dualisms of body/mind, life/intellect, intuition or feelings/rational thought) while seeking new forms of understanding which would recognize the validity of the immediacy of lived experience. At different points, her early ideas resonate with those of Kierkegaard, Husserl, and Heidegger and pre-figure the more recent ideas of theorists who continue to build on their work. At the same time, her attack on dualism pre-figures more recent theories of affect which have had an impact on many fields of thought 'including history, political theory, human geography, urban and environmental studies, architecture, literary studies, art history and criticism, media theory and cultural studies' (Leys 2011: 434). Affect theory challenges the 'primacy of cognition over affect' (Robinson 2013: 38) and argues that in response to any stimulus from the environment:

> There is an *affective appraisal* that concerns those things that *matter* to the organism and that occurs very fast, automatically, and below the threshold of awareness. This affective awareness is *non-cognitive* in that it occurs prior to and independently of any cognitive evaluation. (Robinson 2007: 42–43)

Accordingly, the notion of abstract thought as somehow independent from lived bodily experience has become, for many, hard to maintain. The notion in affect theory that the intellect is in fact influenced by non-conscious bodily reactions to the external environment even before it begins to do its work does not necessarily suggest the primacy of affect over cognition (even though affects are triggered first), but that human thought depends on the interplay of affects and cognition.

The manner in which Zambrano understood and tackled the question of transformation was heavily coloured by her passionate involvement in the political struggle to defend the Spanish Republic in a decade in which, throughout Europe, the conservative forces of the right, in particular fascism, were gaining strength. In the real world, the reaffirmation of lived experience as part of a new understanding of life and politics as dynamic processes, rather than states, was the expression of an ideal to be achieved but one which, in Spain, eventually failed with the imposition of a dictatorship built on an essentially static, dogmatic ideology. The importance of literature to Zambrano was that the works of writers like Galdós and Cervantes preserved and represented that ideal which was in conflict with the social and political reality of their times. Implicit in this is the notion that such texts survive because, as Derek Attridge has argued, the key characteristic of artworks is that they hold out 'the possibility of a repeated encounter with alterity' (Attridge 2004: 28). Attridge also sees the artwork as part of a dynamic process of transformation:

> In the case of most types of invention, once it has brought about change in an individual or a culture its work is done: its effects will continue to be felt through those applications, reproductions, and reworkings. The artistic invention is strikingly different: though it too gives rise to repetitions and developments of various kinds, it retains its inventiveness as long as it finds a responsive audience, which is to say as long as it is not wholly and permanently accommodated. (Attridge 2004: 28)

Zambrano, of course, was not concerned by enquiries into the nature of the artwork or the literary text which have returned to critical debates in recent years but the question of transformation here can be linked to her concern for transformation in relation to man, history, politics, and philosophy. Indeed, when the social and political transformations dreamed of by Republicans in Spain in the 1930s fail to emerge, the potential for transformation remains and retreats into the philosophical and literary spheres in the same way that Zambrano had argued that the counter-Reformation and the decline of the Spanish state had earlier forced *poiēsis* to find refuge in literature. One might argue that something similar happens with Zambrano's thought in exile as her language becomes increasingly metaphorical as a way of expressing and giving shape to her concept of 'poetic reason'. Nonetheless, Zambrano would constantly return to these early ideas on Spain, democracy, and Spanish writers in her later writings. Some twenty years after the Civil War, for example, she would revisit the question of democracy in her book *Persona y democracia* (1958) [Person and Democracy] and, in addition to several essays on Spanish writers, published *La España de Galdós* (1960) [The Spain of Galdós]. In the early 1940s she had also prepared the manuscript of a book entitled *Unamuno y su obra* [Unamuno and his Works] which was only published in 2003 along with other writings on this Spanish philosopher in an anthology edited by Mercedes Gómez Blesa entitled simply *Unamuno*. In exile, however, Zambrano's philosophy developed and changed. One consequence of this is that her later inquiry into the nature of democracy is, in some regards, much deeper but it is also more detached from the real world of politics and relies more heavily on philosophical discussions of the nature of the relationship between the individual and society. These later works, inevitably, have to be read in the context of Zambrano's exile and the impact that this prolonged experience and the defeat of the Republican cause had on her thought, a task which, however, lies beyond the scope of this essay. A study of these later works will reveal other interesting, if different, parallels with aspects of contemporary thought, none of which detracts from the value of Zambrano's early writings on philosophy, democracy, and literature which still have a general relevance today, but also very particularly for a Spain whose new democracy is still relatively young and continuing to come to terms with the country's violent past.

Notes to Chapter 12

1. As Roberta Johnson has noted, 'The intersection of philosophy and literature had a large share in defining Spanish letters in the first third of the twentieth century' (1997: 181).
2. Pérez 1999.
3. Zambrano herself declared that 'el exilio que me ha tocado vivir es esencial. Yo no concibo mi vida sin el exilio que he vivido. El exilio ha sido como mi patria, o como una dimensión de una patria desconocida, pero que una vez que se conoce, es irrenunciable' [the exile I have lived is essential. I cannot conceive of the life I have lived without exile. Exile has been like my homeland, or like one dimension of an unknown homeland which, when once discovered, cannot be renounced] (2000b: 184). José Luis Abellán has argued that when she moved to France in 1964 exile became for her an existential reality and one of the defining aspects of her life (2006: 48). All translations, with the exception of those from *Delirio y destino* are my own.
4. For a consideration of the development of Zambrano's ideas in this area after the fall of the Republic and the beginning of the Second World War, see Soto Carrasco (2010) and dos Santos das Neves (2001).
5. David Carr, the translator, notes that 'the translating difficulties with Geist and its derivatives are too well known to require comment. I have usually opted for "spirit" as the least of several evils. Sometimes "mental" is used for the adjectival form' (Husserl, 1970: 6, n. 5).
6. In everyday language *hombría* means 'manliness' or 'manhood' but is used here in its wider sense as being derived from *hombre* [man] in a general sense to mean mankind.
7. The distinction Zambrano draws between Spain and Europe is not an absolute one as she recognizes in her essay 'La reforma del entendimiento español' [The Reform of Spanish Understanding] that, in spite of cultural and philosophical differences which began with the ascendancy of Cartesian thought, Spain is still fundamentally linked to Western culture (2015: 208).

8. The word 'pueblo' means both people and village or town which gives it a resonance in any nationalist discourse which is impossible to convey easily in English.
9. In her later writings, Zambrano continues to use the word 'pueblo' but often in a more general sense. As she remarks in *Persona y democracia* (1958) [Person and Democracy]: '[d]ecir pueblo es decir *ecce homo*, mas no como individuo, sino en toda la complejidad y concreción del hombre en su tierra, en su tiempo, en su comunidad' [to say 'pueblo' is to say *ecce homo*, but not as an individual, but in all the complexity and concreteness of man in his land, in his time, and in his community] (1988b: 173).
10. For Zambrano, revolution means much the same as constant reform or change as she notes elsewhere that revolution is less about abrupt, catastrophic change than about something continuous which changes from day to day, or even hour to hour (2015: 71).
11. Jacques Rancière talks of 'an "aesthetic of the political", to indicate that politics is first of all a battle about perceptible/ sensible material' (2000: 11). While Rancière's formulation is fundamentally about the way in which the sensible is made visible in different political configurations ('the partition of the sensible that constitutes the political', 17), Zambrano is arguing from a different, and more general, perspective in which the sensible has first to be 'recovered' back into philosophical and political discourse. It is the focus on the sensible which in part characterizes their respective thoughts as modern.

BIBLIOGRAPHY

Works by María Zambrano

1933. 'Señal de vida', *Cruz y Raya* (2 May), 145–55
1937. 'La poesía de García Lorca', in *Antología de Federico García Lorca* (Santiago de Chile: Panorama), pp. 7–14
1949. 'La muerte de un poeta', *Crónica*, 1.3, 5–6
1950. *Hacia un saber sobre el alma* (Buenos Aires: Losada)
1961. 'Carta sobre el exilio', *Cuadernos del congreso por la libertad de la cultura*, 49, 67–70
1962. 'La poesía de Luis Cernuda', Homenaje a Luis Cernuda, *La Caña Gris*, 6, 7 & 8 (Autumn), 15–16
1971. *Obras reunidas* (Madrid: Aguilar)
1977. *Los intelectuales en el drama de España: ensayos y notas (1936–39)* (Madrid: Editorial Hispamerca)
1986A. *Claros del bosque* [1977] (Barcelona: Seix Barral)
1986B. *El sueño creador* (Madrid: Turner)
1986C. *De la aurora* (Madrid: Ediciones Turner)
1987A. *Hacia un saber sobre el alma* (Madrid: Alianza)
1987B. 'La metáfora del corazón [Fragmento]', in *María Zambrano en Orígenes* (Mexico City: Ediciones del Equilibrista), pp. 1–13
1987C. 'Del método en filosofía o de las tres formas de visión', *Suplementos Anthropos*, 2, (March-April), 120–24
1988A. *La confesión: género literario* (Madrid: Mondadori)
1988B. *Persona y democracia: la historia sacrificial* (Barcelona: Anthropos)
1988C. 'Ausencia y presencia', *Philosophica Malacitana*, 1, 7–10
1988D. 'Rosa', *Un Ángel Más*, 3–4, 11–12
1989A. *Algunos lugares de la pintura*, ed. by Amalia Iglesias (Madrid: Espasa Calpe)
1989B. *Delirio y destino (Los veinte años de una española)* (Madrid: Mondadori)
1989C. *Notas de un método* (Madrid: Mondadori)
1991A. *Los bienaventurados*, 2nd edn (Madrid: Siruela)
1991B. *El hombre y lo divino* (Madrid: Siruela)
1992A. *Los sueños y el tiempo* (Madrid: Siruela)
1992B. 'La mirada originaria en la obra de José Ángel Valente', in *José Ángel Valente*, ed. by Claudio Rodríguez Fer (Madrid: Taurus), pp. 31–38
1992C. *Cartas a Rosa Chacel*, ed. by Ana Rodríguez-Fischer (Madrid: Cátedra)
1993. *El hombre y lo divino* (Madrid: Fondo de Cultura Económica)
1994. 'Árbol', *Nostromo*, 19 (6 March), 12
1995A. 'Amo mi exilio', in *Las palabras del regreso*, ed. by Mercedes Gómez Blesa (Salamanca: Amarú), pp. 13–14
1995B. 'Delirio de Antígona' in *María Zambrano: nacer por sí misma,* ed. by Elena Laurenzi (Madrid: Horas y Horas), pp. 66–76
1996. *La Cuba secreta y otros ensayos*, ed. by Jorge Luis Arcos (Madrid: Endymion)
1998. *Los intelectuales en el drama de España* (Madrid: Trotta)

1999. *Delirium and Destiny: A Spaniard in her Twenties*, commentary by Roberta Johnson, trans. by Carol Maier (Albany: State University of New York)
2000A. *La agonía de Europa*, ed. by Jesús Moreno Sanz (Madrid: Trotta)
2000B. 'Amo mi exilio', *Renacimiento*, 184–85
2002. *Cartas de La Pièce: correspondencia con Agustín Andreu*, ed. by A. Andreu (Valencia: Pre-textos)
2004A. *La confesión: género literario* (Madrid: Siruela)
2004B. *Hacia un saber sobre el alma* (Madrid: Alianza)
2004C. *La razón en la sombra: antología crítica*, ed. by Jesús Moreno Sanz (Madrid: Siruela/ Fundación María Zambrano)
2007A. *Algunos lugares de la poesía* (Madrid: Trotta)
2007B. *La aventura de ser mujer*, ed. by Juan Fernando Ortega Muñóz (Málaga: Editorial Veramar)
2008. *España: pensamiento, poesía y una ciudad*, ed. by Francisco José Martín (Madrid: Biblioteca Nueva)
2009. *Las palabras del regreso*, ed. by Mercedes Gómez Blesa (Madrid: Cátedra)
2010. *Esencia y hermosura: antología*, ed. and prologue by José-Miguel Ullán (Barcelona Galaxia Gutenberg/Círculo de Lectores)
2011A. 'La confesión: género literario y método', in *Confesiones y Guías*, ed. by Pedro Chacón (Madrid: Eutelequia), pp. 37–100
2011B. *Escritos sobre Ortega*, ed. by Ricardo Tejada (Madrid: Trotta)
2011C. *Delirio y destino (Los veinte años de una española)* (Madrid: Horas y Horas)
2011D. *Obras completas III. Libros 1955–1973*, ed. by Jesús Moreno Sanz and others (Barcelona: Galaxia Gutenberg/Círculo de Lectores)
2011E. 'El nacimiento de la amistad' [1965], in *Filosofía y educación*, ed. by Ángel Casado and Juana Sánchez Gey (Madrid: Editorial Club Universitario), pp. 73–75
2012A. *Algunos lugares de la pintura*, ed. by Pedro Chacón (Madrid: Eutelequia)
2012B. *La tumba de Antígona y otros textos sobre el personaje trágico*, ed. by Virginia Trueba Mira (Madrid: Cátedra)
2012C. *Cartas inéditas (a Gregorio del Campo)*, ed. by María Fernanda Santiago Bolaños (Ourense: Linteo)
2013. *Filosofía y poesía* (Mexico City: Fondo de Cultura Económica)
2014A. *El exilio como patria*, ed. by Juan Fernando Ortega Muñoz (Barcelona: Anthropos)
2014B. *El hombre y lo divino*, in *Obras completas III. Libros 1955–1973*, ed. by Jesús Moreno Sanz and others, 2nd edn (Barcelona: Galaxia Gutenberg/Círculo de Lectores), pp. 95–359
2014C. *Obras completas VI. Parte I: Escritos autobiográficos. Delirios. Poemas (1928–1990). Parte II: Delirio y destino (1952)*, ed. by Jesús Moreno Sanz and others (Barcelona Galaxia Gutenberg/ Círculo de Lectores)
2015A. *Obras completas I. Libros 1930–1939*, ed. by Jesús Moreno Sanz and others (Barcelona: Galaxia Gutenberg/Círculo de Lectores)
——, and ROSA CHACEL. 2015. *Two Confessions*, trans. and ed. by Noël Valis and Carol Maier (Albany: State University of New York Press)
——, and REYNA RIVAS. 2004. *Epistolario 1960–1989* (Caracas: Monte Avila)

Other Works

ABELLÁN, JOSÉ LUIS. 2006. *Maria Zambrano: una pensadora de nuestro tiempo* (Barcelona: Anthropos)
ADORNO, THEODOR W. 1962. *Prismas* (Barcelona: Ariel)
——. 1981. *Prism* (Cambridge, MA: Massachusetts Institute of Technology Press)

———. 2005. *Negative Dialectics* (New York: Continuum)
AGAMBEN, GIORGIO. 1989. 'Bartleby o della contingenza', in Gilles Deleuze and Giorgio Agamben, *Bartleby: la formula della creazione* (Macerata: Quodlibet)
———. 1998. *Homo Sacer: Sovereign Power and Bare Life*, trans. by Daniel Heller-Roazen (Stanford, CA: Stanford University Press)
ALCALÁ CORTIJO, PALOMA, and OTHERS. 2009. *Ni tontas ni locas: las intelectuales en el Madrid del primer tercio del siglo XX* (Madrid: FECYT)
ÁLVAREZ JUNCO, JOSÉ. 1996. 'The Nation-Building Process in Nineteenth-Century Spain', in *Nationalism and the Nation in the Iberian Peninsula*, ed. by Clare Mar-Molinero and Angel Smith (Oxford & Washington, DC: Berg), pp. 89–106
ANCET, JACQUES, and OTHERS. 1996. *En torno a la obra de José Ángel Valente* (Madrid: Alianza)
ATTRIDGE, DEREK. 2004. *The Singularity of Literature* (London: Routledge)
BACHELARD, GASTON. 1964. *The Poetics of Space*, trans. by Maria Jolas (New York: Orion)
BAHUN, SANJA. 2014. *Modernism and Melancholia: Writing as Countermourning* (Oxford: Oxford University Press)
BALFOUR, SEBASTIAN. 1996. 'The Lion and the Pig: Nationalism and National Identity in Fin-de-Siecle Spain', in *Nationalism and the Nation in the Iberian Peninsula*, ed. by Clare Mar-Molinero and Angel Smith (Oxford & Washington, DC: Berg), pp. 107–17
BALIBREA, MARI PAZ. 2005. 'Rethinking Spanish Republican Exile: An Introduction', *Journal of Spanish Cultural Studies*, 6.1, 3–24
BALLESTEROS GARCÍA, ROSA MARÍA. 2004. 'Maruja Mallo (1902–1994): de las cloacas al espacio sideral', *Aposta. Revista de Ciencias Sociales*, 13, 1–34
BARTHES, ROLAND. 1981. *Camera Lucida: Reflexions on Photography*, trans. by Richard Howard (New York: Hill and Wang)
BATAILLE, GEORGES. 2010. *Las lágrimas de Eros*, introduction by J. M. Lo Duca, trans. by David Fernández (Barcelona: Tusquets)
BATTERSBY, CHRISTINE. 1989. *Gender and Genius: Towards a Feminine Aesthetics* (London: Women's Press)
BEARDSWORTH, SARA. 2005. 'Freud's Oedipus and Kristeva's Narcissus: Three Heterogeneities', *Hypatia*, 20.1, 54–77
BEEVOR, ANTONY. 2006. *The Battle for Spain: The Spanish Civil War 1936–1939* (London: Weidenfeld & Nicolson)
BÉGUIN, ALBERT. 1939. *L'Âme romantique et le rêve* (Paris: Librairie José Corti)
BELTING, HANS. 2005. 'Image, Medium, Body: A New Approach to Iconology', *Critical Inquiry*, 31.2, 302–19
BENEYTO, JOSÉ MARÍA. 2004. 'La multiplicidad de los tiempos: María Zambrano en diálogo con Reinhardt Koselleck, Hans Blumenberg y Emmanuel Levinas', in María Zambrano, *La visión más transparente*, ed. by José María Beneyto and J. A. González Fuentes (Madrid: Trotta-Fundación Carolina), pp. 477–503
BENJAMIN, WALTER. 1998. *The Origin of German Tragic Drama*, trans. by John Osborne (London and New York: Verso)
———. 1999A. *The Arcades Project*, trans. by Howard Eiland and Kevin McLaughlin (Cambridge, MA, & London: Belknap Press)
——— 1999B. 'Little History of Photography', in *Selected Writings. Vol. 2 (1927–1934)*, trans. by Rodney Livingstone and others, ed. by Michael W. Jennings, Howard Eiland, and Gary Smith (Cambridge, MA, & London: Belknap Press), pp. 507–30
———. 2003. *Selected Writings. Vol. 4 (1938–1940)*, trans. by Edmund Jephcott and others, ed. by Howard Eiland and Michael W. Jennings (Cambridge, MA, & London: Belknap Press)

BERG, NANCY E. 1996. *Exile from Exile: Israeli Writers from Iraq* (Albany: State University of New York Press)
BERLIN, ISAIAH. 1980. *Against the Current: Essays in the History of Ideas* (New York: Viking Press)
BERROCAL, ALFONSO. 2011. *Poesía y filosofía: María Zambrano, la Generación del 27 y Emilio Prados* (Valencia: Pre-Textos/Fundación Gerardo Diego)
BLANCO, ROGELIO. 2004. 'La pintura: lugar antropológico privilegiado', in *María Zambrano, 1904–1991: De la razón cívica a la razón poética*, ed. by Jesús Moreno Sanz ([Madrid]: Publicaciones de la Residencia de Estudiantes and Fundación María Zambrano), pp. 663–69
BLASCO PASCUAL, FRANCISCO JAVIER. 1981. *La poética de Juan Ramón Jiménez: desarrollo, contexto y sistema* (Salamanca: Ediciones Universidad de Salamanca)
BLUMENBERG, HANS. 1998. *Paradigmen zu einer Metaphorologie* (Frankfurt am Main: Suhrkamp)
BOEHM, GOTTFRIED. 2009. 'Il ritorno delle immagini', in *Il ritorno delle immagini: il dibattito contemporaneo*, ed. by Andrea Pinotti and Antonio Somaini (Milan: Raffaello Cortina), pp. 39–71
BOLTER, JAY DAVID, and R. GRUSING. 1999. *Remediation: Understanding New Media* (Cambridge, MA, & London: MIT Press)
BOMBACI, NUNZIO. 2007. *La pietà della luce: María Zambrano dinanzi ai luoghi della pintura* (Soveria Mannelli: Rubettino)
BOZAL, VALERIANO. 1995. 'El arte español entre 1920–1957: poéticas de la modernidad', in *Arte en España, 1918–1994 en la Colección Arte Contemporáneo* (Madrid: Alianza)
BRAIDOTTI, ROSI. 2011. *Nomadic Subjects: Embodiment and Sexual Difference in Contemporary Feminist Theory*, 2nd edn (New York: Columbia University Press)
BRUTON, KEVIN J. 1984. 'Luis Cernuda's Exile Poetry and Coleridge's Theory of Imagination', *Comparative Literature Studies*, 21.4 (Winter), 383–95
BUNDGAARD, ANA. 2000. *Más allá de la filosofía: sobre el pensamiento filosófico-místico de María Zambrano* (Madrid: Trotta)
——. 2005. 'Ética y estética de la razón poética', in *Filosofía y literatura en María Zambrano*, ed. by Pedro Cerezo (Seville: Fundación José Manuel Lara), pp. 55–75
BURGOS-LAFUENTE, LENA, and TATJANA GAJIC (eds). 2015. *María Zambrano in Dialogue*, special issue of the *Journal of Spanish Cultural Studies*, 16–24
CABALLERO RODRÍGUEZ, BEATRIZ. 2008. 'La centralidad del concepto de delirio en el pensamiento de María Zambrano', *Arizona Journal of Hispanic Cultural Studies*, 12, 93–110
——. 2014. 'The Cathartic Exercise of Memory in María Zambrano's *Delirio y destino*', in *Memory and Trauma in the Postwar Spanish Novel: Revisiting the Past*, ed. by Sarah Leggott and Ross Woods (Lewisburg, PA: Bucknell University Press), pp. 141–53
CALVO SERRALLER, FRANCISCO. 1988. *Del futuro al pasado: vanguardia y tradición en el arte español contemporáneo* (Madrid: Alianza Forma)
CANO BALLESTA, JUAN. 1972. *La poesía española entre pureza y revolución (1930–1936)* (Madrid: Gredos)
CÁMARA BETANCOURT, MADELINE, and LUIS PABLO ORTEGA HURTADO (eds). 2011. *María Zambrano: palabras para el mundo* (Newark, DE: Juan de la Cuesta)
——. 2015. *María Zambrano: Between the Caribbean and the Mediterranean, a Bilingual Anthology* (Newark, DE: Juan de la Cuesta)
CARANDELL, LUIS. 1983. 'El filósofo de Madrid', *El País: Libros* (8 May)
CAREY, JOHN. 1992. *The Intellectuals and the Masses: Pride and Prejudice among the Literary Intelligentsia, 1880–1939* (London & Boston, MA: Faber and Faber)
——. 2005. *What Good Are the Arts?* (London: Faber and Faber)

CARMONA, EUGENIO. 1993. 'Pintura y poesía en la generación del 27', *Cuadernos Hispanoamericanos. Generación del 27*, 514–15, 103–16

CARRETÓN CANO, VICENTE. 2000. 'Victorina Durán y el círculo sáfico de Madrid: semblanza de una escenógrafa del 27', *El Maquinista de la Generación*, 9, 4–20

CARUTH, CATHY. 1996. *Unclaimed Experience: Trauma, Narrative, and History* (Baltimore, MD, & London: John Hopkins University Press)

CASCARDI, ANTHONY J. 1999. *Consequences of Enlightenment* (Cambridge: Cambridge University Press)

CEREZO, PEDRO (ed.). 2005. *Filosofía y literatura en María Zambrano* (Seville: Fundación José Manuel Lara)

CERNUDA, LUIS. 1973. 'Las ruinas', in *Poesía completa* (Barcelona: Barral), pp. 282–84

CHACEL, ROSA. 1936. *A la orilla de un pozo* (Madrid: Héroe)

——. 1962. 'Luis Cernuda, un poeta', Homenaje a Luis Cernuda, *La Caña Gris*, 6, 7, & 8 (Otoño), 18–19

——. 1972. *Saturnal* (Barcelona: Seix Barral)

——. 1978. *Versos prohibidos* (Madrid: Caballo Griego para la Poesía)

——. 1980. *Timoteo Pérez Rubio y sus retratos del jardín* (Madrid: Cátedra)

——. 1981. 'Luis Cernuda', in *Los títulos* (Barcelona: EDHASA), pp. 85–89

——. 1982. *Alcancía (Ida) Alcancía (Vuelta)* (Barcelona: Seix Barral)

——. 1984. *Acrópolis* (Barcelona: Seix Barral)

——. 1985. *Barrio de Maravillas* (Barcelona: Bruguera)

——. 1989. *Obra completa*, vol. 1 (Valladolid: Centro de Creación y Estudios Jorge Guillén)

——, 1993A. *Obra completa*, vol. 3 (Valladolid: Excma. Diputación Provincial de Valladolid)

——. 1993B. *Obra completa*, vol. 4 (Valladolid: Excma. Diputación Provincial de Valladolid)

——. 1994. *Memoirs of Leticia Valle*, trans. by Carol Maier (Lincoln & London: University of Nebraska Press)

CHACÓN FUERTES, PEDRO. 2011. 'Ramón Gaya — María Zambrano: afinidades electivas', *Escritura e imagen*, 7, 39–58

CIORAN, EMIL. 1981. 'María Zambrano: una presencia decisiva', *Cuadernos del Norte*, 9, 23

CLARK, MICHAEL P. (ed.). 2000. *Revenge of the Aesthetic: The Place of Literature in Theory Today* (Berkeley: University of California Press)

CLOUGH, PATRICIA T. 2008. 'The Affective Turn: Political Economy, Biomedia and Bodies', *Theory, Culture & Society*, 25, 1–22

COLINAS, ANTONIO. 1986. 'Sobre la iniciación (Conversación con María Zambrano)', *Los Cuadernos del Norte*, 7.38, 2–9

COLLIN, FRANÇOISE. 2000. 'Diferencia y diferendo: la cuestión de las mujeres en filosofía', in *Historia de las Mujeres en Occidente. 5. El Siglo XX*, ed. by George Duby and Michelle Perrot (Madrid: Taurus), pp. 319–57

CRUZ, JUAN. 1984. 'María Zambrano pide "un poco de luz y no más sangre" para su tierra', *El País* (27 November), <http://elpais.com/diario/1984/11/27/cultura/470358005_850215.html> [accessed 13 February 2016]

DAL POZZOLO, ENRICO MARIA. 2009. *Giorgione* (Milan: Motta)

DENNIS, NIGEL. 2010. 'En torno a los homenajes de Ramón Gaya', *Turia*, 95, 225–32

——. 2011. 'Ramón Gaya y el Museo del Pueblo de las Misiones Pedagógicas', *Escritura e imagen*, 7, 15–26

DERRIDA, JACQUES. 1982. '"White Mythology": The Discourses of Metaphor and Philosophy', in *Margins of Philosophy*, trans. by Alan Bass (Chicago: University of Chicago Press), pp. 207–72

——. 1993. *Aporias*, trans. by Thomas Dutoit (Stanford, CA: Stanford University Press)

DE TORRE, GUILLERMO. 2002. *Literaturas europeas de vanguardia* (Pamplona: Urgoiti editores)

DEVEREUX, CECILY. 2014. 'Hysteria, Feminism, and Gender Revisited: The Case of the Second Wave', *English Studies in Canada*, 40.1 (March), 19–45
DÍAZ PLAJA, GUILLERMO. 1975. *Tratado de las melancolías españolas* (Madrid: Sala)
DIDI-HUBERMAN, GEORGES. 1992. *Ce que nous voyons, ce qui nous regarde* (Paris: Minuit)
———. 2000. *Devant le temps* (Paris: Minuit)
———. 2008. *La ressemblance par contact: archéologie, anachronisme et modernité de l'empreinte* (Paris: Minuit)
———. 2013. *Cuando las imágenes toman posición. El ojo de la historia, 1* (Madrid: Antonio Machado Libros)
DI PIERRO, EDUARDO GONZÁLEZ. 2010. 'Dos fenomenólogas piensan la república: María Zambrano y Edith Stein', *Open Sight*, 1, 70–83
DI PIPPO, ALEXANDER FERRARI. 2000. 'The Concept of Poiesis in Heidegger's *An Introduction to Metaphysics*', *Thinking Fundamentals, IWM Junior Visiting Fellows Conferences*, IX, 1–33
DOCHERTY, THOMAS. 2006. *Aesthetic Democracy* (Stanford, CA: Stanford University Press)
DOS SANTOS DAS NEVES, MARIA JOÃO. 2001. 'La democracia como sociedad donde no solamente es permitido sino exigido el ser persona', *Thémata. Revista de Filosofía*, 26, 205–12
DUBOIS, PHILIPPE. 1983. *L'acte photographique* (Paris & Brussels: Nathan and Labor)
DURANTE, LAURA MARIATERESA. 2006. 'El primer exilio de María Zambrano: la búsqueda de la soledad', in *Escritores, editoriales y revistas del exilio republicano de 1939*, ed. by Manuel Aznar Soler (Seville: Renacimiento), pp. 59–66
EAGLETON, TERRY. 1990. *The Ideology of the Aesthetic* (Oxford: Blackwell)
ENJUTO RANGEL, CECILIA. 2007. 'Broken Presents: The Modern City in Ruins in Baudelaire, Cernuda and Paz', *Comparative Literature*, 59.2 (Spring), 140–57
———. 2010. *Cities in Ruins: The Politics of Modern Poetics* (West Lafayette, IN: Purdue University Press)
ESCOBAR BORREGO, FRANCISCO JAVIER. 2012. 'Tres lecciones de tinieblas, de José Ángel Valente: naturaleza musical, claves de poética e implicaciones simbólicas', *Enthymema*, VI, 118–91
ESCRIBANO, MARÍA. 2009. 'Maruja clara', in *Maruja Mallo* (Madrid: Ministerio de Cultura/ Fundación Caixa Galicia), pp. 21–31
FERNÁNDEZ MARTORELL, CONCHA. 2004. *María Zambrano: entre la razón, la poesía y el exilio* (Madrid: Montesinos)
FICINO, MARSILIO. 1989. *Three Books on Life*, trans. and ed. by Carol V. Kaske and John R. Clark (Binghamton, NY: Medieval and Renaissance Texts and Studies)
FLATLEY, JONATHAN. 2008. *Affective Mapping: Melancholia and the Politics of Modernism* (Cambridge, MA, & London: Harvard University Press)
FORNIELES TEN, JAVIER (ed.). 2005. *Correspondencia entre José Lezama Lima y María Zambrano y entre María Zambrano y María Luisa Bautista* (Seville: Ediciones Espuela de Plata)
FREIXAS, LAURA. 2004. 'Rosa Chacel', *Letras Libres*, 56–59
FREUD, SIGMUND. 2005. 'Mourning and Melancholia', in *On Murder, Mourning and Melancholia*, trans. by Shaun Whiteside, intr. by Maud Ellmann (London: Penguin), pp. 201–18
FRITZSCHE, PETER. 2011. 'The Melancholy of History: The French Revolution and European Historiography', in *The Literature of Melancholia: Early Modern to Postmodern*, ed. by Martin Midekke and Christina Wald (Basingstoke: Palgrave Macmillan), pp. 116–29
GARDNER, HELEN. 1978. *The Composition of the Four Quartets* (London: Faber and Faber)
GARGANI, ALDO G. 1986. *Lo stupore e il caso* (Rome & Bari: Laterza)
GAYA, RAMÓN. 1960A. *El sentimiento de la pintura: (diario de un pintor)* ([Madrid]: Arion)
———. 1960B. *Il sentimento della pittura*, trans. by Leonardo Cammarano (Rome: De Luca)

———. 1994. *Obras completas. Tomo III* (Valencia: Pre-Textos)
———. 1999. *Obras completas. Tomo I* (Valencia: Pre-Textos)
———. 2006. 'Mi experiencia en las misiones pedagógicas: con el Museo del Prado de viaje por España', in *Las misiones pedagógicas: 1931–1936*, [exhibition catalogue] ed. by Eugenio Otero Urtaza (Madrid: Sociedad Estatal de Conmemoraciones; Publicaciones de la Residencia de Estudiantes), pp. 372–77
GENTILI, AUGUSTO. 1999. *Giorgione* (Florence: Giunti)
———. 2008. 'A proposito di Giorgione: aspirazioni, esiti e limiti dell'iconologia', in *Giorgione entmythisiert*, ed. by Sylvia Ferino-Pagden (Turnhout: Brepols), 105–16
GILBERT, SANDRA, and SUSAN GUBAR. 1988–94. *No Man's Land: The Place of the Woman Writer in the Twentieth Century*, 3 vols (New Haven, CT: Yale University Press)
GIBSON, ANDREW. 2011. '"They Came, They Cut Away My Tallest Pines": Tennyson and the Melancholy of Modernity', in *The Literature of Melancholia: Early Modern to Postmodern*, ed. by Martin Midekke and Christina Wald (Basingstoke: Palgrave Macmillan), pp. 101–15
GILSON, E. 1972. *Peinture et réalité* (Paris: Librairie Philosophique)
GINGERICH, STEPHEN D. 2009. 'Europe's Frenzy: European and Spanish Universality in María Zambrano', *The New Centennial Review*, 8, 189–214
GIRARD, ALAN. 1963. *Le journal intime* (París: Presses Universitaires de France)
GLICK, THOMAS F. 1982. 'The Naked Science: Psychoanalysis in Spain, 1914–1948', *Comparative Studies in Society and History*, 24.4, 533–71
GOMBROWICZ, WITOLD. 2006. *Contra los poetas* (Madrid: Sequitur)
GÓMEZ BLESA, MERCEDES. 2007. 'María Zambrano: el delirio y el destino de los Intelectuales Republicanos', in *Las intelectuales republicanas: la conquista de la ciudadanía*, ed. by Mercedes Gómez Blesa (Madrid: Biblioteca Nueva), 131–47
GÓMEZ CANSECO, LUIS. 1993. 'Luis Cernuda en Nueva Inglaterra', *Philologia Hispalensis*, 8, 227–38
GÓMEZ-PÉREZ, ANA. 2001. 'La confesión en *La sinrazón* de Rosa Chacel', *Revista Hispánica Moderna*, 54.2, 348–63
GRAHAM, HELEN. 1996. 'Community, Nation and State in Republican Spain, 1931–1938', in *Nationalism and the Nation in the Iberian Peninsula*, ed. by Clare Mar-Molinero and Angel Smith (Oxford & Washington, DC: Berg), pp. 133–47
GROSZ, ELIZABETH. 1989. *Sexual Subversions: Three French Feminists* (Sidney: Allen & Unwin)
HEGEL, GEORG W. F. 2008. *Outlines of the Philosophy of Right*, trans. by T. M. Knox, ed. by Stephen Houlgate, Oxford World Classics (Oxford & New York: Oxford University Press)
HIRSCHKOP, KEN. 1999. *Mikhail Bakhtin: An Aesthetic for Democracy* (Oxford: Oxford University Press)
HEIDEGGER, MARTIN. 2000. *Introduction to Metaphysics* (Newhaven, CT: Yale University Press)
———. 2001. 'What Are Poets For?', in *Poetry, Language, Thought* (New York: Harper & Row), pp. 87–140
HORKHEIMER, MAX. 1974. *Eclipse of Reason* (New York: Continuum)
HUSSERL, EDMUND. 1970. *The Crisis of European Sciences and Transcendental Phenomenology: An Introduction to Phenomenological Philosophy* (Evanston, IL: Northwestern University Press)
HUTCHINSON, KATRINA, and FIONA JENKINS. 2013. *Women in Philosophy: What Needs to Change* (Oxford and New York: Oxford University Press)
HUYSSEN, ANDREAS. 2010. 'Authentic Ruins: Products of Modernity', in *Ruins of Modernity* ed. by Julia Hell and Andreas Schönle (Durham, NC, & London: Duke University Press), pp. 17–28
IGLESIAS SERNA, AMALIA. 2004. 'María Zambrano y la pintura', in *República de las Letras*, dedicated to María Zambrano, *La hora de la penumbra*, 84–85, 96–103

ILLÁN, MIGUEL. 2002. 'María Zambrano's Phenomenology of Poetic Reason', in *Phenomenology World-Wide*, ed. by Anna-Teresa Tymieniecka (Norwell, MA: Kluwer Academic Publishers), pp. 471–73

IRIGARAY, LUCE. 1985. 'The Eternal Irony of the Community', in *Speculum of the Other Woman* (Ithaca, NY: Cornell University Press), pp. 214–26

——. 1993. *An Ethics of Sexual Difference*, trans. by C. Burke and G. Gill (London: Athlone Press)

JAMESON, FREDRIC. 1972. *The Prison House of Language: A Critical Account of Structuralism and Russian Formalism* (Princeton, NJ: Princeton University Press)

JANÉS, CLARA. 2002–2003. 'Dos fieras mentes de nuestras letras. Rosa Chacel (1898–1994). María Zambrano (1904–1991)', *Las voces del árbol. ADAMAR. Revista de Creación*, <http://www.adamar.org/archivo/ii_epoca/[num12/v3.html> [accessed 12 February 2016]

JIMÉNEZ, JOSÉ. 1996. 'El vuelo de la imagen', in *En torno a la obra de José Ángel Valente*, ed. by Jacques Ancet and others (Madrid: Alianza), pp. 59–74

JIMÉNEZ CARRERAS, PEPITA (ed.). 2008. *Cartas desde una soledad. Epistolario. María Zambrano, José Lezama Lima, María Luisa Bautista, José Ángel Valente* (Madrid: Verbum)

JOHNSTON, PHILIP G. 2002. *The Power of Paradox in the Work of Spanish Poet Antonio Machado (1875–1939)* (New York, Ontario, & Lampeter: Edwin Mellen Press)

JOHNSON, ROBERTA. 1996. 'María Zambrano's Theory of Literature as Knowledge and Contingency', *Hispania*, 79.2 (May), 215–21

——. 1996. '"Self"-Consciousness in Rosa Chacel and María Zambrano', *Bucknell Review*, 39.2, 54–72

——. 1997. 'María Zambrano as Antigone's Sister: Towards an Ethical Aesthetics of Possibility', *Anales de la literatura española contemporánea*, 22, 1–2, 181–94

——. 2012. 'El concepto de "persona" de María Zambrano y su pensamiento sobre la mujer', *Aurora*, 13, 8–17

——. 2013. 'María Zambrano's Solitude: The Silver Age Continued', *Anales de la literatura española contemporánea*, 38.1–2, 149–74

——. 2015. 'María Zambrano's Ideas on the Self and the Other in Light of Jean-Paul Sartre's Existentialism', *Anales de la literatura española contemporánea*, 40.1, 177–206

——. 2016. '"Antigone's Delirium" by María Zambrano', in *Writing Translators, Translators Writing*, ed. by Françoise Massardier-Kenney, Brian James, and Maria Tymoczko (Kent, OH: Kent State University Press), pp. 169–86

JUNG, CARL GUSTAV. 2002. *Answer to Job* (London & New York: Routledge)

KERMODE, FRANK. 1989. *History and Value* (Oxford: Clarendon Press)

KLIBANSKY, RAYMOND, ERWIN PANOFSKY, and FRITZ SAXL. 1964. *Saturn and Melancholy: Studies in the History of Natural Philosophy, Religion, and Art* (New York: Basic Books)

KRAUEL, RICARDO. 2013. *Imperial Emotions: Cultural Responses to Myths of Empire in 'Fin-De-Siècle' Spain* (Liverpool: Liverpool University Press)

KRISTEVA, JULIA. 1984. *Revolution in Poetic Language*, trans. by M. Walter (New York: Columba University Press)

——. 1986. 'A New Type of Intellectual: The Dissident', in *The Kristeva Reader*, ed. by Toril Moi (Oxford: Blackwell), pp. 292–96

——. 1987. *Tales of Love*, trans. by Leon S. Roudiez (New York: Columbia University Press)

——. 1989A. *Black Sun: Depression and Melancholia*, trans. by Leon S. Roudiez (New York: Columbia University Press)

——. 1989B. *Desire in Language: A Semiotic Approach to Literature and Art* (New York: Columbia University Press)

——. 1991. *Strangers to Ourselves*, trans. by Leon S. Roudiez (New York: Columbia University Press)

——. 1995. *New Maladies of the Soul*, trans. by Ross Guberman (New York: Columbia University Press)
——. 1996. *Julia Kristeva Interviews*, ed. by Ross Guberman (New York: Columbia University Press)
——, 2001. *Hannah Arendt*, trans. by Ross Guberman (New York: Columbia University Press)
——, 2004. 'Is There a Feminine Genius?' *Critical Enquiry* 30 (Spring), 493–504
——. 2010. 'Antigone: Limit and Horizon', in *Feminist Readings of Antigone*, ed. by Fanny Soderback (Albany: State University of New York Press), pp. 215–29
——, and MARGARET WALLER. 1982. 'Psychoanalysis and the Polis', *Critical Inquiry*, 9.1, 77–92
LACOUE-LABARTHE, PHILIPPE. 2002. *La ficción de lo político: Heidegger, el arte y la política* (Madrid: Arena Libros)
LAFUENTE FERRARI, ENRIQUE. 1970. *Ortega y las artes visuales* (Madrid: Revista de Occidente)
LAURENZI, ELENA. 2012. 'Desenmascarar la complementariedad de los sexos: María Zambrano y Rosa Chacel frente al debate en la *Revista de Occidente*', *Aurora*, 13, 18–29
LE DOEUFF, MICHÈLE. 2007. *Hipparchia's Choice: An Essay Concerning Women, Philosophy, etc.*, trans by Trista Selous (New York: Columbia University Press)
LEÓN, MARÍA TERESA. 1977. *Memoria de la melancolía* (Barcelona: Laia-Picazo)
LEVINE, CAROLINE. 2007. *Provoking Democracy: Why We Need The Arts* (Oxford: Blackwell)
LEVINE, SAMUEL. 1977. *The Semantics of Metaphor* (Durham, NC: Duke University Press)
LEYS, RUTH. 2011. 'The Turn to Affect: A Critique', *Critical Inquiry*, 37, 434–72
LEZAMA LIMA, JOSÉ. 1972. *Posible imagen de José Lezama Lima*, ed. and prologue by José Agustín Goytisolo (Barcelona: Ocnos Llibres de Sinera)
LLOYD, GENEVIEVE. 2002. *Feminism & History of Philosophy*, Oxford Readings in Feminism (Oxford and New York: Oxford University Press)
LÓPEZ CASTRO, ARMANDO. 2013. 'El enigma de la pintura', in *El canto de la alondra: estudios sobre María Zambrano* (León: Universidad de León), pp. 105–23
LÓPEZ GARCÍA, JOSÉ-RAMÓN. 2013. 'Magda o la amistad: homenaje a Concha de Albornoz de Juan Gil-Albert', in *El exilio literario de 1939, 70 años después*, ed. by María Teresa González de Garay and José Díaz-Cuesta (Logroño: Universidad de la La Rioja, pp. 482–511
LOUGH, FRANCIS. 2002. *Sender, el novelista y las masas*, in *Sender 2001. Actas del congreso centenario celebrado en Sheffield*, ed. by Anthony Trippett (Bristol: HiPLAM), pp. 1–23
——. 2006. 'Sender, Zambrano y la filosofía mística del exilio', in *Escritores, editoriales y revistas del exilio republicano de 1939*, ed. by Manuel Aznar Soler (Seville: Renacimiento), pp. 789–97
——. 2007. 'Éxito, mito e identidad nacional en María Zambrano', in *España en la encrucijada de 1939: exilios, culturas e identidades*, ed. by Mónica Jato Brizuela, José Ángel Ascunce Arrieta, and María Luisa San Miguel Casillas (Bilbao: Publicaciones de la Universidad de Deusto), pp. 69–87
MACEY, DAVID. 2006. 'Rebellion, or, analysis', *Radical Philosophy* 136 (March/April), 44–48
MACOLA, ERMINIA, and ADONE BRANDALISE. 2004. *Psicoanálisis y arte del ingenio: de Cervantes a María Zambrano*, trans. by Pilar Sánchez Otin (Málaga: Miguel Gómez Ediciones)
MAILLARD, CHANTAL. 1992. *La creación por la metáfora: introducción a la razón poética* (Madrid: Anthropos)
——. 1998. 'Las mujeres en la filosofía española', in *Breve historia feminista de la literatura española*, ed. by Iris Zavala (Barcelona: Anthropos), pp. 267–96

MAINER, JOSÉ-CARLOS. 1975. *La edad de plata (1902–1931): ensayo de interpretación de un proceso cultural* (Barcelona: Los Libros De La Frontera)
MALLO, MARUJA. 1939. *Lo popular en la plástica española a través de mi obra 1928–1936* (Buenos Aires: Editorial Losada)
MANGINI, SHIRLEY. 1995. *Memories of Resistance: Women's Voices from the Spanish Civil War* (New Haven, CT: Yale University Press)
——. 1998. 'Women, Eros, and Culture: The Essays of Rosa Chacel', in *Spanish Women Writers and the Essay: Gender, Politics, and the Self*, ed. by Kathleen M. Glenn and Mercedes Mazquiarán Rodríguez (Columbia: University of Missouri Press)
——. 2001. *Las modernas de Madrid: las grandes intelectuales españolas de la vanguardia* (Barcelona: Península)
——. 2009. 'El papel de la mujer intelectual según Margarita Nelken y Rosa Chacel', in *Roles de género y cambio social en la literatura española del siglo XX*, ed. by Pilar Nieva-de la Paz (Amsterdam: Rodopi), pp. 171–86
——, 2010. *Maruja Mallo and the Spanish Avant-Garde* (Farnham: Ashgate)
MARAÑÓN, GREGORIO. 1967–1973. *Obras Completas*, ed. by A. Juderías and P. Laín Entralgo, 10 vols (Madrid: Espasa Calpe)
——, and MARTÍNEZ DÍAZ. 1932. 'Sobre la melancolía involutiva', *Gaceta Médica Española*, 68 (May), 471
MARSET, JUAN CARLOS. 2004. *María Zambrano I: los años de formación* (Seville: Fundación José Manuel Lara)
MARTÍNEZ GARRIDO, ELISA. 2009. 'Between Italy and Spain: The Tragedy of History and the Salvific Power of Love in Elsa Morante and María Zambrano', in *The Power of Disturbance: Elsa Morante's Araceoli*, ed. by Manuele Gragnolati and Sara Fortuna (Oxford: Legenda), pp. 118–27
MASSUMI, BRIAN. 1996. 'The Autonomy of Affect', *Cultural Critique*, 31, 83–109
MATE, REYES. 2006. *Medianoche en la historia: comentarios a las tesis de Walter Benjamin 'Sobre el concepto de historia'* (Madrid: Trotta)
——. 2014. 'Del exilio a la diáspora: a propósito de Max Aub y María Zambrano', in *El exilio español del 39 en México: mediaciones entre mundos, disciplinas y saberes*, ed. by Antolín Sánchez Cuervo and Guillermo Zermeño Padilla (Mexico City: El Colegio de México), pp. 233–60
MATEO, MARÍA ASUNCIÓN. 1993. *Retrato de Rosa Chacel* (Madrid: Galaxia Gutenberg)
MAY, TODD. 2007. 'Jacques Rancière and the Ethics of Equality', *SubStance*, 36, 20–36
MAYHEW, JONATHAN. 2012. 'The Genealogy of Late Modernism in Spain: Unamuno, Lorca, Zambrano, and Valente', *Modernist Cultures* 7.1, 77–99
MCKINLAY, NEIL C. 1999. *The Poetry of Luis Cernuda: Order in a World of Chaos* (London: Tamesis)
MEJÍA BURGOS, OTTO GERMÁN. 2014. 'El proyecto de nación masferreriano y su recepción en la presidencia de Maximiliano Hernández Martínez' (unpublished doctoral thesis, (Universidad Centroamericana 'José Simeón Cañas')
MELZER, ARTHUR M., JERRY WEINBERGER, and RICHARD ZINMAN (eds). 1999. *Democracy and the Arts* (Ithaca, NY, & London: Cornell University Press)
MERLEAU-PONTY, MAURICE. 1963. *The Structure of Behaviour* (Boston, MA: Beacon)
——. 1964. *The Primacy of Perception*, ed. by James M. Edie (Evanston, IL: Northwestern University Press)
——. 1968. *The Visible and the Invisible, Followed by Working Notes*, ed. by Claude Lefort, trans. by Alphonso Lingis (Evanston, IL: Northwestern University Press)
MERMALL, THOMAS. 1976. *The Rhetoric of Humanism: Spanish Culture after Ortega y Gasset* (New York: Bilingual Press)

MICHERON, CÉCILE. 2013. 'Introducción al pensamiento estético de María Zambrano: Algunos lugares de la pintura', *LOGOS. Anales del Seminario de Metafísica*, 36, 215–44

MITCHELL, W. J. T. 1996. 'What Do Pictures "Really" Want?', *October*, 77 (Summer), 71–82

MOLINA FLORES, ANTONIO. 2014. 'Poeta en Oxford: las relaciones entre la poesía española y la poesía europea a través del *Diario anónimo* de José Ángel Valente', in *Tendencias estéticas y literarias en la cultura contemporánea* (Seville: Renacimiento), pp. 31–59

MORAGA, PABLO. 2012. 'El género de la guía en María Zambrano' (unpublished doctoral thesis, City University of New York), <http://search.proquest.com.mercury.concordia.ca/docview/111501842> [accessed 28 December 2015]

MORENO SANZ, JESÚS (ed.). 1996. 'Estudio introductorio: La política desde su envés histórico-vital: Historia trágica de la esperanza y sus utopías', in María Zambrano, *Horizonte del liberalismo* (Madrid: Morata)

——. (ed.). 2003. María Zambrano, *Razón en la sombra: antología crítica* (Madrid: Siruela)

——. 2008. *El logos oscuro: tragedia, mística y filosofía en María Zambrano* (Madrid: Verbum)

——. 2010. 'Destierro y exilio: categorías del pensar de María Zambrano', in *Pensamiento exiliado español: el legado filosófico del 39 y su dimensión iberoamericana*, ed. by Antolín Sánchez Cuervo and Fernando Hermida de Blas (Madrid: Biblioteca Nueva-CSIC), pp. 268–322

MORÓN ARROYO, CIRIACO. 1965. 'Las dos estéticas de Ortega', *AIH. Actas II*, 439–45

MUÑOZ MILLANES, JOSÉ. 2011. 'Los homenajes de Ramón Gaya', *Escritura e imagen*, 7, 161–82

MURCIA SERRANO, INMACULADA. 2002. 'Ramón Gaya: Diario de un pintor 1952–1953: homenaje a la pintura', in *El diario como forma narrativa*, IX Simposio Internacional sobre Narrativa Hispánica Contemporánea IX (El Puerto de Santa María: Fundación Luis Goytisolo), pp. 197–210

——. 2009. *La razón sumergida: el arte en el pensamiento de María Zambrano* (Salamanca: Luso-Española Ediciones)

——. 2011. *Agua y destino: introducción a la estética de Ramón Gaya* (Oxford: Peter Lang)

NIETZSCHE, FRIEDRICH. 1980. *Also sprach Zarathustra. Sämtliche Werke. Kritische Studienausgabe*, ed. By Giorgio Colli und Mazzino Montinari, vol. 4 (Munich: Walter de Gruyter; Berlin & New York: Deutscher Taschenbuch Verlag)

NIKOLCHINA, MIGLENA. 1991. 'Born from the Head: Reading Woolf via Kristeva', *Diacritics* (Summer-Fall), 30–42

NIMMO, CLARE E. 1997. 'The Poet and the Thinker: María Zambrano and Feminist Criticism', *The Modern Language Review*, 92.4, 893–902

OLIVER, KELLY. 1991. 'Kristeva's Imaginary Father and the Crisis in the Paternal Function', *Diacritics* 21.2/3 (Summer-Autumn), 43–63

ORTEGA ALLUÉ, FRANCISCO JAVIER. 1998. 'Vencidos que no han muerto: los exilios de María Zambrano', in *El exilio literario español de 1939: Actas del Primer Congreso Internacional*, ed. by Manuel Aznar Soler (Barcelona: Universidad de Barcelona), pp. 437–46

ORTEGA MUÑOZ, JUAN FERNANDO. 1994. *Introducción al pensamiento de María Zambrano* (Mexico City: Fondo de Cultura Económica)

——. 2006. *Biografía de María Zambrano* (Málaga: Arguval)

ORTEGA Y GASSET, JOSÉ. 1938. 'Concerning Pacifism', trans. and adapted by A. Pastor, *The Nineteenth Century*, 124 (July), 20–34

——. 1957. *The Revolt of the Masses* (New York: Norton)

——. 1966. 'Las dos grandes metáforas', in *Obras completas II*, 7th edn (Madrid: Revista de Occidente), pp. 367–400

——. 2004–2010. *Obras completas*, 10 vols (Madrid: Taurus-Fundación José Ortega y Gasset)

OTTO, WALTER F. 1960. *Dionysos: Mythos und Kultur* (Frankfurt am Main: Vittorio Klostermann)

PARDO, FELIX. 1989. 'Los ensayos de Rosa Chacel: una empresa filosófica', in *Rosa Chacel, Obra completa. Volumen II: Ensayo y poesía* (Valladolid: Excma. Diputación Provincial de Valladolid), pp. 7–43
——. 2001. 'Voces pitagóricas en el pensamiento de Rosa Chacel', *Aurora*, 3, 101–14
PEINADO ELLIOT, CARLOS. 2002. *Unidad y trascendencia: estudio sobre la obra de José Ángel Valente* (Seville: Ediciones Alfar)
PENALVA MORA, VICENTE. 2013. 'El orientalismo en la cultura española en el primer tercio del S. XX: la Sociedad Teosófica española (1888–1940)' (unpublished doctoral thesis, Universidad Autónoma de Barcelona)
PÉREZ, JANET. 1997. 'Razón vital y razón poética: la solución meta-racional de María Zambrano', *Letras femeninas*, 23, 1–2 (Spring-Autumn), 9–25
——. 1999. 'La razón de la sinrazón: Unamuno, Machado, and Ortega in the Thought of María Zambrano', *Hispania*, 82.1, 56–67
PÉREZ SEGURA, JAVIER. 1997. 'La Sociedad de Artistas Ibéricos (1920–1936)' (unpublished doctoral thesis, Universidad Complutense de Madrid)
PIGNATTI, TERISIO, and FILIPPO PEDROCCO. 1999. *Giorgione* (Milan: Rizzoli)
PITTARELLO, ELIDE. 2014. 'María Zambrano ante Giorgione: *La tempesta*', in *Ritratti di donne: studi dedicati a Susanna Regazzoni*, ed. by Silvana Serafin (Venice: La Toletta), pp. 183–98
PLOTINUS. 2015. *Enéadas IV-VI*, trans. and with notes by Jesús Igal (Madrid: Gredos)
PORPHYRY. 2015. 'Vida de Plotino', in Plotinus, *Enéadas I-III*, trans. and notes by Jesús Igal (Madrid: Gredos)
PREZZO, ROSELLA. 2006. *Pensare in un'altra luce: l'opera aperta di María Zambrano* (Milan: Raffaello Cortina)
PSEUDO-DIONYSIUS AREOPAGITA. 2005. *Los nombres divinos*, trans. and notes by Pablo A. Cavallero, revision and commentary by Graciela Ritacco (Buenos Aires: Losada)
——. 2014. *Obras completas*, ed. by Teodoro H. Martín (Madrid: Biblioteca de Autores Cristianos)
RAJEWSKI, IRINA O. 2005. 'Intermediality, Intertextuality, and Remediation: A Literary Perspective on Intermediality', in *History and Theory of the Arts, Literature and Technologies*, 6, 43–64, <http://id.erudit.org/iderudit/1005505ar> [accessed 30 January 2016]
RAMÍREZ, GORETTI. 2004. *María Zambrano: crítica literaria* (Madrid: Devenir)
RANCIÈRE, JACQUES. 2000. 'Literature, Politics, Aesthetics: Approaches to Democratic Disagreement', *SubStance*, 29, 3–24
——. 2009. *The Politics of Aesthetics* (London & New York: Continuum)
——. 2010. *Dissensus: On Politics and Aesthetics* (London & New York: Continuum)
REVILLA GUZMÁN, CARMEN. 1998. 'Claves de la "razón poética"', in *Claves de la razón poética. María Zambrano: un pensamiento en el orden del tiempo*, ed. by Carmen Revilla Guzmán (Madrid: Editorial Trotta), pp. 13–21
——, 2001. 'Amistades intelectuales: la mujer y las mujeres en la obra de María Zambrano', *Brocar*, 35, 91–107
——. 2005. *Entre el alba y la autora: sobre la filosofía de María Zambrano* (Barcelona: Icaria)
——. 2012. 'María Zambrano, discípula de Ortega y Gasset', *Aurora*, 13, 6–7
RICOEUR, PAUL. 1975. *La métaphore vive* (Paris: Seuil)
RIUS GATELL, ROSA. 2003. 'María Zambrano y la enigmática 'Tempesta' de Giorgione', *Aurora. Papeles del "Seminario María Zambrano"*, 5, 22–29
ROBINSON, JENEFER. 2007. *Deeper Than Reason: Emotion and its Role in Literature, Music and Art* (Oxford: Oxford University Press)
RODRÍGUEZ FER, CLAUDIO (ed.). 1992. *José Ángel Valente* (Madrid: Taurus)
ROMERO DE SOLÍS, DIEGO. 2005. 'El corazón en la niebla', in *Filosofía y literatura en María Zambrano*, ed. by Pedro Cerezo (Seville: Fundación José Manuel Lara), pp. 171–252

ROMERO SALVADÓ, FRANCISCO J. 1996. 'The Failure of the Liberal Project of the Spanish Nation-State, 1909–23', in *Nationalism and the Nation in the Iberian Peninsula,* ed. by Clare Mar-Molinero and Angel Smith (Oxford & Washington, DC: Berg), pp. 119–32

ROSSET, CLEMENT. 1974. *La antinaturaleza* (Madrid: Taurus)

ROUSSET, JEAN. 1983. 'Le journal intime, texte sans destinataire?', *Poétique,* 56, 435–43

ROZAS, J. M., and G. TORRES NEBRERA. 1989. *El grupo poético del 27,* 2 vols (Madrid: Cincel)

RUBIO, OLIVIA MARÍA. 1994. *La mirada interior: el surrealismo y la pintura* (Madrid: Tecnos)

RUSSO, MARIA TERESA. 2003. 'Lo invisible sugerido por lo visible: el significado metafísico de la pintura en el pensamiento de María Zambrano', *Aurora. Papeles del "Seminario María Zambrano",* 5, 108–15

SÁNCHEZ CUERVO, ANTOLÍN C. 2010. 'Las metamorfosis del exilio', in María Zambrano, *Pensamiento y exilio,* ed. by A. Sánchez Cuervo, A. Sánchez Andrés, and G. Sánchez Díaz (Madrid: Editorial Biblioteca Nueva), pp. 173–90

——. 2011. 'Pasado inconcluso: las tensiones entre la historia y la memoria bajo el signo del exilio', *Isegoría. Revista de filosofía moral y política,* 45 (julio-diciembre, 653–68

——. 2014. 'El exilio de María Zambrano y la política oculta', *Aurora. Papeles del Seminario María Zambrano,* 15, 56–62

——, and AGUSTÍN SÁNCHEZ ANDRÉS, GERARDO SÁNCHEZ DÍAZ (eds.). 2010. *María Zambrano: pensamiento y exilio* (Madrid: Biblioteca Nueva)

——, and SEBASTIÁN HERNÁNDEZ TOLEDO. 2014. 'La estancia de María Zambrano en Chile', *Universum. Revista de Humanidades y Ciencias Sociales,* 29, 125–37

SCHIESARI, JULIANA. 2011. 'Melancholia and Mourning Animals', in *The Literature of Melancholia: Early Modern to Postmodern,* ed. by Martin Midekke and Christina Wald (Basingstoke: Palgrave Macmillan), pp. 223–39

SEIGWORTH, J., and MELISSA GREGG. 2010, 'An Inventory of Shimmers', in *The Affect Theory Reader,* ed. by J. Seigworth and Melissa Gregg (Durham, NC, & London: Duke University Press), pp. 1–25

SÉRULLAZ, MAURICE. 1963. *Le cubisme* (Paris: Presses Universitaires de France)

SETTIS, SALVATORE. 1978. *La 'Tempesta' interpretata: Giorgione, i committenti, il soggetto* (Turin: Einaudi)

SHOWALTER, ELAINE. 1993. 'Hysteria, Feminism, and Gender', in *Hysteria Beyond Freud,* ed. by Sander L. Gilman and others (Berkeley, Los Angeles, & London: University of California Press, 1993), 287–335

——. 2007. *The Female Malady: Women, Madness and English Culture 1830–1980* (London: Virago)

SIMMEL, GEORG. 1923. 'Lo masculino y lo femenino: para una psicología de los sexos', *Revista de Occidente,* 1.5, 218–36

SMITH, ANNE-MARIE. 1998. *Julia Kristeva: Speaking the Unspeakable* (London: Pluto Press)

SOPHOCLES. 2008. *Antigone, Oedipus the King and Electra,* trans. by H. D. F. Kitto (Oxford and New York: Oxford University Press)

SOTO CARRASCO, DAVID. 2010. 'Historia y violencia: Walter Benjamin y María Zambrano', *Thémata. Revista de Filosofía,* 43, 417–34

STEINER, GEORGE. 1984. *Antigones* (Oxford: Oxford University Press)

STEVENS, WALLACE. 1990. *Opus Posthumous.* (New York: Random Penguin House)

SUREDA, J., and ANA MARÍA GUASCH. 1987. *La trama de lo moderno* (Barcelona: Akal)

TEJADA MÍNGUEZ, RICARDO. 2011. 'Roma 1956: Ramón Gaya, puente entre Tomás Segovia y María Zambrano', *Escritura e imagen,* 7, 59–75

TOVAR, ANTONIO. 1960. 'Antígona y el tirano o la inteligencia en la política', in *Ensayos y otras peregrinaciones* (Madrid: Guadarrama), pp. 15–31

TRAPIELLO, ANDRÉS. 2000. 'Solo pero no de espaldas: Ramón Gaya y las ciudades', in Ramón Gaya, *El pintor en las ciudades: 4 Mayo-2 Julio 2000* (Valencia: IVAM), pp. 11–27

TRÍAS, EUGENIO. 1999. *La razón fronteriza* (Barcelona: Destino)

ULACIA ALTOLAGUIRRE, PALOMA. 1990. *Concha Méndez. Memorias habladas, memorias armadas* (Madrid: Mondadori)

VALENDER, JAMES. 1998. 'Luis Cernuda y María Zambrano: simpatías y diferencias', in *Homenaje a María Zambrano: estudios y correspondencia*, ed. by James Valender (Mexico City: Colegio de México), pp. 165–97

—— (ed.). 2001. *Una mujer moderna: Concha Méndez en su mundo (1898–1986)* (Madrid: Amigos de la Residencia de Estudiantes)

VALENTE, JOSÉ ÁNGEL. 1968. *Breve son* (Madrid: El Bardo)

——. 1976. *Interior con figuras* (Barcelona: Ocnos, Barral Editores)

——. 1978. 'Del conocimiento pasivo o saber de quietud', *El País*, 26 November

——. 1980. *Punto cero: poesía 1953–1979* (Barcelona: Seix Barral)

——. 1981. *Tres lecciones de tinieblas*, with illustrations by Baruj Salinas, 2nd edn (Barcelona: La Gaya Ciencia)

——. 1982. *La piedra y el centro* (Madrid: Taurus)

——. 1985. *Entrada en materia*, ed. by Jacques Ancet (Madrid: Cátedra)

——. 1988A. *El fulgor*, 2nd edn (Madrid: Cátedra)

——. 1988B. *Lectura en Tenerife* (Santa Cruz de Tenerife: Universidad Internacional Menéndez Pelayo)

——. 1989A. *Al dios del lugar* (Barcelona: Tusquets)

——. 1989B. *Cántigas de alén*, trans. by César Antonio Molina, preliminary study by Claudio Rodríguez Fer (Barcelona: Àmbit Serveis Editorials)

——. 1990. *Los ojos deseados*, with illustrations by Guillermo Pérez Villalta (Madrid: Instituto de Estética y Teoría de las Artes)

——. 1991. *Variaciones sobre el pájaro y la red, precedido por La piedra y el centro* (Barcelona: Tusquets)

——. 1992A. *Lectura de Paul Celan: Fragmentos*, Hojas de Poesía, nº II, Instituto de Bachillerato 'Francisco Giner de los Ríos' (Segovia: Pavesas)

——. 1992B. *No amanece el cantor* (Barcelona: Tusquets)

——. 2000. *Fragmentos de un libro futuro* (Barcelona: Galaxia Gutenberg/Círculo de Lectores)

——. 2001A. *La voz de José Ángel Valente: poesía en la Residencia* (Madrid: Publicaciones de la Residencia de Estudiantes)

——. 2001B. *Obra poética 2: material memoria (1977–1992)*, 4th edn (Madrid: Alianza)

——. 2002. *Elogio del calígrafo: ensayos sobre arte* (Barcelona: Galaxia Gutenberg/Círculo de Lectores)

——. 2004. *La experiencia abisal* (Barcelona: Galaxia Gutenberg/Círculo de Lectores)

——. 2008. *Obras completas II. Ensayos*, ed. by Andrés Sánchez Robayna, with an introduction by Claudio Rodríguez Fer (Barcelona: Galaxia Gutenberg/Círculo de Lectores)

——. 2011. *Diario anónimo (1959–2000)*, ed. by Andrés Sánchez Robayna (Barcelona: Galaxia Gutenberg/Círculo de Lectores)

——. 2014. *Palais de justice*, ed. by Andrés Sánchez Robayna (Barcelona: Galaxia Gutenberg/ Círculo de Lectores)

——, and JOSÉ LEZAMA LIMA. 2012. *Maestro cantor: correspondencia y otros textos*, prologue by Juan Goytisolo, introduction and notes by Javier Fornieles Ten (Seville: Espuela de Plata)

VALIS, NOEL. 2015. 'Introduction', in *Two Confessions: María Zambrano and Rosa Chacel*, trans. by Noel Valis and Carol Maier (Albany: State University of New York, Albany)

VELÁZQUEZ DELGADO, JORGE. 2007. *Fragmentos de la modernidad: filosofía de la historia e imperativo de la modernidad en José Ortega y Gasset y María Zambrano* (Buenos Aires: Ediciones del Siglo)

VIDAL, CARME. 1999. *Maruxa Mallo* (Vigo: Ediciōns a Nosa Terra)

VILLENA, LUIS ANTONIO DE. 2002. *Luis Cernuda* (Barcelona: Omega)
VIRNO, PAOLO. 2003. *El recuerdo del presente: ensayo sobre el tiempo histórico* (Barcelona: Paidós Ibérica)
WARDROPPER, BRUCE W. 1969. 'The Poetry of Ruins in the Golden Age', *Revista Hispánica Moderna*, 35.4 (1969), 295–305
WHITE, DAVID. 1977. *Heidegger and the Language of Poetry* (Lincoln: University of Nebraska Press)

INDEX

Abellán, José Luis 198
Acedia 107, 109, 119
Las adelfas 127
Adorno, Theodor 8, 90–91, 99, 137
aesthetic turn 11, 186,-187, 188
affective turn 4, 109, 110, 113, 138, 186–87, 195, 196–97
Agamben, Giorgio 52, 168, 183, 192, 196
Alarcón, Araceli 114
Alberti, Rafael 3, 20, 28
Albornoz, Álvaro de 77
Albornoz, Concha de 6, 7, 16–19, 28, 30, 32, 77–78
Alianza de Intelectuales para la Defensa de la Cultura 2
Almería 64, 66–67, 70, 126
Alonso, Ángel 37
Altolaguirre, Miguel 3, 21, 29
Andalusia 63, 145–46
Andreu, Agustín 137
Antigone 2, 9, 52, 122, 124–26, 128–37, 140–55, 183
Aranguren, José Luis 23, 68
Arendt, Hannah 1, 2, 12, 52
Aristotle 108, 142, 156
art criticism 5, 10, 34–48, 101–04, 121, 163–70, 196
Athena 124, 133, 137
Atheneum 2, 15–16, 18, 25, 26, 30, 33
Attridge, Derek 11, 197
St Augustine 43, 44, 49, 177
autobiography 4, 5, 16, 21, 22, 25–29, 38, 53, 60, 110, 125–26, 145, 165, 169, 170–72, 182, 198
avant-garde 2, 5, 6, 7, 16, 22, 26, 28, 34, 36, 37, 38, 39, 40, 44–47, 64, 189
Azaña, Manuel 114
Azorín 2, 154

Bachelard, Gaston 143
Bahun, Sanja 107, 116
Balibrea, Mari Paz 12, 176
Baroque 36, 37, 39, 48
Barral, Carlos 65
Baudelaire, Charles 102, 103, 111, 117, 195
Bellini, Giovanni 160
Belting, Hans 158, 159
Benjamin, Walter 17, 21, 31, 52–53, 61, 79, 98, 107, 108, 110, 117–20, 160, 187
Berenguer, Dámaso 17
Berg, Nancy E. 178
Bergamín, José 3, 64, 114, 182
Bergson, Henri 185
Berlin, Isaiah 188

Berrocal, Alfonso 77, 87
Besteiro, Julián 114
Bible 134, 172, 178, 179
birth 4, 67, 84, 129, 148–50, 166, 174
Bizet, Georges, *Carmen* 188
Boehm, Gottfried 157–58, 160
Bozal, Valeriano 39
Braidotti, Rosi 8, 182
Braunschweig (Brunswick) 167
Breton, André 20, 40, 43
Buenos Aires 21, 31, 32, 50, 78
Bundgaard, Ana 12, 48, 50, 52, 73, 94, 103, 108, 111, 156
Buñuel, Luis 127
  Le Chien Andalou 127

Caballero, Beatriz 29, 137
Calderón de la Barca, Pedro 87
Calvert, Casey 71
Campoamor, Clara 17
Camus, Albert 3, 63
Cancioneros 36
Capitalism 56, 193, 196
Caruth, Cathy 183
Castro, Rosalía de 68
Catharsis 57, 84, 117, 137
Celan, Paul 73
Central University of Madrid 15–16, 25, 28, 185
Cernuda, Luis 3, 7, 18–20, 30, 32, 77–88
Cervantes, Miguel de 61, 194, 197
  Don Quixote 194–95
Cézanne, Paul 100
Chacel, Rosa 3, 5, 6, 7, 12, 15–33, 68, 109, 114, 116, 120, 136
Chacón, Pedro 161
Champourcín, Ernestina de 17
Chile 12, 20, 53, 61, 62, 63, 145
Christianity 30, 49, 56–57, 58, 71, 74–75, 109, 128, 136, 137, 138, 168, 195
Cioran, Emil 3, 4, 95
Cixous, Hélène 9, 123–24
Cocteau, Jean 49, 98
Colette 1, 12
Communism 20, 55, 193–94
Complutense University Madrid 18
confession 42–43, 49, 120
consciousness 7, 9, 35, 43, 49, 52, 93, 97–98, 101, 103, 125, 135, 137, 140, 147–55, 176

Costafreda, Alfonso 114
Counter-enlightenment 188
Creacionismo 81
Critical Theory 11, 52, 55, 56, 57, 61, 157, 186
Croce, Elena 3
Cruz y Raya 2
Cuba 3, 7, 63, 77, 78, 140, 147, 171
   Havana 3, 8, 21, 29, 30, 44, 49, 78, 124, 137, 161
Cubism 35–36, 38, 39, 40, 161, 163

Dalí, Salvador 127
Dal Pozzolo, Enrico Maria 164
Dante 195
Dasein 42, 180, 194
De Chirico, Giorgio 47
del Campo Mendoza, Gregorio 15
Deleuze, Gilles 183
delirium 9, 25, 37, 67, 81, 99, 104, 125–27, 132, 134–38, 147, 149, 180
democracy 11, 16–17, 20, 53–54, 61, 122, 157, 176, 185–99
Derrida, Jacques 77, 87, 139
Descartes 42, 43, 115, 141, 198
Dialectics 90, 114, 143, 160, 172–73
Díaz Plaja, Guillermo 109
Diderot, Denis 86
Didi-Huberman, Georges 160, 165–66, 169
Dieste, Rafael 20, 21, 114
Di Pippo, Alexander 194
Docherty, Thomas 186, 187–88, 192, 196
Dostoevsky, Fyodor 49, 57
dreams 29, 35, 37, 39, 40, 52, 57, 59, 64–65, 68, 79, 83, 84, 87–88, 98, 102–03, 113–14, 130, 134, 143, 146–47, 151, 158, 162, 166, 191, 197
Dresden 167
Dürer, Albrecht 109
Duque, Aquilino 66

El Greco 37
El Liberal 16, 24
El Sol 63, 127
Eliot, T. S. 8, 91
elitism 186, 189
Enjuto Rangel, Cecilia 81, 83, 86, 87, 88
Enlightenment 2, 7, 47, 59, 86, 107, 123, 154, 187, 188
Epistemology 49, 146, 173, 180, 186
Eros 8, 63–76
Escorial 122
Escribano, María 19
Escuela de Vallecas 21, 31
Ethics 1, 5, 6, 10, 25, 52–53, 75–76, 85–87, 103, 124–25, 128, 134–35, 171–84, 191
Europe 3, 24, 41, 44–45, 50, 54, 58, 110, 186–90, 193–98
exile 1, 2, 3, 4, 6, 7, 9–11, 18, 20, 21, 28, 30–32, 34, 37, 48, 52–53, 61, 76, 78, 86, 92, 108, 110, 116, 124, 126, 127, 129, 131, 133, 135, 136, 138, 152, 153–54, 157, 159–60, 161, 169–70, 171–84, 185–86, 189, 197–98
existentialism 28, 34, 41–42, 44, 49, 59, 87, 113, 136, 169, 198
Expressionism 35, 47

Falange 3, 122, 136
Fascism 7, 8, 20, 21, 40, 54– 62, 189, 190, 193, 196, 197
Federación Universitaria Escolar (FUE) 16, 29
Feijóo, Benito Jerónimo 127
Feminism 1, 2, 4, 5, 9, 22, 23, 26, 31, 122–37
Fernández, Luis 37–38, 39, 48
Fichte, Georg Friedrich 141
Ficino, Marsilio 109
Flâneur 17, 21, 26, 29
flapper 22
Flatley, Jonathan 107, 109, 110, 117, 119
Florence 161
Franco, Francisco 3, 6, 20, 30, 53, 56, 185, 193
Frankfurt School 56
French Revolution 193
Freud, Sigmund 40, 44, 49–50, 108–10, 114, 115, 119, 120, 127–29, 137, 138, 177
Freudianism 44, 115, 127, 128
Fundación María Zambrano 4, 66

García Lorca, Federico 12, 15, 61, 63, 97, 98, 102, 123, 136, 145
   and duende 123
García Morente, Manuel 63
Gaya, Ramón 3, 10, 37, 159–63, 169
Gender 2, 6–7, 9, 12, 16, 19, 21–27, 29, 31, 41, 43, 96, 122, 123–25, 128, 129, 133, 136, 183
Generación del 1898 60, 121, 188
Generación del 1927 3–4, 16, 36–37, 127
Geneva 3, 8, 63, 64, 66, 67, 68, 70, 71, 126
Gentili, Augusto 164, 167
Gestapo 68, 125
Gil de Biedma, Jaime 3, 65, 68
Gingerich, Stephen 187, 188
Giorgione 10, 164–70
   The Tempest 10, 164–70
Girard, Alan 112
Giraudoux, Jean 23
Gnosticism 30, 64
Golden Age 12, 48, 185
Gombrowicz, Witold 8, 89–91
Gómez Blesa, Mercedes 30, 62, 108, 11, 198
Gómez de la Serna, Ramón 2, 143
Góngora, Luis de 36
Goya, Francisco de 37
Greek mythology 46–47, 50, 58, 67, 124, 168
Gris, Juan 38–39
Guillén, Jorge 3
Guillén, Nicolás 3

Habermas, Jürgen 51

Hades 69, 96, 122
heart 9, 73, 139, 141–45, 154–55
Hegel, Georg Wilhelm Friedrich 58–59, 122, 124–25, 130, 133, 137
Heidegger, Martin 1, 8, 89–91, 103, 141, 180, 194–96
Hermeneutics 7, 10, 52, 53, 59, 134, 156, 157, 159, 164, 169
Hernández, Miguel 20, 114
Herrera Petere, José 114
Hippocrates 109
historical reason 29
Hitler, Adolf 103, 193
Hölderlin, Friedrich 89, 103
Holocaust 183
hombría 60, 189, 196, 198
Homo sacer 174, 183
Hora de España 3, 6, 12, 30, 31, 53, 72, 77
Horkheimer, Max 55–56
Huidobro, Vicente 53, 81
Husserl, Edmund 141, 154, 187, 188, 196, 198
Huyssen, Andreas 79, 86
hybridization 10, 156, 160
hysteria 9, 122, 127, 134–38

Iconic turn 10, 157–70
Idealism 7, 40, 41, 44, 46, 47, 49, 56–58, 59, 141, 156, 188, 191, 194
Impressionism 35, 36
Ínferos 148–49
Institución Libre de Enseñanza 28, 60–61, 64
Instituto Escuela 6, 16
Ínsula 68
intrahistoria 37, 60, 123, 154, 175, 183
Irigaray, Luce 9, 124, 134
Ismene 128–30, 138, 151

Jameson, Fredric 139
Janés, Clara 31
Jesus Christ 162
Jiménez, Juan Ramón 123
Jiménez Fraud, Alberto 64
Job 10, 68, 174, 179–82, 184
St John of the Cross 72
Johnson, Roberta 9, 29, 31, 88, 113, 120, 128, 137, 182, 198
Jung, Carl-Gustav 176, 170

Kant, Immanuel 51, 63, 195
Kent, Victoria 17
Kierkegaard, Søren 137, 183, 196
Klein, Melanie 1, 12, 129
Krauel, Ricardo 121
Kristeva, Julia 1–2, 4, 5, 9, 12, 107–10, 119, 120, 122, 123, 125, 129–32, 133–36, 137, 138
  and abjection 129, 131, 136, 137
  and chora 130, 138

La Nación 55
La Pièce 8, 65–66, 68
La sinrazón 32 (Chacel), 127 (Sánchez Mejías)
Lacan, Jacques 75, 129, 137, 138, 160
Lam, Wilfredo 40, 50
Laurenzi, Elena 23, 24, 31
León, María Teresa 16, 28, 109
Levine, Samuel 139
Lezama Lima, José 3, 7, 8, 12, 31, 67, 71, 76, 126, 127, 128
Liberalism 11, 20, 29, 31, 52, 54, 55, 61, 94, 136, 190, 192–93, 196
Liga de Educación Social 16
literature 4, 10–11, 61, 102, 137, 185–99
Litoral 36
Logos 56, 102, 151, 154, 155, 156, 157
Lope de Vega, Félix 36
Lyceum Club 2, 6, 17, 21, 30, 87

Machado, Antonio 2, 11, 12, 15, 27, 53, 61, 63, 71, 114, 123, 127, 185, 187, 194–95
Machado, Manuel 127
Madre España 53
Madrid 2, 4, 6, 7, 12, 15–19, 21–23, 26, 28, 29, 30, 31, 32, 33, 63, 64, 66, 72, 157, 161, 164, 169, 185
Maeztu, María de 15
Maier, Carol 5, 12, 27, 29, 32
Maillard, Chantal 2, 12, 154
Mainer, José-Carlos 185
Mallo, Maruja 6, 16, 19, 20, 21, 28, 29, 30, 31
Manrique, Jorge 195
Marañón, Gregorio 15, 32, 110, 114, 127
Martínez Garrido, Elisa 126
Mary Magdalene 162
Marset, Juan Carlos 15, 64, 85, 116
mask 46–47, 50, 57, 99, 104, 111, 119, 127, 150
May, Todd 195
Mayhew, Jonathan 8, 123, 136
Mckinlay, Neil C. 86–87
melancholy 8, 9, 107–21
Melville, Herman, *Bartleby, the Scrivener* 168
memory 32, 52, 53, 85, 97–98, 160, 164–65, 167, 175–84
Méndez, Concha 6, 16, 17, 19, 21, 28, 29, 31
Mérimée, Prosper 188
Merleau-Ponty, Maurice 9, 139, 141, 150, 151, 155, 160, 166
Mermall, Thomas 138
metaphor 4, 9, 52, 73, 94, 101, 124, 139–55, 156–58, 161–63, 165, 169–70, 197–98
  see also ruins; heart
Metaphysics 1, 11, 38, 41, 43, 47, 59, 66, 75, 89, 94, 103, 156–58, 161–62, 164, 166, 169, 186, 191, 193
Mexico 3, 21, 30, 44, 63, 66, 72, 77–78, 155, 159, 160, 161, 171, 182
Miró, Joan 40, 49, 71
Misiones pedagógicas 3, 159

modernity, crisis of 6, 15, 22, 36–37, 44, 55–56, 79, 107–14, 117–20, 123, 176, 187, 192
Molinos, Miguel de 8, 66, 68, 70–71
Moraga, Pablo 108, 111
Morante, Elsa 126
Morelia, University of 3
Moreno Sanz, Jesús 4, 12, 20, 30, 50, 52, 62, 108, 111, 136, 185
Muñoz Millanes, José 159
Murillo, Bartolomé Esteban 159
Mussolini, Benito 193
Mysticism 8, 47, 52, 61, 63–65, 68, 70, 71, 73–75, 95, 102, 123, 162, 163, 164, 175, 180, 186
  see also Miguel de Molinos; St John of the Cross

Nancy, Jean Luc 29
National-Socialism 1, 103
Natura mater 166
Nelken, Margarita 17, 31
Neo-cubism 161, 163
Neoplatonism 49, 188
Neruda, Pablo 20, 21, 53, 120
Nietzsche, Friedrich 15, 21, 34, 35–36, 46–47, 48, 59, 63, 157
Nimmo, Clare E. 123, 136
nostalgia 35, 133, 177–78, 183

Oedipus 131, 132, 137, 148, 151, 152
Ontology 25, 26, 32, 42, 118, 154, 156, 166, 175, 192, 196
Orígenes 3, 115, 139, 146
Orpheus 69, 76
Ortega Allué, Javier 172, 180, 181
Ortega y Gasset, José 1, 2, 6–9, 16–17, 19, 22–24, 27, 29, 31, 32, 34–35, 40, 42, 45, 50–51, 54–56, 61–63, 66, 94, 100–03, 114, 120, 123, 127, 139–42, 146, 185–86, 188
  La deshumanización del arte 6, 34, 42, 45, 50, 186
  La rebelión de las masas 54, 55, 76, 186

painting 10, 21, 30, 37–40, 44–49, 101, 156–70
  see also Cubism; Surrealism; avant-garde; Ramón Gaya
Palencia, Benjamín 21, 31
Papeles de Son Armadans 184
Paris 3, 10, 16, 20, 30, 39, 48, 68, 77, 111, 124, 125, 161, 185
Parmenides 195
Paz, Octavio 3, 4
Peninsular War 188
Pérez, Janet 88, 139, 195, 198
Pérez Galdós, Benito 61, 194–95, 197–98
  Fortunata and Jacinta 194–95
  Misericordia 61, 194–95
Persephone 131, 133, 147–48
Phenomenology 2, 29, 123, 139, 140, 143, 145, 158, 162–63, 165, 166, 180, 187
Phidias 47

Picasso, Pablo 37, 48
Pittaluga, Gustavo 3, 128
Pizarro, Miguel 15, 33, 63, 71
Plato 21, 40, 49, 51–52, 74, 96, 130, 137, 177–78, 187–89, 191, 194
  Timaeus 130
Plotinus 74
poetic reason (*razón poética*) 4, 7, 9, 10, 11, 12, 17, 19, 20, 29, 51–62, 82, 88, 93, 103, 111, 123, 128, 137, 139, 154, 156, 162, 163, 178, 179, 186–88, 195, 198
Poïēsis 194, 197
poetry 1, 11, 21, 29, 30, 36, 37, 46, 64, 73–74, 89–104, 120, 178–79, 187, 193–96
  see also José Ángel Valente; Luis Cernuda; Pablo Neruda
Post-structuralism 139, 140
Prado Museum 25, 29, 159
Pre-Socratics 194
Primo de Rivera, Miguel 17, 29, 60, 185, 190
Psychoanalysis 5, 9, 41, 49, 56–57, 122–38
  see also Kristeva; Freud; Lacan; Klein
Puerto Rico 3, 63, 66
Pythagoras 19, 31, 195

Quimera 68

Raciovitalismo 34, 61, 123
Rancière, Jacques 186, 195, 199
Rationalism 9, 11, 17, 19, 34–35, 36, 43–44, 46, 47, 51, 61, 90, 98, 115, 120–21, 123, 187, 192–93
Rawls, John 51
Reconquista 172
Reformation 36, 188, 197
Rembrandt 159
Renaissance 49, 56, 164
Residencia de estudiantes 16, 26, 64
Residencia de Señoritas 2, 6, 15, 17–18
Restauración, régimen de la 32, 182, 190, 193
revelation 10, 42, 54, 60, 66, 72, 74, 82, 99, 112, 150, 156, 158, 160, 162–63, 165, 174, 180–81
Revilla Guzmán, Carmen 12, 29, 32, 85, 186
Revista de Occidente 2, 6, 12, 16, 21, 31, 127
Ricoeur, Paul 10, 156
Rimbaud, Arthur 97
Rivas, Reyna 136
Romancero 36
Romanticism 40–42, 55, 60–61, 75, 84, 91, 93, 95, 109, 142, 165, 188
Rome 3, 10, 16, 23, 65, 70, 82, 114, 126, 132, 135, 148, 158, 161
Rosenzweig, Franz 7, 56
Rousset, Jean 112
ruins 4, 7, 11, 12, 53, 77–88, 90, 116–17, 118

sacrifice 10, 58, 148–49, 173, 175
Salinas, Baruj 73, 163
Sánchez Mejías, Ignacio 127

Sartre, Jean-Paul 120, 141, 154
Scheler, Max 23
Second Republic 1, 3, 7, 17–18, 20, 21–22, 25, 29, 30–32, 52–54, 62, 64, 152–53, 155, 157, 159, 161, 185, 189, 190, 193, 196, 198
Séjourné, Laurette 135
Semiotics 5, 9, 136, 138
Seneca 52, 61, 137
Showalter, Elaine 127, 135, 137
Simmel, Georg 22–23
Sophocles 122, 124 -125, 128–29, 131, 132
Soriano, Juan 50, 64, 161
soul 23, 29, 39–43, 45, 49, 51, 74–75, 79, 86, 96, 112, 133, 139, 141, 147, 154, 158, 165–66, 173, 176, 178, 183, 188, 190
Spanish Civil War 2, 7, 22, 25, 28, 30, 32–33, 48, 52, 54, 56, 60, 62–63, 76, 77–78, 126, 148, 171,185, 189–90, 193, 195, 196, 198
Spinoza, Baruch 35, 48, 66, 95
Stalin, Joseph 193
Steiner, George 137
Stevens, Wallace 8, 91
Surrealism 6, 19, 20–21, 29, 39, 40–44, 47, 49, 57

Tanizaki, Junichiro 63
Tarde, Gabriel 55
tertulias 2, 16, 18, 19, 77
   de la Cacharrería 6, 16, 28
   Café Pombo 2
   Granja del Henar 2, 18
Theosophy 20, 30
   Timæus 130
Tintoretto, 161
Titian 159, 167
Tovar, Antonio 122–23, 128, 136
Trauerspiel 111, 120
trauma 7, 8, 10, 29, 86, 125, 126, 173–74, 176, 177, 183
Trueba Mira, Virginia 136, 145–46, 148, 154

Ullán, José Miguel 12, 65
Unamuno, Miguel de 2, 8, 15, 37, 50, 60–61, 63, 114, 120, 123, 136, 154, 183, 185, 188, 198
   Del sentimiento trágico de la vida 185
   see also intrahistoria; generación de 1898

Valis, Noël 5, 6
Valender, James 21, 77–78, 87
Valente, José Ángel 3–4, 8, 12, 31, 63–76, 108, 111, 123, 136
Valéry, Paul 98, 102–03
Valle-Inclán, Ramón del 2, 48, 63, 71
Velázquez Delgado, Jorge 85, 87

Velázquez, Diego 37, 159, 167
   Las Meninas 176
Vélez-Málaga 4, 63, 66, 68, 145
Venice 160–62, 164, 167–70
Venus 133, 167–68
virginity 122, 124, 132, 146, 147, 155, 189
vital reason (raciovitalismo) 34, 51, 61, 123

Weil, Simone 3
World War I 22, 24, 25, 57
World War II 1, 7, 44, 91

Zamacona, Conchita 18
Zambrano, Araceli 2, 63, 65, 67–68, 70–71, 108, 114–16, 124, 125–28, 129, 135, 136, 137
Zambrano, Blas 2, 15, 28, 63, 114, 115, 126, 185
Zambrano, María:
   La agonía de Europa 44, 50, 117
   Algunos lugares de la pintura 4, 10, 48, 50, 157, 161, 170
   Los bienaventurados 53, 85, 86, 169, 172, 180
   Claros del bosque 4, 9, 41, 64, 66, 67–68, 96, 126, 145, 150
   La confesión: género literario 41–43, 49, 116, 120, 183
   'Delirio de Antígona' 124, 135, 140, 146–48, 155
   Delirio y destino 4, 16, 25–26, 29, 38, 53, 60, 125, 126, 145, 172, 173, 182, 198
   La España de Galdós 61, 198
   Filosofía y poesía 92, 93, 94, 102, 104, 120, 178
   El Freudismo, testimonio del hombre actual 49, 114–15, 128, 138
   'La guerra de Antonio Machado' 53, 194, 195
   Hacia un saber sobre el alma 51, 137, 154, 165
   El hombre y lo divino 46, 53, 54, 58, 59, 68, 71, 78, 88, 95, 111, 118, 136, 184
   Horizonte del Liberalismo 1, 16, 51, 54, 94, 190–91
   Los intelectuales en el drama de España 31, 32, 40, 53, 56, 59, 102, 187, 189–90
   'Nostalgia de la tierra' 6, 11, 34–38, 44–45, 157
   Notas de un método 64, 97, 116, 157, 162, 169
   El pensamiento vivo de Séneca 52
   Pensamiento y poesía en la vida española 2, 37, 61–62, 92–93, 120–21
   Persona y democracia 3, 4, 54, 58, 198–99
   El sueño creador 53, 68, 98, 166
   Los sueños y el tiempo 1, 162
   'Sueño y destino de la pintura' 37, 48, 158
   La tumba de Antígona 9, 52, 122–37, 140, 148, 150
   Unamuno (y su obra) 198
   see also razón poética; metaphor; poetry; literature; art criticism
Zubiri, Xavier 2, 63, 136, 185
Zurbarán, Francisco de 37–39, 48